Marketing Management in Practice
2005–2006

The Chartered
Institute of Marketing

Marketing Management in Practice 2005–2006

John Williams and Tony Curtis

ELSEVIER
BUTTERWORTH
HEINEMANN

AMSTERDAM BOSTON HEIDELBERG LONDON NEW YORK OXFORD
PARIS SAN DIEGO SAN FRANCISCO SINGAPORE SYDNEY TOKYO

Elsevier Butterworth-Heinemann
Linacre House, Jordan Hill, Oxford OX2 8DP
30 Corporate Drive, Burlington, MA 01803

First published 2005

British Library Cataloguing in Publication Data
A catalogue record for this book is available from the British Library

Library of Congress Cataloguing in Publication Data
A catalogue record for this book is available from the Library of Congress

ISBN 0 7506 6649 8

For information on all Elsevier Butterworth-Heinemann publications
visit our website at http://books.elsevier.com

Typeset by Integra Software Services Pvt. Ltd, Pondicherry, India
www.integra-india.com
Printed and bound in Italy

Contents

Preface

welcome to the CIM coursebooks

An introduction from the academic development advisor

In the last 2 years we have seen some significant changes to CIM Marketing qualifications. The changes have been introduced on a year-on-year basis, with Certificate changes implemented in 2002, and the Professional Diploma in Marketing being launched in 2003. The professional Postgraduate Diploma in Marketing was launched in 2004. The new qualifications are based on the CIM Professional Marketing Standards, developed through research with employers.

As a result the authoring team, Elsevier/Butterworth-Heinemann and I have all aimed to rigorously revise and update the coursebook series to make sure that every title is the best possible study aid and accurately reflects the latest CIM syllabus. This has been further enhanced through independent reviews carried out by CIM.

The revisions to the series this year include continued development at – Certificate in Marketing and Professional Diploma in Marketing, and complete rewrites at Professional Postgraduate Diploma in Marketing level to align with the radical overhaul of the CIM syllabus. In particular we have aimed to develop the assessment support to include some additional support for the assignment route as well as the examination, so we hope you will find this helpful.

There are a number of new authors and indeed Senior Examiners in the series who have been commissioned for their CIM course teaching and examining experience, as well as their research into specific curriculum-related areas and their wide general knowledge of the latest thinking in marketing.

We are certain that you will find these coursebooks highly beneficial in terms of the content and assessment opportunities and a study tool that will prepare you for both CIM examinations and continuous/integrative assessment opportunities. They will guide you in a logical and structured way through the detail of the syllabus, providing you with the required underpinning knowledge, understanding and application of theory.

The editorial team and authors wish you every success as you embark upon your studies.

Karen Beamish
Academic Development Advisor

How to use these coursebooks

Everyone who has contributed to this series has been careful to structure the books with the exams in mind. Each unit, therefore, covers an essential part of the syllabus. You need to work through the complete coursebook systematically to ensure that you have covered everything you need to know.

This coursebook is divided into units each containing a selection of the following standard elements:

- o *Learning objectives* – tell you what you will be expected to know, having read the unit.
- o *Syllabus references* – outline what part of the syllabus is covered in the module.
- o *Study guides* – tell you how long the unit is and how long its activities take to do.
- o *Questions* are designed to give you practice – they will be similar to those you get in the exam.
- o *Answers* (at the end to the book) – give you a suggested format for answering exam questions. *Remember* there is no such thing as a model answer – you should use these examples only as guidelines.
- o *Activities* – give you a chance to put what you have learned into practice.
- o *Debriefings* (at the end of the book) – shed light on the methodologies involved in the activities.
- o *Hints and tips* – are tips from the senior examiner, examiner or author and are designed to help you avoid common mistakes made by previous candidates and give you guidance on improving your knowledge base.
- o *Insights* – encourage you to contextualize your academic knowledge by reference to real-life experience.
- o *Key definitions* – highlight and explain the key points relevant to that module.
- o *Definitions* – may be used for words you must know to pass the exam.
- o *Summaries* – cover what you should have picked up from reading the unit.
- o *Further study* – provides details of recommended reading in addition to the coursebook.

While you will find that each section of the syllabus has been covered within this text, you might find that the order of some of the topics has been changed. This is because it sometimes makes more sense to put certain topics together when you are studying, even though they might appear in different sections of the syllabus itself. If you are following the reading and other activities, your coverage of the syllabus will be just fine, but don't forget to follow up with trade press reading!

About MarketingOnline

Elsevier/Butterworth-Heinemann offers purchasers of the coursebooks free access to MarketingOnline (www.marketingonline.co.uk), our premier online support engine for the CIM marketing courses. On this site you can benefit from:

- o Fully customizable electronic versions of the coursebooks enabling you to annotate, cut and paste sections of text to create your own tailored learning notes.
- o The capacity to search the coursebook online for instant access to definitions and key concepts.

    o   Useful links to e-marketing articles, provided by Dave Chaffey, Director of Marketing Insights Ltd and a leading UK e-marketing consultant, trainer and author.

    o   A glossary providing a comprehensive dictionary of marketing terms.

    o   A Frequently Asked Questions (FAQs) section providing guidance and advice on common problems or queries.

Using MarketingOnline

Logging on

Before you can access MarketingOnline you will first need to get a password. Please go to www.marketingonline.co.uk and click on the registration button where you will then find registration instructions for coursebook purchasers. Once you have got your password, you will need to log on using the onscreen instructions. This will give you access to the various functions of the site.

MarketingOnline provides a range of functions, as outlined in the previous section, that can easily be accessed from the site after you have logged on to the system. Please note the following guidelines detailing how to access the main features:

1. *The coursebooks* – Buttons corresponding to the three levels of the CIM marketing qualification are situated on the home page. Select your level and you will be presented with the coursebook title for each module of that level. Click on the desired coursebook to access the full online text (divided up by chapter). On each page of text you have the option to add an electronic bookmark or annotation by following the onscreen instructions. You can also freely cut and paste text into a blank word document to create your own learning notes.

2. *e-Marketing articles* – To access the links to relevant e-marketing articles simply click on the link under the text 'E-marketing Essentials: useful links from Marketing Insights'.

3. *Glossary* – A link to the glossary is provided in the top right-hand corner of each page enabling access to this resource at any time.

If you have specific queries about using MarketingOnline then you should consult our fully searchable FAQs section, accessible through the appropriate link in the top right-hand corner of any page of the site. Please also note that a *full user guide* can be downloaded by clicking on the link on the opening page of the website.

Focus of the module

This module is assessed by either examination or Integrated Project. The module enables students to practise the development and implemention of marketing plans at an operational level in organizations. A key part of the module is working within a team to develop the plan and managing teams, implementing the plan by undertaking marketing activities and projects. Its aim is to assist students in integrating and applying knowledge from all the modules at Professional Diploma in Marketing, particularly as part of a team. The Marketing Management in Practice syllabus requires a broad and practical demonstration of marketing at an operational level and an awareness of the strategic context. It provides an opportunity for students to develop and implement an operational marketing plan, so applying, as part of a team, the theory of research, planning and marketing communications provided in the previous three modules. This module also provides the final assessment of students' ability to create an operational marketing plan. As such, it forms an important measure of the students' ability to meet organizations' requirements of an operational marketer. Marketing Management in Practice is about developing and managing teams to add value to the organization's activities and deliver effective results. Like members of other functions and disciplines within organizations, marketers work towards departmental and broader organizational objectives. They work in teams, both within the marketing function and, importantly, with people in other functions. The context within which marketers are operating is continually changing as a result of both external and internal influences. No organization is detached from international influences, even if the organization does not have to deal with international customers. Organizations source materials from around the globe, access international markets from a desk, compete with other organizations from around the world, and imitate global behaviour. It is therefore appropriate in this module to cover international issues as part of everyday marketing life in organizations. Marketers and marketing managers must be able to work effectively themselves, for example managing time and problem solving. They must also be able to manage and motivate people and teams to produce results. Using Adair's model of leadership, effective team performance is contingent on a balance between:

The needs of the task.
The needs of the individuals within the team.
The maintenance needs of the team as a whole.

The syllabus for the module uses Adair's concept. It provides underpinning theory on managing teams to help with managing individual needs and team needs to get the most from the team. It also provides basic project management techniques to help with managing the task. These two elements provide the final skills and knowledge for marketers to develop and implement marketing plans at an operational level. The remainder of the syllabus for this module is about the development and implementation of an operational marketing plan, including the management of information, communications and human resources. Students should apply (within a marketing team) the theory of marketing research and information, planning and communications covered in the earlier modules. This should be achieved through the vehicle of a project.

Study note © CIM 2005

unit 1
management and marketing roles

Learning objectives

o To describe the nature of relationships with other functions in organizations operating in a range of different industries and contexts (1.1).

o To explain the importance of developing and maintaining effective relationships with people in other functions and disciplines (1.2).

The learning objectives are only partly covered in this chapter and they are a theme throughout the book. Other chapters will also be concerned with these objectives, particularly the chapters that focus on the use of teams and communications.

D Key definitions

Accountability – The extent to which individuals and managers are held responsible for the outcome of the decisions they make.

Autonomy – Independence to make decisions within a decentralized working environment, where decision-making is passed down from the top of the organization to the lower levels.

Fads – Fashions that enter quickly, are adopted with great zeal, peak early and decline very fast.

Flat hierarchy – An organizational structure that provides a wide span of control within only a few layers of organizational hierarchy.

Global firm – A firm that by operating in more than one country gains R&D, production, marketing and financial advantages in its costs and reputation that are not available to purely domestic competitors.

Global organization – A form of international organization whereby top corporate management and staff plan worldwide manufacturing or operational facilities, marketing policies, financial flows and logistical systems. The global operating unit reports directly to the chief executive, not to an international divisional head.

International division – A form of international marketing organization in which the division handles all of the firm's international activities. Marketing, manufacturing, research, planning and specialist staff are organized into operating units according to geography or product groups, or as an international subsidiary responsible for its own sales and profitability.

Marketing database – An organized set of data about individual customers or prospects that can be used to generate and qualify customer leads, sell products and services and maintain customer relationships.

Market research – The process of (1) analysing marketing opportunities; (2) selecting target markets; (3) developing the marketing mix; (4) managing the marketing effort.

Marketing mix – The set of controllable tactical marketing tools – product, price, place and promotion – that the firm blends to produce the response it wants in the target market.

Market segment – A group of consumers who respond in a similar way to a given set of marketing stimuli.

Market segmentation – Dividing a market into distinct groups of buyers with different needs, characteristics or behaviour, who might require separate products or marketing mixes.

Management

Introduction to the book

The coursebook is targeted at assisting you to pass the Marketing Management in Practice examination. The main focus of the CIM Advanced Certificate Course Marketing Management in Practice is on the development and implementation of marketing plans at an operational level in organizations. The Marketing Management in Practice unit helps students to develop and implement marketing plans at an operational level in organizations. A key part of this unit is working within a team to develop the plan and managing teams implementing the plan by undertaking marketing activities and projects. Its aim is to assist students in integrating and applying knowledge from all the units at Professional Diploma, particularly as part of a team. This unit also forms the summative assessment for the Advanced Certificate.

The syllabus is covered in eight units and these cover the main areas that contribute to effective marketing management. A marketing-oriented company needs to align its distinctive competencies with market opportunities but to do this effectively requires a team effort.

Customer focus needs to be shared by the whole organization and is not solely the responsibility of the marketing department in isolation. Achieving an organization-wide sense of shared values and beliefs can take a long time as it may mean changing the structure and culture of the organization. Front-line staff are often the public face of the organization and, as customer service providers, they possess useful information. A key element of a market orientation is intelligence-gathering about customer needs and preferences and what influences them. This should involve people throughout the organization but channelled for analysis towards a particular part of it. This is often a marketing department in larger organizations.

The structure of an organization can be a barrier to success if it separates one department from another. In some organizations, sales, marketing and customer service are organized as a team but finance, human resource management, research and development, production, purchasing and management all affect the marketing effort. To ensure that everyone is working to the same broad objectives as a team, requires good communication and an awareness and respect for each other's contributions. The book looks at these key issues. Unit I introduces the broad subject of management in the context of marketing and marketing management. The diverse roles of marketing management and the various ways in which the marketing function is organized are discussed. Guidance on examination preparation will focus on the examination techniques that will maximize your probability of passing.

CIM Professional Marketing Standards

These set out a competency framework that can be used as the definition of marketing practice and the requirements of organizations that employ marketers. The framework has been developed in partnership with large organizations including multinationals, and is based on competencies defined through marketing job descriptions. This framework defines what marketers in organizations actually do, identifying the knowledge and understanding skills.

What form do the CIM Professional Marketing Standards take?

The Standards are an easy reference matrix, combining 6 key marketing roles and 4 job levels. The marketing roles established through research are:

1. Research and analysis
2. Planning (at an operational marketing level or at a strategic level)
3. Managing brands
4. Implementing marketing programmes (of various types)
5. Measuring marketing effectiveness
6. Managing marketing people.

Managing people and teams

This element provides the underpinning knowledge required for the selection, development and maintenance of effective marketing teams. Marketing teams are operating in an organizational and global context, and how different organizations adopt different approaches to marketing depends on their context and culture. Key Skills – 'Working with others' and 'Improving one's own knowledge and performance'.

Managing marketing projects and activities

Managing the planning and performance of a marketing task by a team requires skills in planning, scheduling, directing, motivating and monitoring. The techniques of project management equip marketing managers to manage marketing activities and projects effectively.

Managing knowledge and delivering market research projects

Knowledge management is about people. People need to be motivated and enthused to share and exchange knowledge. This cannot be done by simply presenting them with a piece of IT equipment. It requires a cultural norm of open communication, informing and sharing knowledge, and motivating and rewarding knowledge-sharing that benefits the business.

Developing and implementing marketing plans

This element requires effective teamwork, and a good understanding of the marketing planning process and techniques to produce successful outcomes.

Studying management

Key issues to bear in mind when studying management are: firstly, although it is possible to identify trends that are occurring in some large well-known companies, this does not necessarily mean that they are occurring everywhere in all sizes and types of companies.

Awareness of similarities and differences

Examples from one sector may not always be appropriate for understanding what happens in other sectors. There are stereotypes about what happens in both the 'private' and the 'public sector' from within each sector. It is important to go beyond the stereotypes to look for similarities as well as differences. Not all private sector management is good and public sector management bad and vice versa.

Culture

What happens in one country may not be easily applied in other countries because it is difficult to transplant all the social and cultural conditions that make a particular initiative or innovation a success. In recent years, there have been many attempts to use Japanese management techniques with varying degrees of success. Much management writing is based on what happens in companies in the USA and the UK, so it is important to be aware of cultural differences and how other countries do things. What works in one context may not work as well in a different context.

When Parker Pen devised advertisements for its ball point pen they were meant to say 'It won't leak in your pocket and embarrass you.' However, in Spanish 'embararzar' means pregnant, not embarrassed and the advertisement was translated as 'It won't leak in your pocket and make you pregnant.' In Chinese, the name Coca-Cola was translated as Ke-kou-ke-la to make it sound similar to the original. However, after printing its signs, the company discovered that, in at least one dialect the phrase means 'female horse stuffed with wax'. In Taiwan, the slogan 'Come alive with the Pepsi Generation' was translated as 'Pepsi will bring your ancestors back from the dead.'

However, language is only one aspect of culture. The term refers to complete way of life of a people: the shared attitudes, values, goals and practices that characterize a group; their customs, art, literature, religion, philosophy, and so on; the pattern of learned and shared behaviour among the members of a group.

Fads and fashions

Writing about management is prone to fads and fashions, with management gurus often very influential in disseminating ideas about what seems to be working. However, not all popular management ideas are effective. Some management ideas have had a negative effect on some organizations. In the early 1990s, the Chief Economist of Morgan Stanley argued strongly in favour of downsizing, saying that it was a cure for companies' problems. By 1997 he had changed his mind and argued, on the contrary, it could be a recipe for disaster. In 1982, Tom

Peters wrote *In Search Of Excellence*, a book that identified 43 successful companies and gave reasons for their success over 20 years. However, many of the companies, including the computer company IBM (see Case study, p. 10) ran into problems not long after the book was published. Peters apologized, saying that 'there are no excellent companies' and now says of his writing 'Some of my stuff is wrong. Some stuff is right, but I hope all of it is provocative.'

Reading 1.1

Boddy, D. (2002) 'Conventional and critical perspectives and studying management', *Management: An Introduction*, pp. 30–32.

What is management?

Management is an inclusive term that is used in a variety of ways. Generally, it is the process of planning, organizing, leading, co-ordinating and controlling aspects of an organization's resources to achieve organizational goals. Different managers have different styles that are formed by their past experience, the nature of the tasks they have to undertake, the context they work in, and the expectations, capabilities and motivation of the people they work with. Studies of management behaviour show that there are wide variations both for the same manager from 1 week to another and between managers in similar jobs. There are also wide differences between managers' jobs in the same country as well as across countries. Individual influences such as gender, age, ethnic background, education, career experience and personality may also have an impact but there is no conclusive evidence about whether and how these factors influence management behaviour. Rosemary Stewart recommended a three-part classification for the analysis of management jobs. She identified:

1. Job demands (what you must do)
2. Job choices (the freedoms you have to decide what to do)
3. Job constraints (the limit on what you can do).

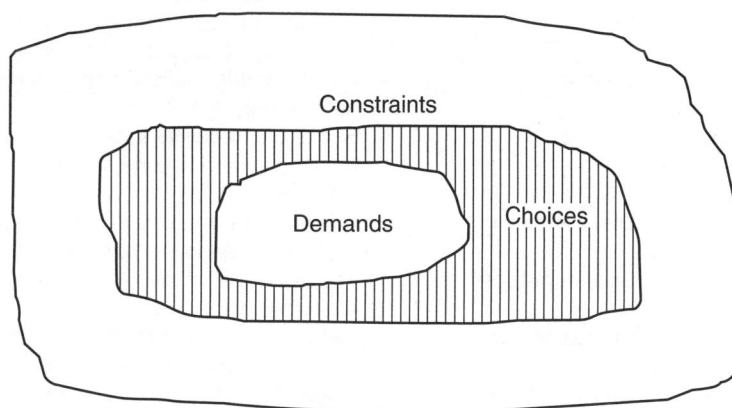

Figure 1.1 The reality of management
Source: Stewart (1963)

Activity 1.1

How would you draw the diagram to represent opportunities, constraints and demands on your own job?

1. *Job demands* – What job activities must not be neglected? What are the targets that you must meet? Who or what defines these demands? – Your manager? Your peers in the organization? People outside the organization? You – your standards or ambitions? Rank them again according to how much attention/time you allocate to each of them. Do these rankings reflect their importance?

2. *Job constraints* – What factors limit you in what you would like to do in your job? Attitudes or expectations of your manager? Your colleagues? People outside the organization? Your organization's policies or procedures? Shortage of other resources? Technology? Your own skills, relationships with other functions in the organization?

3. *Job choices* – What choice do you have over the work that is to be done? When it is to be done? How it is to be done? The standards to which it is to be done? The results that are to be achieved? Over who does the work?

Management roles

Henry Mintzberg analysed the nature of managerial work and concluded that management consisted of a mass of fragmented activities, constant interruption, pressure for immediate answers and reliance on word-of-mouth messages. Managers value 'soft' information, often acquired through gossip, hearsay and speculation. Consequently, important information for the organization is held not necessarily in the memory of its computers but in the minds of its managers. Mintzberg offered a view of management based on 'roles'.

INTERPERSONAL	Figurehead	Performs ceremonial and symbolic duties such as greeting visitors, signing legal documents.
	Leader	Sets the strategic direction of the organization, motivates managers and other staff.
	Liaison	Maintains information links both inside and outside the organization.
INFORMATIONAL	Monitor	Seeks and receives information, scans periodicals and reports, maintains personal contacts.
	Disseminator	Forwards information to other organization members, sends memos and reports.
	Spokesperson	Transmits information to outsiders through speeches, reports and memos.
DECISIONAL	Entrepreneur	Initiates improvement projects, identifies new ideas, delegates responsibility to others.
	Disturbance Handler	Takes corrective action during disputes or crises, resolves conflicts among subordinates, adapts to environmental crises.
	Resource Allocator	Decides who gets resources, scheduling, budgeting, sets priorities.
	Negotiator	Represents department during negotiation of contracts, sales, purchases, budgets.

Figure 1.2 Mintzberg's managerial roles
Source: Mintzberg (1973)

Each of the ten roles covers a different aspect of managerial work. The ten roles form an integrated whole but different managers are likely to give greater prominence to different aspects of the job. For example, sales managers tend to spend relatively more time in their interpersonal roles, while production managers tend to give relatively more attention to the decisional roles. Mintzberg found that the amount of time spent in the three sets of roles varied with the level of the manager. For example, first-line supervisory positions are likely to have more decisional roles (at a day-to-day operational level). Senior managers spend more time on interpersonal roles. Middle managers tend to be more occupied with informational roles. Roles will also change with culture and organizational size.

Activity 1.2

Write some brief notes summarizing what you think 'management' means. What is your experience of management? – As someone who has been managed or when you have managed something or someone. Think of the best manager that you have encountered – what characteristics did they possess? Who was the worst manager you have encountered and what were their characteristics? What conclusions do you draw from this exercise about what makes an effective manager?

Reading 1.2

Boddy, D. (2002) 'The process of management', *Management: An Introduction*, pp. 21–24.

Activity 1.3

This activity asks you, first of all, to try to make a note of everything you do on your next day at work and how long you spend doing it. Draw up a chart with the following headings:

- o Time begun
- o Nature of activity
- o Who was involved?
- o Whether planned or unplanned but occurring as the result of your taking advantage of an opportunity
- o Completed/not completed/deferred/referred elsewhere.

Consider the following questions:

- o How typical a day was this?
- o How much time did you actually spend on what you regard as managerial tasks? You might express this as an approximate percentage of your day at work.
- o What approximate percentage of your time was spent dealing with trivial matters that you feel need not have concerned you?
- o What was the longest period of time you spent on any one task?
- o How many interruptions did you suffer during the day?

o How many of the things you had intended to do during the day did you actually complete?

o How long did you spend at your place of work?

o How much time did you spend on interpersonal roles? decisional roles? informational roles?

o Which of Mintzberg's ten management roles do you perform? What are the most common situations when you would enact these roles?

Marketing management

CIM's definition of marketing is 'The management process which identifies, anticipates and satisfies customer requirements profitability.' This process varies depending on factors such as the size of the organization, the sector in which it is located, the type of work role performed by the manager and the career experience that the marketing manager brings with them. Generally speaking, the smaller the organization the more multifaceted are the roles of the marketing manager.

Marketing titles

Marketing titles and positions vary considerably along with the particular responsibilities that accompany them. They span a range of positions, including marketing director, marketing manager, sales manager, advertising manager, promotion manager and public relations manager. A marketing director is responsible for directing overall marketing policy. Marketing managers work with service or product development, market research and others to develop detailed marketing strategies.

Sales and marketing

As mentioned above, sometimes sales and marketing are combined in one department, section or job description so as to avoid the damaging splits that can sometimes occur when they are separate. Sales and marketing teams should work together creating opportunities for new business, identifying new markets and gathering competitive intelligence. However, they may work quite differently. Sales managers direct the efforts of sales professionals by assigning territories, establishing goals, developing training programs, and supervising local sales managers and their personnel. Sales teams need immediate information to close sales quickly whereas marketing teams are often focused on longer-term results. Differences in approach between sales and marketing can create barriers to sharing information and make it difficult to close sales.

Working across organizational boundaries

Marketing management has an important role in working across organizational boundaries to help prepare managers to develop strategies for their products and services, and incorporate marketing into the corporate strategy. This means that marketing managers need to work with, for example, colleagues from Human Resources and Finance to deal with recruitment and the reward of staff as well as securing and monitoring budgets and expenditure. If a company has introduced a human resource management approach as opposed to a 'personnel' approach, a manager may find that many of the responsibilities that used to belong to the personnel department have been pushed across to line managers. The following case study describes how marketing management process works in the railway industry. It highlights the need for a marketing orientation across the organization.

Insight

An overview of the Marketing Management process in a railway environment

In railways, departments that play a role in service delivery – Operations, Mechanical Engineering and Civil Engineering – affect the quality of the Seven Ps and have an important influence on the marketability of the railway product. They also have a 'Marketing' role but the Marketing Department has primary responsibility for translating the needs of customers into service requirements and communicating them to service providers. It must also ensure that customer needs are met. The wants and needs of the organization's target customers is the main factor influencing the process of Marketing Management. The development of a strategy to meet the needs of the target market must also adapt to distribution channels, suppliers, competitors and publics. It must also adapt to demographic, economic, political, legal, technological, physical and social forces. Marketing Management must take into account all the factors and forces to develop its strategy to serve the target market.

The case study illustrates the point that a marketing orientation requires all the parts of an organization to work interdependently because they can all have an effect on the marketability of the service. Sometimes, a narrow focus on the demands of particular functional requirements with no regard for the customer or end-user can be bad public relations. For example, the scheduling and duration of maintenance work needs to take into account the impact on the travelling public. Releasing stories about the 'wrong' kind of leaves or snow having an adverse effect on the rail network might be technically accurate but a disaster in public relations terms. For example, as part of an English language programme, the German radio station Bayern Radio carried a story entitled 'Leaves on the track: The story of Britain's railway system' and described a comedian's patter:

> *a leaf grows on a tree. It's very small. It's harmless. You can stick one in your mouth and chew it. But when a leaf falls on a railway line, it can stop the biggest train and make it thirty minutes late. One leaf! And now we have the wrong kind of snow. I mean, what is the wrong kind of snow? Nobody knows, but watch the weather forecast. If it's the wrong kind of snow, do not get on a train.* (Bayern Radio, 1999)

This might be a parody of the technical difficulties experienced by Railtrack but it does show the need to make sure that technical issues are presented in a way that understands the potential impact on public relations.

The following diagram shows an example of a structure for a marketing-oriented organization and the typical marketing roles.

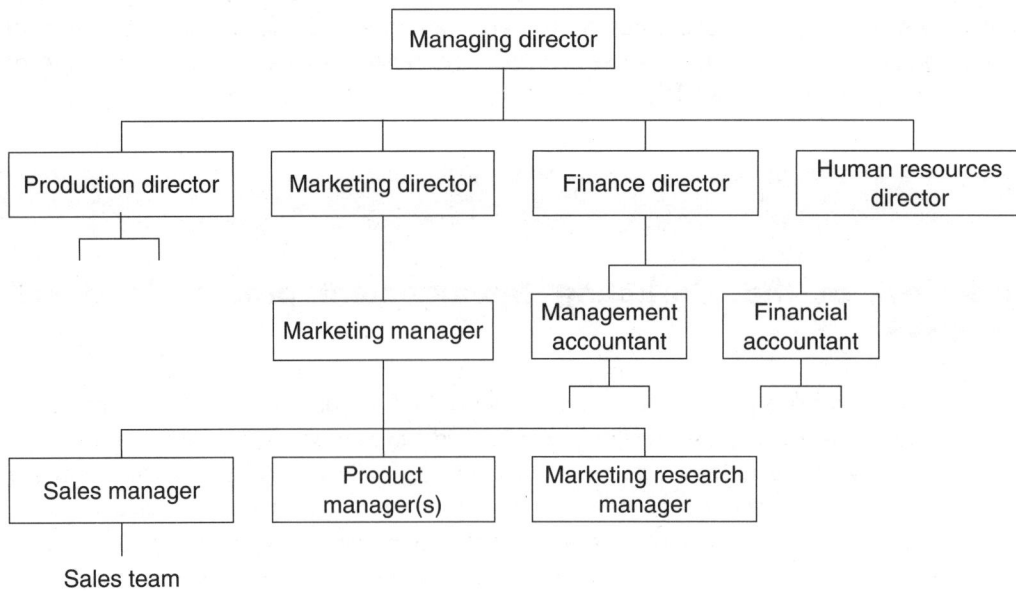

Figure 1.3 Departmentalism by function

In smaller organizations, where these roles exist, they may be carried out by one or two people. The following case study describes how IBM needed to change the structure of its organization to enable people to work together and become more focused on the needs of customers. When you read it, reflect on your own organization and the way that different parts of it work together. Are there any particular arrangements that contribute to successful or unsuccessful collaboration? For example, does the use of IT help or hinder? Is there room for improvement?

Case study

Changing IBM's focus

In the 1990s, IBM faced a difficult competitive environment with demand for its products declining. IBM was used to developing systems and then looking for customers with a problem who would fit the 'solution'. However, it was recognized that helping customers use technology effectively was the critical success factor. 'Solution selling' required a good understanding of the company's capabilities and the ability to integrate these from the different parts of the organization. At IBM, product chiefs and the geographic region heads were the powerful players. IBM's organizational structure stood in the way of providing solutions to customers. Since resources needed mobilising across product and country organizations, there were conflicts. New co-ordinating processes were developed. The sales force had to change from being order takers to becoming consultants and they were re-organized along industry lines. IBM also understood the importance of aligning structure with strategy and encouraged various IBM units to work together.

Source: Adapted from Kumar, Nirmalya (2002) 'The path to change', *Financial Times*, 6 December.

The case study identifies the need for organizations to ensure that their structure fits the strategy that the company is pursuing rather than working against it. It also highlights the importance of being able to draw on resources from across the organization, and to identify and remove any barriers that stand in the way of this. This might involve confronting vested interests and it is important to make sure that solving one problem does not cause another problem somewhere else in the organization. This is looked at in more detail in the unit

'Managing Change'. The functions of marketing vary in different sectors. The following case study is based on marketing legal services and is interesting because sometimes established professions need a lot of convincing that marketing is necessary.

Case study

Marketing legal services

The leading London-based firms have remarkable marketing departments, with extensive budgets, sophisticated technical equipment and talented marketers. Their marketing departments may be broken down into myriad areas including: publications, conferences, desktop publishing and graphics, public relations, internal and external communications, business research, Internet marketing, web and Intranet, and database management. British firms also have additional practice development specialists. The departments are growing in size and results are being tracked to enable the management to see the benefits that the marketing department provides. Marketing departments need to be viewed as knowledge centres and marketers are seen as assets and not cost centres.

Source: 'Growing Your Marketing Department into a Knowledge Management Team: Aim to Hire Assets Not Overheads' by Linda Sedloff Orton, http://www.llrx.com/features/market.htm.

The case study illustrates the importance of trying to assess the value of marketing rather than seeing it exclusively as a cost. This is likely to require a proactive approach to measuring value but there are a wide range of activities that fall under the marketing umbrella. Many people are likely to be surprised at the extent of marketing activity in legal practices. Another issue that is important for considering working relationships is how the function relates to professionals. Professionals tend to value autonomy and having control over their working life. It is not always easy to incorporate them into marketing activities. Throughout the 1980s and 1990s, there were major changes to public sector organization and management. A key aspect of this change was the emergence of a 'new managerialism', that is the importation of modern private sector management techniques which challenged some established principles and practices within the public sector. It was seen as a threat to the traditional dominance of professionalism and professionals.

The digital economy

Communication and information processing technologies are an important tool in many organizations. Company intranets provide an interface for sharing company-wide information and people can access information, collaborate and distribute results anywhere, anytime. High-speed networking capability and software innovations allow work teams to collaborate at a distance, and the growth in the use of ICT also means that the skill mix that people need to perform their jobs is changing.

Organization benefits are:

- New promotional media
- Access to richer and more targeted research data
- Enhanced employee and customer communication
- Ability to customize promotions.

Activity 1.4

Visit the *Lord of the Rings* film website www.lordoftherings.net that supports the film and then go to the *Spiderman* movie website www.spiderman.sonypictures.com/ that supports that film.

Compare the two sites:

- What are the ways used to involve the web viewer and to generate interest in the respective movies?
- What are your views about the potential of this kind of promotional effort?
- How effective is each promotional strategy, given what you have seen?
- What are the types of merchandise each site is selling as part of its merchandising strategy?
- Which site do you think is more effective in marketing terms? What criteria are you using to judge?
- What channel(s) of distribution are being promoted here to purchase this merchandise?

Reading 1.3

Boddy, D. 'Information systems and the process of management', pp. 550–563.

New work practices and implications for management

With the rapid advancements in technology, acceptance of new forms of working from home is set to increase considerably in the future. Teleworking is seen as a way of creating new jobs and increasing flexibility and is now a mainstream form of employment in Europe and the USA. One employee in 20 in the UK is now a teleworker. However, the UK lags behind other parts of the EU where the practice is growing more rapidly. A number of multinational companies have set up teleworking operations around the world and 70 per cent of large companies recognize teleworking. Teleworking is growing rapidly in The Netherlands, Finland and Italy. The public sector is using teleworking, for example in Social Services, Leisure and Environment departments.

Charles Handy wrote *The Age of Unreason* (1991) and predicted a time when new working patterns such as outsourcing, telecommuting and the rise of knowledge workers would become widespread. A number of organizational forms would emerge in an age of unreason.

The Shamrock organization is one that is based on a core of permanent workers supported by outside contractors and consultants used for specific time-limited inputs and part-time help brought in and laid off to cope with peaks and troughs in demand.

The federal organization is a form of decentralization that combines the autonomy of individual parts with the economies of scale that occur because the centre co-ordinates, advises, influences and suggests rather than directs or controls.

The Triple I organizations such as universities and research organizations will try to create value out of knowledge, specifically Information, Intelligence and Ideas. Handy also predicted the growth of Portfolio working which would include paid work and 'free' work encompassing homework, gift work and study work. Paid work is for time given, free work is for results delivered, homework includes the range of tasks carried out in the home. Gift work is work undertaken for charities, neighbours or for the community. The idea of study work is self-explanatory and can take place in and out of the home. A balanced portfolio would comprise elements of each of these types of work in differing proportions for different people.

Activity 1.5

Write a report which explains the likely problems of new work practices for managers and employees. Include the main implications for the business, such as impact on business operations and implications of setting up teleworking.

Equality and diversity

The workforce and working patterns are changing. The working population is getting older and there are more women and men from different cultural and ethnic backgrounds. Employees rightly expect to be treated fairly and considerately. This expectation is generally supported by the law. It is illegal to discriminate against people at work on the grounds of:

Gender
Race
Disability
Sexual orientation (from December 2003)
Religion or belief (from December 2003)
Being or not being a member of a trade union.

From 2006 age will be added. Valuing the diversity of employees is also important from a business point of view. Companies with a diverse range of employees are better able to understand the needs of a diverse range of customers. They are also best placed to recruit and retain staff in an increasingly diverse and competitive labour market. These factors affect company performance.

The role of marketing in the organization

Insight

A survey on Marketing in British organizations by McKinsey & Co. found that the role of marketing was at its most sophisticated in the Business-to-Consumer area (B2C) and the lowest in the Business-to-Business area (B2B). The primary role of marketing for a quarter of all sectors' respondents was promoting sales. But B2C gave greater weight to building brands (28 per cent). Many organizations ran a marketing function without a specific department – 47 per cent for B2C and B2B, and 39 per cent for 'Both'. A specific marketing department was found in 41 per cent of B2C organizations, but in only 15 per cent of B2B and 29 per cent of 'Both'. Almost a third (31 per cent) of all B2B respondents combined marketing with sales or other functions, compared with 23 per cent of 'Both' and only 6 per cent B2C. Less than 10 per cent of respondents stated that marketing does not really exist as a function within their organizations.

Just over half the respondents showed that the most critical change required in their organizations was the need for enhanced collaboration between marketing and other functions. Nearly half of each sector stated that marketing worked with other functions 'most of the time' (45 per cent B2C, 47 per cent both, 46 per cent B2B), and slightly less specified 'all the time' (32 per cent B2C, 29 per cent both, 29 per cent B2B).

Source: McKinsey Marketing Practice, 2002.

The extract from the survey shows that there is a lot of work to be done to improve cross-organization working and, in particular, the way that marketing works with other functions in the organization. This is looked at in greater depth in Unit 3 'Developing the Team'.

Question 1.1

How is marketing activity organized in your organization? How would you describe collaboration? Is it successful? If so, what factors contribute to its success? If not, how could it be improved? The following extract written by a marketing manager shows some of the diversity that exists in marketing jobs.

Insight

I am a marketing manager in a services company. There is a flat hierarchical structure, with a CEO, a layer of senior management and then the rest of us. We are a small team of self-managers and are encouraged to manage our own career-development. We are not issued with job descriptions to demonstrate that the role is dynamic and evolving. We are also encouraged to develop our roles individually rather than have our workload dictated by the management. Our jobs have 'breadth' rather than 'depth' which makes us less specialized but more able to handle *ad hoc* enquiries across different areas and we are each required to turn our hand to whatever situation arises.

Question 1.2

Do you have a job description? – Is it useful or does it gather dust? – Does it accurately reflect what you do? Is it reviewed regularly? – If you do not have one, are there any problems that arise because of it?

Organization culture

Charles Handy reporting the work of Harrison suggests that organizations can be classified under four cultures. He felt that every organization was a different mix of the same four basic cultures.

Power culture

Handy describes this as the Zeus Culture, after the head of the gods, and is an organization dominated by the personality and power of one person, often the owner. The visual image is of a spider's web with power residing at the centre controlled by a single owner or a small group. Power and influence spread out from a central figure or group. The organization is dependent on the ability and judgement of the central power base.

Role culture

Handy calls this the Apollo Culture, after the god of harmony and order, and represents a culture dominated by rules and procedures. Work within and between departments is controlled formally by procedures, role descriptions, lines of authority and well-defined systems. Matters for decision have to be taken up the line and co-ordination is at the top by the senior management group. Role cultures tend to develop in relatively stable environments. The civil service and the IBM of the late 1980s are examples of a role culture.

Task culture

This is called the Athena Culture, after the warrior goddess. It is a culture that is suited to project work and is typical of consultancies and advertising agencies. The visual image used by Handy is a net with its vertical and horizontal lines and, not surprisingly, network and matrix organizations are examples of this kind of culture. People with the necessary skills, sometimes from different levels of the organization, are brought together to work on specific projects. The teams can be formed for specific purposes, disbanded, reformed and reconfigured according to the nature of the work that needs to be undertaken.

Person culture

Handy calls this the Dionysius Culture, where the individual has the freedom to develop their own ideas in the way they want such as in an artists' studio, or a traditional university. In this type of culture it is difficult to manage individuals since there is very little structure and individuals are relatively autonomous to carry out their work in the way that they want. Some consultants, barristers' chambers and universities are examples of such a culture. Typically, individuals work on their own but they do find administrative support useful.

Every organization is different from each other but they are all a mix of the same four basic cultures. The problem is that some organizations get 'stuck' in one of them instead of mixing all four.

Objectives of an organizational structure

Organization structure refers to the pattern of relationships among positions in the organization and among members of the organization. The purpose of structure is to divide work among members of the organization and co-ordinate their activities so that they are directed towards achieving the goals and objectives of the organization. Structure defines tasks and responsibilities, work roles and relationships, and channels of communication. It should embrace:

o Accountability for the areas of work undertaken by groups and individual members of the organization.
o Co-ordination of different parts of the organization and different areas of work.
o Effective and efficient organizational performance, including resource utilization.
o Monitoring the activities of the organization.
o Flexibility in order to respond to changing environmental factors.
o Job satisfaction of members of the organization.

An organization's structure is said to have two major components, these include formalization and centralization. Formalization is the extent to which rules and regulations are used to regulate behaviour. This is affected by the size of the organization because a small shop will not have as many rules as a hospital or an oil refinery. Centralization refers to where decision-making powers lie within an organization. In highly centralized organizations, most decisions are made at the highest level of management and these are communicated to other members. In a decentralized organization, the authority to make decisions is more widespread at all levels of management. Most organizations use a variety of these forms and may combine aspects of both for different parts of the organization.

Hierarchical models of organizations

- Responsibilities and duties are clearly laid down – strong on formalization and strong on centralization.
- Specialized rather than generic roles.
- Vertical rather than horizontal communication.
- Decision-making is strongly centralized at senior levels of the organization.
- Clear lines of accountability between different levels of the hierarchy.
- Clear rules of procedure written down.

Collegial models of organizations

- Authority is generally through expertise and knowledge rather than necessarily through position.
- Weak on decentralization.
- 'Bottom-heavy' – large numbers with the same pay and conditions.
- Common goals and purposes – people work together in teams.
- Formal and informal opportunities to participate in the development of initiatives.
- Employees are autonomous individuals needing a minimum of rules.

Handy's model of organizational culture can be put together with the formalization and centralization dimensions to form a matrix as shown in Figure 1.4:

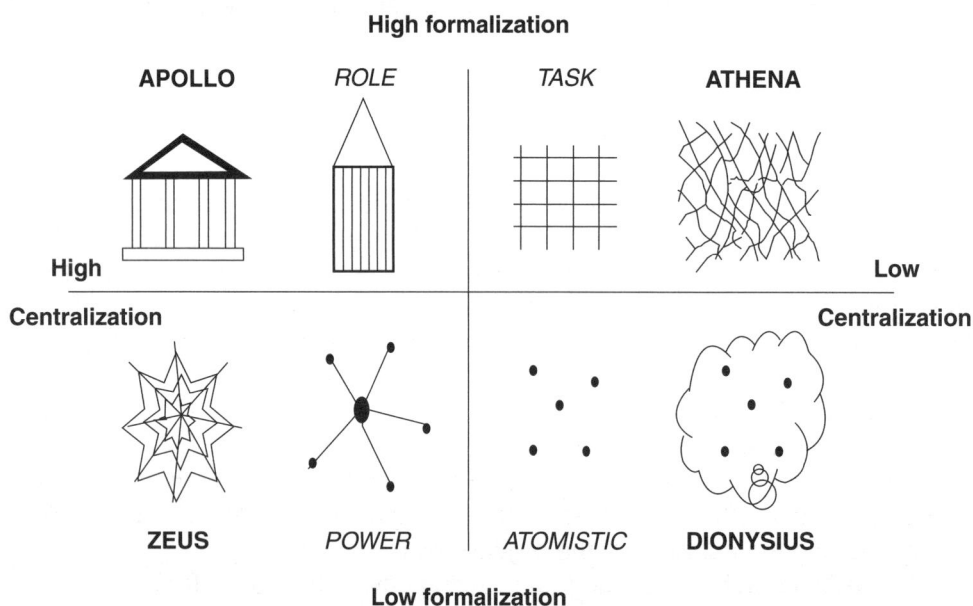

Figure 1.4 Models of organizational culture

The following case study identifies what is needed from an organizational structure and culture in a fast-moving airline industry that can be strongly influenced by external social, political and economic forces.

Case study 1

Singapore Airlines

The Group needs a flexible structure that enables people to work with one another in a co-ordinated and co-operative way. Issues associated with decentralizing a business include: *maintaining lines of communication* – so that people know how other parts of the enterprise are working; *staff motivation* – the structure must provide job satisfaction and be capable of motivating all employees; *achieving goals* – employees need to know the goals set for them; *thinking globally whilst acting locally* – responding to local needs but remaining conscious of the global environment. A flatter organizational structure creates a more dynamic and flexible business, empowering people to make decisions in response to customer needs and to the changing nature of the Group's activity.

The case of Singapore Airlines identifies a range of issues that need to be addressed, particularly the need to balance a range of factors such as knowledge of local markets and also being able to see the 'bigger picture' and the autonomy to make decisions whilst also requiring greater collaboration and co-ordination amongst people. Potentially, these trends could work against each other which is why managers need to be alert and guard against it.

(A) Activity 1.6

Using the key factors identified in the case study above – communication, motivation, achieving goals and, if appropriate, acting locally and thinking globally – analyse the structure of your own organization from the point of view of enabling people with a marketing role to work with one another, and with other people in the organization in a co-ordinated and co-operative way.

Types of organizational structure

Functional

This type of structure groups major functions, for example information, finance, personnel and marketing. The advantages of this kind of structure are that it increases the utilization and co-ordination of groups of people with technical/specialized expertise. It can encourage sectional interests and conflicts, and make it difficult for an organization to adapt to product/service diversification.

Figure 1.5 Traditional organization of marketing departments

Product/Service

This is where there is grouping by service/product. For example, in the Health Service, the structure could have groupings around specialisms such as orthopaedic, surgical, psychiatric, and so on, rather than medical, nursing and paramedical functions.

The following provides an example of a large marketing-oriented organization chart. In this kind of structure, marketing is represented at board level and a Marketing Manager co-ordinates the marketing activity in the organization.

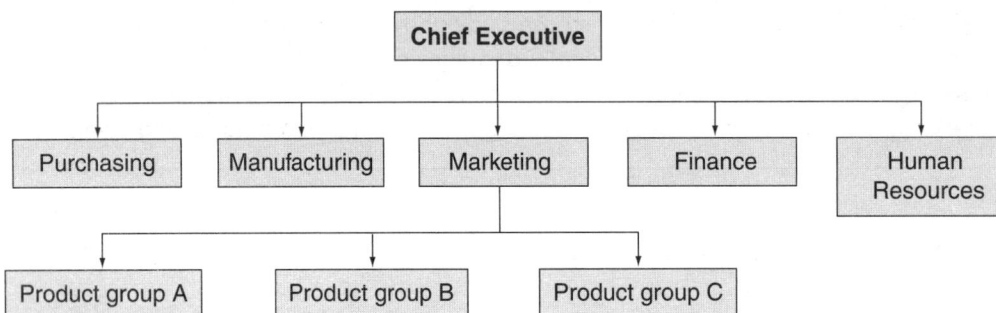

Figure 1.6

Geographical

A nationalized service develops regions or areas; for example, in the NHS there are District Health Authorities, Health Authorities, Primary Care Groups, Hospital Trusts, Primary Care Trusts and Strategic Health Authorities covering regional and local organizations. Such a structure should mean greater responsiveness to local/regional issues and different cultures, national/state laws, and so on. A potential disadvantage is the possibility of localities/regions conflicting with each other. The following two case studies are both examples of very different organizations with a geographical organization structure.

Case study

The Seventh-day Adventist Church is organized with a representative form of church government. This means that authority in the Church comes from the membership of local churches. Four levels of Church structure lead from the individual believer to the worldwide Church organization.

1. The local church made up of individual believers.
2. The local conference, or local field/mission, made up of a number of local churches in a state, province, or territory.
3. The union conference, or union field/mission, made up of conferences or fields within a larger territory (often a grouping of states or a whole country).
4. The General Conference, the most extensive unit of organization, made up of all unions in all parts of the world. Divisions are sections of the General Conference, with administrative responsibility for particular geographical areas.

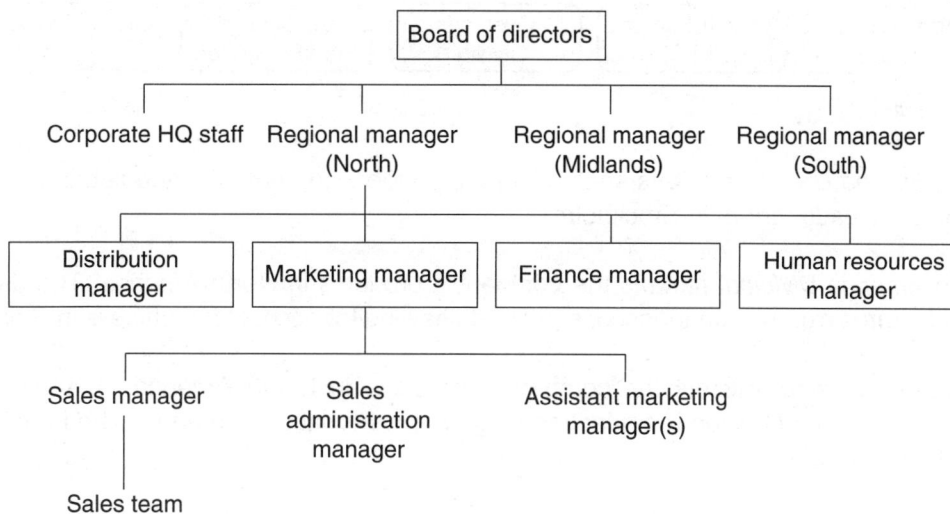

Figure 1.7 Departmentalism by territory

Singapore Airlines uses a geographical structure because it perceives that this makes it easier to customize services to local markets and enable greater responsiveness to customers.

Case study

As a global business with operations in more than 80 countries, Singapore Airlines has also divided up its overseas business by geographical area. For each region, it has created a senior vice president with authority for that region. Being organized geographically makes it easier for a large company to:

o Respond quickly to local issues and problems.
o Build up knowledge of specific markets.
o Tailor its strategies to local conditions, laws and customs.

Within this structure, general managers for each country have the independence to make their own decisions, allowing the organization to respond more quickly and appropriately to market conditions.

Geographical structures

Geographical structures traditionally developed as companies expanded their offerings across territories. There was usually a need to be close to the customer, and to minimize the costs of travel and distribution. Today, the economics of location is important but information technology is making it less important in certain industries. The use of geographical structure depends on the industry. In service industries where the service is provided on-site, geography continues to be a structural basis for many companies. Sales forces and knowledge services like consulting were traditionally managed out of local offices, based on personal relationships and knowledge of the region. However, industry knowledge and expertise are becoming more important. Geographical structures are occurring in industries where the technology is creating a smaller efficient scale and flexible plants, and where customers demand just-in-time delivery.

Swedish match company

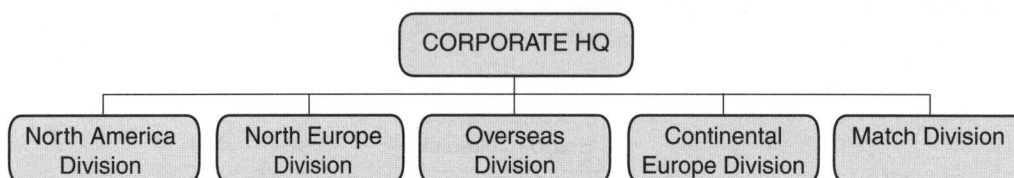

Figure 1.8

North Europe Division markets snuff, cigars, pipe tobacco, matches and lighters in the Nordic countries. Headquarters in Stockholm.

North America Division markets the company's products in North America. The division also manufactures cigars, pipe tobacco, snuff and chewing tobacco. Head office is in Richmond VA.

Overseas Division markets the company's products in South America, Australia, Asia and South Africa. The Division manufactures cigars, pipe tobacco and snuff. The head office is in Rio de Janeiro, Brazil.

Continental Europe markets the company's products in Europe with the exception of the Nordic countries. The Division manufactures cigars, pipe tobacco and lighters. The head office is in Valkenswaard, The Netherlands.

Match Division manufactures matches in Sweden, Brazil, Spain, Hungary, Turkey, Bulgaria, Indonesia and India. The matches are marketed globally through the four geographic divisions: North Europe, Continental Europe, North America and Overseas. The head office is in High Wycombe, Great Britain.

Division structure

This is where the organization is divided into divisions with devolved responsibility for the conduct of their business and financial performance. The grouping of services and/or geography and functionality (but often with functions such as finance, personnel and planning retained at headquarters). This can be suitable for international companies that are highly diversified, working in more than one country, for example, a pharmaceutical company with divisions in each country producing and marketing products developed by the parent company. Divisional structures can be tight or loose, that is, with varying degrees of central control and common service (finance, personnel, computing, etc.). Examples of this kind of structure are General Motors and GEC (UK).

The divisional structure is often developed in response to the difficulties associated with the functional structure. Divisions or business units are set out, each being regarded as a profit centre. Often the divisions are decided upon according to processes, geographic region, product type, or sometimes some combination of two of these. There is often diversity within a division which can be combated by subdivisions (e.g. product divisions further divided according to geographic region), or by having a functional structure within the division. The main advantage is that each division can be managed almost as if it were a separate company, which helps to deal effectively with different products or markets. This division of the company can, however, lead to wasteful duplication of services. This structure is suited to companies which are able to very clearly distinguish between different divisions. When there is confusion as to which division should be responsible for something, it can lead to considerable managerial difficulties. Advantages include improved decision-making, accountability for performance and better co-ordination of functions. The disadvantage is that economies of scale can be lost and rivalry among divisions might be fostered.

Singapore police training command

As the police force is operating in an environment that is changing rapidly, training and continuous learning play an important role in enabling officers to cope with change. Therefore, there is a need to have training capabilities, which enable the organization to monitor and control operational doctrines and translate them into training contents.

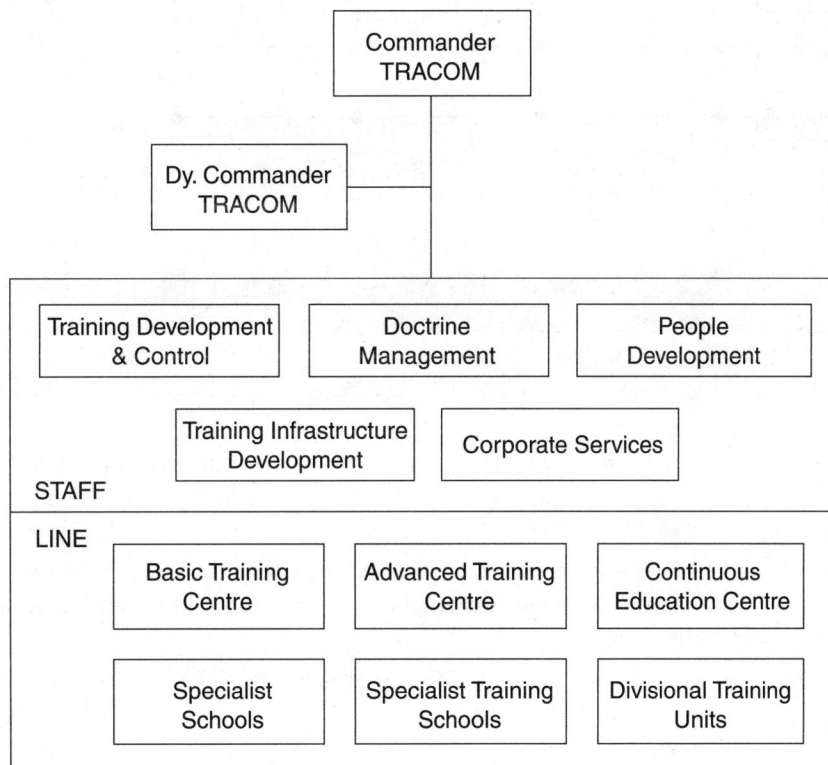

Figure 1.9

Matrix

To make use of both marketing and product know-how, modern companies establish a matrix organization. It should combine product and marketing know-how in a flat hierarchy that is flexible towards market requirements. The matrix approach involves organizing the management of a task along lines that cross normal departmental boundaries so that the ability of product managers and functional managers to communicate with each other is crucial. For example, a new product development team might be formed from an engineer, a research chemist, a marketing manager and a designer. In the matrix, individuals have two or more 'managers', for example, a sales manager will report to the marketing director and the product manager. Once the project has been finished, the team may be disbanded, with the individual members being drafted into other teams or absorbed back into the organizational structure. This kind of structure should ensure that the project is better co-ordinated than with four or five departments contributing occasionally. If many different project teams are organized, it gives more people an opportunity to use their capabilities. It emphasizes that project aims are all-important. The disadvantage is that individuals may suffer if both managers make heavy demands on them and there can be conflict between the project leader and the functional leader. Sometimes there can be a failure to provide clear lines of accountability.

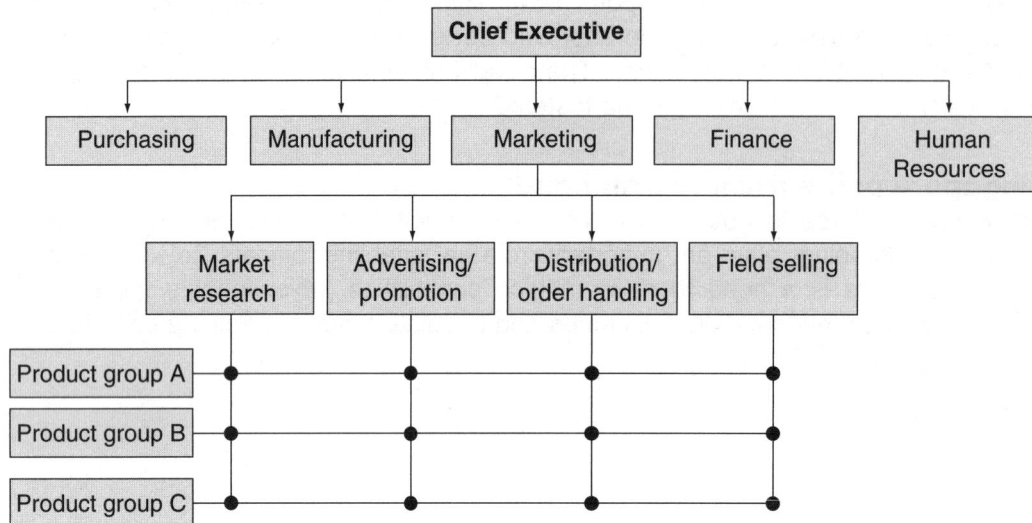

Figure 1.10

Case study 2

BIC

A company's values should help to determine the way it behaves. BIC's values relate to its products, which are:

o *Functional* – designed to perform a specific function well, for example, to draw a line, produce a flame, shave hair. The key to achieving functionality is to adopt the most appropriate design, engineering and technology.
o *Affordable* – achieved by using appropriate design, materials production and distribution channels.
o *Universal* – capable of being used by anyone worldwide, for example, the ballpoint pen, the pocket lighter, the one-piece shaver.

BIC has three core categories for products, based on a global range, designed for mass appeal. BIC then helps local retailers to select the products that best suit their own customers' needs from this range. Each of the product categories is managed by a Category General Manager, who has the overall responsibility for the marketing, development and manufacturing worldwide. In recent years manufacturing operations have been simplified and super-factories serve very large geographical markets. Product distribution is then organized by continent, with country managers reporting to their continental manager. The organization is a matrix structure based on two main lines of communication:

1. By product category
2. By geographical region.

It means that an employee working, say, in a pen manufacturing plant in France would be accountable both within the Western European division and the stationery category.

BIC's matrix structure
Product category:

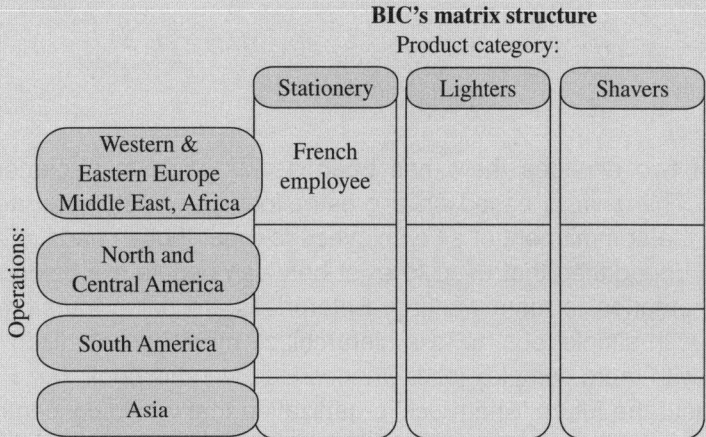

From the BIC case study it can be seen that the matrix structure is aimed at maximizing the benefits of strong product expertise with strong operational structures in each major geographical area.

The problem with all forms of organization structure is how to encourage people to feel that not only do they belong to their part of the organization but also to the whole organization. The Singapore Airlines case study provides an example of how managers are encouraged to have a company-wide focus. Do you have any similar policies in your organization? Do they work? Do they cause unanticipated problems, for example loss of expertise?

Case study 3

Singapore Airlines

A problem that can result from organizing by function is that people know one part of the business but have no experience of the business as a whole. Singapore Airlines has a policy of moving key staff around to provide managers with cross-functional expertise and knowledge of the business as a whole. At the same time, the Group wishes to retain a sense of common purpose. Wherever they work, every employee within the Group is united in a number of other ways, through the Singapore Airlines song, through wearing similar uniforms and through sharing a common business culture, philosophy and goals.

To what extent do you feel that these examples are culturally specific, or would they work anywhere? Obviously, your organization may be too small for this to be a factor but does your own organization have any particular ways of making people feel that they belong to the 'whole' organization?

Question 1.3

Does your organization do anything specific to encourage employees to understand the business as a whole and develop a sense of common purpose?

Reading 1.4

Boddy, D. *Organization and Culture*, Chapter 8, pp. 233–260.

Over the past two decades there has been a change in management practices in many organizations. This shift is based on a greater focus on customers' needs and aspirations, and engaging the commitment of all employees to meet those needs effectively. Typically, the organizational boundaries that used to exist between people are being replaced with internal networks that emphasize team working. Enterprises are being transformed from hierarchical organizations with simple jobs, to less hierarchical, more decentralized and network-oriented organizations with more complex jobs. Charles Handy in his book *The Empty Raincoat* (1990) has written about the future 'Shamrock' organization that would concentrate on fewer full-time people at the core whilst others had to develop 'portfolio' lives, a mix of different bits and pieces of part-time work. However, he felt that people were not being properly prepared for this kind of future.

The following case study shows how a well-known company changed from a traditional functional structure to one based on cross-functional teams. Interestingly, one of the benefits is a cross-company marketing culture.

Case study

Elida Faberge from 'Marketing Department' to 'Marketing Company'

In 1992, Elida Faberge started to bring about a change of approach to meet the needs of a changing environment. The typical organization prior to 1992 was based on a functional structure with the key functions being Marketing, Sales, Commercial, Technical and Personnel. The business was re-organized as a process-based organization. Traditional departments like 'Marketing' were abolished. Work is now planned and implemented by cross-functional teams. New process-based systems of strategic planning and control have been created, which ensure customer requirements are given priority. The cross-functional approach has resulted in a pan-company marketing culture. Training days per employee significantly increased from 7 to 10. Productivity per employee rose by 50 per cent. Numbers of managers reduced by 30 per cent between 1992 and 1994, and then kept at the same level.

Managing yourself

Managing effectively requires knowing yourself and effective managers understand how their behaviour affects others. They are able to adapt their style to the context in which they work. Personal management skills are common to all management jobs at whatever level. The Charities Aid Foundation (CAF) has identified competences in four clusters: managing self, managing others, managing work and technical competences. CAF has identified job competences from level 1 to 5 and, as can be seen below, the position requires competences mainly at level 3. It is unusual for organizations to use this level of detail in identifying the characteristics needed to perform a particular role effectively but the following are the 'managing self' competences required by CAF for a Marketing Co-ordinator position.

Communication   **Level 3**

Takes account of the audience when making presentations. Conveys complex and/or technical information in a clear, concise way. Contributes complete sections of Departmental documents. The job requires provision of written data with in the department.

Creativity   **Level 3**

Rapidly absorbs facts and evidence, and makes considered decisions under pressure. Decisions cover a range of activities where information may not always be available. Awareness of the impact of decisions on others and the business overall.

Motivation   **Level 2**

Adapts approach to meet objectives and pursues key result areas. Looks to recover from setbacks to regain position. Works with a sense of urgency to ensure targets are met and is encouraging to others in the team.

Sharing Knowledge   **Level 3**

Establishes procedures that encourage sharing of good practice across the organization. Formally researches to ensure all information and data is accurate before used by self, team and others. Probes for additional information on clients and issues.

Interpersonal   **Level 3**

Judges and makes inferences about the concerns of others, predicts likely responses and prepares accordingly.

Integrity   **Level 3**

Able to give constructive feedback in a difficult situation and resolve minor discrepancies. Areas of serious concern are relayed to above level.

Figure 1.11 Managing self job competences
Source: CAF

Managing people

The belief that people are the most important asset that an organization has is based on some key assumptions:

o People make the difference and need to be treated as assets, not costs.
o In the light of the importance of people, their management is an issue of strategic importance.
o Managing human resources is too important to be left to personnel managers – it must be an activity undertaken by all managers.
o Managing people, policies and practices needs to be fully integrated with the other aspects of the organization's strategy.

HRM is meant to represent a more strategic approach to the management of people, and its main purpose is to ensure that all people management policies are integrated, coherent, mutually reinforcing and supportive of the strategic direction of the organization. This is why performance management is an important issue – it provides a way of linking individuals and groups with organizational priorities. Central to this is the role of managers who are expected to be much more active in managing the staff in their unit or department to contribute to the organization's effectiveness.

Key marketing roles and tasks

Marketing titles and positions can vary among different organizations and sectors of the economy along with the responsibilities that accompany them. The marketing function can also be organized in different ways depending on factors such as size, management philosophy and type of business.

(A) Activity 1.7

Look for marketing jobs and positions on the Internet and make a note of the skills and working relationships required. See the example below.

As the advertisement demonstrates, the role of a marketing manager can be multifaceted. A summary of some of the main marketing management roles is shown below.

Marketing manager

One of the main responsibilities of a marketing manager is to identify the target market for products and services, devise strategies and select media that will reach and attract the target market. A marketing manager needs to work with a range of people inside and outside the organization on all aspects of marketing. Inside the company the marketing manager may work with the sales force, promotion manager, product development teams and market research. Outside the company this may involve advertising agencies, consultants and market research organizations. This means that marketing managers need to have good people skills. A marketing manager's responsibilities include large-scale customer relationship management, utilizing skills in customer segmentation, customer loyalty, customer satisfaction, database marketing and direct marketing. These jobs may require market research skills or they may be the responsibility of a market research manager.

Advertising

Advertising managers may oversee account services, creative services and media services departments. Planning and managing advertising campaigns and briefing and managing advertising agencies are a key part of the role, particularly in larger organizations. In larger firms, advertising managers oversee in-house accounts, creative and media services departments. An account executive manages the account services department, assesses the need for advertising and, in advertising agencies, maintains the accounts of clients. The creative services department develops the subject-matter and presentation of advertising. A creative director oversees the copy chief, art director and their respective staffs. A media director oversees planning groups that select the communication media – for example, radio, television, newspapers, magazines, Internet, or outdoor signs – to disseminate the advertising. Assessing the effectiveness of advertising is often undertaken in conjunction with market researchers. In a small firm, managers may serve as a liaison between the firm and the advertising or promotion agency to which many advertising or promotional functions are contracted out.

Brand management

Brand managers design and enhance the brand image to support the marketing strategy and plans. They identify the issues to explore with consumers about their brand experiences, and they build the research capabilities to gather that intelligence. Then, with help from each of the company's functions, product development, manufacturing, marketing and sales, they translate this learning into specifications for product development and process design. They also fund the development of brand-building capabilities and track the performance of the functions they oversee. The following two extracts show the developments that are occurring in brands and their management. The developments have implications for the kinds of management skills needed to be a successful brand manager and the trend towards interactive and more customized marketing.

Extended knowledge

The New Brand Management – Traditional brand managers are responsible mainly for managing promotions, advertising and relations with the trade. Often, they have neither the authority nor the skills to articulate the strategic, cross-functional, long-term perspective that is required. It takes someone with the power, skills, perspective and access to information necessary to drive the development of new products and the design of new business processes. What might the new brand-management function look like?

Category Brand Management – Category managers patrol the boundaries and relationships among brands ensuring that a company's brands are not competing with each other.

Corporate Brand Management – A manager must have a holistic perspective on the consumer's experience and on the entire business system that defines a brand. The levels of managerial expertise are higher, and the stakes involved in launching, maintaining and evolving a brand are also higher today compared to the past.

Does this match up with your experience of brand management and brand managers?

Labels like Nike are out of favour on Wall Street – and losing their cool on the high street. On both sides of the Atlantic, the story is the same: It's not easy for a global company whose trainers are on every high street to remain fashionable. Young people like brands that are (a bit) rebellious and Nike is perilously close to being the establishment. A decision was taken in the mid-Eighties to turn the business into 'a marketing-oriented company'. Nike stopped making anything and became a kind of shell, branding and distributing products. An assumption grew up that all products were the same because technology made goods so easy to copy. Values, though, were different. You couldn't copy 'Just do it'. Brands that are seen to be too big and homogenized need to diversify. McDonald's has bought Prêt a Manger, and Coca-Cola hedges its bets by buying up or creating sub-brands. The future for the big brands is to get customers more involved. Megabrands aren't offering what consumers want. Now the challenge is how to involve the consumer and individualize the product.

Source: Geraldine Bedell (2003) *The Observer*, Sunday, 19 January.

Relationship marketing

Gronroos (1994) defined relationship marketing as identifying, establishing, maintaining, enhancing and, where necessary, terminating the relationship with customers and other stakeholders, at a profit. Relationship marketing is focused on maximizing the lifetime value of desirable customers and customer segments. Strategies need to enhance relationships with key 'markets', including internal ones as well as external relationships with customers, suppliers, referral sources, influence markets and recruitment markets. A relationship marketing approach aims to bring the elements of quality, customer service and marketing into an integrated relationship. This helps marketers to focus on maintaining and enhancing customer relationships. The types of interactions that take place between buyers and sellers can be viewed on a continuum, ranging from transaction to relationship.

Transaction marketing	Relationship marketing
Focus more on single sale	Focus more on customer retention
Orientation more on product features	Orientation more on product benefits
Comparatively short timescale	Comparatively long timescale
Little emphasis on customer service	High emphasis on customer service
Limited customer commitment	Higher customer commitment
Moderate customer contact	Higher customer contact
Quality is primarily a concern of production	Quality is the concern of all

Case study

Wal-Mart Stores Inc. has been ranked number one in the USA by Fortune magazine for a second year in a row. Wal-Mart uses one-to-one relationship marketing tactics, executed by the famous Wal-Mart greeter. A greeter at the door thanks customers for coming in, assists with a shopping cart, and provides a 'goodbye thank you' upon departing the store. So why don't others adopt this simple marketing tactic? — because relationship marketing is not as simple as it seems. It takes a type of commitment different than traditional marketing.

Relationship Marketing has 4 key components:

1. It has to be personalized. Personalization can come in the form of a highly targeted direct mail piece, a phone call or e-mail.
2. It has to be targeted. Wal-Mart invests in maintaining relationships with existing customers. By targeting this group, Wal-Mart establishes long-term relationships with their most loyal shoppers.
3. It has to be meaningful. If the Wal-Mart greeter did not look you in the eye while saying 'hello', the greeting would not have a lasting impact.
4. It should be interactive. Many Wal-Mart greeters learn the names of frequent shoppers. It is important to make relationship marketing interactive so you can hear feedback. Don't forget the value of real conversations and face-to-face meetings. There is a reason why Wal-Mart employs more than 164 000 associates 55 and older to greet customers at the door.

Relationship Marketing King Wal-Mart Still No. 1 by Doug Edge, 29 April 2003.

Customer relationship management (CRM)

This is an area of marketing that has been influenced considerably by the availability of IT solutions, particularly large interactive databases to enable companies to gather and maintain large amounts of data about individual customers and enable more individualized marketing. Customer databases and database marketing are the key to effective CRM.

Database uses include:

- Identifying the best prospects
- Matching offers to customers
- Strengthening customer loyalty
- Re-activating customer purchasing.

Relationship marketing sees the concept of ongoing customer loyalty at the core of its customer relationship marketing strategy. The key aims are to ensure existing customers to continue purchase from them on a life-long basis, that is achieving lifetime value to both the customer and the organization, rather than just one-off transactions. Sometimes, organizations concentrate solely on their customers, but there are other important relationships that should be considered. Typically, these groups are known as the stakeholder audience and include the following:

- *Internal Markets* – If employees are treated as customers it should be possible to improve levels of customer service and quality throughout the organization.
- *Influence Markets* – These are any bodies or groups that influence or have the potential to influence the organization's operations. This includes government and regulatory bodies.
- *Employee Markets* – The recruitment, retention and succession of skilled staff are important to the continuing success of the organization and companies need HR strategies to address this.
- *Supplier Markets* – In recent years, there has been a lot more emphasis on partnerships and alliances, and the synergy that is created from different forms of co-operative relationship.
- *Referral Markets* – This is where organizations refer potential customers to third parties, for example, banks may refer mortgage customers to insurance companies and vice versa.

In order to implement successfully the ethos and culture of relationship marketing, the organization needs to look at internal markets – that is the employees and management of the organization. This aspect is considered in more detail in Unit 3 'Developing the Team'.

Knowledge management – At the heart of a CRM implementation is the acquisition of information about a customer, its analysis, sharing and tracking. Employees need to know what actions they need to take as a result of this knowledge.

Database consolidation – The consolidation of customer information in a single database and the re-engineering of business processes around the customer. All interactions with a customer need to be recorded in one place to drive production, marketing, sales and customer support activities.

Integration of channels and systems – Customers should be able to interact with a company through the former's channel of choice. The aim is to integrate all communication channels with the customer database. It also means the integration of CRM with other parts of a company's business systems and applications.

Technology and infrastructure – Tools exist to automate and streamline online customer service but there is a need to ensure that the technology infrastructure is able to cope with increased volumes.

Change management – CRM involves a change in philosophy and attitudes. A process for managing this change is needed to help a company move from a product centric focus to a more customer centric one.

Activity 1.8

Visit CRM Update at http://techupdate.cnet.com/enterprise/0-6133427-724-20156564.html and answer the following questions:

1. The site contains information about CRM. How could a CRM manager benefit from the site?
2. Read one of the related articles on CRM found on the site and describe how a company can benefit from the information you found.

Case study

Sales and marketing

A key aspect of developing and maintaining effective relationships with people in other functions and disciplines within the organization is how the sales and marketing functions work together. This is a critical relationship and can take different forms depending on factors such as the size of the company, number of products and services and the geographical reach of the organization. Greater complexity creates greater demands on the co-ordination of activities.

According to IT market analysis firm Aberdeen Group Inc., as much as 80 per cent of marketing expenditures on lead generation are wasted because these efforts are ignored by salespeople. Marketing teams overlook critical input from salespeople regarding customer data and needs. Marketing exists to support sales. A marketing department can develop a good product strategy, but it is up to sales staff to implement it. And when the marketing and sales departments fail to share the right information, the organization suffers.

Salespeople are required to spend the bulk of their time in the field meeting with customers, in the office on the phone, or at the computer. Marketing people are under pressure to solve challenges quickly and creatively while analyzing the available information on the competition, the marketplace, the company's products and services, and the target audience. They rarely interact with customers, unless it is through second-party reports from surveys or focus group research. To succeed, marketing people and sales staff both need to be involved in the development of sales and marketing programmes and planning marketing activities – from product launches through promotional campaigns – If the sales force is not involved programmes are likely to fail. Sales staff need to share customer insights as well as candid information on the usability and effectiveness of marketing tools and campaigns.

Marketing should present:

o An overview of current business conditions a company faces, including new technological breakthroughs, competitive product launches, and government regulations that will affect customer relations.
o Promotional and advertising programmess in the works, their central messages, key features and launch dates.
o A description of the marketing programmes of major competitors.
o Details about forthcoming press coverage.
o Insight gained from customer feedback from Websites and research.

A sales team should report on:

o Any changes in customer demographics or hot buttons.
o The quality of marketing leads.
o The effectiveness of special promotions.
o Objections raised by customers, and the sales strategies and tactics used to overcome them.
o Feedback on how well marketing messages relate to customers' needs.
o Competitive product or service comparisons as they relate to the company's strengths, weaknesses, opportunities and threats.
o Feedback on the usability of sales tools and materials.
o When you ensure vital information flows between your sales and marketing teams, the resulting marketing campaigns and materials will be right on the money.

Source: http://www.entrepreneur.com/Magazines/Copy_of_MA_SegArticle/0,4453,314251,00.html.

Are there any particular difficulties in how different functions relate to or communicate with each other in your organization?

Are there any particularly successful strategies deployed for overcoming communication problems?

Argos is one of the UK's largest chain stores owned by GUS plc. In the late 1990s a new boss set out to improve its performance by changing the business culture, that is, the values and beliefs shared across the organization. The new culture he wanted to promote was one that was based on:

o Good customer service
o Close teamwork
o Managers being given more responsibility
o All staff showing respect for each other
o All staff wanting to better compete and to improve the business.

The sense in which all employees feel that they work for one organization rather than a particular department or function in an organization is a key aspect of organizational success. A feeling that we are 'all in it together' based on good relationships is likely to be a more effective approach than one where there are a lot of internal rivalries and destructive competition.

Other key aspects of marketing

A marketing manager can find themselves specialising in a particular area of marketing or in a marketing related area such as public relations. The following section provides a brief summary of these areas.

Direct marketing

This develops the direct marketing strategy, ensuring it complements the overall marketing strategy. It requires an understanding of the various channels through which customers can be reached directly. It requires building, developing, maintaining and using large databases. Campaign results and trends need to be analysed and presented to senior management. External agencies need to be briefed and managed.

Internal marketing

Internal marketing is based on the premise that all customer contact employees, supporting service people and the whole organization need to develop a marketing orientation and work as a team to provide customer satisfaction. If employees are motivated, this has positive benefits for the employee–customer relationship. The areas that companies need to pay attention to are: recruitment and training of staff, levels of remuneration, delegation of decision-making to give customer interfacing staff greater discretion to respond to customers, developing and/or introducing systems and technology that are designed to have a beneficial impact on customer service and reducing any mismatch between supply and demand.

Market research

Virtually every company in the UK uses market research and it is one way of keeping the company in touch with its customers. It is often commissioned from external agencies. The main purpose of market research is to provide information about actual and potential customers to support marketing decisions. A marketing manager's responsibilities include large-scale customer relationship management, encompassing the key customer approach and utilizing skills in international marketing, customer segmentation, customer loyalty, customer satisfaction, database marketing and direct marketing. These jobs may be very intensive in market research skills or may be the responsibility of a market research manager. Within market research firms or consulting firms, marketing research managers might specialize in market strategy (including new products and markets), customer satisfaction and customer segmentation (customer care in many consulting firms), service marketing, database or direct marketing and emerging technologies such as e-commerce.

Not-for-profit marketing

Marketing is often criticized for promoting materialism and unnecessary consumption. However marketing can be good or bad depending on who uses it and to what use it is put. Many not-for-profit organizations routinely use marketing to further their mission and goals. Not-for-profit organizations have more 'key publics' that they need to consider compared to commercial organizations. These can be classified as:

- ○ *Beneficiaries* – People who benefit directly from services.
- ○ *Funders* – Funding may be offered and received from many sources. The people providing the funding may have different motives which may raise ethical issues when deciding whether or not to accept funds.
- ○ *Internal staff* – These may be mostly volunteers who undertake the work for a variety of reasons and motivations. This can alter the manager–employee relationship and, for example, volunteers may not want to undertake certain tasks. The manager may not have much leverage beyond personal influence and persuasion. This may be an issue if levels of customer service are compromised by an unwillingness to undertake certain tasks.

Public relations

Public relations managers conduct publicity programmes and supervise the specialists who implement them. They provide advice about pitfalls to avoid and opportunities to pursue. A key part of the role is to monitor and assess PR activity to ensure that it is effective, for example, evaluating advertising and promotion campaigns to see that they are compatible with public relations efforts. Adverse publicity needs to be managed, and media coverage needs to be archived and distributed to managers so that they are aware of what is being written about the company. Keeping track of competitor activity, as reported in various types of publications, is also an important part of the role. Public relations managers may specialize in a specific area, such as crisis management, or in a specific industry, such as health care. They may produce internal company communications such as newsletters and liaise with financial managers to produce company reports. They can also have a role in drafting speeches, arranging interviews and maintaining other forms of public contact.

Product or service management

The original purpose in creating product or service managers was to have someone who would take full responsibility for an individual product or a portfolio of products or services. This meant that the role was there to ensure that important issues were not overlooked. Product management involves monitoring the performance of a specific product or service group in the market place. This makes it possible to avoid having a marketing department that focuses only on a few favoured products or services. The potential benefits of product and service management are:

- ○ Expertise and know-how is acquired about all aspects of a product or service group.
- ○ New product or service development is better oriented towards market requirements.
- ○ A more cost-effective marketing mix for the product group can be developed.
- ○ Changes in the market place that are relevant for the product or service group can be identified more quickly and acted upon.
- ○ Someone is responsible and accountable for the profit generated by the service or product group.

The product manager needs to co-ordinate all activities relating to the product and service. One of the problems often associated with the role is the lack of direct authority compared to functional department heads. This cross-departmental role means that a product or service manager often needs to work by persuasion rather than through direct authority to champion the product internally as well as externally. A service marketing manager's role is often parallel to that of a product manager. For example, on the service side of a computer manufacturer's business, the ongoing servicing of the product and customer over several years may be a much larger piece of business compared to the initial sale.

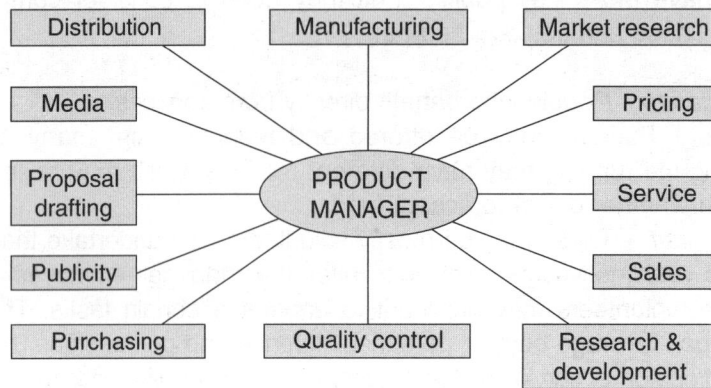

Figure 1.12 The cross-departmental role of the product manager

Promotion management

Promotion managers direct promotional programmes that combine advertising with purchase incentives in order to increase the sales of products and/or services. They direct promotion programmes combining advertising with purchase incentives to increase sales. In an effort to establish closer contact with purchasers, dealers, distributors or consumers, promotion programmes may involve direct mail, telemarketing, television or radio advertising, catalogues, exhibits, inserts in newspapers, Internet advertisements or websites, in-store displays or product endorsements and special events. Purchase incentives may include discounts, samples, gifts, rebates, coupons, sweepstakes and contests.

Social marketing

Social marketing involves the application of marketing principles and techniques, developed in the private sector, to social issues. It has been defined as 'the design, implementation and control of programmes calculated to influence the acceptability of social ideas and involving considerations of product planning, pricing, communication, distribution and marketing research' (Kotler and Zaltman, 1971). They argue that every organization performs marketing-like activities and that marketing has evolved from an economic discipline to one concerned with the relationships of organizations in the broadest sense.

Ⓐ Activity 1.9

Go to the Ben & Jerry's USA home page. Click on 'Company Information' on the menu. Read 'Ben & Jerry's Philanthropy'. Click on the 'Ben & Jerry's Foundation' and read about its mission. How is this website used to identify social causes?

What links are provided to non-profit organization(s) promoting social causes?

How are Ben & Jerry's using their site as a marketing tool to promote and sell their products?

Go to the Ben & Jerry's UK site – What differences do you notice? – How would you account for the differences?

(A) Activity 1.10

You are employed as a Marketing Manager by a service organization that supplies cleaning products and services to commercial premises. Your Managing Director has asked you to prepare a presentation for junior marketing recruits explaining the characteristics of services marketing and how they apply to your organization. Draft a document which details the areas you will need to cover in your presentation.

Summary

o Marketing departments can be organized by:

- Function
- Geographic area
- Products or brands
- Matrix
- Corporate divisions
- Global aspects.

o A marketing manager needs to work with a range of people inside and outside the organization on all aspects of marketing.

o The marketing manager is involved in a wide range of activities, particularly in small organizations.

o The marketing function is organized in different ways in different organizations, depending on factors such as size, geographical spread, management philosophy and type of business.

o A matrix structure is suited for collaborative working focused on projects that cross normal departmental boundaries.

o Managing effectively requires knowing yourself, and effective managers understand how their behaviour affects others and are able to adapt their style to the context in which they work. Personal management skills are common to all management jobs at whatever level.

Further study

Book

Kolter, P. (2000) *Marketing Management: Analysis, Planning, Implementation, and Control*, 10th edition, Englewood Cliffs, New Jersey: Prentice Hall.

Websites

1. Management Learning website: (http://managementlearning.com/art/culttsoc/index.html)
2. Reports, books, newsletters or websites on permission-based e-mail marketing: (http://www. email-marketing-reports.com/report_imt1.htm)
3. Connected in Marketing – A site dedicated to e-marketing: (http://www.cim.co.uk/ece/cfml/ index.cfm)

4. What's New in Marketing Newsletter? (http://www.wnim.com/issue13/pages/index.htm)
5. Free articles: (http://www.marketingprofs.com/intro.asp)
6. Free marketing articles: (http://www.bizweb2000.com/articles.htm)

Hints and tips

o Where possible, include examples from the marketing press, textbooks, journals and Internet to support your examination answers. This is one way of demonstrating your wider knowledge and understanding to the senior examiner.

o Marketing is a practical business so examples that illustrate the way that theory relates to practice will demonstrate your broader knowledge and understanding of marketing.

o Reports from examiners are published regularly and are available to students. These reveal that there are similar concerns and problems occurring frequently across all subject areas. The most common mistakes are caused by a lack of exam technique and examination practice.

o *Not answering the question set* – Examiners are looking for both relevant content and its application in an appropriate context. You must be able to work flexibly with the material you have studied, answering different questions in different ways, even though the fundamental theory remains the same.

o *Presentation and style* – These skills are important to a marketing practitioner. The examiners expect work to be presented in a well-written, professional manner. 'Report' style, using sub-headings and indented numbering for points, and so on looks much more credible than an essay style. This approach allows you to break the work up, highlight the key points, and structure your answer in a logical way. Take care with your grammar and use of language; small errors can change the sense.

o *Timing* – The scarce resource in an examination is time. You must control your time carefully. Read the instructions carefully, identify what has to be done and how the marks are allocated. Spread your time proportionately to the mark allocation. Allow a few minutes at the end to read through your work.

o *Theory without application* – The examiners expect relevant theory to be illustrated with practical examples and illustrations. These can be drawn from your own marketing experience observations, or your reading. A theory paper without evidence of practical appreciation is unlikely to be successful.

Bibliography

Bayern Radio (1999) <http://www.bronline.de/imperia/md/content/bayern/collegegrad/englisch/7.rtf>

Bedell, G. (2003) 'The changing face of the brand', *The Observer*, 19 January, <http://www.observer.co.uk/review/story/0 6903 877476 00.html>

Boddy, D. (2002) 'Conventional and critical perspectives and studying management', *Management: An Introduction*, pp. 30–32.

The Charities Aid Foundation (CAF) *Job Competences*, www.cafonline.org.

Christopher, M., Payne, M. and Ballantyne, D. (2001) *Relationship Marketing: Creating Shareholder Value*, London: Butterworth-Heinemann.

ESCAP: Guidelines for Development of Railway Marketing Systems and Procedures, www.unescap.org/tctd/pubs/marketingtoc.htm.

Gronroos, C. (1994) 'From marketing mix to relationship marketing: Towards a paradigm shift', *Management Decision*, **32**(2), pp. 4–20.

Handy, C. (1976) *Understanding Organizations*, Penguin.

Handy, C. (1991) *The Age of Unreason*, Business Books.

Handy, C. (1995) *Gods of Management: The Changing Work of Organizations*, London: Arrow.

Harrison, R. and Stokes, H. (1992) *Diagnosing Organizational Culture*, San Francisco: Pfeiffer.

Kotler, P. and Zaltman, G. (1971) 'Social marketing: An approach to planned social change', *Journal of Marketing*, **35**, 3–12.

Kumar, Nirmalya (2002) 'The path to change', *Financial Times*, 6 December.

McKinsey Marketing Practice 'Creating leading-edge marketing organizations', <http://www.mckinsey.com/>

Mintzberg, H. (1973) *The Nature of Managerial Work*, London: Harper & Row.

Paraguayan, A., Zeithaml, V.A. and Berry, L.L. (1988) 'SERVQUAL: A multiple item scale for measuring consumer perceptions of service quality'. *Journal of Retailing*, **64**, 13–37.

Peters, T. and Waterman, R.H. (1988) *In Search Of Excellence*, New York: Harper & Row.

Sedloff Orton and Linda (2002) 'Growing your marketing department into a knowledge management team: Aim to hire assets not overheads', <http://www.llrx.com/features/market.htm>

Stewart, R. (1963) *The Reality of Management*, London: Heinemann.

Sample exam questions and answers for the Marketing Management in Practice module as a whole can be found in Appendix 6 and past examination papers can be found in Appendix 7. Both appendices can be found at the back of the book.

unit 2 recruiting the team

Learning objectives

- Describe the functions, roles of marketing managers and typical marketing jobs and the nature of relationships with other functions in organizations operating in a range of different industries and contexts (1.1). This objective was also partly covered in the previous unit.

- Identify and explain the key challenges of managing marketing teams in a multinational or multi-cultural context (1.3).

- Explain how you would use the techniques available for selecting, building, developing and motivating marketing teams to improve performance (1.4).

- This last objective is partly dealt with in this unit and also in the following unit. In this unit, the focus is more upon selecting the team.

Statement of Marketing Practice

Lc.1   Manage a marketing team.
Lc.2   Maintain relationships with other functions and disciplines within the organization.
Lc.3   Encourage and help others to develop their competencies relevant to a marketing role.

D Key definitions

Cultural empathy – An understanding of and a true feeling for a culture.

Cultural environment – Institutions and other forces that affect society's basic values, perceptions, preferences and behaviours.

Cultural universals – Cultural characteristics and attributes that are found in a wide range of cultures: that is, features that transcend national cultures.

Culture – The set of basic values, perceptions, wants and behaviours learned by a member of society from family and other important institutions.

Groupthink – A term to describe one process by which a group can make bad or irrational decisions. In a groupthink situation, each member of the group attempts to conform his or her opinions to what they believe to be the consensus of the group. This results in a situation in which the group ultimately agrees on an action which each member might normally consider to be unwise.

ICT – Information and Communications Technology.

International division – A form of international marketing organization in which the division handles all of the firm's international activities. Marketing, manufacturing, research, planning and specialist staff are organized into operating units according to geography or product groups, or as an international subsidiary responsible for its own sales and profitability.

International market – Buyers in other countries, including consumers, producers, resellers and governments.

Strategic alliance – A formal relationship, short of a merger or acquisition, between two companies, formed for the purpose of gaining synergies because in some aspect the two companies complement each other.

Team selling – Using teams of people from sales, marketing, production, finance, technical support, and even upper management to service large, complex accounts.

Teams

Introduction

A number of factors are contributing to an increasing emphasis on teams, including the increasing availability and affordability of Information and Communication Technology (ICT) and demands for making work more flexible by reducing its dependence on location. Many organizations have flattened their structures and delegated responsibility in order to cut costs and to utilize the skills of the workforce more effectively. Shifting authority and responsibility down the organization allows teams to take over roles and functions previously performed by management. There are also changes in relationships – among employees, between employees and employers, and between all kinds of organizations and their customers and business partners. Companies that formerly developed products solo are now forming development alliances with suppliers, customers, contractors, consultants and even competitors.

Most teams are created to increase productivity, maximize co-operation and communication, and minimize conflict. Work teams, which are part of larger systems like managerial or production systems, perform a wide array of activities within the organization. Teams often have well-defined boundaries, and norms or rules governing interaction and behaviour.

The internal leader may be a full-time team member. Management may appoint an external leader, who serves as co-ordinator, facilitator or mentor. The leadership role may also be shared by several people, or the leader may perform several functions.

Insight

Four Types of Leader

There are two main Leadership Drives:

1. *Dominance* – Desire to dominate (manage) other people.
2. *Eminence* – Desire to achieve status through competition based on ability.

These two drives can be combined in four ways.

And each combination creates a different type of leader.

Type	Dominance drive	Status drive
A: Dominant Boss	high	high
B: Ambitious Professional	low	high
C: Informal Influencer	high	low
D: Reluctant Leader	low	low

Type A: Dominant bosses have the desire to dominate plus the desire to achieve status through competitive striving. Included here are political and business leaders like, Bill Gates and Steve Jobs.

Type B: Ambitious professionals have little interest in dominance over others. They are leaders because they possess some technical ability.

Examples: Faceless technocrats running investment banks and science-based firms. Or colourful creative people who lead media and arts organizations but have no real interest in managing people.

Extreme A's are often followed by B's because B's are not so pushy.

Type C: Influencers do not want to compete because they fear failure. But their high dominance drive makes them want power. So they gravitate to roles in which they have power without responsibility.

They can be cheerleaders for the boss or rebellious dissidents who sit on the sidelines working the crowd against him.

They only become leaders if there is little risk attached (e.g. in organizations which are run collectively or where the leadership role merely represents a higher power).

Type D: Reluctant leaders prefer a safe, rewarding niche free from competition. They become leaders when no one else is available or when the leader role confers little status or power.

They can also come to power via natural succession in a family firm but when they do they are usually awful.

Reluctant leadership is also common in bureaucracies in which people automatically inherit the role via rules of seniority.

Source: Recruiting.com www.recruiting.com/recruiting/2004/12/hrfont_colorred_2.html.

Teams differ in many ways, including size, purpose, type of work performed, structure, leadership, influence and decision-making ability.

Types of teams include:

  o   Natural work group
  o   Management
  o   Project improvement
  o   Process redesign or re-engineering
  o   Cross-functional, for example, design and production include people of various skill levels from throughout the organization
  o   New product and service design teams.

More and more work is performed in new ways, so as to exploit the possibilities of co-operative work across national boundaries and time zones. Many tasks are too complex for individuals to handle alone and teams are potentially more effective in solving problems and learning more quickly than individuals. When a team works well, it can improve problem-solving, become more creative and generate acceptance, support and commitment. However, teams can also be inefficient, indecisive, frustrating and, ultimately, inferior to what a collection of individuals working on their own can accomplish. Equally, some people are more comfortable working on their own than they are in a group.

Teams can be used as *integrating mechanisms* that co-ordinate and integrate information across an organization by enabling co-ordination and integration, or as *self-contained units* (self-managed or autonomous work teams, self-directing teams) that manage aspects of an organization's work.

In knowledge-based organizations both integrating teams and self-contained teams are common and cross-functional project teams are needed to integrate the work of different functions while being as self-contained as possible.

As mentioned previously, a key part of the Marketing Management in Practice unit is working within a team to develop the marketing plan and managing teams implementing the plan by undertaking marketing activities and projects. Unit 4 of this book looks at Project Management in detail but one of the key aspects of project management is the recruitment of a team or teams of people who are able to work together effectively.

Effective product and process development requires the integration of specialized capabilities. This can be achieved, with varying advantages and disadvantages with various team structures.

Clark and Wheelwright (1997) identify four types of project teams:

  1. *Functional teams* – Members are grouped by discipline, working under the direction of a functional manager. Primary responsibility for the project passes sequentially from one function to the next. An advantage of this type of organization is that managers control resources and performance in their functional areas, and team members bring specialized expertise to the project. A disadvantage is that a task must be subdivided according to functions and team members may be judged independently of the success or failure of a project.
  2. *Lightweight teams* – Like a functional team but with a liaison representative. Members stay in their functional areas but each function designates a liaison

person to represent it on, for example, a project co-ordinating team to co-ordinate different function's activities. There is likely to be improved communication and co-ordination compared to a functional team but Project leaders may have no real control.

3. Heavyweight teams, in which the project manager has direct access to and responsibility for the work of all those involved in the project, managed by leaders who may have a higher status than the functional managers. An advantage of this type of team is the integration of a project that may require fewer members compared to a more traditional team. However, it may conflict with the functional organization and be seen as an 'elite' group, alienating the rest of the organization.

4. Autonomous team structure, often called 'tiger teams', in which individuals from different functional area are formally assigned, dedicated, and co-located to the project team. Tiger teams tend to be very focused but it can be difficult to integrate their 'solutions' into the 'parent' organization.

Tiger teams can be used in various aspects of marketing but is particularly suited to customer focused initiatives where quick solutions may be needed. The following extract provides an example of its use in the context of Tiger teams.

Insight

Don't give up on the Hubble Space Telescope and its stunning cosmic images just yet. After NASA's reluctant decision to let one of the most productive and well-known astronomical instruments in history die early, scientists are showing that one of the best inspirations is desperation.

Stunned by the decision, 'tiger teams' of scientists and engineers have been appointed to find technological loopholes in the bad news. The search is on for new power-conserving procedures to extend battery life, ways to keep the telescope pointing at targets with as few as two gyroscopes (two of six are already kaput), and, most daring, 'teleoperated' service robots. Sent on unmanned rockets, they would be controlled from the ground like imitation astronauts to replace batteries and gyros and upgrade cameras and detectors.

But a reprieve is what astronomers want most. With one more round of service plus clever conservation, Hubble might operate until 2011 or longer, says Bruce Margon, the telescope institute's science director. That's when, if current plans hold, the even larger James Webb Space Telescope should be ready to pick up Hubble's torch. 'Do we really want to go several years with no space telescope at all?' he asks.

Effective project management requires planning and co-ordination. In vertical management, employees are organized along top-down chains of command and may have little opportunity to work with other functional areas. In horizontal management, work is organized across various functional groups that work with each other. This should lead to improved co-ordination and communication among employees and managers. When people are able to work horizontally and vertically there are more opportunities to understand the operations of other functions and how they relate to each other. The vertical aspects of organizations can limit the ability of a project manager to pull together the horizontally integrated teams that are often important for project success.

A key characteristic of a team is that the members have a common purpose and the following case study is an example of how teamwork extends to board level.

Case study

Tesco now plays a team game

Tesco has moved from domination by the family of an entrepreneur to management by a team of professionals working closely together. At board level, directors never vote on anything. Instead, they have a discussion and come to a consensus. This is an important part of the teamwork management culture. By visiting stores unannounced, senior executives have close contact with customers and staff, which helps them understand the marketplace. The creation of a management culture based on team-work comes with the following recommendations:

- ○ Discuss and come to a consensus on major boardroom issues.
- ○ Deal decisively with corporate succession; retire senior executives at 60.
- ○ Clearly identify your exact business goal and follow this single-mindedly.
- ○ Understand the retail market in which you are working; never lose touch with your home market.
- ○ Drive the business with research and marketing.
- ○ Keep close to customers and staff; reward customer loyalty.

Source: Maclaurin (1999), 11 Strategic Direction.

The team ideal

Robbins and Finley (2001) in their provocatively entitled book *Why Teams Don't Work: What Goes Wrong and How to Make It Right* maintain that in the 1980s the functional or specialist team worked in its organizational 'silo' in parallel rather than with other teams. These teams included, for example, accounting, finance, advertising and marketing who spoke their own functional language and did not really communicate across their functional boundaries. In contrast, today there is more variety and a cornucopia of different types of teams. For example, there are teams where everyone has the same skills but people perform different tasks, teams where people with different expertise each tackle a different part of a task, functional teams, cross-functional teams, inter-organizational teams and intra-organizational teams. Some teams work together for long periods of time while others form for a week or two then dissolve. There are self-managed teams, leader-led teams and teams where leadership is distributed within the team so that everyone leads. Clearly, what is meant by the concept of a 'team' can vary considerably and cover various organizational arrangements. However, teams are not the answer to all organizational ills and if used inappropriately they can mean that less, rather than more, is achieved.

Insight

The great sin of the age of teaming is to ask teams to do everything. A job done by a team is better than a job done by a single individual. You get that synergy going, you know, all that shared information. The truth is that teams are inherently inferior to individuals, in terms of efficiency. If a single person has sufficient information to complete a task, he or she will run rings around a team assigned the same task.

There are no handoffs to other individuals. No misunderstandings or conflicting cultures. Beware. Teaming can be bad. Sometimes managers prefer teaming because it spreads accountability around, makes blaming more difficult. Or it means hand-picking team members. The saddest thing we hear is 'We were told we had to do everything as a team.' The CEO is all ga-ga about teams, so now unless you do something as a team you're a pariah in your organization. It is team tyranny and people resent it.

Source: Robbins and Finley (2001).

Types of marketing teams

Examples include,

Sales teams which can consist of one or a mix of the following:

- o Field sales people
- o Sales engineers
- o Sales technicians
- o Office sales staff
- o Sales manager
- o Export sales force.

Marketing research teams which can consist of one or a mix of the following:

- o Market analysts
- o Market researchers
- o Interviewers.

Product management teams which can consist of one or a mix of the following:

- o Research and development engineers
- o Design engineers.

Activity 2.1

Identify key stakeholders and their expectations

- o Stakeholders in this exercise are individuals and groups with whom you work to achieve your work objectives. This can include other teams in the organization, for example, support functions such as Finance, HR or suppliers.
- o Who are your key stakeholders and what do you need to do together to produce your product, service, and so on?
- o What are your key stakeholders' expectations of your team and how do you know?
- o What is your team's purpose and role in the organization?
- o What products and/or services do you provide?
- o What skills and capabilities does your team contribute to customer value?
- o Who are your customers?

However, if teams are comparatively inefficient they should be more effective because they enable the collective talents of people to be brought to bear on issues, problems and situations. They can also ensure that the organization presents a consistent and coherent face internally and externally and that plans are developed to make the best use of organizational resources. There are synergies that can be derived from working together that can produce efficiency and effectiveness. Few people could deny that a marketing campaign is more effective if people in the organization are working together to ensure that it is integrated with schedules for production, operations, sales and merchandising.

All parts of an organization should have a common focus and work together purposefully to pursue the organization's overall objectives. In practice, however, relationships between different parts of an organization can be characterized by rivalry and distrust. This can affect all types and sizes of organization and give rise to what is often referred to euphemistically as office politics, or 'the informal and sometimes emotion-driven process of allocating limited resources and working out goals, decisions and actions in an environment of people with different and competing interests and personalities' (Dobson, D. and Dobson, M., 2000). Sometimes conflict arises from differences in view about what is in the organization's best interests; sometimes it is from trade-offs between what is seen to be best for the organization as a whole against what is best for a particular part of it and sometimes it arises from stereotypes and prejudices about the relative worth of different functional specialisms. In organizations staffed by professionals, the conflict can sometimes occur around who feels that they know best about what is in the interests of the customer. The customer might be a patient, a parent, a client or other service-user but in the tradition of paternalistic public services, the professional may feel that they know much better what is best rather than managers, customers or clients.

The wisdom of cross-functional teams

Don H. Lester, an operations manager for Hoechst, developed criteria for staffing cross-functional new product teams.

- o   What team leadership style and level of expertise is required?
- o   What team member skills and expertise are needed?
- o   What is the level of interest in the particular product concept? – is there a Champion? – is there a high level of ownership and commitment?
- o   Motivation – What will motivate individuals to want to take part in the product development project?
- o   Diversity of team members? – The greater the diversity, the greater the range of viewpoints represented.

Source: Lester (1998).

The role of the manager

The role of the manager is important in creating, co-ordinating and maintaining the team. This requires an understanding of the specific skills and abilities of team members, and their ways of working. Managers need to understand their staff and use their influence over the way the team works, transforming them from a group of individuals to a team that is able to work together. It is also the manager's responsibility to oversee the assimilation of new recruits into a team.

Most teams are created to increase productivity, maximize co-operation and communication, and minimize conflict. Work teams that are part of larger systems like managerial or production systems, perform a wide array of activities within the organization. The manager may be a full-time team member. Management may appoint an external leader, who serves as co-ordinator, facilitator, mentor, encourager, cheerleader, or consultant, but not as a foreman or supervisor. The management role may also be shared by several people, or the manager may perform several functions. Teams differ in many ways, including size, purpose, type of work performed, structure, leadership, influence and decision-making ability. Figure 2.1 gives an indication of the range of stakeholders with whom a product manager may need to interact, although the extent to which this might be called a meaningful team is questionable. More realistically it is likely that the product manager and his or her team need to relate these to other teams in the organization and/or, the product manager forms a middle management team with other managers from other functions.

Figure 2.1

Relations between departments in an organization

Managers see teams as a way of accomplishing some or all of the following:

o Providing a structure where people with a range of technical skills, functional specialisms and different perspectives can come together, exchange ideas, learn from each other and, ultimately, provide a better service to internal and external stakeholders.
o Providing a forum in which issues or problems can be aired and dealt with.
o Encouraging acceptance and understanding of a problem and a proposed solution.
o Enable people to develop their roles.

Each part of an organization can have an impact on customer satisfaction. If it has a marketing orientation, all departments should focus on the customer or service-user and work together to meet needs, wants and expectations. An organization with a marketing orientation sees the needs of customers and consumers as central to everything and, depending on size, may have something like the following structural characteristics:

Activity	Function
Identifying customer/consumer needs and wants	Marketing research
Developing products to meet customer/consumer needs and wants	R&D and production
Deciding on the value of the product to customers	Pricing (sales and marketing)
Making the product available to customers at the right time and place	Distribution
Informing customers/consumers of the existence of the product and persuading them to buy it	Promotion

However, there are other orientations and there is little agreement on how much influence and authority marketing should have over other departments.

Different orientations to the market

Sales orientation
When the need is perceived as selling more of a product or service that is already available. They may make full use of selling, pricing, promotion and distribution skills but a sales-orientated business pays little attention to customer needs and wants, and does not try particularly hard to create suitable products or services.

Production orientation
A production-orientated business is said to be mainly concerned with making as many units as possible. By concentrating on producing maximum volumes, such a business aims to maximize profitability by exploiting economies of scale. The needs of customers are secondary compared with the need to increase output. This approach works best when a business operates in high growth markets or where there are few opportunities for economies of scale.

Product orientation
This is a business that focuses exclusively on its own products. They may even be rather arrogant about how good they are. However, a failure to be kept up with developments in the external market or with changing consumer preferences means that it loses business to its competitors.

Kotler (2003) has identified the differences and conflicts of interest that can exist between different functions in an organization. Left to their own devices, departments can interpret organizational goals from their own viewpoint rather than the interests of the whole organization. There is no suggestion that the following descriptions are typical of all organizations but they do occur in some contexts. They should be thought of as worst-case scenarios.

R&D

The drive for successful new products is often hindered by weak working relations between R&D and marketing. This can arise because of different professional and organizational cultures meaning that they operate with different priorities. R&D scientists and technicians may pride themselves more on scientific curiosity and detachment whereas marketing and sales personnel are likely to have a more practical set of concerns and look for products and services with features that can be promoted and sold in the market place. In some companies, R&D and marketing share responsibility for market-oriented innovation. R&D staff take responsibility for innovation and product launch, and marketing staff must take responsibility for new sales features and for correctly identifying customer needs and preferences.

Engineering and purchasing

Engineering is responsible for finding practical ways to design new products and production processes. Engineers, who may be focused more on technical quality and manufacturing simplicity, may be in conflict with the marketing function if they are asked for products with slightly different features, adding to manufacturing complexity. Purchasers want to obtain materials and components in the right quantities and quality at the lowest possible cost. They may have a perception of marketers as people who want products with small quantities of many components rather than large quantities with fewer components. They can also be critical of the forecasting inaccuracy of marketing personnel.

Manufacturing and operations

They may see marketers, stereotypically, as people who complain about delays in production, poor quality control and poor customer service. They may also see marketers as providing inaccurate sales forecasts who promise a higher level of service than is reasonable. Marketers are seen as not particularly interested in production problems but focused much more on the problems of customers who need goods and services quickly, who may receive defective merchandise, and who do not receive the service they need. In marketing-driven companies, the company will do all it can to satisfy its customers but this can result in high and fluctuating manufacturing costs. Organizations that have a balanced orientation ensure that manufacturing and marketing jointly determine what is best for the organization. Managing operations in service industries is concerned with service levels, and it is necessary for marketing and operations to work together. Marketing people must fully understand the capabilities and mind-set of those delivering the service, and continuously try to improve attitudes and capabilities.

Finance

Financial executives evaluate the profit implications of proposed business activity. Marketing executives ask for substantial budgets for advertising, sales promotions and the sales force, without being able to prove how much this expenditure will contribute to the bottom line. They believe marketers are too often tempted to reduce prices to win orders instead of pricing to make a profit. However, marketers can see finance as conservative, risk-averse and the cause of lost opportunities because of a failure to invest in long-term development.

Insight

Marketing Departments Coming Under Greater Financial Scrutiny

27 September 2004 — Within the financial services sector, 94 per cent of marketing heads surveyed say they are under greater pressure than ever to demonstrate a return on investment (ROI) for marketing initiatives, but the majority do not have the tools to accurately track marketing spending and measure returns, according to new research.

The findings come from a survey of 50 marketing directors and managers within the UK financial services sector. The research reveals that while marketing departments are today being held more accountable, even keeping track of spending is difficult with 88 per cent of companies forced to rely on spreadsheets and 80 per cent relying on company-wide financial systems.

Accounting

Accountants may not be very keen on the special deals sales people make with customers because these require special accounting procedures. Marketers may dislike the inflexible way that accountants allocate fixed costs to products and services. They would also like accounting to produce special reports on sales and profitability by segments, important customers, individuals and products, channels, territories, order sizes and so on. Marketers may feel that credit standards are too high and when they do find customers, they may not be able to sell to them because of a low credit rating.

Insight

Achrol and Kotler

The marketing 'department' will become a functional silo, the creator and repository of the firm's marketing skills and knowledge base. It will operate the firm's market information system, databases and analytical models, conduct research commissioned by its process teams or market units and be responsible for environmental scanning. It will be the base for marketing specialists assigned to various teams or units. It will have the opportunity to lead the training and education of technical and non-technical members of the organization in marketing. Its most important function will be to create marketing know-how that operational levels of the organization will find invaluable to their success.

Source: Achrol and Kotler (1999).

Concerns about working in teams

- Few companies know how to properly implement a team process. Many managers lack the necessary skills to provide strong leadership in a team environment.
- Managers too frequently select people in their own image.
- Managers do not understand the strengths of their team members and do not allocate work appropriately.
- Members of unbalanced teams often feel that their particular talents and abilities are not being used to the full. Managers do not know how to motivate people because they do not understand individual needs.
- Groupthink drives out critical judgement, for example illusion of invulnerability, illusion of unanimity, self-censorship.

What are effective teams?

Mike Woodcock identified a number of characteristics in his Team Development Manual, as follows:

Openness and confrontation – Where the team is working well, people can express themselves openly and confront mistakes, confusions or frustrations. Such feedback can be received without recrimination and act as feedback to team members and management.

Support and trust – Trustful working relationships stem from positive orientations to others. In reality there is often too much at stake between people at work (personal rivalry, politics). Concerns such as being helpful, endeavouring to understand the perception and difficulties of others are important for team leaders responsible for giving feedback to members whose actions generate difficulty within the team.

Co-operation and conflict – Helpful competition can stimulate ideas and energy but unhelpful competition and conflicts, hidden agendas and stereotyping of people and problems need to be avoided.

Sound procedures – Effective teams need sound procedures for calling meetings, drawing up agendas, managing meetings, ensuring that follow-up action is implemented. Sound procedures include, for example chairing skills, briefing, summarizing, questioning and exploration skills. Decision-making arrangements also need to be clear. Should the team vote on issues? Does the chair have the final say?

Appropriate leadership – The team leader has to focus on the task, the team and the needs of individuals, ensuring that the team works effectively and efficiently, and achieves its aims and objectives. The range of styles that a leader or manager can use has been captured by Tannenbaum and Schmidt.

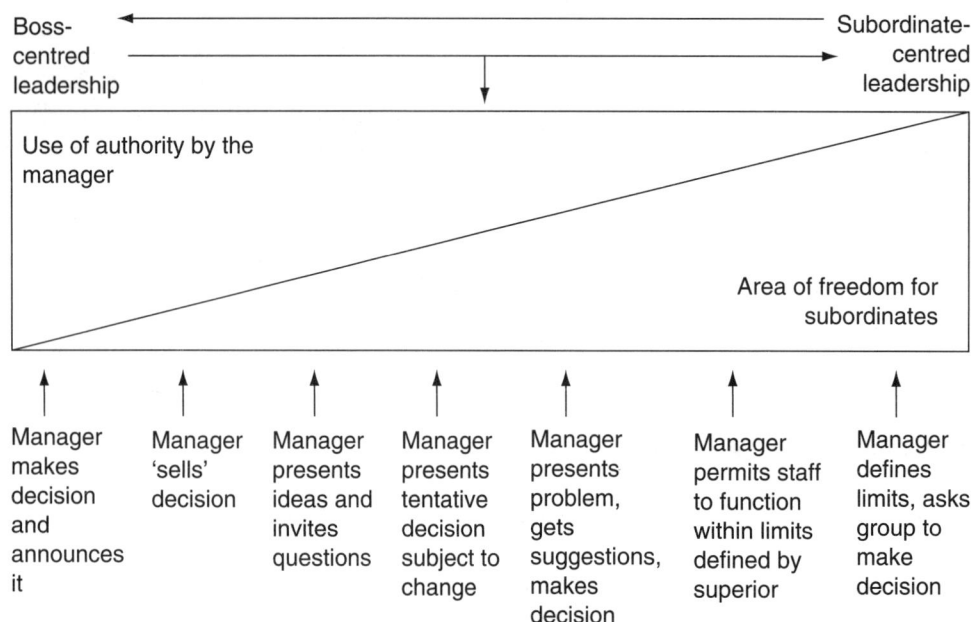

Boss-centred leadership						Subordinate-centred leadership
Use of authority by the manager						Area of freedom for subordinates
Manager makes decision and announces it	Manager 'sells' decision	Manager presents ideas and invites questions	Manager presents tentative decision subject to change	Manager presents problem, gets suggestions, makes decision	Manager permits staff to function within limits defined by superior	Manager defines limits, asks group to make decision

Figure 2.2

There is no one best style to adopt, rather it depends on the nature of the context, the type of work tasks undertaken and the people who make up a team and the relative importance of the decision. Styles are also contingent on factors such as timescales for making a decision.

Therefore, fitness for purpose means that different approaches might be used according to how this range of factors varies.

Regular review – A team regularly reviews where it is going and focuses on issues such as: Are we achieving our objectives? Are we being effective? How well are we working together? How can we improve?

Individual development – Members' needs for growth, all-round ability, satisfaction of needs, opportunity and experience need attention.

Sound inter-group relations – Effective teams have good relationships with other departments/ teams. Each values and respects the other. The respective leaders themselves comprise an effective team. Inter-group processes require shared information and an open approach to problem-solving.

The following case study is an example of an effective team but it is one that is very different from many teams that are found in organizations.

Case study

Team formation at Honeywell Scarborough Manufacturing Operations, Canada

The implementation of an empowered workforce, particularly within a team concept, is anything but quick. The empowered Self-Directed Work Team (SDWT) concept at Honeywell is a major contributor in helping Honeywell to achieve national recognition for quality. In some types of teams, such as task or project teams, team leaders are likely to be required. However, in an SDWT mode, leaders may simply replace the supervisor and, thus, continue the hierarchical structure. SDWT members would probably wait for the leader's guidance, deferring the development of empowering skills. Team leaders are not imposed at Honeywell but individual team members can exercise 'leadership' in particular developed skills and help others with deficiencies.

Source: Department of Indian Affairs, 2001.

(A) Activity 2.2

- ○ Choose a team in your organization.
- ○ What is its function?
- ○ What are the key considerations to take into account in building the team?
- ○ How would you rate its effectiveness using Woodcock's criteria, above?
- ○ What, if any, are the key barriers to effectiveness in your chosen team?

Virtual teams

A virtual team is a group of people who are working together, even though they are not all in the same geographical location. Specifically, teams may be distributed for a variety of reasons:

- Organization-wide projects or initiatives.
- Alliances with different organizations, some of which may be in other countries.
- Mergers and acquisitions.
- Emerging markets in different geographic locations.
- The desire of many people and government organizations for telecommuting.
- The continuing need for business travel and information and communications technologies available to support this travel.
- A need to reduce costs.
- A need to reduce time-to-market.

Team members use communication technologies such as e-mail, videoconferencing and telephone more often than face-to-face meetings to communicate with each other. Common reasons for forming virtual teams are to integrate expertise from different locations, to save on travel time and travel costs, and to build relationships, shared understanding and shared identities across workplaces or organizations. Virtual teams face both the same challenges that traditional teams do and some unique ones such as those relating to communication technologies and working at a distance. The dispersion of team members can make it difficult to establish a strong team identity, and it can be more of a challenge for the team members to work towards a common goal. Examples of virtual teams include a team of people working at different geographic sites and a project team whose members telecommute.

Seven things virtual teams can do to work better:

1. Have face-to-face meetings with all the members as soon as possible after the team is formed.
2. Find ways of building trust between the team members.
3. Clearly define goals, roles and tasks.
4. Ensure all team members are trained in cultural awareness and interpersonal skills.
5. Encourage informal communication between team members.
6. Set standards for responding to communications frequency, and acceptable times to call those in different time zones.
7. Rotate the team members.

Leaders of virtual teams need to be proactive in building the team, and should anticipate and resolve misunderstandings and conflicts before they are allowed to develop. Difficult areas for dispersed teams include co-ordination and collaboration, and dealing with conflict and performance problems when team members cannot be observed directly.

Managing diversity

The trend towards a global economy is bringing people of different ethnic and cultural backgrounds together. The development of greater intercultural understanding should be an important element in all organizations because of the nature of the societies in which we live, the markets in which organizations operate, and the customers and clients that are served. Organizational culture encompasses the shared values, beliefs, behaviour and background of people, and includes race, gender, sexual orientation, age or disability. Ethnocentricity is the inclination for majority group members to view their beliefs, behaviours and values more positively than those of other minority 'out' groups and to evaluate the latter's beliefs, behaviours and values negatively from the perspective of the majority group. The members of virtual teams often include people from different countries, cultures, disciplines or organizations. Such differences mean that people have different expectations, for example, about how things should be done or said, or how people should behave. This can make it difficult to build and maintain trust and personal relationships between the team members. Bringing the team together for face-to-face meetings can help here, but one of the most important things is to ensure that team members have a good degree of cultural and interpersonal awareness and are prepared to give each other the benefit of the doubt and thus avoid a blame culture.

People of different ethnic backgrounds do not always share the same attitudes, values and norms. The contemporary organizational trend is to acknowledge, accept and value the differences among diverse groups. This raises interesting questions about how best to manage people in a workforce which becomes increasingly diverse.

Insight

The term Latino covers some two dozen nationalities, and includes a variety of cultures, physical types and racial backgrounds. Cuban, Mexican, Puerto Rican, Dominican and other Central and South American groups are included under the Latino umbrella. It is the fastest growing minority in the USA and presents some major challenges to marketers. However, there are also common elements such as strong family values, product loyalty and a concern for product quality. Spanish language TV is the best medium for reaching Latinos, who tend to watch more TV than their American counterparts.

Source: Wynter (1997).

One area that has been researched extensively is the contrast between individualism and collectivism. Compared to individualist cultures, collectivist cultures emphasize the needs of the group, social norms, shared beliefs and co-operation with group members. In general, Asians, Hispanics and Blacks have roots in nations with collectivist traditions, while Anglos have roots in the European tradition of individualism. Groups composed of people from collectivist cultural traditions tend to exhibit more co-operative behaviour than groups of people from individualistic cultural traditions.

Geert Hofstede conducted perhaps the most comprehensive study of how values in the workplace are influenced by culture. He analyzed a large data base of employee values scores collected by IBM between 1967 and 1973 covering more than 70 countries, from which he first used the 40 largest only and afterwards extended the analysis to 50 countries and 3 regions. Subsequent studies validating the earlier results have included commercial airline pilots and students in 23 countries, civil service managers in 14 counties and 'elites' in 19 countries. He developed different axes for measuring cultural factors and found considerable differences from one nation to the next.

Power Distance Index (PDI)

This focuses on the degree of equality, or inequality, between people in the country's society. A High Power Distance ranking indicates that inequalities of power and wealth have been allowed to grow within the society. These societies are more likely to follow a caste system that does not allow significant upward mobility of its citizens. A Low Power Distance ranking indicates the society de-emphasizes the differences between citizen's power and wealth. In these societies equality and opportunity for everyone is stressed.

Individualism (IDV)

This is the degree the society reinforces individual or collective achievement and interpersonal relationships. A High Individualism ranking indicates that individuality and individual rights are paramount within the society. Individuals in these societies may tend to form a larger number of looser relationships. A Low Individualism ranking typifies societies of a more collectivist nature with close ties between individuals. These cultures reinforce extended families and collectives where everyone takes responsibility for fellow members of their group.

Masculinity (MAS)

This refers to the degree the society reinforces, or does not reinforce, the traditional masculine work role model of male achievement, control and power. A High Masculinity ranking indicates the country experiences a high degree of gender differentiation. In these cultures, males dominate a significant portion of the society and power structure, with females being controlled by male domination. A Low Masculinity ranking indicates the country has a low level of differentiation and discrimination between genders. In these cultures, females are treated equally to males in all aspects of the society.

Uncertainty Avoidance Index (UAI)

This focuses on the level of tolerance for uncertainty and ambiguity within the society – that is unstructured situations. A High Uncertainty Avoidance ranking indicates the country has a low tolerance for uncertainty and ambiguity. This creates a rule-oriented society that institutes laws, rules, regulations and controls in order to reduce the amount of uncertainty. A Low Uncertainty Avoidance ranking indicates the country has less concern about ambiguity and uncertainty and has more tolerance for a variety of opinions. This is reflected in a society that is less rule-oriented, more readily accepts change, and takes more and greater risks.

Long-Term Orientation (LTO)

This focuses on the degree the society embraces, or does not embrace, long-term devotion to traditional, forward thinking values. A High Long-Term Orientation ranking indicates the country prescribes to the values of long-term commitments and respect for tradition. This is thought to support a strong work ethic where long-term rewards are expected as a result of today's hard work. However, business may take longer to develop in this society, particularly for an 'outsider'. A Low Long-Term Orientation ranking indicates the country does not reinforce the concept of long-term, traditional orientation. In this culture, change can occur more rapidly as long-term traditions and commitments do not become impediments to change.

Hofstede's data revealed an Anglo culture of management based on high individualism, low to medium power distance between bosses and their subordinates, low to medium uncertainty avoidance and high masculinity. However there are also considerable differences within Anglo cultures. Of the 52 countries in his study, Australians were the most likely to say that leaving staff alone to get the job done was the attribute that made for a good manager. Canada ranked next, while the United States was not far behind. In relationships with suppliers, Europeans are more likely to develop a long-term relationship based upon ideas of partnership, whereas both Americans and Australians perceive contracts with suppliers as 'deals'.

How managers see their working lives

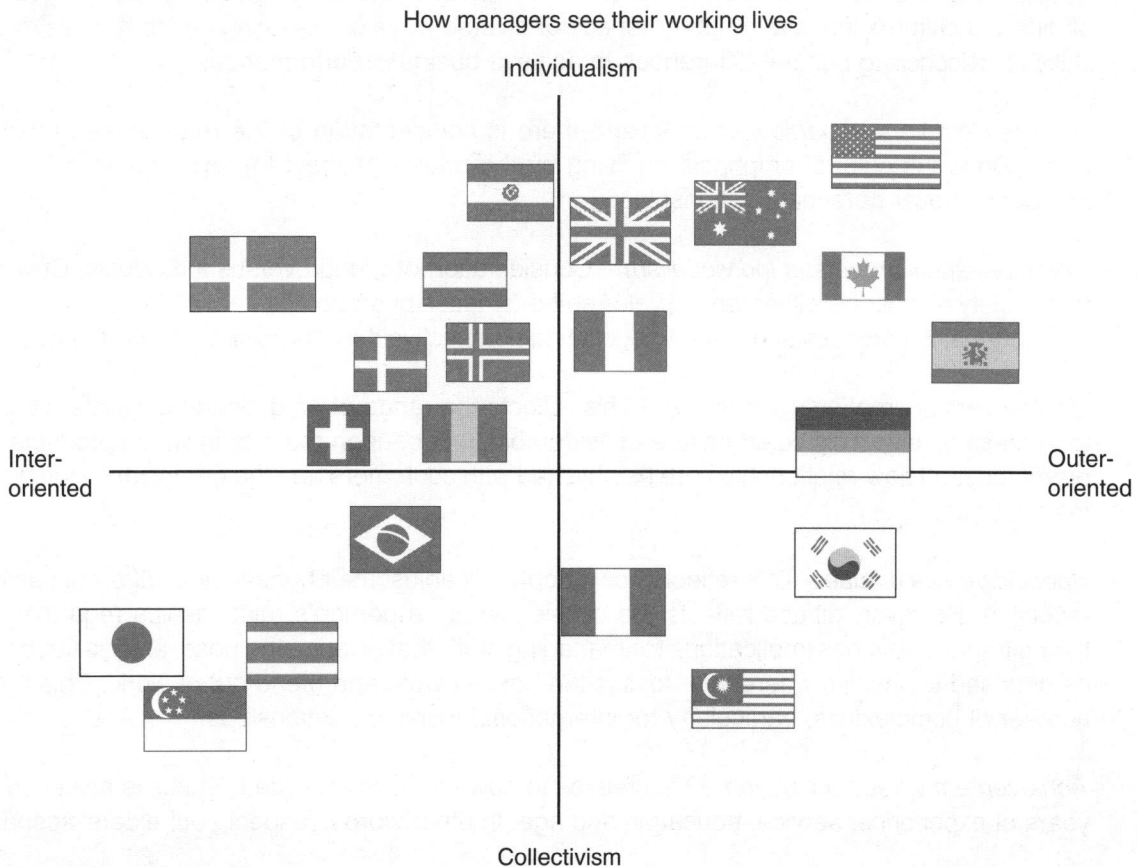

Figure 2.3

International Marketing activities are usually organized in three ways: through export departments, international divisions or a global organization

- ○ A global strategy looks upon the world as single market.
- ○ A multinational strategy treats the world as a portfolio of national opportunities.
- ○ A 'global' strategy is based on standardizing some aspects and localizing other aspects of a Company's products and services.

Source: Bartlett and Ghoshal (1989).

Trompenaars's seven dimensional model

Trompenaars developed a model to analyze cultural differences, the 'Seven Dimensions of Culture Model', to show how managing complexity in a heterogeneous environment is a major challenge for today's international managers and corporate leaders as well as a critical component of long-term success. He explains how reconciling cultural differences will lead to competitive advantage.

He worked for the Royal Dutch Shell Group handling operations in nine different countries and his 15 years of research. His work discusses the implications for managing or being managed, working together, building relationships, team working, negotiating and communicating with people from other cultures. His basic premise is that an understanding of the underlying values of different cultures leads to greater respect for diverse ways of operating and to the desire and skills for reconciling cultural differences to achieve business performance.

Universalism versus particularism – Here there is consideration of the rules versus relationships. Does the cultural emphasis on living by the rules – respect for law, and so on – take precedence over personal relationships.

Communitarianism versus individualism – Consideration of groups versus individuals. Cultures, for a variety of reasons, either tend to value self-orientation or group orientation. This can affect the decision-making process and from a negotiating perspective it is vital to understand the culture.

Neutral versus emotional (affective) – This reflects the range of emotions that people are able to express openly. This could have a considerable impact upon the way in which products are promoted, and how relationships are established with customers and the organizations in which they operate.

Specific versus diffuse – This reflects how people will adjust their behaviour in different settings (specific). However, diffuse reflects the consistency of a person's relationships regardless of their situation. This has implications for managing staff, that is 'once the boss, always the boss', as opposed to specific where 'the boss is the boss in work and friend out of work'. This has a number of complexities, particularly for international working relationships.

Achievement versus ascription – This relates to how status is accorded. Status is achieved via years of experience, service, education and age. In other words 'respect your elders' scenario.

Sequential time versus synchronic time – This is essentially the difference between a sequence of events or simultaneous events. It is a question of being able to juggle a lot of balls in respect of time, or needing to operate in a sequence to differentiate activities. This can indicate a lot about an individual's ability to work individually, within a team, on a self-motivated basis, or on a delegated activity basis.

High context and low context – High context behaviour will have a form of ritual behaviour in everyday life. Priorities, status, and so on will be important. Low context will see little in the way of ritual behaviour and can generally cope with a number of events happening at any one time.

Fons Trompenaars and Charles Hampden Turner (2001) interviewed 15000 managers in 28 countries to explore the cultural differences between what they called universalist societies and particularist societies. In universalist societies people follow the rules and assume that the standards they support are the correct ones. Further, they believe that society works better if everyone conforms to them. Particularist societies believe that particular circumstances are more important than general rules, and that people's responses depend on circumstances and on the particular people involved. In universalist countries written contracts are taken seriously. Teams of lawyers are employed to make sure that a contract is correctly drafted, and once signed it must be policed to ensure it is kept. Particularist countries think that the relationship is more important than the contract and that a written contract is not always necessary – the particular people and the particular situation matter more than the universal rules. Different cultures have different ways of coping with life, a different set of responses to the same underlying dilemmas. In Far Eastern cultures, books start 'at the back' and are read from right to left in vertical columns. To Westerners, this seems a reversal of normal practice. Managers need to display cross-cultural competence and reconcile cultural differences. Successful leaders are those who are flexible, sensitive and skilled enough to be able to ride what they call 'the waves of culture'.

The following Insight illustrates how different cultures look upon teamwork and the difficulties associated with its use in India.

Insight

The magic of teamwork missing in India/Asia

(Sam Pitroda, Chairman & CEO of World Tel)

Lack of teamwork and co-operation

This is a problem in India and wherever Indians work worldwide. If someone is trying to climb higher and achieve more, others drag him down. The signal sent out is, 'I couldn't do it; I wouldn't let you do it and, if by chance you start succeeding, we will all gang up and make sure that you don't get to do it.' Where does this attitude come from?

Hierarchical system

We've had a feudal and a hierarchical social system in which whoever is senior supposedly knows best. However, today, a young computer-trained person may have more answers for an accounting problem than a senior accountant has. Until we are able to leverage this diversity of experience, we will not be able to create and fully utilize the right kind of teams. Because of our background, we often do not learn how to exercise and accept leadership – to lead and to follow simultaneously. In teamwork, everyone needs to be able to do both.

People in India tend to focus on achieving total agreement, which is almost always impossible. They should say 'OK. This is what we agree on, so let's start working on this. What we don't agree on, we will resolve as we go along.'

Activity 2.3

o   Do you have experience of working with international organizations, or does your own organization have international divisions? – If not, try to find out about the business culture in a very different country from the one in which you work.
o   What are the key differences in culture between each country that have an impact on working life, for example, are there different approaches to teamwork, team leadership, management style, delegation, making mistakes?
o   What do you think will be the key differences that would have an impact on the manager's role?

Role of the HRM function

All large organizations have developed HRM departments, and their managers can rely upon the existence of clear personnel policies and back-up through every aspect of concern to personnel management. For many managers, however, there is likely to be little formal support and it is for them to recruit, select and manage. Even for managers with HRM support, there is a need to understand fully the systems and procedures so that they have sufficient understanding to be able to exert control as needed. In this, the relationship with HRM is exactly the same as with any other specialist function.

Recruitment and selection

The process involves clearly defined stages and the use of a systematic approach should ensure that you do not overlook anything important and, significantly, it will reduce the area of subjective judgement where people's biases, prejudices and weaknesses can creep in. This is important for several reasons. Firstly, on grounds of natural justice, there is the obvious point that everyone needs to be treated fairly and equitably. One of the most depressing situations that can arise in organizations is when people are denied opportunities for reasons beyond their personal control such as their age, ethnicity, disability or gender. This may deny the organization the opportunity to appoint the best candidate. Other weaknesses in the recruitment process can mean that weak or unsuitable people may be appointed on superficial criteria. There are also legal, recruitment and poor public relations consequences that can follow if a recruitment process is flawed. Who is the best candidate for a post depends on the nature of the job, the people with whom the person will need to work and interact, and the context in which the work is carried out. It is a matching process between the existing strengths and weaknesses of team members, future requirements of the role, and the qualities and capabilities of the prospective candidates.

Recruiting externally

Businesses could choose to search using the following media:

o   Advertising in papers, magazines or locally
o   Employment agencies
o   Executive 'head-hunters'
o   Job centres
o   Colleges/universities
o   Careers fairs.

These are all useful, but there are some disadvantages:

o   Companies might be overlooking and frustrating talented internal candidates.
o   External recruitment can be expensive.

Internal recruiting

Internal recruiting has traditionally been done by a manager appointing or promoting people. Some organizations use formal internal advertising to find the best candidate. They will advertise on noticeboards, via intranets or newsletters.

Not everyone agrees with formalized internal recruitment:

o   Employees may think it is an empty exercise, believing decisions are already made.
o   Some managers anticipate problems in succession planning if they must use open internal markets.

To avoid problems, businesses can bring someone impartial – managers from other departments, someone from HR – into the procedure. Internal recruitment can be efficient because:

o   The person and the firm know each other.
o   Savings on commercial advertising rates for recruitment can be made.
o   Employees are motivated because they can see the possibility of progression.

Whilst there is a cost in building on existing skills internally, this can be more reliable and less expensive than external recruitment. On the down side:

o Good people outside could be overlooked.
o Unsuccessful internal candidates can feel slighted.
o Entirely new skills may need intensive training.

Advertising and the use of agencies

Advertising is a major marketing activity and marketers use agencies regularly. The concepts of positioning, segmentation and targeting apply just as much to recruitment as to any other form of advertising. The agency's job is to translate your needs into short-listed candidates. The aim is to design an advert so that only those who have a realistic chance of being successful apply for the position. It is as important for unsuitable candidates to rule themselves out as it is to encourage eligible people to apply. Having a large field of candidates is of little use if many of them would stand little chance of being appointed.

Question 2.1

What are the recruitment methods used in your organization for:

o Administrative jobs?
o Sales jobs?
o Professional jobs?
o Managerial jobs?

Applications

After the closing date, a long list of possible candidates can be drawn up. From the long list you can use your personnel specification to compile a short-list. It is good practice to respond to all applicants, but some organizations feel they cannot afford it. Applicants are consumers in the market place so it is important to create a favourable impression with everyone who applies for a job.

Discrimination: what the law says

There are a number of Acts of Parliament which are relevant to the recruitment of staff. The main provisions are the Sex Discrimination Acts of 1975 and 1986, the Race Relations Act 1976, the Race Relations (Amendment) Act 2000 and the Disability Discrimination Act of 1995. These Acts seek to promote equality of opportunity and to ensure that no person is treated less favourably than another person on the grounds of disability, colour, race, nationality, ethnic or national origins, sex or marital status. The Disability Discrimination Act 1995 gives disabled people the right not to be treated less favourably than other job applicants, unless the employer can justify objectively such treatment.

Discrimination

Under the Sex Discrimination Act 1975 and Race Relations Act 1976, the main forms of discrimination are:

Direct discrimination – that is where a woman is treated less favourably than a man or vice versa, a married person is treated less favourably than a single person or vice versa, or someone is treated less favourably on grounds that they are intending to undergo, are undergoing or have undergone a gender reassignment. Direct discrimination can occur where someone is treated less favourably on the grounds of their sexual orientation.

Indirect discrimination – that is applying a requirement or condition which, although applied equally to all groups, is such that a considerably smaller proportion of a particular racial group, sex or married persons can comply with it and which cannot be shown to be justifiable. Possible examples are unjustifiable age limits which could discriminate against women who have taken time out of employment for child rearing and rules about clothing or uniforms which disproportionately disadvantage a particular racial group.

Both types of discrimination are unlawful irrespective of whether there has been any intention to discriminate.

Disability discrimination – While legislation covering discrimination on grounds of race and sex makes discriminatory conduct unlawful, the Disability Discrimination Act 1995 goes further by requiring employers to make 'reasonable adjustments' to the workplace where that would help to overcome the practical effects of disability. Failure to carry out this legal duty amounts to discrimination unless an employer is able to justify it. People with disabilities who feel that they have been unfairly discriminated against can seek redress through the Employment Tribunals.

Sexual orientation

The Employment Equality (Sexual Orientation) Regulations 2003 outlawed discrimination in employment and vocational training on grounds of sexual orientation. The law means that it will be unlawful to deny lesbian, gay and bisexual people jobs because of prejudice. The legislation provides protection throughout the employment relationship – during the recruitment process, in the workplace, on dismissal and, in certain circumstances, after the employment has finished. They apply to terms and conditions, pay, promotion, transfers, training and dismissals.

Religion and belief

The Employment Equality (Religion or Belief) Regulations 2003 outlawed discrimination and harassment on grounds of religion or belief in large and small workplaces in England, Scotland and Wales, both in the private and public sectors. They cover all aspects of the employment relationship and outlaw treating people less favourably than others because of their religion or belief.

Equal pay

The Equal Pay Act 1970, as amended by the Equal Pay Regulations, covers all contractual conditions of service, not only pay. It gives both sexes the right to an 'equality clause', which means that if any term in their contract is less favourable than that in a contract of the opposite sex, it must be modified to make it equitable.

1. 'Like work', that is work of the same or a broadly similar nature.
2. Work rated as equivalent under a non-discriminatory evaluation scheme.
3. Work of equal value in terms of the demands made, for example, under such headings as effort, skill and decision-making.

Job description

A job description is the focus of any employee's relationship with the employer. In establishing what the job is, the manager provides the foundation for all the stages of recruitment, selection, training and appraisal that follow. The job description describes the tasks and responsibilities which make up the job. As well as being a prerequisite to the recruitment process, it provides a standard against which the performance and development needs of the post-holder can be assessed. It also enables the department to focus on the characteristics of the post rather than those of the previous occupant. Job descriptions have several standard components, provided in greater detail as needed:

Job title – Accurate titles reflecting the function and level of the job – modest duties should not have grand titles. 'Engineer' should only describe a qualified engineer.

Position – Stating the job title of the person to whom the employee is responsible as well as those who report to the job holder.

Areas of responsibility – Stating the overall purpose of the job – the principal role of the job holder and the expected contribution to achieving objectives.

Main tasks – Identifying the tasks, grouping together related ones. Includes the objective or purpose of each task but not how it is done.

Description of tasks – In short numbered paragraphs, with no more than two sentences per description. Gives details of measures of work involved and proportion of time involved for any task. Descriptive headings to group together related tasks: organizing or planning.

Special requirements – Equipment, tools, special skills.

Location – of the job and travelling needed.

Special circumstances – Lifting, dangerous or unpleasant conditions, night work, overtime, weekend working.

Challenging aspects of the job – This can be useful in attracting applicants.

What is the overall purpose of the job? – Describe in one sentence, for example, 'to assist the Head of Department in the efficient running of the departmental office'.

What are the main tasks of the job? – Try to use active verbs, for example, 'producing', 'planning', rather than vague terms such as 'deals with', 'handles'.

What are the main responsibilities involved? – 'Responsibilities' define the scope of the job, for example for managing staff, materials, money, and so on.

The key result areas of the job and the standards expected – These may include such aspects as the degree of precision required and/or the consequences of error.

With whom does the post-holder work? – These may include other staff, students, and so on.

Terms and conditions of the post – Unsocial hours, necessity to work regular overtime, and any restrictions on periods during which annual leave can be taken, and so on.

The job description provides a basis for drawing up a 'person specification', that is, the skills and experience required to carry out the duties of the job.

The person specification

Purpose – The person specification forms the basis of the recruitment process from the advertisement through to the final interview stage. It describes the skills, aptitudes and experience needed to do the job and should be based on the job description, rather than a subjective view of the sort of person you would like to see filling the job. Generally, person specifications are laid down under standardized headings.

Qualifications and training

1. *General education* – It may be more appropriate for applicants to have certain levels of literacy or numeracy rather than academic qualifications. If qualifications are stipulated, equivalent qualifications that would be considered must be included.
2. *Specific training* – For example vocational certificates, professional qualifications, apprenticeship certificates, and so on.

Knowledge – This is knowledge without which the job cannot be done, for example, of computer systems. It should not include knowledge that can be imparted in an induction programme.

Experience – Either directly relevant or similar experience in a different environment might be considered. The type, range and depth of experience should be qualified (e.g. staff supervision). Specifying length of experience is usually unhelpful as some people learn more in a shorter time than others will learn in a longer time.

Skills and abilities – This includes such aspects as the ability to communicate effectively, numeracy, analytical skills, attention to detail, and so on. However, these skills must be clearly measurable as part of the selection process.

Special requirements – This should only form part of the specification where it is relevant to the job, for example, a special type of driving licence if fork lift truck driving is to be part of the job, travelling, staying away from home, and so on. The required characteristics are then entered against the appropriate heading, and subdivided into essential and desirable categories. The candidate who meets both the essential and desirable criteria will do the job particularly well, but obviously this person may be hard to find. Training and development may be needed in some areas. The person specification should be realistic. Too high an ideal will mean that potentially good candidates are excluded.

The seven-point plan – This was devised by Alec Rodger who developed a systematic approach for constructing person specifications. Having defined the demands of the job and evaluated the knowledge-base, skills, personal orientations, pre-dispositions and preferred values, the recruiter identifies the ideal 'qualities' needed for the job. Using the seven headings, the aim is to determine whether the candidate satisfies the essential criteria (factors that should disqualify candidates if they do not possess them). Desirable factors are ones that could be developed through training or development activities but could help in the process of distinguishing one eligible candidate from another – Does one candidate present a better profile than another?

1. *Physical make-up*

   What does the job demand in the way of general health, physical strength, stamina, eyesight, hearing, speech, appearance, and so on? Legislation to prevent discrimination has stopped most of the specifications for 'attractive', 'young', and so on. The increasing number of disabled people in the workforce has encouraged many managers to re-evaluate just what physical attributes are necessary for a post.

2. *Attainments*

   What general education, technical knowledge, specialized training and relevant experience are required? To avoid becoming too overpowered by qualifications and diplomas, it is more useful to list specific knowledge areas, for example, a marketing research job holder needs a proven knowledge of statistical sampling techniques. Conversely, sometimes there is an unwillingness amongst employers to recognize the value of working hard to achieve formal marketing qualifications when appointing marketing professionals. Questions need to be asked to establish the job, candidate's experience. Experience indicates knowledge and skill and how these have been used together. Much personal development comes from experience.

3. *General intelligence*

   What level of reasoning and learning ability is required? This can be a difficult area to evaluate since it is subjective in nature. For some jobs, the need is for people who prefer to have clearly structured rules and procedures to follow. For other jobs, the need may be for someone who does not mind ambiguity where little is clear-cut and each situation is different.

4. *Special aptitudes*

   Aptitudes and abilities are difficult to quantify, but they can be specified as the ability to be creative in generating solutions, to work under pressure, to think strategically, to negotiate contracts, and so on. Once specified, it is possible to devise ways for assessment and evaluation.

5. *Interests*

   Are any general interests likely to be relevant to job success?

6. *Disposition*

   Does the job require people to get on with people, to be a self-starter, work on their own initiative, to accept responsibility, to work under pressure, to influence others? What attributes are needed to be able to fit into the culture of the department, section, and so on. Disposition is important when individuals are going to be working as part of a team. An attempt should be made to assess how they might fit in and what contribution they might make. Characteristics such as loyalty and reliability may be more suited to the role of a product manager than to a sales person who needs to be outgoing and independent, self-motivated and confident.

7. *Candidate's circumstances*

   What domestic circumstances are relevant? – daily travel from home to work, time spent away from home on business. Is working overtime possible, if needed? However, care needs to be taken when asking such questions and the following are to be avoided – 'Are you married?', 'Do you have children?' 'Are you intending to start a family?' These are not relevant to the selection decision and could be perceived as discriminatory because they are about the person rather than the ability to do the job.

Munroe Fraser – 5 Point Plan

This focuses more upon a candidate's career to date as an indicator of future potential.

The 5 points:

1. *Impact on others* – Whether a person's appearance and demeanour are important.
2. *Qualifications and experience* – Skills and knowledge required.
3. *Innate abilities* – How quickly and accurately a person's mind works.
4. *Motivation* – The kind of work that appeals to a person and the amount of effort they are prepared to put into it.
5. *Emotional adjustment* – Capability of working with others.

(A) Activity 2.4

Using one of the sets of headings identified above, draw up a person specification for the Media Relations post below:

1. *Job purpose*
   The Media Relations Executive will work in conjunction with the Trust's senior executives to develop and implement a comprehensive communications strategy. This will require building sound media contacts to ensure positive media coverage for the Trust's activities.
2. *Tasks*

   (a) Conduct a comprehensive review of media relations, and provide a diagnostic report for the Board of Directors.
   (b) Develop and implement a Trust media relations strategy.
   (c) Provide a quarterly analysis of media coverage with recommendations to improve coverage.
   (d) Arrange and publicize corporate events and host media representatives.
   (e) Anticipating and responding to events by issuing press releases, giving professional advice and guidance to other Trust managers.
   (f) Co-ordinate press conferences as necessary.
   (g) Provide in-house training on media relations and skills to Trust staff according to need.
   (h) Establish robust relationships with key media representatives.

Preparing for the interviews

- Produce an interview assessment from the person specification to provide a commonality to the evaluations of yourself and any others who are involved.
- Book time for the selection procedure in the diaries of all concerned.
- Reserve special accommodation, equipment, and so on as needed.

Panel interviews

Ideally, the date and time of interviews should be agreed prior to the advertisement for a post and be included in the advertisement. Those on the panel must not be related to or have a personal interest in the appointment of the candidate. All interviewers should be made aware of the responsibilities for equal opportunities. Panel interviews can provide a better picture of a candidate than a one-on-one interview. There is more chance to think about a candidate's responses because the interviewer is more of an observer than a participant. This increases the validity of the assessment. In most one-on-one interviews, the interviewer is often thinking about what question to ask next, rather than listening to a candidate's answer.

Interviewers do not judge answers as much during the response, because others are asking for clarifying information. More in-depth responses are possible. More of the candidate's personality is revealed in a panel interview, especially if most of the questions are about how accomplishments were achieved.

Panel interviews save time. It takes only three or four people 1–2 hours to know a candidate, rather than a whole day. The assessment is more accurate and consistent. Because everyone is using the same information to make an assessment, consistency is achieved. If the panel interview is led by a good interviewer, the information obtained is insightful.

Source: Adler (2002).

The interview room
It is essential that candidates be made to feel relaxed so that a proper assessment of their suitability for the job can be made. In the case of interview panels, care should be taken to ensure that the candidate is not seated too far away from the interviewees so as to feel isolated, nor so close as to be able to read the interviewers' notes.

Planning the interview
For an interview to be successful, it should be conducted in an orderly, empathetic but efficient manner. It is recommended that interviewers should undertake the following preparation:

- Compare the candidate's application form with the person specification and pick out the points which need investigating further, for example experience, qualifications, gaps in a career history and inconsistencies.
- Once the interview panel has done this, they should then prepare a plan of how the interview is to be conducted to ensure that nothing is omitted.
- Questions need to be planned. These should be designed to probe the selection criteria of the person specification; namely a candidate's knowledge, ability and experience. Other questions should be aimed at a more general assessment of the candidate.
- Where a candidate is attending an interview and they have informed you of any disability that they have, which may affect them during the interview process, it is a requirement of the Disability Discrimination Act to carry out 'reasonable' adjustments in order to ensure they can perform to their maximum potential, for example, if access is a problem for a candidate, the interviews should be held in a room accessible to all.
- Identify key questions pertinent to the job that is asked of all candidates. This ensures that they have been asked equivalent and relevant questions.
- Allocate the subjects to be explored. Each interviewer can cover different areas, for example, work experience and training.
- The candidate should have an opportunity to ask questions and interviewers should be prepared for the more obvious ones, such as hours of work and annual leave.

Objectives for an interview

Interviewers should be clear on the objectives of the interview:

o To find out whether a candidate is suitable for the job advertised.
o To find out whether the job and the department/organization are suitable for a candidate's needs (an aspect which is often overlooked).
o To fairly select the most suitable candidate.

Conducting the interview

The interviewer should control the focus of the interview:

o Introduce the members of the panel. Start the interview slowly, to allow the candidate to relax.
o Explain the structure of the interview and what it is trying to achieve.
o Give an overview of the context of and brief background for advertising the job.
o Put the candidate at their ease and begin your questioning by identifying areas that are familiar, for example, his/her present job before working through to the candidate's thoughts on the job for which he/she has applied.

Questioning

Encourage the candidate to speak freely, by asking open-ended questions such as 'tell us what you think about···?' or 'how do you deal with ···?' Closed questions do not encourage the candidate to express his/her opinions in his/her own way.

Open-ended questions start with: 'how', 'what', 'why', 'when' or 'where'.

Behavioural questions are a good way of exploring what candidates have actually done in areas relevant to the job, for example:

'Give us an example from your last job when you had to persuade others to adopt a particular course of action.'

Hypothetical questions, for example, 'what would you do if?', should be used with care.

o Allow the candidate time to think of his/her answers.
o Summarize if you need to clarify ambiguous answers and to keep the interview on course.
o Listen closely to what is being said and how it is expressed; as by observing keenly, an interviewer can pick up clues that will enable him/her to explore an issue in more depth.
o Be aware of your own biases for or against certain types of dress, appearance, and so on as this could impair your judgement on the candidate's ability to do the job.
o Make sure the candidate is aware of any special requirements of the job and that these are acceptable.
o Allow time for the candidate to ask questions and invite him/her to do so.
o Take brief notes which will allow you to return to a point later and to deliberate at the end.
o To make comparative judgements of candidates, you must be able to remember the key points that each candidate made.

Finishing the interview

Once the interviewers have obtained all they need from the interview, they should check that the candidate has no further questions and then signify the end of the interview. They should then:

- o Tell the candidate when he/she can expect to know the outcome.
- o Check the candidate's expenses are covered, if appropriate.
- o Thank the candidate for attending the interview and see him/her out.

Key points

- o Remove as much stress from the interview as possible.
- o Ask open-ended questions.
- o Ascertain all relevant facts, and probe ambiguous or vague answers.
- o Listen to what the candidate has to say.
- o Provide information relevant to the job.
- o Provide opportunities for the candidate to ask questions.
- o Tell the candidate when to expect to know the outcome of the interview.

The interview assessment

When a succession of candidates are seen over a period, it is essential to record accurate views on each immediately after each part of the process. Never allow interviewers to rely on memory.

The interview assessment allows each of your defined categories to be rated and a justification noted. This greatly facilitates the discussions that must take place at the end of the session as the short-list is constructed or the successful applicant is identified. Do not allow any sharing of views about candidates until after individual assessments have been recorded in writing.

Debriefing

Arrange a debriefing to:

- o Short-list or reject candidates
- o Make improvements to the recruitment and selection procedures
- o If possible, provide advice to the unsuccessful candidates – this is good for public relations and is used routinely in the public sector.

Other aspects of interviews

The following examples of different selection techniques are not mutually exclusive and can be used in different combinations with each other.

Second interviews or follow-up interviews

Employers invite those applicants they are seriously considering as an employee following a screening or initial interview. These interviews are generally conducted by middle or senior management, together or separately. Applicants can expect more in-depth questions, and the employer will be expecting a greater level of preparation on the part of the candidate.

One-on-one interviews

Candidates are interviewed by one person. These interviews tend to be more informal; however, it depends on the employer's style. The interviewer will often have a series of prepared questions, but may have some flexibility in their choices.

Group interviews

Employers may bring several candidates together in a group situation to solve a problem. These may be aimed at testing your ability to work in a team environment or other interpersonal or problem-solving skills. It is difficult to prepare for this type of interview except to remember what is being tested and demonstrate team member or leadership skills.

Presentations

Asking candidates to make an oral presentation about a relevant topic can measure both their presentational and analytical skills.

Report writing

Candidates can be asked to write something on or before the interview day. This could test writing skills, subject knowledge or both.

Simulation exercises

An interpersonal exercise with a particular agenda and objectives, to observe how the candidates perform in a typical work situation such as a manager faced with an industrial relations issue.

Group discussions

Typically, all candidates are put together to deal with a particular problem, and are observed and evaluated doing so, such as a planning meeting on next year's appeal.

Psychometrics

These tend to measure current or potential skills levels, or personality profiling, which shows work styles and preferences and can be used to assess how well candidates will fit in to the organization. Psychometric testing describes a range of exercises used by employers to find out about an individual's aptitude or personality. They usually form part of an overall selection process.

Ability tests may consist of one or more of numerical, verbal reasoning, spatial awareness and diagrammatical reasoning. Those used depend on the type of role for which someone is being assessed. Verbal and numerical tests are used in selecting graduates for a wide range of jobs including most business and management functions. Diagrammatic tests are used mainly for computing/IT jobs. The earlier in the selection procedure candidates are asked to sit a test, the more important the results are likely to be to the outcome. Employers who use tests only at second interview stage are likely to look upon the results as one of the number of criteria to be used in the selection process.

Activity 2.5

Verbal critical reasoning

Verbal critical reasoning tests are used to find out how well you can assess verbal logic. They are usually in the form of a passage of prose, followed by a number of statements. Your task is to decide if the statements are 'True', 'False' or if you 'Cannot tell' from the information provided.

Leading scientists defend animal testing

At a recent conference sponsored by a number of leading pharmaceutical companies scientists defended the role of animal testing. The continued use of rabbits, guinea pigs, rats and mice in the development of medicines was strongly endorsed. Many delegates complained that the public did not understand that there were some products which could only be tested on live systems. Also that medical techniques such as kidney transplants would not exist if it were not for pioneering animal testing. The conference confirmed that 2000 animals had been used in tests in the previous year.

New alternative to animal testing discovered

At present there are over 10 000 ingredients available to the cosmetics industry. These can be used in the development of new products, free from the controversy surrounding animal testing. Where testing on live subjects is required this can be achieved by using groups of human volunteers, or methods which mimic the response of a particular protein Vistek which simulates the reaction of the eye. In the future, as has been the case with nuclear weapons, there is also the possibility that all testing will be modelled by computers.

Statements

1. Animal testing is in decline
   True   False   Cannot tell
2. Some products can only be tested on animals
   True   False   Cannot tell
3. Animal experiments and nuclear testing make people angry
   True   False   Cannot tell
4. Vistek is a protein found in the eye
   True   False   Cannot tell
5. Animal testing has been used to develop 10 000 ingredients
   True   False   Cannot tell
6. Kidney transplants were first tested in animals
   True   False   Cannot tell

Numerical critical reasoning

Numerical critical reasoning tests look at how well you can reason with numbers and understand information presented in a numerical form. In this sort of test you are presented with information followed by a number of questions. Your task is to select the right response from a range of possible responses.

Typical behaviour

Employers often want to assess aspects of personality, and in particular the way in which you work in a team situation. One way of doing this is to complete a 'self-report' questionnaire. This asks questions about the sort of role you tend to take when working in a team or group.

1. If it is not at all like you
2. If it is a bit like you
3. In between
4. Quite a lot like you
5. Very like you.

Sample statements

1.	I like to talk about new ways of doing things	1 2 3 4 5
2.	I am good at spotting mistakes	1 2 3 4 5
3.	I prefer to work with people I know well	1 2 3 4 5
4.	I make sure people know what to do	1 2 3 4 5
5.	I often use tried-and-tested methods	1 2 3 4 5
6.	I can be very forceful when I need to be	1 2 3 4 5

Assessment centre approach

One of the advantages of assessment centres is that it allows key job behaviours to be directly observed and measured. An assessment centre is a programme that organizes a range of tests for a group of candidates. The rationale for the approach is that multiple assessment techniques are more valid and reliable compared to single-method approaches such as interviews and personality questionnaires. The following dimensions are often assessed in assessment centres:

o Planning and organizing
o Leadership
o Analytical
o Problem-solving
o Sensitivity
o Decision-making
o Creativity
o Sociability
o Management control and delegating.

Assessors have to demonstrate the capability to observe and record the behaviour of candidates. Video is frequently used to aid assessors in gathering behavioural information. Assessors also need to be able to integrate information from various exercises, to discuss the ratings with fellow assessors and to be able to compare candidate performance.

Online recruitment

Employer website

An employer website may be used as the mechanism for communicating details of job opportunities as well as collecting the data that an organization requires from candidates. Such a website usually provides some or all of the following features for candidates:

- Search for jobs
- Core details of the candidate
- Apply for jobs online
- Set up job 'alerts' (enables the candidate to receive e-mail notification when specified types of jobs become available)
- View status of online applications
- Job basket (allowing a single application to be submitted for multiple job vacancies).

Job boards

A job board is rather like the recruitment advertising section of a newspaper or magazine. It will carry many jobs from a combination of employers and agencies. As with traditional print media, decisions regarding which job boards to use are based on a number of factors: cost, sector, geography and so on. Some job boards offer services such as CV databases that employers and agencies can search. For candidates, job boards offer many of the same features as employer websites mentioned above.

An example of a recruitment process

Online form
MARKETING MANAGER SALARY: £40–50 000

Excellent and rare opportunity to join a dynamic economic regeneration agency. The role will lead to you becoming a team manager, with one direct report, so management skills are a prerequisite. You will have experience in strategic marketing, and be required to write a marketing plan. The ideal candidate will have the relevant experience gained in a similar organization and be looking for a career move which will be both challenging and rewarding. You may apply online or through completing an application form.

Case study

Job: **MARKETING MANAGER**

1) Please complete your contact details: (required)

Full Name:

Email Address:

2) You may upload your own CV, or paste it in the comments box below.

Upload File:

3) Include any additional comments, or type your CV here.

Additional Comments:

Send

Recruitment pack for the position of Marketing Manager

Appointment of Marketing Manager

This pack is designed to tell you more about the role and scope of the post and provides key information about Forward West Midlands, its vision and role in shaping the future of this great and diverse region. I hope that you will find the information is sufficient for you to decide whether you are the right person for this role. If you like working in an ever changing and challenging environment and have the knowledge, skills and abilities outlined in the job description and person specification then we would like to hear from you.

Contents

1. Application form
2. Selection process and timetable

   (a) Additional questions (these can be found on page three and must be answered on the application form – response to question 1, page 9 and question 2, page 10)
   (b) Summary of terms and conditions of employment
   (c) Job description
   (d) Person specification
   (e) Organization chart
   (f) Team structure.

Informational literature

Selection process and timetable

The selection process is conducted and managed by employees of Forward West Midlands Human Resources Department. The manager of the vacant position is fully involved in the process and is responsible for short-listing candidates for the next stage of the selection process. The timetable is as follows:

07-Jan-04 Advertisement appears on www.jobsgopublic.co.uk and www.jobability.com
WC 05-Jan-04 Advertisement appears in Birmingham Post & Mail, Pathfinder, Sunday Times, Marketing magazine
23-Jan-04 is the closing date
WC 26-Jan-04 Selection panel meet to agree which candidates are called for assessment
WC 02-Feb-04 Written invitations are sent out to short-listed candidates
23-Feb-04 Assessment centre takes place.

Application form – additional questions

The following questions are designed to find out a bit more about you and you are asked to provide examples from your past experience (these may include paid and unpaid employment and voluntary activities, etc.) which are relevant to the job you are applying for. The information you provide will make an important contribution to the decision of whom to short-list for the next stage of the selection process.

The questions are:

1. Describe a partnership working arrangement you have put in place. What was it and what was your contribution?
2. Describe a marketing initiative you have been involved in to attract students to a particular educational establishment. What was it and what was your role?

When responding please remember the following: The examples you give must describe what you actually did. Be precise about your contribution to the activities you write about, and also about how you applied your skills. Choose examples, which give you the best opportunity to demonstrate the skills we require. For each example please write about:

What you did.
How you did it.
What the outcome was.

Make your comments as clear and concise as you can. Word count guide: 250–500 words.

Summary of main terms and conditions of employment

Full details will be provided on commencement of employment.

Personal details
You must provide the Agency with reasonable personal information for record purposes and to ensure that the Agency has the details of whom they should contact if, for example, an emergency situation arises.

Induction procedure
The manager of a new employee will provide and co-ordinate a thorough induction to their department, the Agency and their specific job responsibilities.

Training and staff development
The Agency is committed to training and developing all employees to their full potential in order that they may contribute fully to the achievement of the aims, objectives and effectiveness of the business.

Diversity policy
The Agency is committed to equality of opportunity in all its employment practices, policies and procedures. To this end, within the framework of the law, we are committed wherever practicable to achieving and maintaining a workforce, which broadly reflects the area within which we operate. No employee or potential employee will therefore receive less favourable treatment due to their race, creed, colour, nationality, ethnic origin, age, religion, political affiliation, gender, gender reassignment, sexual orientation, marital status, family connections, membership or non-membership of a trade union or, unless justifiable, disability.

Disability
The Agency is committed to supporting colleagues who have a disability and we will arrange for workplace assessments and reasonable adjustments to be carried out at our expense.

Flexible working
For most staff the normal working week will be 37 hours over a 5-day period. You may be required to attend outside of these times if the Agency requires it.

Job description and person specification

1. **Particulars of the job**
    Job title: Market Manager: International Business Marketing Team Leader.

2. **Context**
    Forward West Midlands is a Government-funded Agency with an annual budget of circa £350 million and 150 staff. Forward West Midlands works to enhance the economic prospects of the West Midlands and its population of 5.3 million. Collectively the marketing team are responsible for co-ordinating the delivery of the strategy across the region and for much of its implementation. The team is structured to align with the key audiences of the Regional Marketing Strategy – businesses (internationally, nationally and regionally); business and leisure visitors (domestic and international); students (those in the West Midlands and those who might be attracted to institutions here); the media community (regional, national and international); and the population of the West Midlands.

3. **Job purpose**

To contribute to the promotion of the West Midlands as a region in which to invest to the business community internationally, nationally and regionally by leading all the marketing activity aimed at businesses in the role's assigned territory (Europe including UK, North America or Asia Pacific).

To generate good quality enquiries from potential new inward investors operating in our target clusters within the role's assigned territory who are actively considering or can be persuaded to consider locating in the West Midlands.

4. **Main duties and responsibilities**

   o Contribute to the delivery of the objectives laid out in the Regional Marketing Strategy for changing the perceptions held of the West Midlands by the business community regionally, nationally and internationally by working on the perceptions of target businesses in the role's assigned territory.
   o Tailor the regional offer to businesses in the role's assigned territory and, via a range of marketing activity, generate leads of the quality and quantity required from this territory to maintain the West Midlands' share of investment into our target clusters.
   o Manage and develop the relationships which are key to our success in the role's assigned territory – in the region, in the UK and across the territory itself.

5. **Specific/detailed job responsibilities**

   o Contribute to the delivery of the objectives laid out in the Regional Marketing Strategy for changing the perceptions held of the West Midlands by the business community regionally, nationally and internationally by working on the perceptions of target businesses in the role's assigned territory (20 per cent).
   o Tailor the regional offer to businesses in the role's assigned territory and, via a range of marketing activity, generate leads of the quality and quantity required from this territory to maintain the West Midlands' share of investment into our target clusters (40 per cent).
   o Develop and implement a series of Marketing Plans appropriate to the individual markets within the assigned territory.
   o Lead, coach and develop the teams in the overseas offices in place within the role's assigned territory (25 per cent).
   o Establish clear, stretching but achievable objectives for overseas office staff and review progress through the quarterly review and annual performance appraisal processes.
   o Manage and develop the relationships which are key to our success in the role's assigned territory – in the region, in the UK and across the territory itself (15 per cent).

6. **Resources impacted on**

   Number of staff managed: Around five (although actual number depends on assigned market)
   Budget responsibility: To be confirmed; between circa £1 million and £3 million per annum depending on assigned market.

Person specification

1. Education and qualifications

- Educated to degree level or equivalent demonstrable professional experience.

2. Work experience

- A minimum 5 years' experience in business development, sales, marketing, inward investment, consultancy, account management or similar related experience.
- Ability to produce focused and workable marketing plans.
- Experience operating in the international business environment.
- People management experience.

3. Specific skills, aptitudes and knowledge

- Proven ability to inspire and develop a team.
- People management skills including mentoring, coaching, recruitment and selection and appraisal.
- Ability to prioritize workload and meet tight deadlines.
- To be able to work on own initiative as well as part of a team.
- A strong communicator, with high quality presentation skills.
- Excellent influencing and negotiating skills.
- Ability to think strategically and creatively.
- Ability to engage with senior level business contacts across a broad range of cultures (and specifically those within the assigned territory).
- Understanding of inward investment including the roles of regional partners and other related organizations.

4. Personal qualities

- Professional approach
- Able to listen attentively
- Confident and articulate
- Personable and able to get along with senior business people and partners
- Team player
- Assertive
- 'Can do' attitude
- Commitment to the principles of equal opportunities
- Commitment to the principles of diversity.

5. Other

- Develop and maintain close working relationships with key bodies in the UK and overseas to present the West Midlands and our inward investment service in the most positive light.
- Develop and implement a series of Marketing Plans appropriate to the individual markets within the assigned territory, proactively co-ordinating a range of activities (advertising, direct marketing, events, etc.) aimed to generate quality leads and enquiries.
- Feed resulting enquiries through to the Relationship Manager (Inward Investment) in the appropriate Directorate and work with them on enquiry follow-up as and when required.
- With the International Business Marketing Team Leader and Relationship Managers (Inward Investment) monitor and evaluate the success of lead generation activities in terms of delivering investment and jobs into the West Midlands.

- ○ Establish clear, stretching but achievable objectives for overseas office staff and review progress through Advantage West Midlands' quarterly review and annual performance appraisal processes.
- ○ Provide advice, insight, expertise and mentorship to support overseas staff in contributing effectively to the organization's goals and to their own professional development.
- ○ Maintain an overview of the team's programme of work and monitor individual workloads and reassign tasks if necessary.

6. Resources impacted on

Number of staff managed: Around five (although actual number depends on assigned market)
Budget responsibility: Between £2 million and £4 million per annum depending on assigned market.

Summary

Teams differ in many ways, including size, purpose, type of work performed, structure, leadership, influence and decision-making ability. It is important to recognize that teamworking is not the best solution in every situation, and teams are not always more effective and efficient than individuals working to solve a problem. However, in many business situations, the ability to work in teams is valuable and teams can accomplish more than individuals who plough their own furrow. Criteria for an effective team were identified. An effective team has cohesion and a common purpose. Recruitment and selection guided by a personnel specification and proper preparation for interviews is of key importance. There are a wide range of selection procedures that can be used depending on the nature of the job and its importance to the organization. Recruitment and selection can be expensive but so can appointing the wrong person to a post.

Working with diversity is an important skill for managers and team members, and they need to have good cultural and interpersonal awareness. The differences amongst individuals and groups should be acknowledged, accepted and valued. Working with people in different countries raises particular issues of cultural awareness.

Further study

Read Boddy, D. (2002) *Management: An Introduction*, Chapter 4, 'The international context of management' and Chapter 15, 'Teams'.

Hints and tips

It is always good to demonstrate your broader knowledge of marketing. So try to include examples from the marketing press, textbooks, journals and the Internet to support your answers. This is one way to demonstrate your knowledge and understanding to the senior examiner. Marketing is a highly practical activity and using examples to illustrate theory in practice is important. However, do make sure that your examples are relevant to the question in hand. Many questions do not explicitly ask for examples, but, where it is appropriate, do use them.

Bibliography

Achrol, R. and Kotler, P. (1999) 'Marketing in the network economy', *Journal of Marketing*, **62**, 146–163.

Adler, L. (2002) *Hire with Your Head*, New York: John Wiley & Sons.

Ashton, C. (1998) Strategic considerations in facilitative evaluation approaches, [Internet] The Action Evaluation Project. (Available from www.aepro.org/inprint/conference/ashton.html [23 April 2000]).

Bartlett, C.A. and Ghoshal, S. (1989) *Managing Across Borders*, Cambridge, Mass: Harvard Business School.

Department of Indian and Northern Affairs, Canada (2003) <http://www.ainc-inac.gc.ca>. These ideas are adapted from the Department of Indian and Northern Affairs' website.

Department of Indian Affairs (2001) www.nqi.ca/english/ex8_spring_2001_empowerment.htm.

Dobson, D. and Dobson, M. (2000) *Enlightened Office Politics*, AMACOM.

Earley, P.C. (1993) 'East meets west meets mid east: Further explorations of collectivist and individualist work groups', *Academy of Management*, **36**(2), pp. 319–348.

Hamel, G., Doz, W.L. and Prahalad, C.K. (1991) 'Collaborate with your competitors and win', *Harvard Business Review*, **67**(1), pp. 133–139.

Hofstede, G. (2001) *Culture's Consequences, Comparing Values, Behaviors, Institutions, and Organizations Across Nations Thousand Oaks*, CA: Sage Publications.

Hofstede, G. *Cultures and Organizations: Software of the Mind* (London: McGraw-Hill, 1991; New York: McGraw-Hill, 1997). Entirely re-written third Millennium edition, by Hofstede, G. and Gert, J. forthcoming (New York: McGraw-Hill, 2004).

Katzenbach, J.R. and Smith, D.K. (1993) *The Wisdom of Teams*, Harvard Business School.

Kotler, P. (2003) *Marketing Management*, 11th edition, Prentice Hall.

Lester, Don H. (1998) 'Critical success factors for new product development', *Research Technology Management*, January–February, pp. 36–43.

Maclaurin, I. (1999) 'Strategic direction', *Human Resource Management International Digest*, July/August.

Pettigrew, A. and Whipp, R. (1991) *Managing Change for Competitive Success*, Oxford: Basil Blackwell.

Robbins, H.A. and Finley, M. (2001) *The New Why Teams Don't Work: What Goes Wrong and How to Put it Right*, San Francisco: Berrett Kohler.

Trompenaars, F. and Hampden, Turner, C. (2001) *21 Leaders for the 21st Century: How Innovative Leaders Manage in the Digital Age*, London: Wiley & Sons. This is the latest book from the authors. Their best known book is *Riding the Waves of Culture* (1997), Nicholas Brealey Publishing.

Wertheim, E.G. (2000) Surviving the group project: A note on working in teams. [Internet] <http://www.cba.neu.edu/_ewertheim/teams/ovrvw2.htm> [20 April 2000].

Wilcox, D. (1994) 'The guide to effective participation', *Partnership*, Brighton, UK. (Available at www.partnerships.org.uk/guide/index.htm.)

Wynter, Leon E. (1997) 'Business and race: Hispanic buying habits become more diverse', *Wall Street Journal*, 8 January, B1.

Sample exam questions and answers for the Marketing Management in Practice module as a whole can be found in Appendix 6 and past examination papers can be found in Appendix 7. Both appendices can be found at the back of the book.

unit 3 developing the team

o Explain how you would use the techniques available for selecting, building, developing and motivating marketing teams to improve performance. This objective was partially covered in the previous unit (1.4).

o Allocate and lead the work of marketing teams, agreeing objectives and work plans with teams and individuals (1.5).

o Respond to poor performance within a marketing team by minimizing conflict, supporting team members, overcoming problems and maintaining discipline (1.6).

o Evaluate individual and team performance against objectives or targets, and provide constructive feedback on their performance (1.8).

Statements of Marketing Practice

Lc.1 Manage a *marketing* team.

Lc.2 Maintain relationships with other functions and disciplines within the organization.

Lc.3 Encourage and help others to develop their competencies relevant to a *marketing* role.

Study Guide

Teams – Differ in many ways, including size, purpose and type of work performed, structure, leadership, influence and decision-making ability.

Types of teams include:

1. Natural work group
2. Management
3. Project improvement
4. Process redesign or re-engineering
5. Cross-functional, that is, design and production include people of various skill levels from throughout the organization
6. New product and service design teams.

Stages of team development

In the 1960s, Psychologist B.W. Tuckman developed this model and suggested that there are four team development stages that teams have to go through in order to be productive (Tuckman, 1965).

Some teams may go through the four stages fairly rapidly and move from forming through to performing in a relatively short space of time. A lot depends on the composition of the team, the capabilities of the individuals, the tasks at hand, and the team management and leadership.

Forming

Polite but not yet trusting. Formalities are maintained and members are treated as strangers. This can be a stressful phase when new teams come together. Everyone is a bit wary of each other, particularly if they do not know anyone and particularly if the manager is new. At this stage, each individual tends to want to establish his or her personal identity within the group.

Storming

Testing others. Members start to communicate their feelings but probably do not yet view themselves as part of the team. Most groups go through a conflict stage when initial consensus on purposes, leadership, norms of behaviour and work is challenged and re-established. No matter how clear the team was in relation to the goals, roles and rules during the forming stage, it is often the case that individual interpretations of these are somewhat different in reality. At this stage, personal agendas are revealed and a certain amount of interpersonal hostility is generated. If successfully handled, this period of storming leads to a new and more realistic setting of objectives, procedures and norms. This stage can be important for testing the norms of trust in the group.

Norming

Valuing other types. People feel part of the team and realize that they can achieve work if they accept other viewpoints. Norming is characterized by acceptance. The group needs to establish norms and practices. When and how it should work, how it should take decisions, what type of behaviour, what level of work, and what degree of openness, trust and confidence is appropriate. Whereas in the storming stage, people were apt to rebel very quickly; this is not the case now and if someone has a grievance, complaint or suggestion then the proper processes are used. Goals are understood and roles are clarified. The rules and regulations are being adhered to and people are working together positively. Relationships become stronger as people are more aware of each other.

Performing

Flexibility from trust. The team works in an open and trusting atmosphere where flexibility is the key, and hierarchy is of little importance. Not every team makes it to this stage. Many get stuck at norming and although everything appears normal, there is a lack of momentum and motivation towards achieving all the important team goals. At the performing stage, team members are focused on team goals and are aware of the strengths and weaknesses of the team. Only when the three previous stages have been successfully completed, will the group be at full maturity and be able to be fully and sensibly productive. Some kind of performance will be achieved at all stages of the development but it is likely to be impeded by the other processes of growth and by individual agendas.

Roles in a team

Based on research with over 200 teams conducting management business games at the Administrative Staff College, Henley, in the UK, Belbin (1996) identified nine team types. People usually have a mix of roles and will have dominant and sub-dominant roles.

Co-ordinator

The co-ordinator is a person-oriented leader. This person is trusting, accepting, dominant, and is committed to team goals and objectives. The co-ordinator is someone tolerant enough to always listen to others, but strong enough to reject their advice. This is a person who calls meetings, keeps people on track and pays attention to group processes. For example, the co-ordinator makes sure that everyone is involved and notices when someone is upset. Some of the things that successful co-ordinators try to do are:

- o Focus team on task
- o Engage participation from all members
- o Protect individuals from personal attack
- o Suggest alternative procedures when the team is stalled
- o Summarize and clarify the team's decisions.

Shaper

The shaper is a task-focused leader who has a high motivation to achieve and for whom winning is the name of the game. The shaper is committed to achieving ends and will 'shape' others into achieving the aims of the team. He or she will challenge, argue or disagree and will display aggression in the pursuit of goal achievement. According to Belbin, two or three shapers in a group can lead to conflict and in-fighting.

Plant

The plant is a specialist idea maker characterized by high IQ and introversion, while also being dominant and original. The plant tends to take radical approaches to team functioning and problems. Plants are more concerned with major issues than with details.

Weaknesses are a tendency to disregard practical details and argumentativeness.

Resource investigator

The resource investigator is the executive who is never in his room, and if he is, he is on the telephone. The resource investigator is someone who explores opportunities and develops contacts. Resource investigators are good negotiators who probe others for information, and support and pick up other's ideas and develop them. They are characterized by sociability and enthusiasm, and are good at liaison work and exploring resources outside the group.

Weaknesses are a tendency to lose interest after initial fascination with an idea, and they are not usually the source of original ideas.

Company worker/implementer

Implementers are aware of external obligations, and are disciplined, conscientious and have a good self-image. They tend to be tough-minded and practical, trusting and tolerant, respecting established traditions. They are characterized by low anxiety and tend to work for the team in a practical, realistic way. Implementers figure prominently in positions of responsibility in larger organizations. They tend to do the jobs that others do not want to do, and do them well: for example, disciplining employees. Implementers are conservative, inflexible and slow to respond to new possibilities.

Monitor evaluator

According to the model, this is a judicious, prudent, intelligent person with a low need to achieve. Monitor evaluators contribute particularly at times of crucial decision-making because they are capable of evaluating competing proposals. The monitor evaluator is not deflected by emotional arguments, is serious-minded, tends to be slow in coming to a decision because of a need to think things over and takes pride in never being wrong.

Weaknesses are that they may appear dry and boring or even overcritical. They are not good at inspiring others. Those in high-level appointments are often monitor evaluators.

Team worker

Team workers make helpful interventions to avert potential friction and enable difficult characters within the team to use their skills to positive ends. They tend to keep team spirit up and allow other members to contribute effectively. Their diplomatic skills together with their sense of humour are assets to a team. They tend to have skills in listening, coping with awkward people and to be sociable, sensitive and people-oriented.

They can be indecisive in moments of crisis and reluctant to do things that might hurt others.

Completer/finishers

The completer/finisher dots the i's and crosses the t's. He or she gives attention to detail, aims to complete and to do so thoroughly. They make steady effort and are consistent in their work. They are not so interested in the glamour of spectacular success.

Weaknesses, according to Belbin, are that they tend to be overanxious, and have difficulty letting go and delegating work.

Specialist

The specialist provides knowledge and technical skills within the team. They may be introverted and anxious but tend to be self-starting, dedicated and committed.

Significance of Belbin team roles

Where there is an uneven spread of roles in a group there may be problems in addressing the task allocated. Team members need to be aware of their main team role, know their second-best role and see if these can complement the other group members' roles. In this way, an effective team can be constructed. A person's team role may alter over time and he or she may play different roles in different teams.

There is a tendency in top teams for too many 'shapers' and 'plants' with few if any 'completer/finishers'. This means that everyone likes to talk, wants their own ideas to be accepted by all and relies on others to take the follow-through actions. Another role that is often lacking in top teams is that of 'monitor/evaluator' – this person may be perceived as trying to prevent things from happening by introducing balance and reality into the discussions.

Specific teams

Knowing the predominant Belbin roles of your team may provide an explanation as to why a particular team does not work well. Where there is a role that is not fulfilled at all in the team, then either the leader will need to ask someone to take on the role, or it needs to be covered by the team members.

Leadership and management of teams

Not all leaders are managers and not all managers are leaders. However, managers can be leaders and vice versa. Leadership is derived from an Anglo-Saxon word meaning the road or path ahead. Managing comes from a Latin word 'manus', meaning hand, and is more associated with handling a system or machine of some kind. There have been many descriptions of how the two differ, for example, consider the following list:

Managers
- Administer and copy
- Maintain
- Focus on systems and structure
- Rely on control
- Short-range view – bottom line
- Ask how and when
- Accept the status quo
- Classic good soldier
- Do things right.

Leaders
- o Innovation and originality
- o Develop
- o Focus on people
- o Inspire trust
- o Long-range view – the horizon
- o Ask what and why
- o Challenge the status quo
- o Own person
- o Do the right things.

Source: Bennis (1994).

As indicated above, some managers will do some of the same things that leaders do and vice versa. It is more a question of the balance of activities that comprise a job, and the expectation is that leaders would spend more time focusing on the strategic direction of the organization. However, there are many different theories about leadership and in the 1980s a new paradigm emerged called transformational leadership as opposed to transactional leadership. The relative instability and unpredictability of the environment has given rise to this new conception of leadership, and there is a premium on leadership to ensure that an organization can adapt to and be successful in a world of constant change. The transformational leader motivates and inspires staff and ensures that staff understand the vision for the future of the organization.

Five characteristics of leadership
- o *Challenging the process* – encouraging others to develop new ideas and judicious risk taking.
- o Inspiring a shared vision about the future.
- o *Enabling others to act* – encouraging collaboration, co-operation, building teams and empowering others.
- o *Modelling the way* – planning and reviewing progress and taking corrective action in a way that gains the respect of others. Clear about values and act in a manner consistent with them.
- o Recognizing and celebrating others' achievements.

Source: Kouzes and Posner (2002).

Transactional marketing

Transactional marketing emphasizes the exchange of product for money. It focuses on the individual sale, promotes product features and places relatively little emphasis on customer service. Relationship marketing, on the other hand, focuses on product benefits and is geared towards long-term retention of customers.

Transactional marketing is a relatively low cost way to go to market because there is no need to invest a great deal of time or money in sales people and support personnel. Its main disadvantage is that it generates little customer loyalty. If customers have a bad experience or perceive a marginally better deal elsewhere, they are quick to leave. Because customers are heavily influenced by price, profit margins tend to be slim. Relationship marketing requires a greater investment in sales and service resources, and is more complicated to implement. The pay-off is that customers are more loyal and less likely to jump to a competitor on a whim.

Relationship marketing

1. Make it easy for customers to reach you. For example, automated answering services can be confusing by offering endless choices which, in effect, tell customers that its their responsibility to figure out who can help them.
2. Do not wait for customers to contact you. The conversation you have today may include information that you can use in the future.
3. Anticipate customer needs. This is a natural outgrowth of keeping in touch with customers and listening to what they say.
4. Be the expert in your field. In transactional marketing, customers figure out what they need; in relationship marketing, you help them make the right choice.
5. Sell benefits, not features. A feature describes a product but a benefit describes what a product does for the customer.
6. Make it right if you make a mistake. Dissatisfied customers who make a complete break with a supplier rarely come back.
7. Empower sales and service personnel to make decisions. If customers hear 'I'm not authorized to do that', it tells them that they are not important enough to talk to someone who can make a simple decision.
8. One size doesn't fit all. You may need to work with key customers to modify your offering to meet their needs.
9. Don't let the salesperson become the company. Make sure that at least one other person is versed in the needs of key customers.

Source: Relationship Marketing by Daniel J. Ott, Director of Sales & Marketing, Tramont Corporation (Ott, Daniel, J., 1999).

While it is difficult to identify precise types of businesses in which relationship marketing is most appropriate, there are some companies that by their very nature are likely to practise purely transactional marketing. A self-service fuel station is a good example. A customer fills up his fuel tank, pays for it and leaves. There is no further interaction between the buyer and the seller until the next purchase, if there is one. The station offers its products, posts the price and takes the next person in line. There is no serious attempt to develop a long-term relationship with a customer. Transactional marketing makes sense with a product like petrol. Customers tend to purchase commodities based almost entirely on price and convenience, provided the product meets some basic quality and performance standards (see Table 3.1).

Table 3.1 A comparison of transactional and relationship marketing

	Transactional marketing	**Relationship marketing**	
Purpose	Make a sale (close a deal)	Create a customer	
Status of sale	Sale as end result	Sale as beginning of relationship	
Business defined by	Products	Customer relationship	
Status of price	Price as input	Price as outcome of negotiations and joint decision-making	
Communication	Aimed at aggregates of customers	Targeted and tailored	
Marketer valued for	Products and prices	Present and future problem-solving capability	
Objective	Increase number of customers and sales	Satisfying existing customers and retaining them	
Buying orientation	Procurement orientation	Supply management orientation	
Process	Discrete transactions	Repeat transactions	
Relationship	Arm's-length, often adversarial relationship; Distributive negotiations, focus on price	Management of external resources	Integration and co-ordination of purchasing with other functions within the organization as well as other firms in the value network
Buyer influence	Little, if any, input concerning to what, when and what quantity to acquire	Draw upon resources of suppliers to gain quality improvements and cost reductions (TQM, JIT)	Measures like co-developing
Focus	Minimizing price paid	Reduce total costs associated with use of product/service	Obtain maximum benefits relative to costs and price from an offering
Central objective	Obtain best deal in terms of price, quality, availability	Improve productivity by: Improving quality	Focus all of the firm's efforts on delivering value to end-users
	Maximize power over suppliers	Reducing total costs co-operating with suppliers	Concentrate the firm's own resources on a set of core competencies
	Avoid risk wherever possible		Build a supply network that efficiently completes required business processes
			Sustain highly collaborative relationships with select supplier firms

Team leadership

John Adair's (1988) Action-Centred Leadership model is based on three parts:

1. Defining the task
2. Managing the team or group
3. Managing individuals.

People need to be briefed properly about the objectives that need to be achieved, what needs to be done, why, how and when. The extent to which all of this needs to be spelled out by the leader or manager will depend on the people involved, the work context and the nature of any particular tasks. In a situation where there is an expectation that tasks will be delegated, there is no need to go into great detail about how something should be done because this will be the responsibility of the person carrying out the task. The purpose of the business is to deliver something of value to people. The leader is responsible for ensuring that the marketing task determines what that value is, and then organizes work in the most effective and efficient way to deliver it (see Figure 3.1).

Figure 3.1 Team Leadership: John Adair, *What a Leader has to do?* (1988)

Marketing tasks

These could include:

○ Identifying market conditions.
○ Identifying segments to target and buyer behaviour.
○ Identifying competitive responses to customer needs and their competitive position.
○ Designing products/services that match customer needs.
○ Designing integrated marketing communication activities that educate and motivate internally, and that generate awareness and stimulate interest and action externally.
○ Building, maintaining and protecting the brand and competitive position.
○ Co-ordinating the delivery of value to customers.
○ Measuring the effectiveness of marketing activities.

Responsibilities as a manager for achieving the task

○ Making the plan
○ Allocating work and resources
○ Controlling quality and rate of work
○ Checking performance
○ Adjusting the plan – setting standards.

Responsibilities as a manager for the team

- ○ Maintaining discipline
- ○ Building team spirit
- ○ Encouraging, motivating, giving a sense of purpose
- ○ Ensuring communication within the group
- ○ Training the group.

If teams are to perform, a manager needs to:

- ○ Communicate his or her expectations
- ○ Set clear objectives
- ○ Assign tasks and responsibilities
- ○ Establish performance standards and targets
- ○ Measure effectiveness.

Responsibilities as a manager for each individual

- ○ Attending to personal problems
- ○ Recognizing and using abilities
- ○ Developing and training.

While teamwork is important, teams comprise individuals, each of whom has strengths and weaknesses, aspirations and ambitions. Ensuring that the individual gains job satisfaction and is able to develop in their role is a shared responsibility between the manager/leader and the team member. The rotation and delegation of tasks, reward and recognition all play a part in helping to keep the individual motivated to give their best.

Insight

The 12-minute interview

A regular meeting with an employee to talk one-on-one about issues, problems and progress in work and the workplace.

Why should it be used? – To make sure that employees have direct contact with the team leader. Talking to staff regularly encourages each employee to contribute to the team effort. If time is invested, it will help to avoid losing touch with people when it is a busy time.

How can this tool help? – One of the concerns of front-line staff is a lack of direct contact with their supervisor or manager. This tool helps to build meeting time into the daily routine.

How does it work? – Create a rotating schedule so that, for example, every day at a particular time the team leader meets with a different member of staff.

Doing – Ensure that 12 minutes at the set hour. Do not try to control the session; what is important will come up.

Follow-up – Once the 12-minute interview becomes part of workplace culture, it will enable better and more planned use of time. Staff will keep note of questions, problems and issues that can be addressed during their regular interview and only ask for special meetings for more urgent or complex matters.

National UK management standards

The national management standards include an element on leading the work of teams and individuals to achieve their objectives. A competent manager must show, amongst other things, that he or she manages the performance of teams and individuals. It covers allocating work, agreeing objectives, and setting out plans and methods of working. It also involves monitoring and evaluating the work of the team and its members, and providing feedback to them on their performance.

Allocating responsibilities

In order to allocate work to teams and individuals, the manager needs to decide with the team how to distribute tasks and responsibilities. This means ensuring that the allocation makes best use of team members' abilities, and provides opportunities for them to learn and develop in their roles. The manager needs to make it clear what is expected of team members. Where resources are limited, a manager may have to prioritize objectives or reallocate resources while minimizing the disruption this may cause.

Objectives and work plans

In order to agree objectives and work plans with teams and individuals, they need to be SMART, that is, specific, measurable, realistic, time-bound and consistent with the organization's overall objectives and policies. Ways of working need to be explained, and there is a need to update objectives and work plans in the light of progress and changes. In order to assess the performance of teams and individuals, the manager needs to make it clear why performance is monitored and assessed. Individuals and teams need to be encouraged to evaluate their own performance wherever possible.

Feedback

Regular feedback based on objective assessments of performance needs to be given. This should acknowledge achievements and provide constructive suggestions and encouragement. Individuals and teams should have the chance to respond to feedback and suggest how they could improve their performance.

Core functions of leadership

Adair sets out the core functions of leadership that are central to the Action-Centred Leadership model (see Figure 3.2):

- o *Planning* – Seeking information, defining tasks, setting aims, initiating – briefing, task allocation, setting standards.
- o *Controlling* – Maintaining standards, ensuring progress, ongoing decision-making.
- o *Supporting* – Individuals' contributions, encouraging, team spirit, reconciling, morale.
- o *Informing* – Clarifying tasks and plans, updating, receiving feedback and interpreting.
- o *Evaluating* – Feasibility of ideas, performance, enabling self-assessment.

The Action-Centred Leadership model, therefore, does not stand alone, it must be part of an integrated approach to managing and leading. There should be a strong emphasis on applying these principles through training.

Adair's Leadership Checklist

	Key Functions	Task	Team	Individual
C o m m u n i c a t i o n	Define objectives	❑ Clarify task ❑ Obtain information ❑ Identify resources and constraints	❑ Assemble team ❑ Give reasons why ❑ Define accountability	❑ Involve each person ❑ Gain acceptance
	Plan & Decide	❑ Consider options ❑ Establish priorities ❑ Plan time	❑ Consult ❑ Encourage ideas ❑ Agree standards	❑ Listen ❑ Assess abilities ❑ Delegate ❑ Agree targets
	Organize	❑ Establish control ❑ Brief plan ❑ Obtain feedback	❑ Structure ❑ Answer questions ❑ Prepare and train	❑ Check under-standing ❑ Counsel ❑ Enthuse
	Control & Support	❑ Maintain standards ❑ Report progress ❑ Adjust plan if necessary ❑ Set personal example	❑ Co-ordinate ❑ Maintain external co-operation ❑ Relieve tension	❑ Guide and encourage ❑ Recognize effort ❑ Discipline
	Review	❑ Evaluate results against objectives ❑ Consider action	❑ Recognize team's success ❑ Learn from setbacks	❑ Appraise performance ❑ Identify further training needs ❑ Aid personal growth

Figure 3.2 Adair's leadership checklist

Generic role definition for Team Leaders (Armstrong, 1996)

Purpose of role – To lead teams in order to attain team goals and further the achievement of the organization's objectives.

Key result areas:

- o Agree targets and standards with team members which support the achievement of the organization's objectives.
- o Plan with team members work schedules and resource requirements which will ensure that team targets will be reached, indeed exceeded.
- o Agree performance measures and quality assurance processes with team members.
- o Co-ordinate the work of the team to ensure that team goals are achieved.
- o Ensure that the team members collectively monitor the team's performance in terms of achieving output, speed of response, and quality targets and standards.
- o Agree with team members any corrective action required to ensure that team goals are achieved.
- o Conduct team reviews of performance to agree improvement plans.
- o Conduct individual reviews of performance to agree areas for improvement and personal development plans.
- o Recommend appropriate team performance rewards and individual rewards related to the acquisition and effective use of skills and capabilities.

Capabilities:

- o Builds effective team relationships, ensuring that team members are committed to the common purpose.
- o Encourages self-direction amongst team members but provides guidance and clear direction as required.
- o Shares information with team members.
- o Trusts team members to get on with things – not continually checking.
- o Treats team members fairly and consistently.
- o Supports and guides team members to make the best use of their capabilities.
- o Encourages self-development by example.
- o Actively offers constructive feedback to team members, and positively seeks and is open to constructive feedback from them.
- o Contributes to the development of team members, encouraging the acquisition of additional skills and providing opportunities for them to be used effectively.

Motivation

One of the best-known theories is McClelland's motivational theory (McClelland *et al.*, 1953) which is based on three types of motivational need that are found to varying degrees in all workers and managers.

Achievement motivation – The 'achievement motivated' person seeks attainment of realistic but challenging goals, and advancement in the job. There is a strong need for feedback about achievement and progress, and a need for a sense of accomplishment.

Authority/power motivation – The 'authority motivated' person needs to be influential and effective to make an impact. There is a strong need to lead and for their ideas to prevail. There is also motivation and need towards increasing personal status and prestige.

Affiliation motivation – The 'affiliation motivated' person has a need for friendly relationships and is motivated towards interaction with other people. The affiliation driver produces motivation, and need to be liked and held in popular regard. These people are team players.

Most people possess and exhibit a combination of these characteristics. Some people exhibit a strong bias to a particular motivational need, and this affects their behaviour and working/ managing style. McClelland felt that people with a strong 'achievement motivation' made the best leaders although there was a tendency to demand too much of their staff in the belief that they too are highly achievement-focused and results-driven.

McClelland suggested that for achievement-motivated people:

- o Achievement is more important than material or financial reward.
- o Achieving the aim or task gives greater personal satisfaction than receiving praise or recognition.
- o Financial reward is regarded as a measurement of success, not an end in itself.
- o Security is not the prime motivator, nor is status.
- o Feedback is essential, because it enables measurement of success, not for reasons of praise or recognition (the implication here is that feedback must be reliable, quantifiable and factual).

o   Achievement-motivated people constantly seek improvements and ways of doing things better.

o   Achievement-motivated people will logically favour jobs and responsibilities that naturally satisfy their needs, that is, offer flexibility and opportunity to set and achieve goals, for example, sales and business management, and entrepreneurial roles.

McGregor XY Theory

In 1960, Douglas McGregor advanced the idea that managers had a major part in motivating staff. He divided managers into two categories – Theory X managers who believe that their staff are lazy and will do as little as they can get away with; and Theory Y managers who believe that their people really want to do their best in their work. Theory X managers believe that staff will do things if they are given explicit instructions and plenty of stick if they do not do what they are supposed to do. Theory Y managers believe their people work their best when empowered to make appropriate decisions.

Achievement-motivated people tend towards X-Theory style, due to their high task focus.

1.   *Theory X assumptions*:

    (a)   People inherently dislike work
    (b)   People must be coerced or controlled to do work to achieve objectives
    (c)   People prefer to be directed.

2.   *Theory Y assumptions*:

    (a)   People view work as being a natural activity
    (b)   People will exercise self-direction and control towards achieving objectives to which they are committed
    (c)   People learn to accept and seek responsibility.

Since McGregor, Theory Z has been advanced by William Ouchi. This is Theory Y on steroids, and states that employees crave responsibility and opportunities for growth all the time. It is strongly influenced by Japanese management styles.

Hertzberg motivators and hygiene factors (Hertzberg *et al.*, 1959)

Hertzberg (1959) constructed a two-dimensional paradigm of factors affecting people's attitudes about work. He concluded that such factors as company policy, supervision, interpersonal relations, working conditions and salary are hygiene factors rather than motivators. According to the theory, the absence of hygiene factors can create job dissatisfaction, but their presence does not motivate or create satisfaction. In contrast, motivators are elements that enriched a person's job; he found five factors in particular that were strong determiners of job satisfaction: achievement, recognition, the work itself, responsibility and advancement. These motivators (satisfiers) were associated with long-term positive effects in job performance while the hygiene factors (dissatisfiers) consistently produced only short-term changes in job attitudes and performance, which quickly fell back to its previous level.

Satisfiers describe a person's relationship with what he or she does, many related to the tasks being performed. Dissatisfiers, on the other hand, have to do with a person's relationship to the context or environment in which he or she performs the job. The satisfiers relate to what a person does while the dissatisfiers relate to the situation in which the person does what he or she does. A manager may not be able to easily influence all the hygiene factors of a person's job but he or she can have a big influence on many of the motivators.

1. *Motivator factors that increase job satisfaction*:

    (a) Achievement
    (b) Recognition
    (c) Work itself
    (d) Responsibility
    (e) Advancement
    (f) Growth.

2. *Hygiene factors – absence of 'good' factors can create job dissatisfaction*:

    (a) Company policy
    (b) Working conditions
    (c) Salary
    (d) Peer relationships
    (e) Security.

Source: Frederick Hertzberg, *Work and the Nature of Man* (1966).

Equity theory

Adams' Equity Theory is based on the principle that individuals want a fair balance between the inputs, or what they give to their job, and the outputs, or what they get from it. Employees develop a view of what is fair by comparing their own situation with other people who they regard as 'referents'. Typical inputs might be effort, loyalty, hard work, commitment and skill. Typical outputs are obvious ones such as pay and expenses and also more intangible ones such as recognition, praise, responsibility, sense of achievement, and so on.

If people feel that their inputs outweigh the outputs then they may become demotivated. In this situation, some people switch off and do the minimum that they can, or even become disruptive. Others aim to seek to improve the outputs by making pay claims or looking for other work. The key aspect of the theory is that extrinsic rewards such as level of pay are neither motivating nor demotivating in themselves. Rather it is how fair we perceive them to be when we compare ourselves with significant others, that is, people who we feel should be paid less than or about the same as ourselves, or people whom we expect to be paid more than us.

If we feel that inputs are fairly and adequately rewarded by outputs (the fairness benchmark being subjectively perceived from market norms and other comparable references) then we are happy in our work and motivated to continue inputting at the same level.

Creating a culture of teamwork

To make teamwork happen, these actions need to occur:

○ Leaders need to communicate the clear expectation that teamwork and collaboration are expected. No one completely owns a work area or process all by himself. People who own work processes and positions are open and receptive to ideas and input from others.
○ Leaders and managers model teamwork in their interaction with each other and the rest of the organization. They maintain teamwork even when things are going wrong, and the temptation is to slip back into former behaviour.

o Teamwork is rewarded and recognized. The lone ranger, even if he or she is an excellent producer, is valued less than the person who achieves results with others. Compensation, bonuses and rewards depend on collaborative practices as much as individual contribution and achievement.

o The performance management system needs to emphasize and value teamwork. Often 360 degree feedback is integrated within the system; this feedback from colleagues, direct reports and managers can have a powerful impact on work behaviours.

o Teams need to be formed to solve real work issues and to improve real work processes. Provide training in systematic methods so that the team expends its energy on the project, not on how to work together to approach it.

o Hold department meetings to review projects and progress, to obtain broad input, and to co-ordinate shared work processes. If group members are not getting along, examine the work processes they mutually own. The problem may not be the personalities of the people. Rather it may be the fact that they often have not agreed on how they will deliver a product or a service or the steps required to get something done.

o Celebrate group successes publicly.

o A team leader should be focused on achieving the task, building and maintaining the team and developing the individual.

Managing team behaviour

Behaviour to avoid is self-serving behaviour that has nothing to do with the team performing. For example:

o *Attention getting* – nobody seems interested in what I have to say.
o *Aggression* – don't care what you say, you're wrong.
o *Withdrawal* – we're getting nowhere, why don't we each work on the problem by ourselves.

Managing team behaviour requires skill and a clear understanding of what is required. Again good communication skills can significantly improve team behaviour. Communication skills that help encourage team members to focus on the task include:

o *Initiating* – where shall we start?
o *Clarifying* – isn't Jo suggesting that···?
o *Direction* – don't you think we should be moving the discussion along?
o *Information seeking* – don't you have some sales figures on···?
o *Information giving* – the latest marketing research report shows···

Building and maintaining the team

Most teams are created to increase productivity, maximize co-operation and communication, and minimize conflict. Work teams, which are part of larger systems like managerial or production systems, perform a wide array of activities within the organization. Teams usually have well-defined physical and task boundaries, matching technical systems, and norms or rules governing interaction and behaviour. The internal leader may be a full-time team member. Management may appoint an external leader, who serves as co-ordinator, facilitator, mentor, encourager, cheerleader or consultant. The leadership role may also be shared by several people, or the leader may perform several functions.

Characteristics of good team building

- High level of interdependence among team members.
- Team leader has good people skills and is committed to team approach.
- Each team member is willing to contribute.
- Team develops a relaxed climate for communication.
- Team members develop a mutual trust.
- Team and individuals are prepared to take risks.
- Team is clear about goals and establishes targets.
- Team member roles are defined.
- Team members know how to examine team and individual errors without personal attacks.
- The team has capacity to create new ideas.

There are two critical elements to effective team building: a connection between all members of the team, and a shared understanding between the leadership and each team member.

Team building

The Six Deadly Sins of Team Building (Bacal, 2002).

If the need for team development is recognized, there are some pitfalls to avoid.

1. *Lack of a model* – It is not uncommon for people leading a team-building process to focus on a single aspect of team functioning. Often the emphasis will be on communication practices, to the exclusion of other elements that are critical to team success and effectiveness. A one-dimensional team-building process may increase frustration, and destroy the credibility of the process.
2. *Lack of diagnosis* – Each team is different. Each team has distinct strengths and weaknesses, and team building must build on these specific strengths and address weaknesses. Without knowing these strengths and weaknesses, the team-building leader runs the risk of using a process that will be irrelevant.
3. *Short-term intervention* – It is not uncommon for a manager to arrange for a team-building day, without developing a longer term strategy for team development. At best, a single day on its own will result in a brief motivational surge that quickly fades. At worst, the day will bring to light issues that cannot be solved during that day, and are left to fester.
4. *No evaluation of progress* – It is common for team-building efforts to take for granted that things are improving without putting in place a mechanism for regular evaluation of team functioning. The team-building leader must be able to identify barriers so that the team can work to eliminate them.
5. *Leadership detachment* – Management sometimes enters into team building in a somewhat detached way. The detached manager treats it as something that will help others change, so that the team will function more effectively. However, team effectiveness cannot be improved unless the manager is willing to look at his or her contributions to the team. Management usually has to change too.
6. *Doing it all internally* – Team building generally will not succeed unless conflicts and problems can be brought into the open and dealt with properly. The problem is that poorly functioning teams are characterized by a climate of blame, defensiveness and a lack of ability to deal with conflict. Poor teams lack the ability to improve themselves.

Conclusion – Whether you are leading team-building activities, or hiring someone, it is important that you stay away from the six deadly sins.

Insight

The stand-up

A tool to help create a group identity and a sense of shared purpose.

A regular, standing-up, 15-minute team session.

To make sure that everyone is aware of all the important things in your workplace that affect you and your work.

How can it help?

It helps to address the 'Why am I never told?' syndrome. The stand-up is an easy way to make sure that everyone is up-to-date. There is no time for long descriptions of the progress of each person's work.

How does it work?

It requires a shared understanding among the members of your group about what this 'anti-meeting' should accomplish and how it works.

Planning

There is no chairperson and no agenda but only raise those items that concern the whole group. Meet regularly in a central location where everyone has room to stand.

Doing

Keep it simple, optimistic, focused and fun. It is better to say nothing than to talk about something of no concern to the group. Talkers learn to listen and listeners have an opportunity to talk.

Conflict in organizations

Conflict is inevitable but it can be minimized, diverted and/or resolved. Workplace conflict can lower morale and productivity, increase turnover and employee burnout, and add greatly to sick pay costs. Some conflicts are good and some not so good. Conflict occurs naturally when people interact, and teams, organizations and even individuals can grow as a result of the new ideas and the new ways of thinking that can emerge through conflict. However, conflict can also be destructive for individuals and for organizations. Organizational change can require members of an organization to work together in new ways and under new rules. Competition can exacerbate personality conflicts and the complexities of communication can make it more difficult for culturally, economically and socially diverse workers to resolve the issues and problems they encounter on the job.

Source: Lankard Brown (1998).

Conflict occurs when individuals or groups are not obtaining what they need or want and are seeking their own self-interest. Sometimes the individual is not aware of the need and unconsciously starts to act out. Other times, the individual is very aware of what he or she wants and actively works at achieving the goal.

Beginnings of conflict:

Poor communication
Seeking power
Dissatisfaction with management style
Weak leadership
Lack of openness
Change in leadership.

Conflict indicators:

o   Body language
o   Disagreements, regardless of issue
o   Withholding bad news
o   Surprises
o   Strong public statements
o   Airing disagreements through media
o   Conflicts in value system
o   Desire for power
o   Increasing lack of respect
o   Open disagreement
o   Lack of candour on budget problems or other sensitive issues
o   Lack of clear goals
o   No discussion of progress, failure relative to goals, failure to evaluate the superintendent fairly, thoroughly or at all.

Conflict is destructive when it:

o   Takes attention away from other important activities
o   Undermines morale or self-concept
o   Polarizes people and groups, reducing co-operation
o   Increases or sharpens difference.

Conflict is constructive when it:

o   Results in clarification of important problems and issues
o   Results in solutions to problems
o   Involves people in resolving issues important to them
o   Causes authentic communication
o   Helps release emotion, anxiety, and stress
o   Builds co-operation among people through learning more about each other
o   Joining in resolving the conflict
o   Helps individuals develop understanding and skills.

Some strategies for dealing with conflict

1. *Non-verbal alert* – Non-verbal behaviour can be an early warning sign of conflict. Ask people to verbalize their feelings wherever possible.
2. *Team development phase* – See (p. 81) the Tuckman forming, storming, norming, performing model. Sometimes conflict is predictable because that is what happens at one particular phase of group development.
3. *Resort to authority* – This means bringing in someone using a legitimate power base (and perhaps other power bases) to lay down the law. This may be necessary if team members are playing destructive roles.

4. *Planning* – Planning techniques, such as task scheduling, timelines and project diaries and meetings may provide an authoritative and neutral way of sequencing tasks to be performed by different individuals or sub-groups, thus reducing potential for conflict.

5. *Use communication skills more effectively* – Sometimes it is best to utilize what you know about good communication skills. Try to control destructive role-playing. Acknowledge individuals by praising their input.

6. *Conflict management techniques*

   (a) Collaborating: win/win
   (b) Compromising: win some/lose some
   (c) Accommodating: lose/win
   (d) Competing: win/lose
   (e) Avoiding: no winners/no losers.

Collaborating

I win, you win

Fundamental premise – Teamwork and co-operation help everyone achieve their goals while also maintaining relationships.

Strategic philosophy – Working through differences will lead to creative solutions that will satisfy both the parties' concerns.

When to use:

- o When there is a high level of trust.
- o When you don't want to have full responsibility.
- o When you want others to also have 'ownership' of solutions.
- o When the people involved are willing to change their thinking as more information is found and new options are suggested.
- o When you need to work through animosity and hard feelings.

Drawbacks:

- o Takes lots of time and energy.
- o Some may take advantage of other people's trust and openness.

Compromising

You bend, I bend

Fundamental premise – Winning something while losing a little is OK.

Strategic philosophy – Both ends are placed against the middle in an attempt to serve the 'common good' while ensuring each person can maintain something of their original position.

When to use:

- o When people of equal status are equally committed to goals.
- o When time can be saved by reaching intermediate settlements on individual parts of complex issues.
- o When goals are moderately important.

Drawbacks:

- o Important values and long-term objectives can be derailed in the process.
- o May not work if initial demands are too great.
- o Can create cynicism, especially if there is no commitment to honour the compromise solutions.

Accommodating

I lose, you win

Fundamental premise – Working towards a common purpose is more important than any of the peripheral issues.

Strategic philosophy – Appease others by downplaying conflict, thus protecting the relationship.

When to use:

- o When the issue is not as important to you as it is to the other person.
- o When you know you can't win.
- o When it's not the right time.
- o When harmony is extremely important.
- o When what the parties have in common is a good deal more important than their differences.

Drawbacks:

- o One's own ideas don't get attention.
- o Credibility and influence can be lost.

Competing

I win, you lose

Fundamental premise – Associates 'winning' a conflict with competition.

Strategic philosophy – When goals are extremely important, one must sometimes use power to win.

When to use:

- o When you know you are right.
- o When you need a quick decision.
- o When a strong personality is trying to steamroller you.
- o When you need to stand up for your rights.

Drawbacks:

- o Can escalate conflict.
- o Losers may retaliate.

Avoiding

No winners, no losers

Fundamental premise – This isn't the right time or place to address this issue.

Strategic philosophy – Avoids conflict by withdrawing, sidestepping or postponing.

When to use:

o When the conflict is small and relationships are at stake.
o When more important issues are pressing and you don't have time to deal with this one.
o When you see no chance of getting your concerns met.
o When you are too emotionally involved and others around you can solve the conflict more successfully.
o When more information is needed.

Drawbacks:

o Important decisions may be made by default.
o Postponing sometimes makes matters worse.

Source: Culbert (2002).

Groupthink

Groupthink is a concept that was identified by Irving Janis, referring to faulty decision-making in a group. Groups experiencing groupthink do not consider all alternatives, and they desire unanimity at the expense of quality decisions. Janis listed seven symptoms that show that consensus seeking has led the group astray. The first two stem from overconfidence in the group's prowess. The next pair reflect the tunnel vision members use to view the problem. The final three are signs of strong conformity pressure within the group.

o Incomplete survey of alternatives
o Incomplete survey of objectives
o Failure to examine risks of preferred choice
o Failure to reappraise initially rejected alternatives
o Poor information search
o Selective bias in processing information at hand
o Failure to work out contingency plans.

Case study

An illustration of groupthink
Report of the presidential commission on the space shuttle Challenger disaster

1. *Illusion of invulnerability* – Despite the launch pad fire that killed three astronauts in 1967 and the close call of Apollo 13, the American space programme had never experienced an in-flight fatality. When engineers raised the possibility of catastrophic O-ring blow-by, NASA manager George Hardy nonchalantly pointed out that this risk was 'true of every other flight we have had'. Janis summarizes this attitude as 'everything is going to work out all right because we are a special group'.

2. *Belief in inherent morality of the group* – Under the sway of groupthink, members automatically assume the rightness of their cause. At the hearing, engineer Brian Russell noted that NASA managers had shifted the moral rules under which they operated: 'I had the distinct feeling that we were in the position of having to prove that it was unsafe instead of the other way around.'

101

3. *Collective rationalization* – Despite the written policy that the O-ring seal was a critical failure point without back-up, NASA manager George Hardy testified that 'we were counting on the secondary O-ring to be the sealing O-ring under the worst case conditions'. Apparently, this was a shared misconception. NASA manager Lawrence Mulloy confirmed that 'no one in the meeting questioned the fact that the secondary seal was capable and in position to seal during the early part of the ignition transient'.

4. *Out-group stereotypes* – Although there is no direct evidence that NASA officials looked down on Thiokol engineers, Mulloy was caustic about their recommendation to postpone the launch until the temperature rose to 53 degrees. He reportedly asked whether they expected NASA to wait until April to launch the shuttle.

5. *Self-censorship* – We now know that Thiokol engineer George McDonald wanted to postpone the flight. But instead of clearly stating 'I recommend we don't launch below 53 degrees', he offered an equivocal opinion. He suggested that 'lower temperatures are in the direction of badness for both O-rings···' What did he think they should do? From his tempered words, it's hard to tell.

6. *Illusion of unanimity* – NASA managers perpetuated the fiction that everyone was fully in accord with the launch recommendation. They admitted to the presidential commission that they didn't report Thiokol's on-again/off-again hesitancy with their superiors. As often happens in such cases, the flight readiness review team interpreted silence as agreement.

7. *Direct pressure on dissenters* – Thiokol engineers felt pressure from two directions to reverse their 'no-go' recommendation. NASA managers had already postponed the launch three times and were fearful that the American public would regard the agency as inept. Similarly, the company's management was fearful of losing future NASA contracts. When they went off-line for their group meeting, Thiokol's senior vice president urged Roger Lund, vice president of engineering, to 'take off his engineering hat and put on his management hat'.

8. *Self-appointed mindguards* – 'Mindguards' protect a leader from assault by troublesome ideas. NASA managers insulated Jesse Moore from the debate over the integrity of the rocket booster seals. Even though Roger Boisjoly was Thiokol's expert on O-rings, he later bemoaned that he 'was not even asked to participate in giving input to the final decision charts'.

Conflict within groups or teams can often lead to bad decision-making and problem-solving, rash decisions, inadequate consideration of alternative solutions and poor perception of what is happening in a given situation.

Source: Griffin (1999).

Developing the team

Activity 3.1

Here is an activity for evaluating your team. Circle the number that is appropriate for your team. What are your priorities for development? – You could also ask a trusted colleague to complete a form like this about you so that you can compare your responses with his or her perceptions. If there were large gaps in perception you might want to pursue this further to understand why your perceptions are different.

Evaluate your team development

Rating team development

How do you feel about your team's
progress? (Circle rating).

1. Team's purpose

I'm uncertain   1 2 3 4 5   I'm clear

2. Team membership

I'm out   1 2 3 4 5   I'm in

3. Communications

Very guarded   1 2 3 4 5   Very open

4. Team goals

Set from above   1 2 3 4 5   Emerged through team interaction

5. Use of team member's skills

Poor use   1 2 3 4 5   Good use

6. Support

Little help for individuals   1 2 3 4 5   High level of support for individuals

7. Conflict

Difficult issues are avoided   1 2 3 4 5   Problems are discussed openly and directly

8. Influence on decisions

By few members   1 2 3 4 5   By all members

9. Risk taking

Not encouraged   1 2 3 4 5   Encouraged and supported

10. Working on relationships with
others

Little effort   1 2 3 4 5   High level of effort

11. Distribution of leadership

Limited   1 2 3 4 5   Shared

12. Useful feedback

Very little   1 2 3 4 5   Considerable

Learning in teams

Team learning is essential for organizational learning. Learning between teams, and the structures for this shared learning, is how organizational learning builds. Different people learn in different ways and therefore a training programme that suits one type of person might not suit another. Training should contain a variety of activities so that everyone finds something that is suitable for them. One of the best-known approaches to learning styles is the work of David Kolb through his 'Learning Styles Inventory'. Peter Honey and Alan Mumford published *The Learning Styles Questionnaire* (1982) which extended Kolb's work.

Learning styles
Activist

- Learns best from short here-and-now tasks.
- Tries anything once and is enthusiastic about new activities.
- Throws him/herself into action-based courses, games and exercises.

Reflector

- Learns best from standing back and observing what's happening.
- Prefers to collect and analyse data before coming to a conclusion.
- Enjoys watching people in action.
- May not enjoy interacting with a computer screen.

Theorist

- Learns best when reviewing content in terms of a system, model or theory.
- Tends to be detached and analytical.
- Emphasizes rationality and logic.

Pragmatist

- Learns when there is an obvious link between the subject matter and a problem, or opportunity on the job.
- Searches for new ideas and the chance to apply them to a relevant situation.
- Likes to get on with things, rather than having long, open-ended discussions.

Insight

Training and development

In the last 12 months prior to the survey:

88 per cent of employers had provided any job-related training.

55 per cent of employers had provided off-the-job training. The average amount is 2.3 days per employee. The average per trainee is 8.2 days.

78 per cent of employers had provided on-the-job training for their employees.

30 per cent of employers helped employees learn things not directly connected to their job.

NVQs/SVQs are the initiatives with the highest level of awareness.

Source: Learning and Training at Work, 2001, DfES David Spilsbury IFF Research Ltd.

Induction training
All new employees need some form of introduction to the organization and the job. A well-planned system of induction provides regular training and/or development sessions. For example, large department stores have a continuing programme of induction with a new course

starting every week and special provision for part-time workers. This leaves individual managers in the comfortable position of receiving staff who have at least received training that is specific to their job. Some training, such as health and safety awareness, should be given to all employees.

In larger organizations line managers may take responsibility for monitoring and encouraging each individual at their place of work and for off-the-job training. However, there may be a specialist training and development section that is usually part of the Human Resources Department.

The benefits of training and development

- ○ *Improved motivation* – Individuals see their skills base extending and their promotion prospects being enhanced.
- ○ *Lower turnover* – Opportunities for self-improvement, leads to people staying longer in one employment.
- ○ *Higher levels of performance* – Trained and motivated staff are more likely to give of their best, which, in the end, justifies the training budget.

Insight

The most successful teams are those who have demonstrated the greatest commitment to their people. They are the ones who have created the greatest sense of belonging. They have done most in-house to develop their people

Source: Bill Walsh, Head coach San Francisco 49ers, Quoted in the *Harvard Business Review*.

On-the-Job training (OJT)

Although people's learning styles differ, learning theory suggests that most people learn and retain more through doing and practicing activities. OJT is the most common form of training in organizations. To be effective it needs to:

- ○ Be properly planned and specified in advance
- ○ Take place at trainees' normal work positions
- ○ Be accepted that there will be 'downtime' when little is being produced by the people carrying out the training.

It is often carried out with a line manager or other experienced staff but often they will not have received any training in this role so the quality can be variable. OJT is not always the best approach to developing broader transferable skills but it is good for job-specific skills. Training that takes place at or near the job can be more easily tailored to meet specific needs and arranged at convenient times. The involvement of colleagues, supervisors or managers in OJT can also help to build a strong team spirit. OJT is often associated with the development of new employees, but it can also be used to update and widen the skills of existing employees.

Off-the-Job training and development

A key issue is making sure that the event matches up to the values the organization is trying to promote and the expectations of the staff who are taking part in the training. One aspect of this is the venue and, for example, if the intention is to focus on customer care it is important that the participants are treated well as customers. Everything about the training needs to model the behaviour it is trying to promote.

Case study

McDonald's puts great emphasis on OJT as a training handbook. Staff are given a training card on which to record their achievements. They are expected to check with their managers to ensure progress is properly recorded and that they gain experience in all work areas. New employees are teamed up with a 'buddy', a member of the training team. Job rotation is practised and there are 19 work areas to which staff can be assigned.

Observation and questioning are used to assess staff and two observations must be passed before someone is regarded as 'competent'. Restaurant managers spend a lot of time on a one-to-one basis with new recruits. Managers have training responsibilities and can spend 60 per cent of their time on the floor with the crew. Their own training involves learning everything a crew member needs to know and further classroom training.

Online training and education

Online training can be used as a supplement to face-to-face encounters. In some instances, instructors can supplement their material by placing related material on the web. Some uses include:

- ○ Aspects of induction training which are routine and technical such as health and safety procedures.
- ○ Business training on procedures used to protect information within the company.
- ○ Teaching the use of common business applications, such as Microsoft Office.

Managers need to understand their own Learning Style preferences and those of the people they manage. Responses to e-learning may be according to Learning Style preference. E-learning is more likely to deliver knowledge-type learning, rather than skills development. It may not be the most suitable answer to a particular individual's learning needs.

Evaluation of training

Most management and employee training is only assessed by the individuals involved in the process and much of the feedback is taken from questionnaires. Although many organizations have developed strategies for developing managers, the evaluation of their training and development is often ineffective. Over a decade ago, research undertaken in the UK entitled 'Training in Britain: A Study of Funding, Activity and Attitudes' revealed that 85 per cent of UK employers made no attempt to assess the benefits gained from undertaking training. The reasons for this are:

- ○ Difficulty in quantifying the effects.
- ○ Difficulty in disentangling the effect of a number of variables which might affect performance.
- ○ Cost of evaluation that could outweigh the value of the benefit achieved.
- ○ Sensitivity of the trainers who are keen to ensure that their training is shown to have had a positive effect.

The ultimate goal of training and development is to effect change in an individual's knowledge, understanding, skills and behaviours. However, for practical reasons of time and resources, often it only focuses on knowledge and to a lesser extent on understanding.

A model of effective evaluation: Joyce and Showers model

The first of five components of this model is the presentation of theory or the description of a new skill or behaviour deemed useful or desirable.

The second component of the Joyce and Showers model is demonstration or modelling of the new strategy or skill. This could be achieved by observing someone.

The third component is initial practice in a protected or simulated setting – most often in a workshop session. The individual or the group participates, trying out the new skill.

The fourth component is providing structured and open-ended feedback about performance.

The fifth component is coaching. As the new idea or skill is being applied and tried in a real setting, follow-up help with implementation is given to the participant.

When participants were given only the first component, a description of the new skill, 10 per cent of the persons could transfer or use the skill in the workplace. When the second component, demonstration of the skill, was included, 2–3 per cent more persons could perform the skill in the classroom. When practice, the third component, was added, 2–3 per cent more transfer occurred; similarly, when the fourth component, feedback, was included, another 2–3 per cent transfer occurred. Thus, four components resulted in 16–19 persons out of 100 able to perform the new skill in the classroom. However, when coaching, the fifth component, was part of the staff development process, up to 95 per cent of the participants transferred the skill into their actual practice. The coaching component was a critical one in effecting a change in the skills of an exceedingly large number of persons.

Coaching

Coaching is a learning opportunity and individual learning preferences need to be considered as part of this. To be an effective coach, the team leader needs to build trusting relationships. Focused listening is one of the most important skills for establishing such a relationship.

There are three levels of understanding and skill required for effective coaching:

- Recognizing managerial situations as opportunities
- Creating an effective learning process
- Establishing an acceptable helping relationship.

Organizational benefits of coaching

- To improve individual performance – to expand an individual's range of skills, knowledge and insight in order to help them do the job better
- To provide a supportive working environment
- To value people
- To improve communication
- To promote effective teams
- To ensure appropriate allocation of tasks and projects
- To develop managerial skills, for example, to improve the skills of team leaders

- o To expand the range of skills, knowledge and insight of someone in order to enhance their prospects for a different job
- o To develop people for more senior jobs
- o To increase organizational effectiveness and efficiency
- o To enable best use of resources.

Benefits of coaching to the individual

- o Support for individual learning needs – tackling the tasks and the issues that concern people in their day-to-day job.
- o On-the-job development for both coach and individual – it can be a learning experience for both participants in the opportunity to reflect on skills, knowledge and behaviour.
- o Increased motivation.
- o Improved capability at work.
- o Potential to support career development.

Some of the skills needed for coaching

- o Communication – listening skills, for example, active listening, reflective listening, open listening
- o Appropriate questioning strategies
- o Giving feedback
- o Negotiating and agreeing objectives
- o Analytical skills, evaluative skills – ability to reflect and learn from experiences and encourage others to do this.

Activity 3.2

Tick any items where you feel you have a need for coaching. Put them in order of priority for you. Next to your priorities, write the names of people in your organization who might help you with these activities. Work out a strategy for approaching the people concerned.

Coaching checklist

1. Providing guidance and support —— ——
2. Helping to get the 'big picture' in the organization —— ——
3. Helping with networking/making contacts —— ——
4. Interpreting organizational politics —— ——
5. Translating organizational jargon —— ——
6. Being a sounding-board for action plans —— ——
7. Appraising/reviewing performance —— ——
8. Providing day-to-day advice on problems —— ——
9. Listening and questioning —— ——
10. Being a resource person – able to point to opportunities/learning resources
11. Evaluating progress.

Mentoring

Mentoring can be provided in various ways but its aim is to develop people and organizational effectiveness.

Management development

Torrington and Hall (1998) show that management training and management development can be differentiated in four important ways:

1. Management development is a broader concept. It is more concerned with developing the whole person rather than emphasizing the learning of narrowly defined skills.
2. Management development emphasizes the contribution of both formal and informal work experiences.
3. The concept of management development places a greater responsibility on managers to develop themselves than is placed on most employees to train themselves.
4. Although in training generally there is always a need to be concerned with the future, this is especially emphasized in management development. Managers are developed as much for jobs they will be doing, as for jobs that they are doing. Both the managers and the organization benefit from this approach.

K Shoes first implemented teams in 1990, and 45 per cent of the employees are in teams of 5–8 people. Their responsibilities include: managing team resources based on marketplace demand for styles of shoes, understanding the business and marketplace issues and their impact on demand, and the handling of materials and equipment budgeting. Other responsibilities are controlling team profit and loss, identifying team training needs, and conducting cross-training and problem-solving during non-production time. Also described in the case study are the training and compensation of teams, member selection, performance evaluation and the impact of teams on the organization.

The primary benefits of undertaking a management development programme for the individual is the modification of their management style, technical or professional skills, while the primary benefits for the organization of such a programme focus on its ability to act as a catalyst in transforming the organization by providing the skills and knowledge to manage innovation and change (Doyle, 2000). These benefits are complementary in developing both the individual and the organization. A significant trend in management development in the 1990s has been the move away from case-based programmes to problem-solving, focusing on real-life issues.

1. The individual participating must see the issue involved as important.
2. It must involve some analysis.
3. It must involve some aspect of creativity.
4. There must be practical application of the suggested improvement.

Goals of management development

Given that there is some uncertainty about what successful managers actually do, it is difficult to establish clear goals for management development. In general, however:

o Management development will focus on the abilities to do, rather than on pure knowledge.
o Management development will focus on the needs of individuals and tailor 'developmental opportunities for each'.
o Individuals will be expected as a matter of course to take the initiative in their own self-development.

Performance management

The performance management process usually begins with an analysis of the job. Standards of minimum acceptable performance are developed and standards for performance which exceed expectations may also be set to encourage the employee to strive for even better results. Performance management is based on a systematic approach to improving individual and team performance in order to achieve organizational goals. It encompasses processes that aim to improve the performance of both the individual and the organization by, for example, coaching and encouraging the individual, by ensuring that the organization learns from the process and by providing a means of aligning the interests of the individual with those of the organization. It is concerned with creating a shared vision of the purpose and aims of the organization, helping each employee to understand and recognize their part in contributing to achieving them.

Evaluation of team performance

When a team approach to work is in place, the focus of performance management is on the accomplishments of the team as well as the individual's contributions to those accomplishments. Team effectiveness is improved when both team and individual performance are recognized as significant and factored into the performance management process. Team performance standards refer to skills which make employees effective team members as well as the standards expected of individuals. Performance management of a self-directed work team may be undertaken by the team itself but this can vary from organization to organization, or department to department. The organization should provide guidelines and a framework for that performance management, but within this, the team may be responsible and accountable for its own performance. A self-directed work team may be able to describe its own jobs, set its own standards, give feedback to its own members about work performance and team skills, appraise itself and identify and support the training and development needs of its members. However, this is likely to be a rare occurrence because of the greater demands of accountability that have developed in the past couple of decades.

The ability to provide effective observation and feedback is important because it is through observation that areas for improvement can be identified and the team made aware of them. Whether the team is self-directed and managing its own performance, or team members that report to one or more line managers, teams will benefit from observation and feedback. If the team as a whole has a formal reporting relationship with a line manager, he or she will be concerned with observing and giving feedback about the work-related behaviour and outputs of the team as a whole, as well as that of individual team members. If team members report to different line managers, or if the line manager is not present when the team does its work, he or she will need to establish procedures and relationships for learning about the work the team is doing and how it is working together. This could involve receiving input from the team leader, team members and customers of the team.

Performance standards and statistical data relating to the achievement of objectives and targets help in providing 'objective' feedback. However, statistics never speak for themselves and should only be used as the platform for a discussion as to why targets have or have not been reached. There may be a host of extraneous and unforeseen factors that have influenced the attainment of targets. For example, no one could have predicted what would happen to the airline industry in 2001 when the Twin Towers were attacked in New York. Another source of feedback for teams is customers. This feedback may come in a variety of forms: surveys, feedback cards, suggestion boxes, in-person interviews, telephone interviews, and focus groups.

When the basis for appraisal is the performance of individual team members, the incentive to work effectively with other team members may be missing. Because of this some organizations appraise team performance and not individual performance but this can undermine a sense of individual responsibility. Some organizations appraise team performance and individual performance. The main issues regarding the performance management of teams relate to the variety of reporting relationships and degree of independent responsibility that teams may exercise, as well as the need to reinforce team values and efforts without undermining individual responsibility. Typically, a line manager will be involved in some or all of the following activities:

o   Allocating work to teams and individuals
o   Agreeing objectives and work plans with teams and individuals
o   Assessing the performance of teams and individuals
o   Providing feedback to teams and individuals on their performance
o   Dealing with poor performance in a team
o   Supporting team members who have problems affecting their performance
o   Implementing disciplinary and grievance procedures
o   Dismissing team members whose performance is unsatisfactory.

Constructive feedback
Feedback is a way of learning more about ourselves and the effect our behaviour has on others. Constructive feedback increases self-awareness, offers options and encourages development.

Start with the positive
Most people need encouragement to be told when they are doing something well. If the positive is identified at the beginning, negative points are more likely to be acted upon.

Be specific
Generalized comments are not very helpful. Try to be specific about particular examples of behaviour that are not acceptable. Try to identify what a person did well or behaviour that can be praised.

Refer to behaviour that can be changed
Give feedback about something that the person can change.

Offer alternatives
If you give negative feedback, suggest what the person could have done differently. Turn the negative into a positive suggestion.

Be descriptive rather than evaluative
Tell the person what you saw or heard and the effect it had on you rather than merely saying that something was good, bad, and so on. Explain fully.

Own the feedback
All that anyone is entitled to give is their own experience, of that person, at a particular time. Comments such as 'you always · · ·' or 'you are · · ·' as if they are agreed statements about what a person is like are not productive. It is important that we take responsibility for the feedback that we offer.

Leave the receiver with a choice
Feedback which demands change may meet with resistance. Skilled feedback offers people information about themselves in a way which leaves them with the choice about whether to act on it or not. It can help to examine the consequences of any decision to change or not to change.

Team reward

Team reward aims to reinforce behaviour which leads to effective teamwork. It encourages group endeavour rather than just individual performance. Most team reward systems emphasize team pay rather than non-financial rewards. However, teams may respond to all types of reward from pay, bonuses and public recognition. An advantage is that team pay can encourage co-operative work and behaviour, and develop self-managed and directed teams.

In 2001, the Chartered Institute of Personnel and Development (CIPD) conducted research into reward management in 970 organizations in the United Kingdom – the findings included information on team reward. Team bonuses were present in only 18 per cent of organizations and performance related increases were present in less than 57 per cent of organizations.

Team pay works best if teams stand alone with agreed targets and are composed of people whose work is interdependent. For it to work well, everybody must understand and accept the targets and the reward must be linked clearly to effort and achievement.

Teams may be able to plan and implement their own improvement programmes if they receive feedback and meet regularly to discuss performance. Team reward is a way for organizations to demonstrate that they value teams and individuals who perform well, and that high levels of performance are important. The quality of teamwork depends on:

- Culture
- Structure and operating processes
- Values
- Performance management
- Management style
- Employee development programmes.

Discipline

A disciplinary interview can be thought of as having three stages:

Establishing the gap – Future performance is the main concern, so any discussion about present behaviour should be focused on changes that are needed for the future and how to achieve them. It is important to be specific about concerns and to provide evidence or examples of how there is a gap between present behaviour and what is required.

Exploring the reasons for a gap – It is important to allow the person subject to a disciplinary interview to explain the circumstances and to put forward their point of view about the gap. This may uncover problems or issues that the manager is unaware of but will need to be dealt with in some way, for example, suggesting that they seek advice and guidance or specialist help.

Eliminating the gap – There will need to be agreement to a plan of action that may involve training. Arrangements for keeping the situation under review will need to be agreed, and the person should be aware of how and when their performance is going to be monitored. The aim is to help facilitate an improvement in performance.

Summary

Members of a team can contribute to it in two distinct roles: their professional or technical role (production, sales, etc.) and their team role. The effectiveness of the team will depend on the extent to which its members correctly recognize and adjust themselves to the relative strengths within the team. Each team needs a balance of team roles and the optimum balance will depend on the tasks that the team needs to perform and its objectives. Personal attributes fit some roles well but limit the ability to succeed in other roles.

Further study

Read Boddy, D. (2002) *Management: An Introduction*, Chapter 13, 'Motivation' and Chapter 15, 'Teams'.

Hints and tips

If you are asked to interpret some information, it usually means that you need to explain the meaning of it, making it clear that you understand the data provided. This is a likely scenario if undertaking Marketing in Practice. This exam will contain data that needs interpreting.

Bibliography

Adair, J. (1988) *Effective Leadership*, London: Pan.

Armstrong, M. (1996) *A Handbook of Personnel Management Practice*, London: Kogan Page.

Bacal, R. (2002) 'The six deadly sins of team building', <http://www.work911.com/articles/teambuidingsins.htm>

Belbin, R., Meredith (1996a) *Management Teams: Why they Succeed or Fail*, London: Butterworth-Heinemann.

Belbin, R., Meredith (1996b) *Team Roles at Work*, London: Butterworth-Heinemann.

Bennis, Warren, G. (1994) *On Becoming a Leader*, 2nd edition, New York: Perseus.

Challenger Disaster, *A First Look at Communication Theory*, 3rd edition, McGraw-Hill.

Culbert, H. (2002) 'Conflict management strategies and styles: Improving group dynamics', <http://home.snu.edu/>

Doyle (2000) *Value-based Marketing: Marketing Strategies for Corporate Growth and Shareholder Value*.

Griffin, Em. (1999) 'Report of the presidential commission on the space shuttle', www.firstlook.com

Herzberg, F. *et al.* (1959) *The Motivation to Work*, New York: John Wiley.

Kouzes, J.M., Posner, B.Z. (2002) *The Leadership Challenge*, 3rd edition, New York: Jossey Bass.

Lankard Brown, Bettina (1998) 'Conflict management', <http://ericave.org/docs/conflict.htm>

McClelland, D. *et al.* (1953) *The Achievement Motive*, New York: Appleton Century Crofts.

McGregor, D. (1960) *The Human Side of Enterprise*, New York: McGraw-Hill.

Ott, Daniel, J. (1999) <http://www.egsa.org/powerline/past/MA99relmktg.htm>

Tuckman, B.W. (1965) 'Developmental sequences in small groups', *Psychological Bulletin*, **63**, pp. 384–399. Tuckman later revised his model to include a fifth stage but this is not as well known as his 4 stage model. See Tuckman, B.W. and Jensen, M.A.C. 'Stages of small group development revisited', *Groups and Organization Studies*, **2**, pp. 419–427.

Sample exam questions and answers for the Marketing Management in Practice module as a whole can be found in Appendix 6 and past examination papers can be found in Appendix 7. Both appendices can be found at the back of the book.

unit 4 managing change

Learning objectives

Explain the sources and nature of change affecting organizations, and the techniques available for managing change (1.7).

Related Statement of Marketing Practice

Lc.4 Embrace change and modify behaviours and attitudes.

Introduction

Organizations face change all the time, driven by internal and/or external influences. Most changes in organizations are minor and incremental. A few changes are major and involve completely new ways of operating. Managing change means taking active control of change because many problems are those of adaptation, that is they require of the organization only that it adjusts to an ever-changing set of circumstances. Factors from outside the business include: technological developments, changing market conditions, such as exchange rate movements, supplier price increases and demand from customers for new services, legislation, such as the working time regulations and the minimum wage. Factors from inside the business include: personnel changes, such as key employees leaving and new senior appointments. New management processes such as customer service initiatives are also a source of change, and there are constant pressures to improve efficiency in both the public and private sectors.

How is the UK changing?

o Women are now having fewer children than ever before. The birth rate is now fairly stable and is predicted to remain so, although it was declining for most of the twentieth century.

o The UK population is now living for longer than ever before. Average life expectancy in 1999 was 75 years for men and 79–80 years for women. This compared to 70 years for men and 76 years for women in 1979.

o A culmination of a population that is living longer and having fewer children will create a society with a declining workforce supporting a growing population of dependants (over 65's and under 16's).

o By 2014 it is expected that the proportion of the population over 65 years will exceed that under 16 year olds.

o The average size of the UK household is getting smaller. In 2001, 64 per cent of households in the UK were one- or two-person households, compared to 44 per cent in 1961.

o The increase in the number of households in the UK now exceeds the growth rate of the population.

o Working hours in the UK are amongst the highest in Europe. Men are more likely to work longer hours than women.

o The most common length of the working week for men is 40 hours, followed by 60+ hours (1.5 million men), while women tend to work less than 40 hours a week although there is a wide distribution. More women than men work part-time which in part reflects the still apparent difference in gender roles, but this is changing.

o Although we have less 'free' time, more of us have access to technology that can make life easier. Most people own washing machines, microwaves and telephones, whilst almost 3/4 of households own cars. Other products such as dishwashers and home computers have still to reach universal ownership, however, ownership continues to increase at a relatively fast pace.

Source: Office of National Statistics/General Household Survey.

Factors driving change

The macro-environment

This includes all factors that can influence an organization, but that are out of their direct control. A company does not generally influence any laws (although it is accepted that they could lobby or be part of a trade organization). It is continuously changing, and the company needs to be flexible to adapt. There may be aggressive competition and rivalry in a market.

The PEST analysis is a useful tool for understanding market growth or decline. A PEST analysis is a business measurement tool. PEST is an acronym for Political, Economic, Social and Technological factors, which are used to assess the market for a business or organizational unit.

The PEST analysis headings are a framework for reviewing a situation, and can be used to review a strategy or position, direction of a company, a marketing proposition, or idea.

PEST is useful before SWOT because it helps to identify SWOT factors. There is overlap between PEST and SWOT, in that similar factors would appear in each. PEST assesses a market, including competitors, from the standpoint of a particular proposition or a business. SWOT is an assessment of a business or a proposition, whether your own or a competitor's. PEST becomes more useful and relevant the larger and more complex the business or proposition, but even for a very small local businesses a PEST analysis can still throw up significant issues that might otherwise be missed. The four dimensions of PEST vary in significance depending on the type of business, for example, social factors are more obviously relevant to consumer businesses or a B2B business close to the consumer-end of the supply chain.

Political
- o Ecological/environmental issues
- o Current legislation home market
- o Future legislation
- o European/international legislation
- o Regulatory bodies and processes
- o Government policies
- o Government term and change
- o Trading policies
- o Funding, grants and initiatives
- o Home market lobbying/pressure groups
- o International pressure group.

Economic
- o Home economy situation
- o Home economy trends
- o Overseas economies and trends
- o General taxation issues
- o Taxation specific to product/services
- o Seasonality/weather issues
- o Market and trade cycles
- o Specific industry factors
- o Market routes and distribution trends
- o Customer/end-user drivers
- o Interest and exchange rates.

Social
- o Lifestyle trends
- o Demographics
- o Consumer attitudes and opinions
- o Media views
- o Law changes affecting social factors
- o Brand, company, technology image
- o Consumer buying patterns
- o Fashion and role models
- o Major events and influences
- o Buying access and trends
- o Ethnic/religious factors
- o Advertising and public.

Technological
- o Competing technology development
- o Research funding
- o Associated/dependent technologies
- o Replacement technology/solutions
- o Maturity of technology
- o Manufacturing maturity and capacity
- o Information and communications
- o Consumer buying mechanisms/technology
- o Technology legislation

- o Innovation potential
- o Technology access, licensing, patents
- o Intellectual property issues.

Insight: Technology

- o At the end of 2003, 1 in 2 UK homes had Internet access, compared with 1 in 10 in 1999. Regular adult Internet use has also grown significantly, rising to 56 per cent in 2003, representing consistent year-on-year growth of over 5 percentage points. Sixty one per cent of the population reports that they have used the Internet at some time.
- o Increased ease of physical access has fostered this progress. Over £400 million has been invested in the national network of 6000 UK online centres, located in local libraries. Ninety six per cent of Britain's population are aware of a place where they can access the Internet.
- o Eighty per cent of the population has access to a mass-market broadband solution; from less than 50 000 in 2000 there are now over 2.6 million broadband subscribers in the UK.
- o e-Commerce has become more popular. In 2000, 28 per cent of Internet users had purchased goods or services online; by 2003 this figure had reached 52 per cent.
- o UK's lowest income households are, at 12 per cent of the population, over 7 times less likely to be online than those in the top income group, of whom 86 per cent have home Internet access. While over 78 per cent of 16–24 year olds are regular Internet users, only 16 per cent of those over 65 are online.
- o Fewer than 1 in 12 Internet users have ever carried out an online transaction with the government. This, despite the following facts: over two-thirds of government services are now online; every local council has a website; and more than 3000 .gov.uk websites have surfaced.
- o The government pledges that every home in Britain will have access to online services by 2008. The plan includes both narrowband and broadband services as well as digital terrestrial, cable, satellite TV, and next-generat The IT Workforce.

Globalization

Globalization is helping to remove restrictions on where people can go, what they can buy, where they can invest, and what they can read, hear or see. Economic integration is driven by two forces: advances in technology and decisions to liberalize trade. Globalization means that there is always the threat of substitute products and new entrants. The wider environment is also ever changing, and the marketer needs to take account of changes in culture, politics, economics and technology.

However, there are unanswered questions concerning those people who lose out economically, socially and culturally. Globalization has had a mixed press and has been violently denounced at demonstrations during World Trade Organization meetings. The growth in availability of Fair Trade products signals greater interest in the ethics of trade. Critics argue that globalization has led to rising global inequality and exploitation of the poor by transnational companies.

Supporters of globalization argue that the number of people in extreme poverty – living on less than a dollar a day – fell from about 30 per cent of the world population in 1980 to 20 per cent in 1997, according to the World Bank. They also argue that the relatively rapid growth of China and India has led to an improved income distribution, not a deterioration.

A series of corporate scandals that began with the collapse of Enron has caused a crisis of legitimacy and the business of wealth creation has been tarnished. At Enron, this took the form of generating phony profits, whilst at WorldCom, accountants turned operating expenses into capital assets.

The micro-environment

This environment influences the organization directly. It includes suppliers, consumers and customers, and other local stakeholders. Micro-environment describes the relationship between organizations and the driving forces that control this relationship. It may be more of a local relationship, and the organization may be able to exert its influence. Some external influences like globalization affect all organizations, directly or indirectly, whilst other influences may be more specific to particular sectors. For example, at present the Government has a 'modernization agenda' that claims to be aimed at improving public services, as the following case study demonstrates.

Case study

The public sector is faced with the challenge to improve the service it delivers to its customers. A gap has opened up between what commercial services can deliver and what we can expect from public services. For example, two-thirds of the people in this country now own mobile telephones and the cost of calls has fallen by nearly one-quarter over the past 2 years. We can buy cheap fresh food from around the world at any time of the day or night at a local supermarket or, if we prefer, over the phone or the PC. Meanwhile, it is still difficult to find a public library open before or after work or at any time on Sundays, and GP surgery hours are similarly limited. For increasing numbers of us today, the widening gulf between what we can buy as customers and what we get as public service users has created a credibility gap. Moreover, the public sector must serve all sections of society, not just those with money in their pockets. Change is not a simple, linear process, and improving the experience of users requires not only changes to systems and procedures in what are often huge, complex and interdependent organizations, but also changes in the attitudes and behaviour of individual members of staff. Change is painful and destructive as well as positive and creative. It challenges vested interests: personal, professional and institutional. Change is unavoidable; potentially both exciting and rewarding, but at the same time a messy and difficult enterprise, frequently confounding the intentions of managers, politicians and policymakers. There is no magic formula for change management, but there is a body of useful experience about what works and that can help build long-term capacity for the future.

Source: Managing for Excellence in the NHS (2002) Department of Health.

Managing change can be aided by undertaking a stakeholder analysis:

Stakeholder analysis

Stakeholder analysis is the technique used to identify the key people who have to be won over. By communicating with stakeholders early and frequently, you can ensure that they fully understand what you are doing, and understand the benefits of your project – this means they can support you actively when necessary.

Identifying your stakeholders

The first step in your stakeholder analysis is to brainstorm who your stakeholders are. As part of this, think of all the people who are affected by your work, who have influence or power over it, or have an interest in its successful or unsuccessful conclusion.

- o Your line manager
- o Shareholders
- o Senior executives
- o Your co-workers
- o Suppliers
- o Your team
- o Interest groups
- o Customers
- o The public
- o Prospective customers
- o Future recruits.

Prioritize your stakeholders

You may now have a long list of people and organizations that are affected by your work. Some of these may have the power either to block or advance. Some may be interested in what you are doing, others may not care. For example, your line manager is likely to have high power and influence over your projects and high interest.

Key questions that can help you understand your stakeholders

What interest do they have in the outcome of your work? Is it positive or negative?
What information do they want from you?
How do they want to receive information from you? What is the best way of communicating your message to them?
What is their current opinion of your work? Is it based on good information?
If they are not likely to be positive, what will win them around to support your project?
If you don't think you will be able to win them around, how will you manage their opposition?
Write your responses to these questions.

Estimate attitude and confidence in a particular change

Estimate the stakeholder's attitude, from supportive to opposed

- o Strongly in favour
- o Weakly in favour
- o Indifferent or undecided
- o Weakly opposed
- o Strongly opposed.

How confident you are about your estimate

- o Fully confident
- o Reasonably confident (some missing information, perhaps)

o   An informed guess
o   Wild guess.

Your best estimate of the influence of the stakeholder

H – High; this person or group has power of veto, formally or informally.
M – Medium; you could probably achieve your goals against this person's or group's opposition, but not easily.
L – Low; this person can do little to influence the outcomes of your intended actions.

Plan strategies

Plan your strategies for approaching and involving each person or group. It usually takes the form of obtaining more information, or of involving the stakeholder in the planning for the change. Highly influential people need to be involved in some way, or their influence needs to be neutralized. The people or groups who require the most attention are those who are influential and opposed to change.

The internal environment of the organization

As mentioned above, factors that are internal to the organization are known as the 'internal environment', these can include, for example, personnel changes or new management processes or demands to improve efficiency. They are sometimes ascertained by applying what is called the 'Five Ms' which are (Wo) Men, Money, Machinery, Materials and Markets. The internal environment is as important for managing change as the external. Change is likely to be needed when, for example, responding to newly identified markets, or taking up the cost-saving opportunities offered by new technologies. They may be sponsored by a 'champion', perhaps a new Managing Director or Marketing Director.

Insight: Today's world of work in the UK

o   Today's world of work is much less satisfying to employees than the one they were experiencing 10 years ago. What is also striking is the apparent but significant deterioration that has taken place among workers in having any sense of a personal commitment to the company that employs them. Today's managerial rhetoric emphasizes the importance of enhancing human capital, the concept of partnership at work, the need to improve the learning and skills of employees as well as provide a wider range of benefits and incentives to attract and retain staff.

o   The survey provides little evidence, however, that many of these progressive ideas usually associated with enlightened human resource management techniques are being translated into practical measures that are ensuring the growth of more high commitment workplaces.

o   The largest falls in job satisfaction over the number of hours worked was the most pronounced at both ends of the occupational grading – among senior managers and professionals and the unskilled and semi-skilled. The disgruntled manager has joined the disgruntled manual worker, at least in complaints about the long hours culture.

o   Most people still leave their homes for paid employment. In fact, a larger proportion of workers were employed in one specific workplace in 2000 (78 per cent) compared with 10 years ago when 76 per cent were. Only 3 per cent of employees said they worked partly at home in 2000 and a further 1.1 per cent solely or mainly at home. The overwhelming majority of workers in Britain do not feel insecure in their jobs.

- o We have much greater job stability, longer employment tenure and far less evidence of new forms of flexible employment contracts than many may realize. The extent of labour flexibility is also questionable in the way that work is being organized. The overwhelming majority of managers, administrators and professionals see their job as having a career structure with a clearly recognized promotion ladder. By contrast only a tiny minority of manual workers take any similar view of the career potential in their jobs and they are becoming a dwindling part of the labour force with the advance of information technology.

- o The most striking sign of significant workplace innovation can be seen in the dramatic growth in the proportion of workers across all occupational categories who now make use of modern technology in the jobs they do. The use of computers and other forms of information technology at work, advanced significantly during the 1990s.

- o But many employers have not yet recognized that the emergence of a more demanding work-force in future will mean they will have to adopt a more sensitive attitude towards how their employees should be treated. The survey suggests that while a trend exists to greater freedom for the worker on the job, the degree of control and surveillance by management has also increased.

- o We do not have the flexible labour market which we think other European countries ought to admire and emulate. On the contrary it is hard not to draw the conclusion that we need to reappraise our whole approach to employment.

- o *Policies* – If employees are going to co-operate in a positive and active manner with the management of workplace change they are going to need a greater sense of well-being, status and control over the work they perform.

Source: Robert Taylor (2002) Britain's World of Work – Myths and Realities.

Implications for marketing

Some of the implications have been discussed in other units, for example being sensitive to cultural differences when working in a multinational environment and the impact of information and communications technology on approaches to marketing. Marketing management is the process of planning and executing the conception, pricing, promotion and distribution of goods, services and ideas, to create exchanges with target groups that satisfy customer and organizational objectives. The emphasis is shifting from transaction-oriented marketing to relationship marketing, and organizations need to retain customer loyalty through continually satisfying their needs in a superior way.

Marketing teams must implement processes that co-ordinate all marketing and sales activities and achieve the level of data access, collection and sharing that is critical to consistent messaging, lead tracking, sales conversion and ongoing marketing intelligence. With the availability of websites, e-mail and mobile devices, and the introduction of high-powered packages for targeting customers, marketing should be easier than ever. However, the increase in marketing contact causes prospects to feel overloaded, reducing response rates and the value of marketing effort. Lack of co-ordination further erodes marketing effectiveness.

Marketers need to know when to:

- o Cultivate large markets or niche markets
- o Launch new brands or extend existing brand names
- o Push or pull products through distribution
- o Protect the domestic market or penetrate aggressively into foreign markets
- o Add more benefits to the offer or reduce the price
- o Expand or contract budgets for sales force, advertising and other marketing tools.

A product is anything that can be offered to a market for attention, acquisition, use, or consumption that might satisfy a want or need.

Insight

A CIPD survey (Whittington and Mayer, 2002) confirms that reorganizations are more successful when the commitment of employees is directly engaged. Yet, they continue to be a top-down, project-driven process where people often take second place to changes in structures and systems. This can have a detrimental effect. For example, fewer than half of the 800 reorganization initiatives covered by the survey delivered the required improvement in internal flexibility or increased customer responsiveness. Most businesses undergo a major reorganization at least once every 3 years. The increasing complexity of business and the intensity with which knowledge flows is placing organizational design high on the executive agenda. With the potential to maximize or destroy value, redesign is not a one-off episode; it is a high-stakes activity that managers must repeatedly engage with. Neither is it only about getting the structure right. One challenge emerging from the survey is how to manage three streams of integrated activity: changes in the structure, processes and human capability. Doing this successfully requires a sophisticated leadership that strikes the right balance between project discipline and employee involvement. Reorganizations are typically managed within project disciplines, with a clear statement of objectives, defined timescales and milestones. The image of the chief executive redrawing the lines of the organization chart on the back of a cigarette packet is a fading one. Adopting project disciplines pays, and is more likely to lead to successful outcomes. Redesigns that featured strong project discipline and employee involvement were more likely to deliver both direct bottom-line benefit, and improved morale and retention. But the survey found that employees had a say in the design in less than a third of all reorganizations, and in only a half were there consultations about how the final organizational design could be implemented.

The change problem

At the heart of change management lies the change problem. It might be large or small in scope and scale, and it might focus on individuals or groups, on one or more divisions or departments, the entire organization, or on one or more aspects of the organization's environment. Problems may be formulated in terms of 'how', 'what' and 'why' questions. Which formulation is used depends on where in the organization the person posing the question or formulating the problem is situated, and where the organization is situated in its own life cycle.

Relationship marketing

Key dimensions that provide a basis for a relationship:

- o *Reliability* – ability to perform the promised service dependably and accurately.
- o *Responsiveness* – willingness to help customers and provide prompt service.
- o *Assurance* – knowledge and courtesy of employees, and their ability to inspire trust and confidence.
- o *Empathy* – caring, individualism, attention the firm provides its customers.
- o *Tangibles* – physical facilities, equipment and appearance of personnel.

Relationship marketing and mass customization

Mass customization enables companies to focus on what customers want, rather than what the company can produce. It also allows companies to produce individually tailored products. There is a longer history of using this approach with services such as banking stockbroking rather than products. Mass customization is also more common in b2b and the simplest approach is to design a product that buyers can customize themselves. Dell Computers allows the buyer to design an individual computer and then track it through to delivery. Much of Dell's production, up to the point of final assembly, is outsourced which means that suppliers at every link in the chain need good timely information about what customers want, and when. Speed and good communications are essential if mass customization is to work.

The Age of E-tail conveys the message that the future of shopping is online and the result of this will be the need for companies to offer almost everything in ways that are specifically tailored to the customer. Personalized products such as cars and PCs are made to individual specifications and soon all successful e-tailors will offer almost everything tailored individually to the customer. E-tailors need repeat business to achieve profitability but e-customers are fickle.

Making change

The U.S. Mint needed an enterprise resource planning (ERP) system that would let our business units get at all the customer information hidden in our systems. And we had just 12 months to get it up and running. Three years into the process, we kept running into the wall of our systems. Even though the customer data was there, only a few people had access to it. The biggest challenge was to convince them to sacrifice some of their most talented people to the project. If I could do it all over again, I'd spend more money educating the organization on what life was going to be like after the implementation. We invested a lot in training, but we probably should have spent twice as much time and money. To other executives, I would say, the most critical thing is to start with a business requirement. What does your business lack that such a solution will provide? If the business requirement doesn't justify the pain, don't do it.

Source: Adapted from Philip Diehl, Making Change: HEADFIRST. zwww.darwinmag.com\read\ 060100\head_content.html.

Because change causes fear, a sense of loss of the familiar, for example, it takes time for employees to understand and commit themselves to it in a meaningful way. Some writers (Bacal, 2000) argue that people tend to go through stages in their attempts to cope with change.

Stage 1: Denial

One way that people cope with change is to deny that it is happening, or that it will continue or last. People tend to avoid dealing with the fear and uncertainty of prospective change because they are hoping they would not have to adapt. This stage is difficult because it is hard to involve people in planning for the future. Moving out of the denial stage occurs when they see tangible evidence that things are different.

Stage 2: Anger and resistance

When it is no longer feasible to deny that something is happening or has already happened, people may move into a state of anger, accompanied by forms of resistance. Leadership is needed to help people work through this and on to the next stage. If leadership is poor, anger and resentment may last indefinitely.

Stage 3: Exploration and acceptance

This is the stage where people are beginning to develop a better understanding of the change and are more willing to explore further, and to accept it. They are more willing to participate in the process.

Stage 4: Commitment

This is the stage where people are willing to work towards making it succeed. They have adapted sufficiently to make it work. While some changes, for example downsizing, may never be accepted, eventually people do commit themselves to making the organization effective within the constraints arising from the change. The change process can take some time to stabilize.

The following insight highlights some of the problems that people leading change may face.

Insight

New or different ideas often run into trouble before they reach fruition. However, change leaders need to help teams overcome blocks to change.

Forecasts fall short – A plan is needed but it is difficult to predict timing and cost. Change leaders need to accept departures from plans.

Expect the unexpected – A new path is unlikely to run straight and every change brings unanticipated consequences. Change leaders need to respond, to make adjustments and to make their case.

Momentum slows – You do not have solutions to problems, and the team is discouraged and enmeshed in conflict. Critics emerge. Even if a coalition has been built and key stakeholders are involved, you will be challenged. When the impact of change becomes clear, those threatened by it will formulate objections. This is when change leaders need to respond, remove obstacles and push forward. Actual progress will produce more believers than doubters.

Source: Adapted from Kanter, Rosabeth Moss (1999) 'The enduring skills of change leaders', *Leader to Leader*, **13** (Summer 1999), 15–22.

Change management: the skill requirements

Managing the kinds of changes encountered by and instituted within organizations requires an unusually broad and finely honed set of skills, chief among which are the following:

Political skills

Organizations are first and foremost social systems. Without people there can be no organization. Organizations are intensely political. Change agents need to understand it.

Analytical skills

A rational, well-argued analysis can be ignored and even suppressed but not successfully contested and, in most cases, should be successful. If not, the political issues have not been properly addressed.

Why do people and organizations resist change?

Many writers argue that constant innovation is the best way to secure both the individual and the organizational success. Roffe (1999) offers three scenarios:

1. *Incremental change* – here it is the little, unnoticed changes that make the biggest differences
2. *Discontinuous change* – it is different this time because the response needed is not related to a familiar pattern
3. *Radical change* – where 'upside-down' thinking is needed.

In a general sense, entrepreneurial-type managers are thought to be best suited to anticipating the need for, and then leading, productive change. Innovative firms take an 'integrative' approach to problem-solving by showing a willingness to see problems as a whole, and in their solutions to move beyond received wisdom, to challenge established practices and generally view change as an opportunity rather than a threat. This approach requires the skill to: persuade people to invest time and resources in new and possibly risky initiatives, manage problems arising from team-working and employee participation, and understand how change is designed and constructed in an organizational context.

Firms that use compartmentalized structures are more likely to see problems in isolation and out of context. Here, it is unlikely that organizational effort will be devoted to the problem as an integrated whole and the outcomes will reflect this.

Complacency at the top is also a common reason for poor performance. To break free, decentralization is important so that entrepreneurial managers in less senior roles feel that they have the authority and resources to exploit their ideas.

Case study

Decide exactly what you want – Unclear goals create unclear outcomes. Succumbing to the temptation to start work without thought and planning wastes energy and produces disillusionment. Clear goals direct energy, give a sense of purpose and provide a context for resolving any problems.

Decide that you really want the change – Don't see the change as an option, decide that it must happen. Believe that there is no alternative, no matter how busy the organization, no matter what might crop up 2 months from now. If there is an alternative, don't bother starting. Many change projects start life as 'a pretty good idea' that is 'probably worth the effort in the long run'. All too often, people begin with the intention of seeing if anything crops up later along the line. Such saintly efforts are easy prey for people keen to play the role of change assassins. Don't let your project take a mugging.

Own it – Someone must make this change happen and take responsibility for everything it produces – whether the consequences are anticipated and manageable, or not. Someone has to be clearly identified with the project, not only when it is fashionable and full of hope and the best players, but also when it begins to annoy people and your best people leave to work on something that 'cropped up later'.

Be realistic – The change may be as painful and costly for you as for the people around you. The pain and cost may come before, during or after the project – but come it will. Realism means understanding the volume of work involved in keeping individuals and organizations aligned with the change vision, especially when their instincts are screaming at them to get back to the old way of doing things.

Understand what blocks change – Become fascinated by the current practices or behaviours in your organization that resist change. Get to know them intimately. Give power to the strong and take power from the weak. In this context, strong means the positive things you want to achieve. Praise them, reward them, reinforce them, celebrate them, repeat them and publicize them when they happen. By contrast, punish old behaviours when they happen – and make it clear why you have corrected them.

Be positive – Attitude and self-belief are drivers of change. Don't play the 'but' or 'maybe' game; doubt slaughters change. Try not to be side-tracked by fear.

Be optimistic – 'If you want to achieve excellence, you can get there today. As of this second, quit doing less than excellent work.' So, allegedly, said Thomas Watson, the founder of IBM.

Deciding to make a change takes an instant – but sustaining it is the challenge. Most change programmes are long and complex. Some are so long that there's a good chance that you won't be around to see it end, while some change destinations alter as the project is in motion. So focus on the journey as well as the destination.

Be aware – raise awareness by asking key questions.

What is happening to take us towards the goal?

What happened last week that failed to move us forward, or took us down old paths that we agreed we wanted to change?

What can each of us do next week that will move us towards our goal?

Let it happen – It seems a contradictory thing to say, as I do, both that a clear sense of what you want gives you a motivating direction and purpose, and that you should let go of what will happen. Allowing your purpose to unfold as it will is an exhortation to 'stay flexible'.

Source: Adapted from Firth (2003), www.treefrog.ws.

Internal marketing

Preparing for change
- Current attitude of staff?
- How big a change is needed?
- Who are the 'influencers'?
- How big is resistance likely to be?

Internal marketing is an important 'implementation' tool. It aids communication and helps to overcome resistance to change. It informs and involves staff in new initiatives and strategies. Internal marketing has a structure similar to external marketing. The main differences are that the customers are the employees.

The marketer's skills are traditionally associated with the interface between organization and customer/consumer. But management also have a need to communicate with those within the organization – and those stakeholders associated with it. It is unlikely that an organization will be truly successful unless these buy in to management plans. There needs to be a common focus, and goals need to be understood and accepted. The prime marketing skills are communication – marketers are the specialists in identifying target audiences, assessing needs and in managing communications plans. Applying these skills internally means that a consumer-centred approach, with the employees identified as the consumers, needs to be adopted.

Internal marketing

You should be able to demonstrate that you are able to use marketing communications techniques for an internal marketing plan to support the management of change within an organization. The basis of internal marketing is focusing on the relationship that exists between the organization and its employees. One of the success factors for the implementation of the marketing plan is to treat internal staff as if they are customers who all need the same consideration and attention as external customers. The aim of internal marketing is to develop a unified sense of purpose among employees. It plays an important role in ensuring that the organization is marketing- and customer-focused. Internal marketing is based on a communications programme, and there are a number of steps that an organization can take in order to achieve internal synergy and employee co-operation:

- Creating an internal awareness of the corporate aims, objectives and overall mission
- Determining the expectations of the internal customer
- Communication to internal customers
- Changes in tasks and activities
- Internal monitoring and control.

It is as important to segment the market internally, as it is segmented externally. A key aim of the marketing plan should be the successful motivation and retention of the internal customer so that the organization can meet the needs of the external market.

Internal marketing aids communication and can help to overcome resistance to change. It can be used to help inform and involve staff in new initiatives and strategies.

The Internet can help to foster the sharing of information but an extranet, that is a computer network that provides communication across selected organizations, enables sharing in a more controlled and secure manner. Often, companies use extranets as part of a search for better ways to communicate with their channel members and reduce costs. Because the extranet is interactive and easily accessible, it has the potential to transform the way channel members communicate with each other. For example, it can make information sharing and communication frequency more timely than the same information obtained from more traditional methods of communication.

Internal relationship marketing techniques

Internal marketing projects can be considered in four phases:

Understanding the nature of the internal market
An assessment phase that aims to find out the attitudes and beliefs of employees and managers towards each other, the company, customers and marketing mix components.

Communicating with staff
A review of communications activities and their effectiveness, including a 'mapping' of communications channels.

Developing the plan
Devising strategies for meeting the objectives of the internal marketing campaign.

Evaluation
Evaluating the success of the plan according to the set objectives.

Internal marketing can contribute to helping organizations achieve good relationships with their external customers. The key success factors of internal marketing success are:

o   Create an internal awareness of the corporate aims, objectives and overall mission.
o   Determine the expectations of the internal customer.
o   Communicate to internal customers.
o   Provide appropriate human and financial resources to underpin the implementation of the marketing strategy.
o   Provide training in order that employees have the appropriate skills and competences to undertake the task at hand.
o   Implement a change in tasks and activities appropriate to the objectives of the organization.
o   Provide a structure whereby cross-functional integrated teams across business units can work together, in order to aid communication of business activity relating to the achievement of corporate goals.
o   Provide the systems and processes that enable successful delivery of services and products, enabling employees to successfully implement them and achieve organizational success.
o   Maximize the opportunity for customer interaction through effective management of service levels, for example response times, reply processes.
o   Internal monitoring and control.

For internal marketing to be successfully implemented, a planned approach is essential to allow evaluation and measurement of the successful execution of a plan. The plan could be designed with the following headings:

o   Internal vision
o   Aims and objectives
o   Internal marketing strategy

  o   Segmentation, targeting and positioning
  o   Marketing programme (to include all elements of the marketing mix)
  o   Implementation.

Managing the implementation of internal marketing (Jobber, 1995)

  o   Set objectives for internal marketing, for example to persuade 100 staff to join a new Performance-Related Pay (PRP) scheme.
  o   Tactics would include an internal application of the marketing mix, and could include staff forums, presentations, an intranet, away days, videos, personal visits by company directors or newsletters.
  o   Evaluation would consider the take up of PRP against your objectives, attendees at away days, visits to an intranet page and so on.

Internal marketing involves selling marketing plans to key internal staff or employees. Piercey and Morgan's model (Piercey and Morgan, 1997) of internal marketing indicates the implications for the marketing mix.

Price – this relates to the benefit to the employee of taking this marketing planning information on board. It relates to the personal psychological cost of adopting different key values, and changing the way jobs are done. Often it requires asking managers to step outside their comfort zones with new methods of operation.

Place/Distribution – this concerns the physical and socio-technical venues at which organizations will have to deliver the product and its communications – that is where should employees be targeted, for example Internet, staff canteens, and so on.

Promotion/Communication – this is the most tangible aspect of internal marketing – communication media and the messages used to inform and persuade employees. There will be work on the attitudes of the key personnel in the internal market place and two-way methodology must be employed.

Service quality is influenced by employees because of the inseparability of services production and consumption in relation to the provider, that is staff. Good communication, motivation and training are central to service quality, and this is influenced by internal marketing.

Internal marketing is like 'change management'. Firstly, internal customers need to be identified. As with external customers, they will have their own buyer behaviour, or way of 'buying into' the changes which you are charged to implement. As Jobber (1995) explains, three different segments, namely 'supporters', 'neutral', and finally 'opposers', can be targeted. Each segment requires a slightly different internal marketing mix to achieve the internal marketing objectives.

For example, if the change was that a company was to relocate closer to its market, 'supporters' could be targeted with information about lower property prices; 'neutral' internal customers could be targeted with incentives such as better rewards. With 'opposers', a choice would need to be made between inaction or forcing acceptance of change. It depends on a calculation of what the impact would be between these two courses of action.

Critical incidents can also be used to improve service quality. For a critical incident report to be useful, at least three pieces of information must be collected:

1.   A description of the situation that led to the incident
2.   The actions of the focal person in the incident and
3.   The results or outcomes of the incident.

How to plan for a change programme

The approach needs to be properly considered before starting the implementation. The climate needs to be accepting of change.

- Appoint a change agent, or champion for change that will help to ease changes through.
- Audit the skills and capabilities of the team. Train and develop as necessary.
- The change must be correctly marketed to your target audience.
- Decide upon the plan.
- Work out a realistic budget and keep to it.
- Try to anticipate the arguments against change.
- Ensure that there is a receptive climate towards the proposed change.
- Identify a champion or a team of champions that will help to promote change and oversee its implementation.
- Audit team capabilities and competences and identify any gaps that may need to be filled through training and development.
- Market the change to the target audience.
- Develop the plan, including a budget.
- Try to anticipate arguments against change, and identify positive responses to them.

Before we can effectively market our libraries to our customers, we have to market within to library staff. Each member of staff markets the library with every single interaction they have with customers. Friendly staff can often make up for short-comings elsewhere in the service. Staff are also the most potentially damaging part of the marketing equation. Customers do not always notice good service, but they invariably notice and remember poor service, which is often a consequence of limited interpersonal skills. If employees do not care about their company, they will in the end contribute to its demise. Even if you don't have the time, staff, or budget for a formal, full-blown marketing plan, you can make progress on internal marketing.

Step 1: Staff buy-in

Get staff involved, energized, and feeling ownership for your library. Your staff members have a personal stake in your library, and therefore in this process. Every customer interaction is a marketing moment.

Step 2: Mission statement

Do you have a mission statement? Does it explicitly support the mission of your organization? The needs of your customers? Link the work of individual staff members to your mission. Post your mission statement prominently in your library; use it on documents such as fax cover sheets, e-mail, business cards, and so on.

Step 3: Image/Brand

A brand is the emotional connection you have with your customers.

Your library's image is created by the collective actions of library staff.

What expectations do you want to create for your customers?

How will you deliver on those expectations?

Step 4: Identity

Create an identity for your library – Place your identity stamp on intranet banner ads, library brochures and publications, presentations, e-mail signatures, and partner intranet sites.

Step 5: Key customer messages

Identify the key messages you want to communicate to your customers, for example I know the library has an intranet site; I can easily navigate the library's site; I know the library staff can provide consulting and analysis for my projects.

Step 6: Vision

Do you have a vision of where your library is going? What it will look like in 2 years? In the real world, you need to have a clear picture of your vision – and then communicate that vision to your staff.

What will success look like? – library staff will understand that they are selling or hurting your library during every interaction with customers? – feel increased personal ownership for your library? – know how your mission supports your organization's goals?

In conclusion, every customer interaction is a marketing moment. All staff must know, support, and be able to articulate your library's mission, vision, and key customer messages.

Source: Adapted from Internal Marketing: Inside Job Laura Zick, Library and Information Services, Lilly University, Eli Lilly and Company. http://www.sla.org/division/dpht/Spring2003/presentations2003/Laura_Zick.ppt.

Activity 4.1

Think about a change which has recently been introduced in your organization. Would you say it was marketed effectively internally?

What was the change?

What was effective about this approach?

How could this approach have been improved?

Planning for internal marketing

Internal marketing requires a similar kind of approach to that used in external marketing. An internal marketing audit is needed to discover who comprises the target audiences and to identify what are their needs. Channels of communication, both formal and informal, need to be identified. The same kind of questions that are used in any marketing audit can be used. Payback will be in terms of commitment rather than cash. Objectives should be SMART but couched in terms of changed behaviour rather than increases in market share and so on.

Strategy

Establishing a strategy for change will require a long-term view to be taken. What is the long-term need, and what are the short-term issues? Within the long-term strategic goal(s) will be the short-term need to introduce new products, to change operating procedures and so on. New product introduction may not be seen as an internal issue but internal staff need to know about, and be familiar with, new products before the outside world is notified. (One can be sure the telephone calls will start within hours of a launch. Internal staff must not respond 'Is that one of our products? I didn't know.')

Targets

Just as in marketing communications, there is need to identify target audiences. These will range from internal groupings such as individuals, sections, departments, and so on to include those 'exterior' stakeholders such as the organization's shareholders, bankers, lawyers, agencies, consultancies and so on. An internal marketing communications plan can be far more complex than one used to promote a product. The target audiences are more diverse.

Promotion

Two-way communication means that the target audience members should be able to have some input into proposed change. Internal communication media includes meetings, newsletters and noticeboards, but there is a need to achieve impact. Change has to be marketed effectively, and training and development offers a good opportunity to do this.

Price

Faced with 'selling' an idea or proposal to senior managers, the same process should be adopted but the needs of the management team and the stakeholders need to be considered, and benefits such as raised profitability quantified and communicated. The price to an internal audience is measured in terms of inconvenience, extra work, coping with unfamiliarity and so on. The question 'Why bother?' must be answered, and answered well.

Product

The product consists of market strategies and the marketing plan. Therefore, the 'product' needs to be 'sold' in terms of values, attitudes and behaviour to employees so that they can buy into it.

Place

For the internal marketer, place can be interpreted as when and where a change will be introduced. For example, it may be better to introduce a new computer system in the off-season rather than at peak times.

Promotion – As has been said above, promote the benefits to those in each target audience.

Process – All aspects of the change need to be thought through carefully, piloted, evaluated, modified and re-piloted. It should ease the burden of adapting to change and, if possible, should simplify an employee's task. The introductory process, similarly, should be timetabled and then managed so that what is announced actually happens when and how it should.

Participants – All involved, from top management to junior staff, must follow the same procedures. If a senior manager does not comply it is unlikely that others will bother.

Case study

Employees are the company. Particularly in the services sectors, they represent the culture, the brand and the customer experience with the company. Employees are the best form of marketing during change. If people don't feel good about the change, customers will know it quickly.

Segment the benefits of the change. What factors are beneficial to employees, shareholders, customers and other stakeholders? Use these benefits to create key messages about the changes to be marketed to the appropriate audience.

Be truthful and genuine. It only takes one example of misdirection or dishonesty to create employee distrust of management's messages. Spin is spin, and people generally know when they are being spun. Be willing to show that a particular change isn't necessarily 'good' for everyone.

Change requires strongly embracing the future and a quick release of the past. Keep the organization's 'eyes' looking forward. Keep it thinking about what the customer wants. Those who have worked at the company for a long time tend to pull the company back into issues of tradition. Customers care little about the past. What will you do for them today or tomorrow?

Focus communications around the people who will remain after any staffing cuts or changes.

Deal with 'survivor syndrome', that is the phenomenon of those who keep their jobs feeling guilty that they have kept their jobs while many lose theirs.

Focus the organization externally. Work to eliminate the inwardness that comes with change.

Recognize that change is a personal issue. It involves a loss of control and employees, once content with their careers, now have to ask 'Will I have a job when this is finished?'

Make changes quickly, decisively and as fairly as possible. Spreading bad news over a longer period is more painful than making that one decisive action.

Focus on customers. Show a true concern for customer issues, but the change is not a customer vote. Communicating to your people, who will in turn reassure your customers, is the best defence.

Source: Adapted from Change Marketing: The Universal Truths for Marketing the Benefits of a Merger/ Acquisition (Bedford Consulting Group, June 2002).

Summary

Change is a natural part of the environment, but is seldom popular and is often resisted. Change, as a process, can and should be managed. It is as much subject to management planning and control as any other process. All change should be taken seriously, and planned and implemented with care. Major changes include a switch from a product/sales to a marketing/customer approach, and from a domestic to an international orientation. Internal marketing is of crucial importance in securing change and is best handled from a corporate level, possibly with marketers seconded for the purpose. Change always requires a price to be paid in human terms.

Bibliography

Bacal, R. (2000) 'Understanding the cycle of change and how people react to it', www.work911.com/articles.htm.

Bedford Consulting Group, (June, 2002) www.bedfordgroupconsulting.com.

Firth, D. (2003) '10 rules of change', *People Management*, 6 March.

Grove, A.S. (1999), 'Managing segment zero', *Leader to Leader*, **11**, Winter.

Jobber (1995) *Principles and Practicing of Marketing*, McGraw-Hill.

Kanter, Rosabeth Moss (1999) 'Enduring skills of change leaders', *Leader to Leader*, **13**, Summer, pp. 15–22.

Kanter, R.M. (1999) <http://drucker.org/leaderbook/L2L/summer99/kanter.html>

Piercey, N. and Morgan, N. (1997) 'Internal marketing', *International Journal of Bank Marketing*.

Whittington, P.R. and Mayer, M. (2002) *Organising for Success*, London: CIPD.

Sample exam questions and answers for the Marketing Management in Practice module as a whole can be found in Appendix 6 and past examination papers can be found in Appendix 7. Both appendices can be found at the back of the book

unit 5 project management

Learning objectives

- o Describe the main stages of a project and the roles of people involved at each stage (2.1).

- o Describe the main characteristics of successful and less successful projects and identify the main reasons for success or failure (2.2).

- o Explain the importance of, and techniques for, establishing the project's scope, definition and goals (2.3).

- o Use the main techniques available for planning, scheduling, resourcing and controlling activities on a project (2.4).

- o Explain the importance of preparing budgets and techniques for controlling progress throughout a project to ensure it is completed on time and within budget (2.5).

- o Explain the main techniques for evaluating the effectiveness of a project on its completion (2.6).

Statements of Marketing Practice

Jc.1 Plan *marketing* projects and prepare budgets.

Jc.2 Manage and report on delivery against plan and objectives.

Kc.1 Define measurements appropriate to the plan or business case and ensure they are undertaken.

Kc.2 Evaluate activities and identify improvements using measurement data.

D Key definitions

Business case – This is used to define the information that justifies the setting up, continuation or termination of the project. It answers the question 'Why should this project be undertaken?' It can be updated at key points throughout the project.

Critical path – The series of tasks that must be completed on time for a project to finish on schedule. Each task on the critical path is a critical task; any delay to it would delay the project's schedule. Often displayed as:

Critical path analysis – A method for scheduling when tasks will happen. Comprising of a forward pass and a backward pass, it determines how quickly and how slowly the tasks can be accomplished.

Customer – Customer is used to represent the person or group who has commissioned the work and will be benefiting from the end results.

Gantt chart – A graphical representation of the project's current schedule. It will often contain bars for normal tasks, summary tasks, milestone tasks, and slack values. Gantt charts are also referred to as bar charts as they depict task bars against a timescale.

PERT analysis – Is a simple form of quantitative risk analysis and can be applied to a schedule to help estimate the duration of a task. After the entry of optimistic, pessimistic and expected durations for each of the tasks, Microsoft Project will calculate a weighted average of the three durations, and determine a single duration estimate for each task. Gantt charts can display the results of critical path analysis taking all tasks at their optimistic, pessimistic and expected values. A button on the analysis toolbar provides access to PERT commands.

Product, deliverable or outcome – Terms used to describe everything that the project has to create or change, however, physical or otherwise these may be. Results of projects can vary from physical items such as buildings to intangible things such as culture change.

Programme – This is a collection of projects that together achieve a beneficial change for an organization.

Project objectives – Three basic objectives that a project must meet to ensure its successful conclusion:

1. Time objective
2. Cost objective
3. Quality objective.

Project objectives are often a contractual agreement between the project manager, the project's sponsor and the project's stakeholders.

Project definition – What a project will deliver and how it will be judged.

Project resources – Work, time and cost are resources of the project that are consumed in its execution. For example, doing some work will take some time and incur some cost, as its accomplishment adds to meeting the project's overall objectives.

> **Supplier** – This refers to the group that is providing specialist resources and skills to the project, or goods and services, to create the project outcome required by the customer and user(s).
>
> **User** – A user is the person or group who will use or operate the final product. In some situations, the customer and the user may be the same group of people.

Introduction

Some of the underpinning knowledge for this is covered in other modules and units, and a key part is contained in the final unit – Developing marketing plans. When studying the Marketing Management in Practice module, CIM recommends that two-thirds of the sessions should be allocated to a significant practical project involving the formulation and implementation of an operational marketing plan. This should cover the management of information, communications and human resources. The emphasis should be the application of this theory within a marketing team. A typical project will consist of:

- o Planning the project to be undertaken to meet the brief given.
- o Undertaking the task. This will involve collecting and analysing information and developing a marketing plan.
- o Planning, scheduling and resourcing marketing activities within the plan, identifying and overcoming problems during implementation.
- o Measuring and evaluating the outcomes.
- o Reflecting on the performance of the team and the individuals in it.

The basic approach to project management should be the same regardless of the type of project or sector in which the project is carried out. Services marketing professionals, in particular, are facing greater complexity in managing programmes and projects. Typical marketing programmes within large IT services organizations involve teamwork with different functional areas such as research and development, training, manufacturing, communication, as well as with business partners. Global marketing organizations require managing collaboration across numerous cultures and time zones.

What is a project?

The application of knowledge, skills, tools and techniques to a broad range of activities. Project management knowledge and practices are best described in terms of their component processes, for example initiating, planning, executing, controlling and closing.

Overview

Project management
It should be collaborative
The methodology should be capable of being applied to any project
It should be results-oriented
It should be easy to use.

Stages of a project
In recent years, project teams and a project management approach have become common in many organizations. The Initiation – The limits, constraints and priorities need to be defined.

Planning

Team members need to be selected
Scope of the project should be defined
Potential 'risks' identified and planned for
Resources required determined.

Execution

Deliverables created
Progress monitored and communicated
Issues resolved and changes managed.

Closeout

Customer satisfaction measured
Lessons learned, analysed.

Criteria for success

Customer satisfaction – expectations need to be managed
Organization satisfaction – for example profit, development of capability
Team learning – can lessons be learned and taken forward to other projects.

Reasons for failure

Lack of appropriate expertise and approach from the project leader
Lack of support from project sponsor – need to communicate resources needed and reasons
Lack of ability/necessary expertise of team members – need to select carefully
Lack of 'buy-in' from end-users – need to involve them in the project.

Scope, definition and goals

Project name
Business case
Objectives
Deliverables
Identify customers' requirements and needs
Resources needed
Planning, scheduling and resourcing.

Project plan

Who – recruit the right skill base
How – identify the interim deliverables
When – schedule of delivery
How much – the costs.

Budgets

Staff costs
Overheads
Equipment needed
Outside services
Supplies
Travel.

Controls
   Project team meetings
   Regular reviews
   Team member accountability
   Milestones
   Stakeholder meetings.

Post project evaluation
   Customer and stakeholder evaluation
   Reviewing final status report with project team
   Recording lessons learned
   Reviewing final report with sponsor
   Celebrating success.

Seven steps to success
   1.   Use an effective method
   2.   Invest in planning
   3.   Involve the customer
   4.   Make it manageable
   5.   Involve the team
   6.   Communicate effectively
   7.   Learn from mistakes.

Project management may not always come easy to marketers, who may want to focus more on the 'creative' side of the work. Without a project management method, those who commission a project, those who manage it and those who work on it will have different ideas about how things should be organized and when the different aspects of the project will be completed. Those involved will not be clear about how much responsibility, authority and accountability they have and, as a result, there will often be confusion surrounding the project.

A project should possess identifiable goals, and a definite starting and finishing point. Project goals should be defined clearly. The major constraints on the completion of projects are time, resource availability and the need to achieve the required standard of performance for the project.

While marketing projects are getting more complex, marketing managers need to demonstrate a clear and strong return on marketing investment (ROI). One response to these pressures is the establishment of a 'project management office' – a team of people that uses management methodologies and tools. Although such a structured approach might not be necessary or appropriate for every organization, many marketing professionals need to understand project planning and implementation.

Feasibility studies

Before a project is given the go-ahead, a feasibility study might be conducted before the launch of a project. Support for a project could be important, so the aim of a feasibility study is to carry out a preliminary investigation to help determine whether a project should proceed further and how it should proceed.

The questions asked and the focus of a study will depend upon, for example, such things as the nature of the project that is being contemplated, the risk factors involved and its cost. The cost of carrying out a feasibility study needs to be weighed against the cost of a project not delivering what is expected of it. There is no point in carrying out an actual feasibility study if the cost of it would exceed the actual cost of the project. In this situation, the feasibility of a project would need to be determined in other ways on the basis of information that is already available.

However, a feasibility study will need to consider the following:

Cost – Is it within the budget set by the organization or within the capabilities of the organization to finance it?

Timing – Are there any time constraints and will it be possible to complete the project within these constraints?

Performance – Will the project deliver the benefits that are claimed for it?

Effect on the organization – Is it feasible in the context of the organization and the effect which it will have upon it? – Does it fit the culture of the organization? – Will it draw resources away from other important activities?

Resourcing – Are the necessary skills, technology and physical infrastructure available? Or, if not, can they be easily recruited?

Stages of a project

Project definition

Once the project has received formal approval to proceed, the objectives of the project and how the work will be undertaken can be determined. The project manager will carry out this work, in consultation with the client, and any sub-project manager if there are sub-projects. Large projects may be divided into sub-projects, with each sub-project requiring its own sub-project definition. The aim is to identify all prerequisites are in place. Before a definition can begin, there should be a project brief or terms of reference signed off by all parties involved in the project and giving the authority to proceed.

This is the stage where objectives, assumptions and constraints need to be identified so that everyone can be clear about the basis on which the project will proceed. As the project gets underway, there are likely to be changes to it because it is very difficult to know everything at the outset. Some of the assumptions made may need to change in the light of experience or, for example, the availability of resources or key personnel, and the original scheduling may need to be revised. All this is easier if the objectives, assumptions and constraints have been identified in the first place.

A project covers interrelated activities or tasks with definite start and finish times, identifiable objectives and an integrated system of complex but interdependent relationships. An activity or task is a unit of work whose scheduling is overseen by a project manager.

Projects have three elements:

1. Budget
2. Schedule
3. Deliverables.

The aim of project management is to ensure the effective scheduling of tasks and use of resources to deliver the objectives of a project on time, within cost constraints and with outcomes that meet the needs of the end-users.

Determine project scope

Determining the scope of the project helps to clarify objectives and set the boundaries of the project. It is often useful to state limitations, that is what the project will not cover.

Project brief

A project brief should take the objectives and translate them into targets and goals. Any key constraints should also be identified and stated at this stage. This brief should be agreed by the client and communicated to the project manager. Success criteria should be established for the project, preferably criteria that are tangible and measurable. The success criteria should be provided in response to the conditions adhering to the project.

Contents of a project brief

A project brief will identify:

- ○ *Objectives* – Why you are doing it, as listed in the client requirements definition, the business benefits that the project will provide when it is completed – often broken down to three basic project objectives: Time, Cost and Quality.
- ○ *Scope* – Project boundaries.
- ○ *Deliverables* – What it will provide.
- ○ *Accountability* – Success criteria.

How you will be performing it – major milestones, change control procedures.

- ○ *Constraints* – Question of how would you know if your project had been successful
- ○ *Assumptions* – Listed unknowns about the project
- ○ *Resources*.

Key personnel – Who is responsible for what? Who are the stakeholders?

Objectives – Three basic objectives that a project must meet to ensure its successful conclusion:

1. Time
2. Cost
3. Quality.

The objectives form the basis of the project's strategic information. They also relate to one another; for example, a reduction in time may incur additional cost or may reduce overall quality. Project objectives are often a contractual agreement between the project manager, the project's client and the project's stakeholders.

The client is one of the project's stakeholders who will receive the benefits that the project will provide. He usually provides or authorizes the terms of reference and communicates strategic information to and from the project manager. Stakeholders are individuals or organizations with a vested interest in a project. The most obvious stakeholder is the sponsor.

Assumptions

Project assumptions can be checked with stakeholders who can critique them and, if necessary, a revised set of assumptions agreed when there are changes. A schedule can be revised when new information becomes available.

Areas where assumptions may need to be made include:

o The materials, resources, people and equipment that will be available.
o How long particular tasks will take to complete – Are the assumptions based on realistic information or are they the result of inspired guesses?
o How important is cost to the project – What are the arrangements if a budget needs to be increased?
o Will all the project tasks be completed in the timescale available and to an acceptable quality level?
o Are the project aims deliverable in line with what the key stakeholders are expecting?
o What are the management arrangements for overseeing the project – Will there be a steering group to whom the project director or manager will report?
o What kinds of reports will be needed, by when?

Constraints

There can be constraints on the completion of projects, arising from the different objectives of:

o Timescale
o Resource availability
o Quality factors
o Human factors
o *Performance specifications* – These may be set out in terms of the ability to deal with certain demands. For example, this could be number of patients or transactions processed, or the number of enquiries dealt with.
o *Specific quality standards* – This could relate to technical standards and tolerance, or may be the achievement of a favourable report from an outside inspection agency.
o *Meeting deadlines* – For example, a new system may need to be implemented, ready for the start of the financial year, or a new development may have to meet time requirements as laid down in contract specifications.

Calculate resource requirements

Calculate requirements for each time period. Identify needs for each resource type (e.g. systems analyst, user staff) and identify needs for special skills or scarce resources.

Calculate costs

Calculate costs for the sub-project. This should include 'hardening up' items such as cabling, training, and so on for which an order of costs had been produced previously.

Determine overall costs of the project

The cost/benefit justification should have already been stated in the feasibility study. This stage provides the opportunity to review the case in the light of more detailed information. An important criterion may be to complete the project within a cost limit or budget which has been determined. Additionally, there may be requirements in terms of the ongoing cost of the completed project. For example, a new system may be required to make savings for the organization on a continuing basis.

Deliverables

A deliverable is a tangible verifiable outcome of work done to produce a product or service. To be verifiable, the deliverable must meet pre-determined standards for its completion, such as design specifications for a product or a checklist of steps that is completed as part of a service. Deliverables have external stakeholders who receive the finished product or service such as customers and internal stakeholders like a project manager and team members who work directly on the deliverable. A project may have only one or many deliverables.

Define key project tasks

To help in breaking a project down into smaller and more manageable pieces of work, the project's objectives and scope are broken down into more detail in terms of duration, work and links. The most common approach is to plan from the overall objective and then to break this down into sub-objectives (or phases). Sub-objectives may relate to products, functions, disciplines and cost areas. The sub-objectives need to be broken down further into lower levels of detail until quantifiable tasks are at the bottom of the structure. The smaller the task, the more accurately it can be estimated. Tasks should be allocated to a named person, group or organization for implementation.

Once a project's tasks have been defined, the next stage is to determine how the tasks relate to one another. This creates sequences of tasks within the project and identifies when each of the tasks can occur.

In determining the sequence of tasks – the tasks that must be accomplished before a particular task can take place – its predecessor(s) needs to be identified. This technique is known as precedence analysis and is the common way of determining how tasks relate.

These relationships are referred to as dependencies or precedences, and when planning a project it is important to establish the order of precedence of dependent activities, and to establish those activities which can be performed in parallel with other activities.

Not all tasks within a project start at the same time. There will always be some form of sequence. The simplest relationship is where the commencement of one task depends upon the completion of just one task that precedes it. This is a dependent relationship.

Building a project plan

The complexity of the project plan will depend on the size of the project, as larger projects demand greater planning and structure than smaller ones. Software such as Microsoft® Project can be used to build project plans and will help with listing the project tasks, organize them into phases, schedule tasks, set dependencies, deadlines and constraints, and specify and assign the resources to tasks.

If the timeline indicates that the project will run over its deadline, a check should be made to ensure that resources are not under- or overallocated. Resolving this is called Resource Levelling and it may assist in sorting out the timeline. If it does not work, more resources may be needed. However, adding another person to a task does not necessarily mean that the task will necessarily be completed more quickly if the person needs to be trained and familiarized with the specific project. It may also slow down an existing member of the team if they need to brief and coach the newcomer. The timeline might be shortened through working overtime, though excessive overtime reduces productivity. If this does not work and the deadline really is unmovable, the project requirements may need to be back to meet the date. When the project plan is agreed, it becomes a baseline that can be used to compare with the progress of the project.

Determine work structure

Large projects are more likely to be successful if they can be divided into smaller units of work (sub-projects). Identify tasks which can be arranged into logical groups to form sub-projects. Grouping could be on the basis of, for example:

- o Tasks Relating to one functional area
- o Tasks To be performed by staff in one geographic location
- o Tasks Relating to a particular deliverable
- o Tasks To be performed by team members belonging to the same division or department.

Ensure project structure and responsibilities are established.

Determine management systems

These will vary according to the size and nature of the project but should always include:

- o A progress control system for recording planned and actual times. This could be an automated system or a manual one.
- o Agreed procedures for formal review and agreement of each project deliverable.
- o Scheduled management checkpoints.

If the project is divided into sub-projects, it is important that consistent management systems are used across them all.

Assign sub-project managers where appropriate. Clarify composition and responsibilities of the project steering group, and responsibilities of the project sponsor and the project manager.

Produce a project organization structure to show reporting lines.

Assemble and organize the project team

Projects are sometimes carried out by a team of people assembled for that specific purpose. The activities of this team may be co-ordinated by a project manager. Project teams may consist of people from different parts of the organization, and in some cases, people from different organizations. The selection of the team will be dependent upon the skill requirements of the project, and upon the matching of those to individual members of the team. Within a project, roles and responsibilities define the relationships between the project team and the work that has to be done. Project work is often multifaceted, requiring a combination of skills and activities for planning, execution and completion. Every key project activity should be clearly defined in terms of roles and responsibilities. Some team members will have dual responsibilities of involvement in the project, in addition to a commitment to other projects or management of a functional area on a day-to-day basis. It is at this stage that a project manager should be appointed and responsibilities made explicit for all members of the team.

Project scheduling

Scheduling the project
The aim is to ensure that resources are available when they are needed. This needs to be checked before building a project plan.

Creating a cost schedule

This phase is primarily concerned with attaching a timescale and sequence to the activities to be conducted within the project. Materials and people needed at each stage of the project are determined, and the time each is to take will be set. When resources are assigned to tasks, they create measurable work. This work in turn can incur cost. One common occurrence when working with resource assignments is that demand will invariably exceed supply. Some key people will be overworked and others will have time to spare. This inefficiency can be overcome by firstly looking at how people are utilized, and then by looking at the tasks within the project and determining how much free time (slack) they possess. Once these factors are understood, actions can be taken and decisions can be reached regarding who does what (most efficiently), when.

Resource conflicts

If resource demand exceeds supply, this is known as a resource conflict and needs to be resolved. An assignment is the relationship between a task and a resource. This relationship creates work – somebody doing something to achieve the objective of the task. Work, time and cost are resources of the project that are consumed in its execution. Doing some work will take some time and incur some cost.

Milestones

Milestones – measurable objectives that signal the completion of a major deliverable and indicate that you have reached a significant point in the project. Milestones can be established quickly if the project is on schedule, and can be useful when reporting on progress to management and clients.

Milestones are used to signify that something significant has been completed or something significant is ready to occur; for example, the start or beginning of a phase or the achievement of a key deliverable. The milestones and the information that need to be received and provided for different parts of the project need to be agreed with the project stakeholders. The information can be strategic and tactical.

Strategic

Strategic information would normally be provided for and by key stakeholders and would include:

- o Timing reports for the start and finish of major project phases
- o Start and finish dates for discrete tasks within a project phase
- o Cost schedules summarized by phase
- o Start and finish dates for tasks assigned to a particular skill or resource
- o Milestone date schedules a task's sub-deliverables, or a to-do list.

Tactical

Tactical information would normally be shared between the project manager and members of their workgroup. This should include:

- o Start and finish dates for discrete tasks within a project phase
- o Cost schedules summarized by phase
- o Start and finish dates for tasks assigned to a particular skill or resource.

Gantt charts

Gantt charts are particularly helpful when scheduling and controlling a project which has a number of repetitive activities within it. The graphic display afforded by the Gantt chart not only helps the operations management of the project but also helps to co-ordinate the various activities in an efficient way.

The Gantt chart takes its name from Henry Gantt, the American engineer who created it. It is a technique that can be used for sequencing project activities. The chart is the most common report in all project management systems. It is a form of bar chart with horizontal bars drawn against a timescale for each project activity. The length of each bar represents the time taken to complete an activity.

To construct a Gantt chart, the various activities are listed on a vertical axis, and the horizontal axis is used to represent time. Activity precedences are taken into account by starting a horizontal bar to represent the next activity at an appropriate point after its preceding activities, that is those activities which must take place before the next activity can start, have taken place. Normally, this would be at the earliest time that it could start after its preceding activities had finished.

The timescale should cover the duration of the project – from the start to the project finish date. In between these dates, it should be divided into equal increments. Gantt charts are sometimes known as milestone plans and they provide a useful way of monitoring the progress of a project (Figure 5.1). The advantages of using them are:

- All activities are planned for
- The sequence of activities is accounted for
- The activity time estimates are recorded
- The overall project time is recorded.

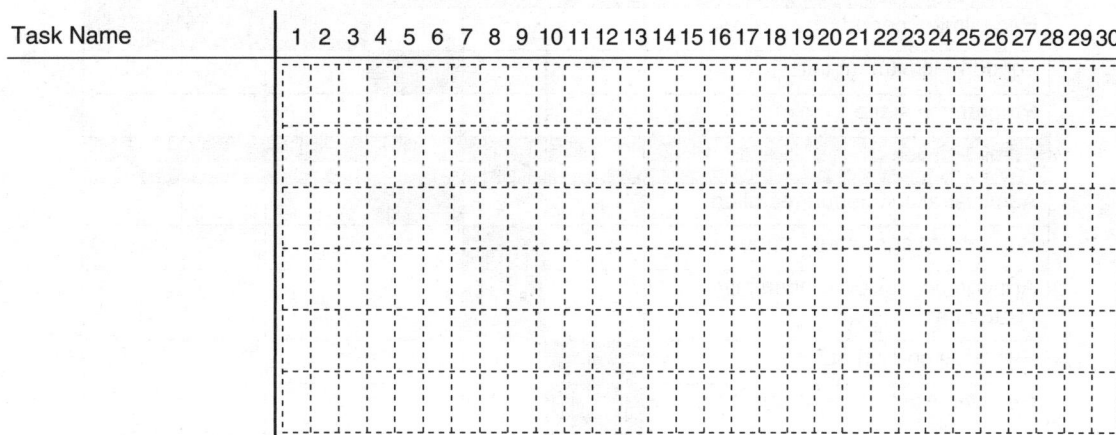

Task Name	1 2 3 4 5 6 7 8 9 10 11 12 13 14 15 16 17 18 19 20 21 22 23 24 25 26 27 28 29 30

Figure 5.1 A Gantt timescale of 30 days

Once the chart's timescale has been created, tasks can be added. These tasks should be the complete list of sub-tasks as described within the network diagram, or from the lowest level of the outline (Work Breakdown Structure). The chart's timescale can be in days, weeks, months and so on. It must be linear and in equal increments, for Figure 5.2 increment per day or one increment per week.

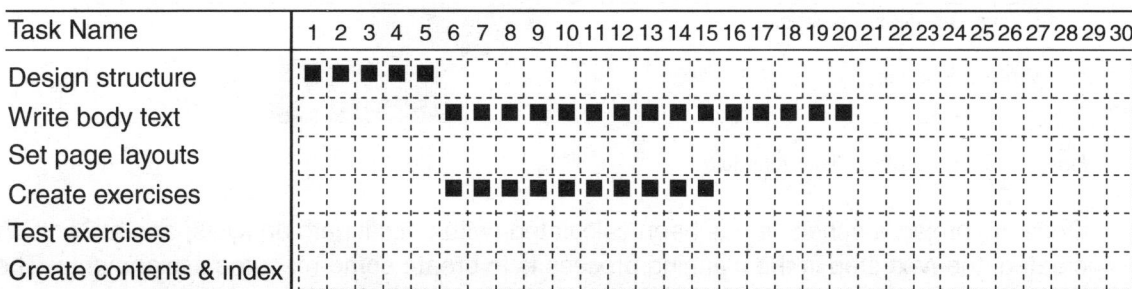

Task Name	1 2 3 4 5 6 7 8 9 10 11 12 13 14 15 16 17 18 19 20 21 22 23 24 25 26 27 28 29 30
Design structure	■ ■ ■ ■ ■
Write body text	■ ■ ■ ■ ■ ■ ■ ■ ■ ■ ■ ■ ■ ■ ■
Set page layouts	
Create exercises	■ ■ ■ ■ ■ ■ ■ ■ ■ ■
Test exercises	
Create contents & index	

Figure 5.2 Example of a schedule for developing an online course

147

Displaying link lines between tasks

When a Gantt chart has a lot of links between tasks (especially cross-project links), the chart can become very busy with detail. When producing a Gantt chart for a client or a sponsor, decide if it is appropriate to tell them how tasks relate. They probably only need to know when tasks are scheduled to occur.

MONTH	APR	MAY	JUNE	JULY	AUG	SEPT
Marketing						
Broadsheet advertisements			■			
Face-to-face meetings with clients			■			
Direct mailing inserts into Marketing Success			■			
Arrange corporate ID		■				
Arrange printing of business cards		■				

	APR	MAY	JUNE	JULY	AUG	SEPT
		■				
Recruitment						
Recruitment period				■	■	■
London recruitment fair			■			
Programme starts						
Administration						
Administration support recruited			■			
Partnership agreement signed		■				
Arrange professional indemnity insurance		■				
Purchase domain name	■					
Register with Data Protection Act	■					
Finance						
Arrange online credit card payment system	■					
Arrange bank loan	■					
Website						
Design website	■					
Design activities for website		■				
Write web guide			■	■		

Figure 5.3 Six month activity schedule

Once the project's schedule has been calculated (with critical path analysis) and a Gantt chart created, the next step in the planning process is to create some resource assignments. These assignments add the people dimension – someone doing something. What is important is a general understanding of the relationship between the task (something that needs to be achieved) and the resource (the individual that performs the work to achieve the task's objective). Gantt charts also provide a summary of the project as a whole, and can be used as a rough and ready means of assessing progress at the project control phase. At any date, the project manager can draw a dateline through the Gantt chart and see which activities are on time, which are behind schedule and generally record project status against plans.

Activity 5.1

Choose a project that you will be involved with at work and, construct a Gantt chart which will provide an overview of the planned project.

When do you anticipate that you will start?

How soon could the project be completed?

Which activities need to be completed on time in order to ensure that the project is completed as soon as possible?

Show the shortest time it will take to complete the project.

Network analysis

The first step in network analysis is to divide the project into discrete 'activities' and 'events'. An event marks a point in time equating to the start or finish of an activity. An activity is a task or combination of small tasks that occurs between two events. Any activity that can be disaggregated and described by activities and events may be analysed within a network. The two most common and widely used project management techniques that can be classified under the title of Network Analysis are Programme Evaluation and Review Technique (PERT) and Critical Path Method (CPM).

PERT/CPM

There are six stages common to both PERT and CPM:

1. Define the project and specify all activities or tasks.
2. Develop the relationships amongst activities. Decide upon precedences.
3. Draw network to connect all activities.
4. Assign time and/or costs to each activity.
5. Calculate the longest time path through the network: this is the 'critical path'.
6. Use network to plan, monitor and control the project. A network diagram is used to express how all the tasks in a project relate to each other. It helps to show how all the project tasks interrelate. A network diagram is also good for showing cross-project links.

Both models can help to answer the following questions for projects with thousands of activities and events, both at the beginning of the project and once it is under way:

1. When will the project be completed?
2. What are the critical activities (i.e. the tasks which, if delayed, will affect time for overall completion)?

149

3. Which activities are non-critical and can run late without delaying project completion time?
4. What is the probability of the project being completed by a specific date?
5. At any particular time, is the project on schedule?
6. At any particular time, is the money spent equal to, less than or more than the budgeted amount?
7. Are there enough resources left to complete the project on time?

Probability analysis

Once the expected completion time and variance have been determined, the probability that a project will be completed by a specific date can be assessed. The assumption is usually made that the distribution of completion dates follows that of a normal distribution curve. If the project is to be completed in a shorter time, what is the least cost means to accomplish this and what are the cost consequences?

Critical path analysis

This is a method for scheduling when tasks will happen. A critical task is one that must be completed on schedule for the project to finish on time. If a critical task is delayed, the project finish date might also be delayed. A series of critical tasks make up a project's critical path.

As the tasks within a project have links between them, they cannot all happen at the same time. Critical path analysis (CPA) can be used to determine what can happen when. It calculates how quickly and how slowly the tasks can be performed, taking into account the sequence of tasks and the interrelationships between them. Gantt charts are created as a result of CPA.

Critical path analysis is a procedure that calculates a project's schedule. Taking each task in turn, it first calculates how quickly the task can be accomplished – its early start and early finish dates. Once all these dates have been calculated, the project finish date can also be determined. With this finish date known, CPA can then calculate how slowly each task can be accomplished (late start and late finish dates). Once all this information is known for each task, CPA will also calculate the slack that the task possesses.

The objective of CPA is to determine times for:

ES = Earliest Start Time. This is the earliest time an activity can be started, allowing for the fact that all preceding activities have been completed.

LS = Latest Start Time. This is the latest time an activity can be started without delaying the start of following activities which would put the entire project behind schedule.

EF = Earliest Finish Time. The earliest time an activity can be finished.

LF = Latest Finish Time. The latest time that an activity can finish for the project to remain on schedule.

ZS = Activity Slack Time. The amount of slippage in activity start or duration time which can be tolerated without delaying the project as a whole.

Once these values are known, the overall project can be analysed. The critical path is the group of activities in the project that have a slack time of zero. This path of activities is critical because a delay in any activity along it would delay the project as a whole. Finding the critical path is a major activity in controlling a project. Managers can derive flexibility by identifying the non-critical activities and replanning, rescheduling and reallocating resources such as manpower and finances within identified boundaries.

PERT

The major difference between CPM and PERT is that the latter employs three time estimates for each activity. Probabilities are attached to each of these times which, in turn, is used for computing expected values and potential variations for activity times. CPM assumes that activity times are known and fixed, so only one time estimate is given and used for each activity. The three time estimates specified for each activity in PERT are:

1. The optimistic time
2. The most probable time
3. The pessimistic time.

The optimistic, most likely, and pessimistic time estimates are used to calculate an expected activity completion time which, because of the skewed nature of the beta distribution, is marginally greater than the most likely time estimate. In addition, the three time estimates can be used to calculate the variance for each activity. The formulae used are as follows:

When using PERT, the expected times are calculated first from the three values of activity time estimates, and it is these values that are then used exactly as in CPM. The variance values are calculated for the various activity times and the variance of the total project completion time is the sum of the variances of the activities lying on that critical path.

Reviewing progress

It is the job of the project manager to make sure that the project stays on track and the deliverables meet the specifications detailed in the project definition document, as well as managing client expectations by keeping all relevant parties informed about the project's status. The project has a greater chance of success if the client is actively involved. The broad aims of reviewing are to:

Compare – Find variances between the baseline schedule and actual progress – cost variances and work variances.

Evaluate – Are the project's objectives still able to be met? Do the variances indicate the development of a trend?

Decide – Perform a 'what-if' analysis to overcome the variances and get the project back on track. This is a method of experimentation to determine the optimum schedule of tasks or utilization of resources. A 'what-if' analysis may need to be carried out more than once.

Inform – Inform all project team members of revisions to the project's schedule, individual schedules and deliverables met. If certain tasks or resources are constantly going over budget or always taking longer than planned, could a trend be developing?

Managing communication

Effective communication with the relevant parties is the key to a successful project. The project manager should develop a communications plan in order to gather progress information from the team, supply timely reports and gather feedback from the management and the client.

Collecting information from team members

Regular contact is needed with individual team members to evaluate the status of their work and to deal with any questions they have or issues that need to be resolved. There is no need to waste time by insisting on written reports when information can be gathered easily in other ways from face-to-face meetings, e-mail or telephone calls.

Information should be gathered at regular intervals and any issues that are raised by the project team should be dealt with promptly.

Project meetings

Project meetings give the team, including management and the client representative, an opportunity to evaluate the project's status as a whole and to highlight issues that the team as a whole need to deal with. These meetings provide an opportunity to raise issues that concern the big picture even if they are only noted to be dealt with at a later time.

Reports to management and the client

Depending on the size of the project, status reports should be submitted to the management and the client to keep those who do not attend the project status meetings up to date. These may not be necessary for small projects, but for medium and large projects bi-monthly or monthly reports would be appropriate.

Managing client expectations

Managing client expectations is one of the tasks of the project manager and the project definition document is a tool that is useful in this process. By identifying clear project deliverables and constraints, the client should know what to expect from the outset of the project.

Once the project is under way, you then need to carefully manage scope change. Any changes to scope, whether suggested by the client or a member of the team, should be carefully discussed with the client. Pros and cons of the change should be weighed up, and if it is decided to go ahead, a formal scope change document should be presented to and signed by the client.

Managing the project plan

The progress of the project can be tracked by noting the status of each task at regular intervals. Software such as Microsoft Project offers three methods for tracking progress:

1. *Percentage of work complete* – This is the least accurate but fastest way to track. Asking team members to report their progress according to this method can result in misleading reports due to the human tendency to at times be 'almost done' for prolonged periods.
2. *Actual work completed* – This is more accurate, but also more time consuming.
3. *Hours of work completed per time period* – This is the most accurate but most time consuming, as people need to specify the exact hours they have worked in particular time periods.

Adding tasks

Sometimes the project will demand the addition of tasks that had not been previously identified, or the scope of the project may have changed. The project plan will need to be adjusted to create a new baseline.

Take note of when milestones are met and review the plan to ensure that it will meet the delivery date. If not, remedial action will be needed. Problems with the budget need to be resolved quickly, so it needs to be reviewed on a regular basis and reports submitted to the relevant parties.

Managing the scope of the project

The project manager is in charge of managing the scope of the project, so that only what was agreed is delivered unless changes have been formally agreed. The project manager needs to ensure that everybody involved remembers the project objective.

Mission creep occurs when the client or team members lose sight of the agreed project objectives. This can be avoided by creating a clear and unambiguous project and scope definition at the outset, and by constantly referring to this definition during the course of the project. The project's scope may also change upon request. Changing the scope of a project often means that a client has asked for extra work.

Budgeting

A budget is an expression of an organization's planned activities and serves a number of purposes. It is a forecast of the resources likely to be available to the organization and a plan for utilizing these resources to achieve the organization's objectives. It is also a framework for authorizing the expenditure of resources and for maintaining control over that expenditure.

Budgeting is the most common control mechanism of any planning process. Control is based on comparing actual against planned expenditure and investigating any variances calculated. It is important that sales and production targets are met and budgeting provides a standard against which the performance of the organization as a whole and the performance of individuals may be judged.

Budgeting systems also need to be flexible in enabling resources to be deployed quickly in response to changing demands from the environment and also motivate staff to use resources effectively and efficiently.

The control process

Monitoring and control effectively contains four key activities:

1. Development or adjustment of marketing objectives
2. Setting of performance standards
3. Evaluation of performance
4. Corrective action.

The first stage in the process after setting the objectives, by which performance will be measured, is setting performance standards. Performance standards are principally the level of performance against which actual performance can be compared. In the main, performance standards are presented in the form of budgets. The sole purpose of this will be to ensure that the amount of money given over to expenditure is not exceeded and that the proposed targets for income and profit are actually achieved. There are a number of methods of measuring performance overall, such as performance management. This consists of reviewing performance, giving feedback and, if necessary, re-examining and re-setting objectives and targets. To make monitoring easier, budgets are often broken down into a number of smaller manageable areas, often termed cost centres. For each of these, planned income and expenditure are monitored and compared with the actual results. In some organizations, each function may be a cost centre. For example, headings on a monthly or annual budget report could be as shown in the following table:

INCOME BUDGET – Marketing and sales division

Income	Actual year	Month	Budgeted amount	Variance under	Variance over
Sales					
Interest earned					
Sales commission					
Licence fees					
Royalty payments					
Property rentals					
Total Income					

EXPENDITURE BUDGET – Marketing and sales division

Income	Actual year	Month	Budgeted amount	Variance under	Variance over
Sales					
Rent					
Advertising					
PR					
Sales promotions					
Travel					
Sales commission					
Total Expenditure					

Variance analysis

One of the main things that control is likely to expose is constant variances from the planned budget. Variance analysis is used along with budgetary control. It compares a planned budget with an actual budget and seeks to explain any variations from what has been planned. A variance in itself is not good or bad, it is the interpretation and explanation of why there is a variance that will determine whether it is good or bad. As mentioned previously, figures do not speak for themselves, they need to be interpreted. The key to using variance analysis as a control tool is to be aware that variance in budgets is inevitable.

Benchmarking

In the words of Drummond and Ensor, *Strategic Marketing Planning and Control*, benchmarking is defined as

> *A systematic and ongoing process of measuring and comparing an organization's business processes and achievements against acknowledged process leaders and/or key competitors, to facilitate improved performance.*

Benchmarking is concerned with demonstrating a commitment to continuous improvement and show that the organization is a learning organization, willing to learn from past mistakes and also past successes and develop an approach to best business practice. It falls into three categories:

1. *Competitive analysis* – reviewing on an ongoing basis competitor activities in order to learn from their success.
2. *Best practice* – here the organization should involve itself in reviewing the best way of undertaking activities across the whole of the organization.
3. *Performance standards* – ensuring that targets are either met or surpassed.

Managing quality

The project manager should ensure that the project's quality standard is understood by everyone concerned and that deliverables meet that standard. Checklists and regular reviews focusing on the subject can assist in this process.

Post project reviews

Some issues to consider:

○ Were the main objectives met?
○ Was enough time allocated to each task?
○ Were there any warning signs that were ignored?
○ Did everyone understand the project definition and their roles?
○ Was the project on time and to budget and why?
○ Was the relationship with the client satisfactory, or did unforeseen problems arise?
○ Was the quality control process sufficient?

Successful project management

The effectiveness of project management is critical in assuring the success of any substantial undertaking. Areas of responsibility for the project manager include planning, control and implementation.

Knowledge, skills, goals and personalities are all factors that need to be considered within project management. The project manager and his/her team should possess the necessary interpersonal and technical skills to control the project activities.

The stages of implementation must be identified at the project planning phase. In addition to planning, the control of the project is also a necessary condition of success. This means adequate monitoring and feedback mechanisms to facilitate comparisons of progress against projections. Monitoring and feedback also enables minor problems to be anticipated and addressed before they become major ones. Consulting with end-users is important for ensuring the success of a project.

(A) Activity 5.2

Can you think of any examples where your organization needs to respond to change and a project management approach may be valid?

The reasons for project failure

Common reasons are as follows:

- Project goals are not clearly defined.
- The assumptions that are made at the outset of the project are incorrect but remain unchallenged.
- The project team is not sure of the project objectives or the deliverables.
- The planned schedule overruns.
- The budget is exceeded.
- Lack of co-ordination of resources and activities.
- Lack of communication with interested parties, leading to products being delivered that are not what the customer wanted.
- Poor estimation of duration and costs, leading to projects taking more time and costing more money than expected.
- Inadequate planning of resources, activities and scheduling.
- Lack of control over progress, so that projects do not reveal their exact status until too late.
- Lack of quality control, resulting in the delivery of products that are unacceptable or unusable.

Problems with project goals

- The project sponsor or client has an inadequate idea of what the project is about at the start.
- Failure of communication between the client and the project manager. This may be due to a lack of technical knowledge on the part of the client or an overuse of jargon by the project manager.
- Specifications may be subject to constant change. This may be due to problems with individual clients, decision-making processes at the client's end, or environmental changes. For example the government may change the basic 'rules of the game' before the completion of the project.
- The project goals may be unrealistic and unachievable, and it may be that this is only realized once the project is under way.
- Projects may be complex and objectives may contradict each other.

There are perhaps two stages which can help in ensuring that goals are properly defined and achievable:

Ensuring that the client specification is clear and understandable. To do this the following objectives of the project must be established:

- What is it that the organization is setting out to achieve or is being asked to achieve?
- Will the suggested project fulfil these objectives?
- Have all the alternatives been considered, and is the chosen option the best one available?
- Have the full effects of the project, both inside and outside the organization, been considered?

Constraints on the completion of projects
Time

The definition of a project stated that it was an activity which had a defined beginning and ending point. Most projects will be close-ended in terms of there being a requirement for completion by a certain point of time. This point may be the result of an external factor such as new legislation, or may be derived from organizational requirements. It may also be partly determined by other constraints. There is likely to be some relationship between the time taken for a project and its cost. A trade-off between the two constraining factors may then be necessary.

Resource availability

There is likely to be a budget for the project and this will clearly be a major constraint. Cost constraints may be set in a number of ways, for example as an overall cash limit or as a detailed budget broken down over a number of expenditure headings. Labour resources in particular may be a limiting factor on the completion of the project. Whilst the overall resource available may be, in theory, sufficient to complete the project, there may be difficulties arising out of the way in which the project has been scheduled. That is, there may be a number of activities scheduled to take place at the same time and this may not be possible, given the amount of resources available.

Quality factors

Whether the project delivers the goods to the right quality. There are techniques which can be used to overcome the problems referred to above. These include:

- ○ Budgeting and the corresponding control of the project budget through budgetary control
- ○ Procedures
- ○ Project planning and control techniques such as Gantt charts and network analysis.

The various constraints on project completion are likely to be interlinked with each other. For example, problems with time constraints or resource constraints may be overcome by spending more through working overtime, employing more people or purchasing better machines. Budget problems may have a knock-on effect on the achievement of deadlines.

Provided the project is not too complex in its activity relationships or simply too big to be mapped on reasonably sized graph paper, Gantt charts can be very useful tools for the project manager and are graphically superior to the network analysis methods of CPM and PERT.

They allow the critical activities to be found, that is those activities which must be performed on time if the project duration is not to increase, and any 'slack' or 'float' in the sequence of activities can easily be shown.

By timetabling the activities by horizontal bars whose lengths represent the activity times, the earliest completion date for the entire project can be mapped out by the Gantt chart, and then used as indicated above by the operations manager to check on progress as the project proceeds.

Management of projects

Gantt charts, PERT, CPM and other scheduling techniques have proven to be valuable tools in the management of large and complex projects. A wide variety of software packages are available for project managers, for use on micro or larger computers, to assist in the handling of complex network problems. PERT and CPM, however, cannot ever purport to be able to solve all project scheduling and management problems in service or manufacturing industries. Good management practices, clear responsibilities for tasks, and accurate and timely reporting systems are the most essential qualities for successful project completion. As useful as these techniques are, they are only tools to assist the manager in making better, more calculated decisions in the process of conducting large-scale projects.

The role of the project manager falls into three areas:

1. Management of stakeholders
2. Management of the project life cycle
3. Management of performance.

Management of stakeholders

Stakeholders' interests must be monitored to ensure that their:

- Interest and support is maintained
- Views and ideas are being adequately reflected in the project development
- Personal success criteria are being pursued and achieved.

Management of the project life cycle

Feedback systems need to be set up to monitor key areas.

Management of performance

This is the least tangible but possibly the most important of the three categories. How it is tackled will depend upon what kind of project is being carried out. It is likely that they will work apart most of the time, meeting up only occasionally and meeting only with the project manager from time to time. Issues that need to be considered are:

- How to get the best out of the team when they are together
- Ensuring people work when the team is apart
- Disseminating information and keeping everyone informed is important
- Ensuring continuing commitment by the team
- Communicating change to team members quickly and effectively
- It is important to look at the team and also for the project leader to look at his or her own performance.

Project management and network techniques such as CPM and PERT are valuable tools for showing relationships between project activities, and identifying critical activities but the management of people is a major factor in whether a project will be a success or not. The ability to motivate staff, to create the structures and conditions in which they can be motivated and work effectively, and dealing with any people problems that arise are also essential features of project management. The human factors are as important as having the right tools and techniques. Working in teams and motivation have been looked at in other chapters so they would not be repeated here, but they are very important.

Five rules for delivering criticism

Project managers need to create and maintain good working relationships but they also need to monitor others' performance and act if there is a problem.

1. *Think it through before you say something* – A problem worth solving demands concentrated attention and focus to gain desired outcomes. This may mean not saying anything at all until you have mentally rehearsed your delivery and envisioned the receiver's response.
2. *Criticize in private* – Public criticism offends the receivers and observers. When a problem arises during a team meeting, acknowledge it and say that this is something that needs to be addressed 'later' 'without taking up everyone's time'.
3. *Respond to problems in a timely fashion* – Realize your own propensity to put off discussing problem behaviours. Remember the difficulty in reconstructing problems because everyone remembers them differently. Compare that to the benefits of a timely focus on correcting one problem at a time.

4. *Criticize without comparison* – Broad, unfavourable comparisons mean that individuals will end up finding fault with you rather than dealing with the ambiguous criticism levied at them.

5. *Criticize with specificity, not labels* – Examples of specific behaviours are: inaccuracy, lateness, absenteeism, interrupting, missed timelines, incompleteness, incorrectness, assumptions, data, and so on. Criticism or feedback that cites specific examples such as these requires no interpretation of meaning. A missed commitment is a missed commitment. These concrete descriptions focus on quantifiable problems and achievable improvements.

Source: Paris (2000).

Activity 5.3

For a project that is already under way in your organization, identify the key areas requiring monitoring, and suggest the kind of information and procedures that would be involved.

Differences between a functional manager and a project manager
A functional manager is likely to be a specialist in the area being managed, such that when technical knowledge is required or a difficult issue arises in an area, he should be able to make some realistic recommendations about how to tackle it (Meredith and Mantel, 1995).

Responsibilities of a project manager
o   To plan the project, soliciting the active involvement of all functional areas involved, in order to obtain and maintain a realistic plan that satisfies their commitment for performance.
o   To control the organization of human resources needed by the project.
o   To control the basic technical definition of the project, ensuring that 'technical' versus 'cost' trade-offs determine the specific areas where optimization is necessary.
o   To lead the people and organizations assigned to the project at any given point of time. Strong positive leadership must be exercised in order to keep the many disparate elements moving in the same direction in a co-operative manner.
o   To monitor performance, costs and efficiency of all elements of the project and the project as a whole, exercising judgement and leadership in determining the causes of problems and facilitating solutions.
o   To complete the project on schedule and within costs, these being the overall standard by which performance of the project manager is evaluated.

The skills of a project manager
The PM is expected to integrate all aspects of the project, to ensure that the proper knowledge and resources are available when and where needed, and above all to ensure that the expected results are produced in a timely, cost-effective manner.

A project manager is more likely to be a generalist who is required to bring together a number of functional areas, each comprising specialists in their own fields. The PM's task is to bring them together to form a coherent whole. The project manager needs to be able to synthesize a wide range of information, whereas a functional manager must be more skilled in analysing a narrower area. The functional manager needs a depth of experience whilst the project manager needs breadth. The authors argue that an analytical approach breaks a system down into smaller and smaller parts, but a systems approach tries to understand the links between different elements. However, there is no doubt that an effective project manager needs the skills of analysis and synthesis.

159

Skill dimensions that a project manager needs to use at different points in the project management cycle (Elbeik and Thomas, 1998):

Administrator

- o Accomplishment of project tasks and goals
- o Strong management of repetitive tasks and procedures
- o Adhering to routines and systematic controls
- o Focus on stability and consistency
- o Able to meet deadlines and cope with workloads
- o Organizing skills
- o A concern for detail and accuracy.

Analyst

- o Strong problem-solving orientation
- o High level of critical thinking ability
- o Ability to synthesize other people's thought and actions
- o A strategic outlook – able to see the 'bigger picture'
- o Able to balance short-, medium- and long-term requirements.

Negotiator

- o Influencing and persuasion skills
- o Diplomatic
- o Willingness to challenge and tackle others
- o Able to 'read' situations and identify motives and needs
- o Determination to achieve objectives.

Verbal communicator

- o Able to present arguments persuasively
- o Able to communicate effectively with people from different backgrounds and levels of seniority
- o Effective range of responses to most situations and able to think on his or her feet
- o Able to secure people's attention
- o Political sensitivity.

Written communicator

- o Able to keep written communications brief and to the point
- o Able to express complexity in a form that makes it accessible to the audience for whom it is intended
- o Can write persuasively
- o Can write with accuracy and precision
- o Political sensitivity.

Listener

Those who are answering questions need to be convinced that someone:

- o Is listening to them
- o Is interested in what they say
- o Understands what they are saying
- o Active listening is the skill of demonstrating to the person who is speaking that you are listening
- o Empathy and the ability to develop rapport.

Motivator

o Commands respect
o Persuasive and influential
o Able to enthuse people
o Highly developed interpersonal skills
o Able to achieve results through others
o Different people may respond to various techniques of persuasion in different ways, and it is important to know how to approach people so that they will be motivated to take appropriate action.

Decision maker

o Capable of making decisions in the face of incomplete information
o Able to absorb a lot of information and identify what is significant about it
o Able to keep project aims and objectives in mind and avoid becoming bogged down in detail.

Three questions face the PM at the outset of a project:

1. What needs to be done?
2. When must it be done?
3. How are the resources needed by the project to be obtained?

Using IT
Computer software for project management

A wide variety of software packages is available to help with the scheduling and controlling of projects. Examples of the kind of software which an organization uses are:

o ABC Flowchart
o Harvard Project Manager III
o On-Target
o Microsoft Project
o Suretrak
o Project Scheduler V5
o Super Project V2
o Time Line
o InstaPlan.

Managing large team projects

When managing a project it may be necessary to bring together partner firms, suppliers, subcontractors and team members who do not sit in the same building, or even in the same state or country. This presents challenges of monitoring, managing and integrating:

o Information flow (up, down and across the team)
o Scheduling, change control and logistics
o Work planning and staffing requirements.

All project team members need to be able to contribute their part of the project at the right time and place. This synergy of time, information and action depends on communication, collaboration and reporting. All of this is influenced by software capabilities.

Using a workgroup messaging system

The success of a project often depends on quick and effective communication between team members. Members of a team can be linked through a workgroup messaging system; for example, Microsoft Project allows for almost instant exchange of project information. A workgroup messaging system is a network that is used to send and receive information about task status and assignments. Each team member should have access to this network, and be able to receive and send workgroup messages.

PRINCE

PRINCE (Projects in Controlled Environments) is a project management method covering the organization, management and control of projects. Since its introduction, PRINCE has become widely used in both the public and private sectors. Although PRINCE was originally developed for the needs of IT projects, the method has also been used on many non-IT projects. PRINCE2 is designed as a generic approach for the management of all types of projects. Each process is defined with its key inputs and outputs together with the specific objectives to be achieved.

Project evaluation

The main reasons for project evaluation and feedback are:

o To ensure that the project remains on track
o To confirm whether the project meets user needs
o To determine whether the project delivers value for money
o To transfer the knowledge and any lessons from one project to other projects.

One reason for carrying out evaluation as an ongoing process during the project, rather than as a single post project evaluation at the end of the project, is to ensure that important information and lessons are not forgotten.

Post Project Review

A Post Project Review is performed by a project team at the end of the project's life cycle to gather information on what worked well and what did not, so that future projects can benefit from that learning. Participants in the Post Project Review process are members of the project team, key stakeholders and users of the project deliverables or results. Lessons learned from the Post Project Review should be archived so that it is easy for project team members, process improvement teams and managers to find useful information. This is a formal review of a programme or project. It helps to answer the question of whether what was planned for has been achieved and if not, what should be done? It is undertaken when there has been time to demonstrate the business benefits.

Outputs and outcomes

There is a difference between outputs and outcomes. It is often possible to identify outputs during and not long after a project has been completed. With outcomes it takes longer to assess the impact of a project because objectives are often long term as well as short term. Implementation of outcomes-based monitoring can be difficult because while an organization may be able to control inputs (which resources are allocated in what amounts at what times to what activities) and to some degree outputs (in terms of products that are controlled by the organization), it cannot control the outcomes (impact) of a project. Traditionally, success is measured by input-output analyses. Thus, for example, an anti-smoking campaign may be measured to see how many column inches of press coverage and other media coverage is generated (an output) but does it stop people smoking and lead to healthier people (an outcome)?

Post Implementation Review (PIR)

The scope of the PIR will be dictated largely by the business case that will have identified the areas of business change and where benefits were to have been realized. A PIR will usually include an assessment of:

o The achievement (to date) of objectives
o Costs and benefits to date against forecast, and other benefits realized and expected
o Alignment with the overall business strategy
o Ways of maximizing benefits and minimizing cost and risk
o Business and user satisfaction.

Common problems

There are a number of common problems that may be encountered in carrying out PIRs. These include:

o When more than one organization is involved there may not be a common standard for measuring and recording the benefits and costs.
o A lack of documentation about aims and objectives.
o A lack of baseline measures. Measures of success can only be made accurately by comparing the level of performance before the project implementation against that at the time of the PIR.
o Management of expectations. The review process may lead to raised expectations of changes that may cost more to implement than the value of the benefits they would deliver.
o An organization may be too busy to undertake a systematic PIR and lessons may not be learnt or passed on when another project is implemented.

Some key success factors

o Focus on achieving continuous improvement through direction setting, evaluating achievements and identifying improvement actions.
o Performance management and measurement is an integral part of the business life cycle, helping the organization to evolve and change.
o Openness to constructive criticism and advice.
o Management commitment and readiness to learn lessons by adopting recommendations.

The Post Implementation Review/Post Project Review

The purpose of the Post Project Review is to find out whether the expected benefits of the project have been realized and if lessons learned from the project will lead to recommendations for improvements.

Fitness for purpose checklist:

Are all benefits mentioned in the Project Brief and is the Business Case covered?

Does it describe each achievement in a tangible, measurable form?

Are there recommendations in any case where a benefit is not being fully met, a problem has been identified, or a potential extra benefit could be obtained?

Has this been conducted as soon as the benefits and problems can be measured?

Was this scheduled in the project/programme plan?

Project review checklist

When the project was complete, did the project outcomes meet user requirements without additional work?

How close to scheduled completion was the project actually completed?

What factors enabled the team to stay on schedule?

What factors caused delays?

Overall, what did you learn about scheduling on this project that will help you on the next project?

Budget

How close to the budget was the final project cost?

What did you learn about budgeting that will help you on the next project?

Team issues

What did you learn about staffing that will help you on the next project?

What worked or didn't work about team communications?

What was effective or ineffective about how information was distributed? Did you have the right skill mix?

Managing relationships

What lessons did you learn about managing the working relationship with your client?

What lessons did you learn about managing working relationships with other departments or divisions?

What techniques or systems did you develop for this project that could be used on other projects?

List any recommendations you have for future development.

If you could do the project again, what would you do differently?

Summary

In recent years, project teams and a project management approach have become common in many organizations. The basic approach to project management should be the same regardless of the type of project or sector in which the project is carried out. Project management is associated with a precise set of techniques, definitions and practices that can be used. These are all useful and demonstrate how a systematic approach can be used. However, skills in managing people are equally important. Many people are involved in managing projects as only part of their job and have to carry it out alongside other activities. A project should possess identifiable goals, and a definite starting and finishing point. Project goals should be defined clearly. Managing stakeholders' expectations is a major part of a project manager's role. The major constraints on the completion of projects are time, resource availability and the need to achieve the required standard of performance for the project.

Further study

Read, Elbeik and Thomas (1998) *Project Skills*, Chapters 2–4.

Hints and tips

It is useful to have an overview of the principles and techniques of project management. There are no surprises in the techniques that are used and they can be applied to a wide variety of situations where a systematic approach is needed.

Bibliography

Elbeik, S. and Thomas, M. (1998) *Project Skills*, Oxford: Butterworth-Heinemann.

Meredith, J. and Mantel, S. (1995) *Project Management – A Managerial Approach*, New York: Wiley.

Paris, Claudine, E. (2000) <http://www.4pm.com/>

Sample exam questions and answers for the Marketing Management in Practice module as a whole can be found in Appendix 6 and past examination papers can be found in Appendix 7. Both appendices can be found at the back of the book.

unit 6
market research

○ Explain the concept of information and knowledge management highlighting the role of marketing and employees within the organization (3.1).

○ Design a research project aimed at providing information as part of a marketing audit or for marketing and business decisions (3.2).

○ Manage a marketing research project by gathering relevant information on time and within the agreed budget (3.3).

○ Make arrangements to record, store and, if appropriate, update information in the market information system (MkIS) – a database created for a purpose or another system (3.4).

○ Analyse and interpret information and present, as a written report or oral presentation, appropriate conclusions or recommendations that inform the marketing and business decisions for which the research was undertaken (3.5).

○ Give examples of the application of information and knowledge management (3.6).

○ Design a research project aimed at providing information as part of a marketing audit or for marketing and business decisions.

○ Review and evaluate the effectiveness of the activities and the role of the individual and team in this process (3.6).

Key skills

Communication

○ Develop a research brief

○ Develop a research proposal or plan

○ Present research results to decision-makers

○ Present and justify a marketing or communications plan

○ Produce effective marketing communications

○ Assess the impact of a campaign.

Study Guide

In order for organizations to make informed decisions about the future, information is needed about a wide range of issues. This unit looks at information and knowledge management, and market research. Marketing research provides a useful link between the supplier and the customer by keeping up to date with customer needs and wants. The unit also looks at the range of issues that needs to be taken into account when conducting a market research project, and in using the results of such projects.

Knowledge management

In recent years, the concept of knowledge management has become widespread in the business and management literature. Given marketing's focus on the effective gathering, analysis and use of information to yield insights into the behaviour of consumers in different markets, it is an important area. As with many business concepts, it is more common to read about it than to find concrete examples in the workplace. Thus, although there is agreement that it is a 'good thing', implementing a system for managing knowledge is by no means a straightforward proposition.

Knowledge management is concerned principally with how people are managed to collaborate and share their knowledge. Managing knowledge is concerned with developing a culture where people within the organization are willing to share knowledge so that the organization can be successful. This may involve changing the culture of the organization and putting processes in place to enable knowledge creation and transfer.

Knowledge management is the process through which organizations generate value from their intellectual and knowledge-based assets. This involves sharing them among employees, departments and sometimes with other companies. Knowledge-based assets can be explicit or tacit. Explicit assets usually refer to items that can be documented and archived such as patents, trademarks, business plans, marketing research and customer lists. Tacit knowledge refers to the know-how contained in people's heads. The challenge consists of being able to recognize, generate, share and manage it. ICT tools such as databases, access tools, e-learning applications, e-mail, groupware, instant messaging and related technologies, synchronous interaction tools, and search and data mining tools can all help to facilitate the dissemination of tacit knowledge but identifying it in the first place is a major challenge for most organizations.

Differences between data, information and knowledge

Data is unorganized words, numbers and images. It has no meaning and context. Information is data that has been organized or categorized and has meaning or value added to data. Knowledge refers to the use of information. Therefore, organizations can gather/capture information about their customers and competitors but they can only become knowledge driven only if they have the systems in place to use the information. Whether the organization becomes a knowledge-driven organization depends on leadership, culture and trust. Organizations such as management consultancies and R&D centres rely almost completely on their employees' skills and know-how for their success. Knowledge-intensive firms need employees who are able to spread knowledge across organizational boundaries.

However, the following case study provides an indication of some of the barriers to sharing knowledge across organizations.

Case study

Why ideas don't travel well

There are a number of reasons why good ideas that emerge in one part of an organization don't get picked up elsewhere. These include:

o *'What's in it for me?'* – To get people to transfer or take on a good idea there must be something in it for them, which could be recognition, thanks, career progression or learning.

o *The 'not invented here' syndrome* – Why should I learn from people I don't know much about? How do I know that what worked there will work here?

o *Lack of leadership* – Many leaders do not spend any time promoting idea-sharing or rewarding those who contribute to it.

o *Lack of time* – This is often a way of saying 'not enough of a priority'.

o *Failure to apply learning design expertise* – Good ideas or business practices are turned into long documents that capture facts but are not designed to help people learn.

o *Lack of context sensitivity* – Many organizations believe that what works well in one part of the organization (often the biggest part, such as the home country) can be applied without any modification in very different business environments.

o *Underinvestment in facilitating knowledge transfer* – Leaders may say that 'sharing best practice' is a business priority but fail to give anyone the accountability or resources to make it happen.

All companies contain knowledge that they need to exploit and new technology makes it easier to share it. For example, conference calls mean that several people in different places can talk together and videoconferencing means they can see each other while they talk. Electronic databases make it possible to store vast amounts of knowledge, to which others can be given access. E-mail means people can communicate quickly, cheaply and over long distances. Company intranets mean staff can be given access to more information more quickly, and extranets enable organizations in the marketing channels to communicate more effectively.

Data mining can help businesses to handle and interpret large volumes of data so as to develop marketing, customer relationship and communication strategies. Advanced software can be used to analyse a terabyte of data – the equivalent of a million floppy discs – in a fraction of the time needed for human analysis. One of the challenges for companies that are serious about knowledge management is how to address the people and cultural issues. In an environment where an individual's knowledge is valued and rewarded, establishing a culture that promotes sharing can be difficult. It can seem as if people are being asked to give up something that enhances their value as individuals. Companies that manage knowledge most effectively tend to have three main characteristics:

1. Knowledge management programmes that are an intrinsic part of their overall business strategy.
2. Human resources and information technology policies that support the sharing of information.
3. A corporate culture that encourages staff to share what they know.

Case study

Nokia dominates the world mobile phone industry with a market share of around 35 per cent. One of the keys to its success is its focus on knowledge management, on making sure that all parts of the organization communicate continuously with each other and with their suppliers. A large part of Nokia's success is ensuring that different groups constantly share their knowledge. A user-interface team is an eclectic group, made up of engineers, graphic designers, psychologists, sociologists and even a theatre director, who look at how people use mobile phones. While the design team thinks about what the phone should look like and the manufacturing group considers how it could be made, the user-interface team worries about how the customer will interact with it. While technology, such as e-mail, is important, it is not the foundation of the company's knowledge management. What is crucial is the constant attempt to break down barriers – between designers and engineers, or between factories and suppliers – and this is a task that never ends. What is important is seeking out the knowledge contained within the company and making it available to others in the organization so that they could use it. Many companies run up against a problem: their staff do not want to share what they know. They want to keep it for themselves. This is the most substantial obstacle to knowledge management.

'Do's' and 'don'ts' for effective knowledge management

1. The idea is to improve something or create new value so start with the business itself, the role of knowledge in it and work from there. Focus knowledge building on tools that justify the investment:

   (a) *In-house Yellow Pages* – This system connects inquirers to experts and experience you can use, reduces errors and guesswork, and prevents the reinvention of countless wheels.

   (b) *Lessons learned* – Insist that no project is complete until time has been spent providing insights into what went right and wrong and guidelines for others undertaking similar projects. Allow access via the company intranet.

   (c) *Competitor intelligence* – Organize a database of customers, competitors and suppliers so that they are searchable and widely accessible and in a consistent format.

   (d) Use technology to its fullest, but don't use it in place of human contact. In particular, don't rely on databases, encyclopedias, and libraries if there aren't 'librarians' who can help with navigation through the sea of information.

2. Share with people how the company makes money. Many people are not aware of how this is achieved.
3. Deal fully with the obstacles to sharing knowledge inside the organization.
4. Get learning out of the classroom and into the marketplace. Action learning with project teams is a very powerful way to learn.
5. Speed up knowledge flows. Encourage interactions via e-mail, in-house training programmes, cross-functional projects, and sharing best practices across departments and business units.
6. Don't manage knowledge for the sake of managing knowledge.
7. Leverage the knowledge you have. The most important function of knowledge management systems should be connection of people to people, of questions to answers.
8. Technology is an enabler but don't think about knowledge management or knowledge management technology until it is clear what needs to be enabled.

169

Information

In his book *Marketing Research*, Alan Wilson (2003) identifies three main areas where information is needed by marketers if decisions are to be effective – information about customers, other organizations and the marketing environment.

Customers

Who are customers? – what are their characteristics? – what are the main influences on what, where, when and how they buy or use a product or service.

Other organizations

Comparison of performance relative to other organizations is used in the private and the public sector to improve competitiveness or, generally, to improve the quality of services. Benchmarking is an example of this.

It involves learning, sharing information and adopting best practices to bring about step changes in performance.

> *Improving ourselves by learning from others.*

Most organizations tailor definitions of benchmarking to suit their own strategies and objectives.

> *Benchmarking is simply about making comparisons with other organisations and then learning the lessons that those comparisons throw up.* (*Source*: The European Benchmarking Code of Conduct)

> *Benchmarking is the continuous process of measuring products, services and practices against the toughest competitors or those companies recognised as industry leaders (best in class).* (*Source*: The Xerox Corporation)

Benchmarking usually encompasses:

Regularly comparing aspects of performance (functions or processes) with best practitioners
Identifying gaps in performance
Seeking fresh approaches to bring about improvements in performance
Following through with implementing improvements and
Following up by monitoring progress and reviewing the benefits.

Although benchmarking involves making comparisons of performance, it is not:

Merely competitor analysis – Benchmarking is best undertaken in a collaborative way.
Comparison of league tables – The aim is to learn about the circumstances and processes that underpin superior performance.
A quick fix, done once for all time – Benchmarking projects may extend over a number of months and it is vital to repeat them periodically so as not to fall behind as the background environment changes.
Copying or catching up – In rapidly changing circumstances, good practices become dated very quickly. Also, the fact that others are doing things differently does not necessarily mean they are better.

Spying or espionage – Openness and honesty are vital for successful benchmarking.

Source: Public Sector Benchmarking Service, 2004.

Marketing environment

The environment consists of many influences that are beyond the power of organizations to shape and control but have an impact on the organization. This includes factors such as social changes in the size and composition of households, age structure, legal framework, government policies and guidelines, economy and technology. The power of alliances such as NAFTA, the European Union and ASEAN means that individual countries are less able to influence the trading environment in any significant way. Changes have to be monitored so that an organization can keep track of present and future trends and try to anticipate the implications of them.

Market Information System (MkIS)

Information underpins successful marketing and can be of strategic importance as well as contributing to tactical and operational decision-making. Kotler defines an MkIS as:

> ... *consisting of people, equipment and procedures to gather, sort, analyse, evaluate and distribute needed, timely and accurate information to marketing decision makers.*

A typical MkIS comprises:

The Marketing Research System – The system used for gathering information about specific issues that are of interest to a marketer such as testing products and evaluating the success of communications strategies.

Marketing Intelligence System – For example, published data, including government statistics, research reports, the national and trade press. A Market Intelligence System (MkIS) gathers and processes critical business information, transforming it into intelligence to support marketing decisions.

Decision support system – The tools needed to make sense of data, statistical packages, the intranet and other tools that help marketers make decisions.

Internal records – Sales records, account records, and other information that is available in the company.

Source: Housden, 2003.

An MkIS can contain many different sources and types of information and, for example, it has a role in support of information gathering, evaluation, processing, dissemination, analysis and control. A good MkIS should encourage people throughout the organization to focus externally and provide quick, efficient and cost-effective information that is easily accessible. It can serve a number of purposes – it can help sales and service personnel in the field who want pricing information; marketers and planners who want to know about market and product trends so as to be able to develop marketing plans and adjust the marketing mix; and directors and senior managers who are interested in market developments that affect investment and other strategic decisions. Knowing what kind of information to obtain and how to make effective use of it are key skills of strategic marketing.

Marketing research is an important element of the MkIS and is concerned with the provision of information about markets and customers and how they may or do react to different marketing strategies. Marketing intelligence is concerned with information available from the marketing environment and may be less focused on immediate decision-making. Marketing productivity analysis uses internal information to quantify marketing inputs and outputs, for example measuring the response to a promotional campaign. Marketing modelling may involve, for example, the synthesis of profile and transaction information to develop profiles of individual customers. The MkIS is concerned with many areas of data collection.

(A) Activity 6.1

How would you respond to these questions if they were asked about your organization?

Some questions for establishing the scope of an MkIS

What types of decisions need to be made regularly?

What types of information are needed to make these decisions?

Is this information available in a timely fashion?

What types of information are needed but aren't available at the moment?

What information is needed on a daily basis? weekly? monthly? yearly?

What reports are needed on a regular basis?

What types of data analysis programs need to be made available?

What are the four most helpful improvements that could be made in the present marketing information system?

The critical function is how the organization uses information not the information system used to develop the information or the technology supporting it. Short-term advantage can accrue from IT but the results are not sustainable. Since the early 1980s, competitive advantage's focus has moved towards systems and away from technology. Systems that enable a business to create value for its customers include customer relationship management, supply chain management and knowledge management.

MkIS and CRM trends

The development of technology is bringing closer the time when a company's information systems will lead to the generation of integrated profiles of individual customers. However, there are considerable difficulties in realizing the potential of technology. Whilst it is an important tool for marketers, human factors will always have a big influence on how effectively technology is utilized. The following trends are mostly enabled by increased technological capacity but still need an appropriate organizational structure and culture in order for any benefits to be realized.

1. *Highly successful companies will invest more in customers, not less* – Successful companies will focus on using customer information and applying technology and strategies to keep high-value customers, convert moderate-to-low-value customers to higher value, and minimize investments in customers that detract value.

2. *Companies will compete for customer share, not market share* – Companies will need to focus on how they are going to increase or maximize the individual share of each customer's spending by managing and increasing the value delivered to each customer.

3. *CRM will evolve to CVM* – Customer value management (CVM) will become the standard approach to maximizing the return on customer investments. The measurement of customer value will evolve from revenue-based metrics to individual customer profitability.

4. *Companies will heighten their focus on data analysis and organization to avoid information roadblocks* – Companies will place a much greater emphasis on the analysis and organization of data so they can better differentiate their customers, establish clear customer value (profitability based) segments, and create richer and more measurable marketing campaigns.

5. *Companies will realize customer satisfaction doesn't translate to loyalty* – Companies will no longer be able to assume that a satisfied customer will remain a loyal customer. That's because people often make purchasing decisions based on shifting and migratory preferences with satisfaction being just one factor among many.

6. *Companies will focus on thoughtware, not software* – There's a reason why 55–75 per cent of current CRM projects don't meet their objectives. It's because companies often confuse CRM strategy with technology implementation, when in fact, CRM is a broader business strategy that technologies can enable.

7. *Companies will stitch their customer channels together* – The trend will be to create seamless interplay among all customer channels (customer service, field service, Web, marketing, sales, etc.) in order to create a consistent experience for customers regardless of how they choose to interact with an organization. As these channels are integrated, the marketer will have one comprehensive view of the customer.

8. *Companies will embrace PRM as a means to maximize value to end-customers* – Organizations finally integrate their customer channels and focus on partner relationship management (PRM), a strategy to better serve end-customers by leveraging a company's business partner network.

9. *Companies will create CRM platforms* – We will start to see the integration and convergence of the Internet platforms with CRM platforms.

10. *Companies will shift to a long-term focus* – Organizations will think about long-term application viability, and focus on IT strategy to enable integrated CRM solutions.

Source: Adapted from Braun Consulting (www.braunconsult.com).

Relationship marketing (RM) and customer relationship management (CRM)

Customer relationship management is a subset of RM and focused on the management of customer relations only. Relationship marketing is a broader type of marketing, encompassing relationships with customers, suppliers and intermediaries as well as strategies for the overall picture. Internal marketing can also be regarded as a sub-type of RM, focusing on the relationships within the company. A database is a tool in RM and might be able to provide information about trends that will help an organization to individualize its offer. Customization involves creating products and service offers specific for a particular individual or target group rather than analysing buying patterns to produce a 'best-fit' option. Thus, a prerequisite of customization is a detailed understanding of clients' needs and wants and this poses a considerable challenge for a marketing information system.

Market research

This is dealt with in more detail in the CIM Advanced Certificate book, *Marketing Research and Information 2004–2005*, Butterworth-Heinemann. A market research project should include some form of a marketing audit, that is an appraisal of an organization's marketing activities. This involves a systematic assessment of marketing plans, objectives, strategies, programmes, activities, organizational structure and personnel. There are a number of models that can be used for a marketing audit, for example a SWOT analysis or a PESTLE can each yield useful data that can inform an audit. The marketing audit and the models that contribute to it are discussed in Unit 8.

Objectives

Are the marketing objectives of your department consistent with the overall company objectives?
Should these objectives be altered to fit changing environmental variables?
Are objectives consistent with one another?
How do objectives relate to marketing strengths and market opportunities?

Strategy

What is the relationship between objectives and strategies?
Are resources sufficient to implement the strategies?
What are the company's weaknesses?
How do you compare your strategies with those of competitors?

Product decisions

How are new products developed within your business unit?
How are existing products evaluated?
How are products phased out of the line?

Pricing decisions

How are pricing decisions made?
How do pricing decisions reflect the influences of competitors and the concerns of channel members?

Distribution decisions

How are channel members selected, evaluated and dropped, if necessary?
How are channel members motivated?
How are decisions to modify channel structures reached?

Promotion decisions

How are promotion mix decisions made?
How are salespeople selected, monitored and evaluated?
How are pay-offs associated with promotional efforts estimated?

Market information

How is marketing research information transmitted to, and used within, the business unit?
Is a global information system in place?

Activities and tasks

How are tasks scheduled, described and planned? How are the responsibilities of individuals determined?

What spans of supervision, reporting relationships and communication patterns exist? How are they evaluated?

Personnel

What level of competence has been attained by personnel in each position?

Are remedies to problems, if necessary, being planned? What are they?

What is the state of morale? motivation? What are the present plans in these areas?

Describe career development paths. Have potential replacements for personnel in key positions been identified?

Benchmarking

Another complementary approach to an audit would be to use a benchmarking approach that compares one organization with another that is regarded as being very successful. Obviously, in some organizations, this can be difficult because of commercial sensitivities and the need to retain competitive advantage. However, a table could be constructed that could compare the organization along the dimensions that are felt to be important for marketing. The precise details will vary for each organization but, for example, it might look something like Table 6.1.

Table 6.1 Comparing the organization with high and low performing organizations

Poor	Good	Excellent
Product driven	Market driven	Market driving
Mass-market oriented	Segment-oriented	Niche-oriented and customer-oriented
Product offer	Augmented product offer	Legendary

The EFQM Excellence Model

Another way of contributing to an audit is to use a recognized quality model. Usually, these kind of models are very comprehensive and too detailed for a marketing audit because they cover the whole of an organization's activities. One of the most widely used models in the private and public sectors is the EFQM Excellence Model. It was introduced at the beginning of 1992 as the framework for assessing applications for the European Quality Award. It is a non-prescriptive framework that recognizes many approaches to achieving sustainable excellence. Increasingly, organizations use the outputs from self-assessment as part of their business planning process and as a basis for reviewing the organization.

Within this non-prescriptive approach, there are some Fundamental Concepts which underpin the model. It is a non-prescriptive framework based on nine criteria. Five of these are 'Enablers' and four are 'Results'. The 'Enabler' criteria cover what an organization does. The 'Results' criteria cover what an organization achieves. 'Results' are caused by 'Enablers', and feedback from 'Results' helps to improve 'Enablers'. The model is based on the premise that:

'Excellent results with respect to Performance, Customers, People and Society are achieved through the enablers of Leadership driving Policy and Strategy, which is delivered through People Partnerships, Resources, and Processes' (Figure 6.1).

175

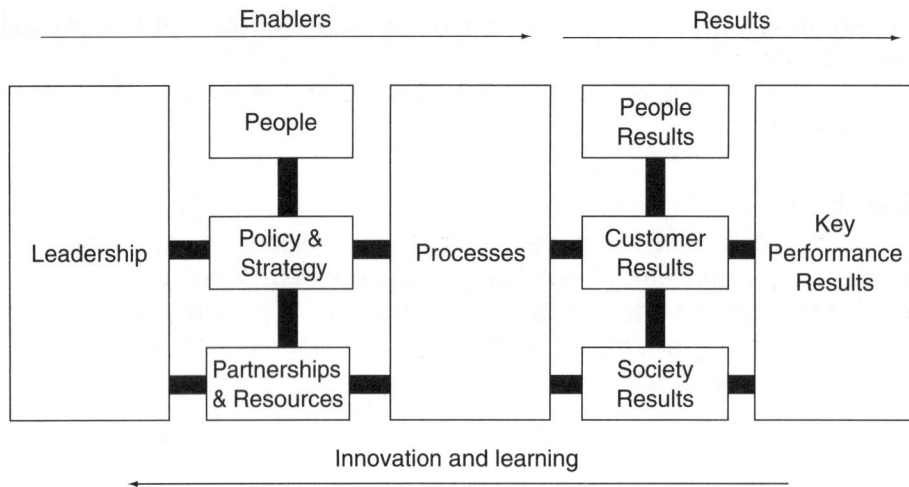

Figure 6.1
Source: http://www.efqm.org.

Results orientation – Achieving results that delight all the organization's stakeholders.

Customer focus – Creating sustainable customer value.

Leadership and constancy of purpose – Visionary and inspirational leadership, coupled with constancy of purpose.

Management by processes and facts – Managing the organization through a set of interdependent and interrelated systems, processes and facts.

People development and involvement – Maximizing the contribution of employees through their development and involvement.

Continuous learning, innovation and improvement – Challenging the status quo and effecting change by using learning to create innovation and improvement opportunities.

Partnership development – Developing and maintaining value-adding partnerships.

Corporate social responsibility – Exceeding the minimum regulatory framework in which the organization operates and strives to understand and respond to the expectations of their stakeholders in society.

An example – Partnerships and Resources Element of the EFQM Model
How is information and knowledge managed in the organization?

Areas to address
This could include:

- How information and knowledge is collected, structured and managed in support of policy and strategy?
- How unique intellectual property is cultivated, developed and protected in order to maximize value?
- How appropriate access to relevant information and knowledge for both internal and external users is provided?
- How the organization seeks to acquire and use information and knowledge effectively?

   o How the organization assures and improves the validity, integrity and security of its information?

   o How the organization generates innovative and creative thinking within the organization through the use of relevant information and knowledge resources?

RADAR

The method of assessment is based on the RADAR model, which looks at the evidence of what the organization achieves. This is based on documenting what it sets out to do, what evidence there is that its aims and objectives are actually translated into practice; whether it assesses the appropriateness of its approach and how successful its reviews have been. In this way, the self-assessment goes beyond what an organization claims it is doing to look for evidence that it is actually being implemented in practice.

Results – What an organization achieves.

Approach – What is it we are trying to do in order to address the issue?

Deployment – How widely is the approach used across the organization?

Assessment – Do we ever think about how appropriate the approach is?

Review – Can we/do we measure success of the approach?

An example of the kind of format in which information could be collected is as follows:

Table 6.2 Recording the outcomes of the process

Review your descriptions of the approaches as a whole, then record your views on where things have been successful, where improvements could be made and actions to be taken based on this analysis

Strengths (+) Areas for improvement (–)

Activity 6.2

Use the 'How' questions above (Areas to address) to find out how your organization acquires and uses information. What are the strengths and weaknesses of its approach and how could it be improved?

Introduction to marketing research

Market research is a cost-effective way of finding out what people believe, want, need or do. It is information that cannot usually be obtained from any other source. Until recently, limited budgets kept most types of market research out of reach of small organizations, but through the Internet there are more research options. The most important role of market research is to minimize risk by researching a product or service before it reaches the market. Thus, market research is a fundamental part of the marketing planning process.

Marketing research

This links the consumer, customer and public to the marketer through information used to:

- o Identify and define marketing opportunities and problems.
- o Generate, refine, identify and evaluate marketing actions.
- o Monitor marketing performance.
- o Improve understanding of marketing as a process.

Market research

- o Specifies the information required to address these issues.
- o Designs the method for collecting information.
- o Manages and implements the data collection process.
- o Analyses the results.
- o Communicates the findings and their implications.

Source: American Marketing Association.

The term 'marketing research' covers market research, marketing research, product research and research to support pricing, distribution and promotional activity. Market research is used to supply information about the market for particular products and services. Therefore, market research has a narrower focus compared to marketing research.

Characteristics of good marketing research

Scientific method – The principles are careful observation, formulation of hypotheses, prediction and testing.

Research creativity – Research should develop innovative ways to solve a problem.

Multiple methods – The research should use more than one method to increase confidence in the results.

Interdependence of models and data – A recognition that data is interpreted from underlying models that guide the type of information sought.

Value and cost of information – A concern for estimating the value of the research against its cost. Costs are easy to determine but the value of the research is harder to ascertain.

Ethical marketing – Marketing research should be conducted according to a recognized code of practice that respects informants.

The most important distinguishing characteristics of marketing research are that:

- o Its primary objective is to apply research methods to the collection of information that will help in describing and understanding markets, planning strategies and monitoring outcomes.
- o In most cases, it achieves this by studying relatively small, and usually representative, samples of the relevant populations.
- o It is primarily, but not exclusively, concerned with analysing and reporting on aggregated groupings of those interviewed; it does not report information which can be linked to identifiable individuals.

o It guarantees the confidentiality of the information provided by respondents. Such information can be disclosed only with the respondent's consent, and then only for research purposes and to research organizations involved in the project.

Marketing research is concerned with a one-way channel of communication, from respondents to the client via the confidential filter of the researcher. It does not provide a facility for any form of commercial or similar communication in the opposite direction, from client to individual respondent, nor does it seek to influence the respondent's views or behaviour as a result of the research.

The characteristics of direct marketing are different from those of marketing research

o The primary objective of direct marketing is to conduct promotional and selling activities directed at specific individuals and organizations. Marketing analysis provides aggregated and cross-analysed information of various kinds – but this is normally a secondary rather than the primary objective of collecting the data, and does not affect the other characteristics of direct marketing referred to here.

o It normally involves the collection and use of personal data from very large numbers of the general population or from as many as possible of a specific group (e.g. customers). The emphasis is on maximizing the total number of the target audience covered rather than on the representativeness of the final data.

o The data collected is purposely stored and made use of on an individually identified, disaggregated basis since it would not otherwise be fully exploitable in direct marketing.

o Since the personal data collected is permanently linked to the individuals who have supplied the data, there can normally be no guarantee of anonymity. In many cases, the personal data will be made available to a variety of users, most often for non-research purposes such as promotion and direct selling.

o Unlike marketing research, direct marketing is usually a two-way process whereby the individual who provides the data receives promotional and/or sales approaches based on the use of that data. Direct marketing is a form of 'commercial communication'.

Stages in the marketing research process

Stage 1 – Defining the marketing problem to be addressed and research objectives

This includes specifying the objectives of the specific research project or projects, to formulate the problem precisely. The art is to strike a balance between too broad and too narrow a definition of a problem. Too broad a definition can lead to a lot of information that is superfluous, whilst too narrow a definition means that some necessary information about issues that impact on the subject is not collected. It depends on how much is known about the problem. If relatively little is known, exploratory research may be used, for example qualitative research as well as secondary research. Some research is causal – its purpose is to test a cause and effect relationship. A marketing problem needs to be formulated as a marketing research problem. So, for example, a marketing problem might be that sales are too low but the marketing research problem could be to assess customer perception of the price of the product in terms of its perceived value relative to the competition.

Sometimes, a researcher will be designing a research programme according to a research brief. However, the brief may not exist in a definitive form, and the researcher may need to work with the client to refine it and make sure that it can be operationalized.

Research briefs

When drafting a research brief for an agency to respond, as much detail as possible should be given. This helps to refine and clarify thinking about the project, including the target audience, the kinds of questions and issues that ought to be addressed, and why. Specify the deliverables expected. Below is a checklist of questions which could be used by the researcher to draw out the background to design a research programme.

Checklist to guide a researcher when taking a brief

History

- ○ How long has the company been established?
- ○ How long has it concentrated on its present product/service range?
- ○ Has the company always been sited in its present location?
- ○ What factors have influenced its location?

Company background

- ○ What is the principal business of the company? What are its subsidiary activities?
- ○ What is its total turnover?
- ○ Describe any holding companies/subsidiary companies.
- ○ How many employees are there at the establishment?

Product details

- ○ What are the important products (or services) in the range (by size, capacity, shape, material, etc.)?
- ○ What proportion of the total turnover does each of the above groups account for?
- ○ To what extent are the products standard/custom built?
- ○ What proportion of an assembled product is made in-house or bought out?
- ○ How important are spares in terms of revenue versus profit?
- ○ Are any of the products built under licence?

Pricing

- ○ What are the prices for each of the important products or services?
- ○ How do prices compare with those of the competition?
- ○ Is there a published price list?
- ○ What is the discount policy?
- ○ What power does the sales representative have to alter prices?
- ○ How price-sensitive is the product?

Sales force

- ○ Number of representatives.
- ○ Are they a general or a specialized sales force – in what way are they specialized?
- ○ How many calls a day do they make?
- ○ Does the salesforce bring back orders or, are they sent in independently?

Markets

- ○ What are the major user markets for the products?
- ○ What proportion of total sales are to each of these markets?

○ Are any markets known for the product, where the company currently does not/cannot sell?

○ Which markets are believed to offer the greatest scope for expansion of sales?

Decision makers

○ Who are the key decision makers who specify and buy this type of product? What roles do they play?

○ What do decision makers look for from suppliers? PROBE price, quality, delivery, sales service?

Competition

○ Who are the most important competitors? Where are they based?

○ What is their rank order/market share?

○ What is each company's (including the client's) perceived strengths and weaknesses?

○ To what extent do competitors rely upon this market for their turnover and profit?

Quality

○ Where does the product fit against the competition in its quality?

○ What are the special features of its quality?

○ Where is it weak on quality?

○ How long will the product last?

○ When it finally fails, why will it do so?

Deliveries

○ What is the current delivery period?

○ What is the competition's delivery?

○ What is the ideal delivery?

Distribution

○ How is the product distributed?

○ What proportion goes direct/indirect? What is the policy which leads to this split (e.g. size of account – OEM versus replacement, etc.)?

○ What are distributors' margins?

○ What other products do distributors sell?

○ Do distributors actively sell, or just take orders?

○ Who are the major distributors

 – used by the company?
 – not used by the company?

○ What is the average size of a direct account and a distributor account?

Promotion

○ How big is the promotional budget?

○ How does this break down between: (a) media (b) exhibitions (c) PR (d) print (e) direct mail (f) websites?

○ Which media are used? Which are most successful?

○ What proportion of sales leads come from promotion? How many? What is their quality?

○ Which exhibitions are attended? What is their perceived value?

○ What opportunities exist for e-commerce?

Other data

Full details of names (initials as well) of persons present at briefing; date of briefing; address of company; address to which proposals should be sent; how many copies of the proposal are required to be sent.

Preparing a research proposal

Having received the brief, the researcher, whether in-house or from an agency, must submit a written proposal to the sponsor which states an appreciation of the problem, the objectives, the research method and the timing. If an agency is preparing the proposal, a statement of cost must be given. An in-house job may omit this but many managers still like to see an estimate as a benchmark to compare with other surveys and as a perspective that they can use to relate to the size of any decision which may be taken. If the proposal is accepted, it becomes the contract between the researcher and the sponsor.

The following case study is an extract from one of the many produced by the US Department of Commerce. Note what it says about the importance of language even though English is spoken in both countries. When conducting market research that has an international focus, all the cultural factors that were mentioned in previous units need to be taken into account.

Entering the UK market

The British still tend to buy package tours put together and advertised in catalogues and brochures by tour operators. Travel agents use these catalogues and brochures to help clients choose where to go and to decide virtually every detail of their vacation.

Tour operators and travel agents therefore are pivotal in the U.K. travel industry. Consumer marketing should be the last, never the first, step.

It can be a costly error to assume that, because English is a shared language, materials developed for the U.S. market are automatically suitable for use in the U.K.

Many words have subtly or radically different meanings in U.K. and American English, which can lead to confusion or misunderstanding. For example, 'cheap' in American parlance is often used to mean 'inexpensive'. To a Briton, however, 'cheap' means 'shoddy'. 'Homely' to an American means 'ugly'; to a Briton it has the very positive meaning of 'homelike'. 'Mean' to an American means 'unkind', while to a Briton it means 'tight with money'.

Source: STAT-USA on the Internet, US Department of Commerce, http://strategis.ic.gc.ca/.

Stage 2 – Develop the research plan and determine research design

This involves developing an efficient plan for gathering the necessary information. A marketing manager needs to know the cost of the research before agreeing it can go ahead. One of the issues to be considered is what is the need for primary and/or secondary research. If primary research is needed, then what type? Research design specifies the type of research required. Secondary research usually precedes primary research to see whether the problem that needs to be investigated can be addressed without having to spend resources on acquiring primary data.

Exploratory research

The goal of exploratory market research is discovery. The underlying questions are 'What is new?' and 'What are we missing?'. The goal of confirmatory techniques is resolution: 'Is this the right choice?' 'What results can we expect?'. Exploratory market research is used to broaden a vision, whilst confirmatory research is used to narrow options and concentrate efforts (McQuarrie, 1996).

Exploratory and confirmatory market research techniques are used at different stages in a research project's decision cycle (Table 6.3). The decision cycle calls for sequential market research activities and questions as the research design and strategy are developed and implemented. Each activity requires different market research techniques as the researcher's informational needs change from initial exploratory information to final confirmatory information.

The four decision cycle activities in Table 6.3 are further described in relation to each activity's objectives and suggested market research techniques.

Research design

Table 6.3 Four decision cycle activities

Activity/Questions	Objectives	Techniques
Scan the environment How are we doing? What is going on? Supporting: Focus groups, surveys	Identify, describe, monitor	Main: Secondary research, user visits
Generate options What are the possibilities? Supporting: Secondary research	Generate, define, explore	Main: User visits, focus groups
Select an option What is the explanation? Which option is best? Supporting: Secondary research	Evaluate, test, select, prioritize	Main: Experiments, surveys, choice models, usability tests
Evaluate success What will we achieve? How are we doing? Supporting: User visits	Measure, track, assess	Main: Surveys, secondary research

Source: Adapted from McQuarrie (1996, p. 24).

A survey of the literature will usually precede all research designs.

This is to:

- ○ Learn from previous research in the area.
- ○ Prevent expensive primary research being undertaken when research results are available.

Surveys of people with particular experience, or knowledge of the subject under investigation should be undertaken. For example, interviews of commercial directors to find out about trends in football merchandising. Examine the best and the worst examples to see if any conclusions may be made. For instance, a detailed investigation of top and bottom salespeople to try to understand the factors that contribute to success or failure.

- o Repeated investigations over time; for example, monthly opinion surveys of consumers.
- o Single investigation; for example, a single survey of 100 business leaders to find out their attitudes to the training of their employees. Field experiments are carried out in the normal context, such as in a store, while a laboratory experiment is undertaken in an artificial environment.
- o A field experiment is where, for example, the store changes the price of products in store and assesses changes in the quantity and value purchased. In this context, the experiment is in a normal environment and the consumer is unaware that it is taking place.

Sampling

Organizations will target specified customer groups for their marketing activity. These customer groups, or segments, will be the basis on which any marketing research is undertaken. They will be the focus of any sampling activity. The potential population in this context could be any target group ranging from large populations, such as the potential purchasers of television sets, to relatively small markets, such as widescreen plasma TV sets. Sampling allows conclusions to be drawn about the wider market, without the need to talk to everyone in the marketplace. Sampling estimates the numbers, attributes and beliefs of a population. The key to a good sample is to define the population of customers that are of interest and to select enough random members of that population. If the attitudes of buyers to a new type of hand-held computer were needed before planning a marketing campaign, the target population will be those who are affluent. This target population could be found, for example, by buying a mailing list from a computer magazine and specifying postcodes in a 30-mile radius of the store with the highest incomes.

However, what you really need to know is who has the highest disposable income with an interest in electronic gadgets. This may not coincide with the most affluent. A young person in a well-paid job, living at home with his parents may have more disposable income than an older person with twice the annual income. Therefore, you might want to cross-refer salary data with other data relating to marital status and age. However, marital status is not much of a guide to anything because many people are unmarried but living with partners. These latter points serve to illustrate the complexity of some of the factors when drawing up a relevant valid and reliable sample. The main decisions to be made when selecting a sample are:

1. The process by which the sample is to be selected is known as the sample design. The quality of all statistical analyses and procedures is governed by the quality of the sample data. If the sample data is not representative of the population, analysing the data and drawing conclusions from it will be unproductive and invalid. A representative sample will require the introduction of randomness in the sampling procedure.
2. From which list to draw a sample? This involves selecting a sample frame (i.e. a list of all members of the population) – unless people are just being interviewed randomly in the street.
3. How large a sample to select?

Sample design

The main approaches to sample design:

- o Non-probability sample design.
- o Probability sample design.

A key issue is the cost of sampling versus the benefits. The main difference between probability and non-probability sampling is that with the former the result of a sample can be projected to the whole population whereas this cannot be done with non-probability samples.

Probability samples

Probability sampling requires the researcher to know the size of the population, and for each individual in the population to have a known and equal chance of being selected (using a sampling frame). The most commonly used sampling frames are telephone numbers and postcodes. There are four major ways to contact those being surveyed:

1. Telephone
2. Personal (e.g. door to door)
3. Mail
4. Internet.

Telephone, mail and e-mail provide the most control over the characteristics of those who are surveyed. The Internet and e-mail are the cheapest, and the respondents may not be representative of your target population.

Random sample – Everyone has the same chance. The advantage of the random sample is that it is the best representation of the population that can be obtained. The disadvantage is the difficulty of obtaining an entire population list. It works better with a small population because it is easier to get hold of that list.

What does it mean to be random?

Stratified random sample – The population is divided into groups/levels of interest, for example socio-economic status. This is a more representative type of sample.

Cluster sampling – This is based on sub-sets of the population, for example geographic regions.

Non-probability samples

These are samples in which you do not know what is the chance of being selected. The precise size of a population or even who is in the population is not known. Examples of non-probability samples include:

Convenience sample – Samples are selected for interviews based on the ease of finding a sample from the researchers' point of view, that is from their convenience. They are not random and they use readily available subjects, for example students.

Quota sample – Respondents are recruited because they possess particular characteristics – perhaps they may be selected on the basis of age or gender if these are believed to be important influencing factors in purchase decisions. Different individuals with different characteristics are sampled to meet the quota – for example gender: 50 male, 50 female. This type of sample design attempts to reflect key attributes of the general population in the selection of the sample to be researched. It is a common sampling technique used by commercial marketing research companies.

Judgement sampling – In this approach, the researcher believes that the results of the research will be improved if some judgement is exercised in selecting a sample, may be by asking 'experts'.

Stage 3 – Data collection methods

Market research works because, by talking to a relatively small number of people, it is possible to find out about a far larger number, but it only works if the people who are interviewed (the sample) are a representative subgroup of the total group of interest (the universe), and if the right questions are asked. The universe might be the population as a whole or, parents, car drivers, the elderly, shoppers, voters, IT managers and so on.

There are four basic data collection methods employed for surveys: (1) personal interviews (2) telephone interviews (3) mail surveys and (4) Web-based surveys. The choice of the data collection method will depend on the objectives of the survey, and the relative importance of factors such as level of accuracy required, the amount of data to be collected, the sample bias acceptable, the budget required, speed and any administrative issues.

Primary data is information collected for a specific purpose

An example is the research required to identify the market for an innovative new product. It is unlikely that such research has previously been undertaken. Therefore, it is specially commissioned and, generally, the results belong to the organization commissioning the work. However, some research firms will conduct limited and less expensive primary research with the requirement that they can make the results available to other companies. More affordable primary research methods – both qualitative and quantitative – are available online as well. Inexpensive ways to conduct qualitative research via the Internet are through do-it-yourself online focus groups.

Compared with primary research, secondary research is generally:

- ○ Quicker
- ○ Cheaper
- ○ Less relevant to the topic under investigation
- ○ Out of date if it refers to fast-changing contexts or issues.

As someone else has conducted the secondary research, users of this material must look carefully at how the data was derived and how valid and reliable are the conclusions.

The following case study is an example of primary research with a difference. Does this count as market research?

Case study

What women want?

Leslie Blodgett uses QVC to sell cosmetics, and to reach out to customers who tell her what sells and what doesn't. Using on air calls to cosmetic groupies in private homes, Blodgett asks viewers what they like and don't like, what new products might work, what old ones should come back. Blodgett claims that the ivory tower marketing research ruins brands because they are so far away from the customer.

Source: Forbes, 12 November 2001, p. 124.

(A) Activity 6.3

What do you see as the advantages and disadvantages of this kind of research? What kind of factors would you need to guard against before deciding to invest in developing new products?

Competitive analysis of French children's clothing market

New products should be aggressively marketed to appeal to French children's tastes and to influence their fashion preferences. The media has a tremendous impact on French children. Music and television are influential at an early age, and are thus excellent means for promoting products that are specifically directed towards children. According to analysts, children spend an average of 2 hours per day watching television. Additionally, 25 per cent of French children have their own television sets. US imports are expected to grow, given the fact that French children are greatly influenced by American trends and television. The easy-to-wear clothing of American colleges and the street wear of large cities appear especially attractive to French children. As a result, US products such as T-shirts, polos and jackets with names of football teams or American colleges are in high demand. Proof of the success of American brands in France can be seen in the opening of a Gap store for children in Paris. There appears to be numerous opportunities for US companies to successfully penetrate the French children's wear market.

(A) Activity 6.4

Identify secondary research sources for your organization's products, services and markets. List specific reports that would be useful for marketing.

Evaluating secondary information

1. *What was the purpose of the study*? – Was it undertaken by an impartial source or by a pressure group that is attempting to put across a particular point?
2. *Who collected the information*? – In the UK, it is possible to obtain statistics on the number of vegetarians from the Vegetarian Society or from the meat industry. These two sources of information do not provide the same estimate for the number of vegetarians!
3. *What information was collected*? – Figures from two sources may differ because of the use of different sources of information, or because different timescales are used. However, sometimes it can be because each wants to prove a point.
4. *When was the information collected*? – If there has been a recent food scare, for example mad cow disease, consumption levels of beef will be low and consumption of substitutes will be high.
5. *Is the information consistent with other information*? – Most secondary information tends to be quantitative rather than qualitative.

Quantitative data

- o Tends to be on large numbers of people.
- o Findings are expressed numerically.
- o Concerned with 'how many', 'how often' and 'what' rather than 'why'.
- o Quantitative research problem: How many consumers buy the company's shampoo?

Qualitative
- ○ Fewer people.
- ○ Deals with data that is difficult to quantify – concerned with 'why' rather than 'how many', or 'how often'.
- ○ Concerned with attitudes and motivations.
- ○ Qualitative research problem: What shape of bottle do consumers find appropriate for the brand values we are trying to communicate?

Primary research
There are four main types of primary research:

1. Surveys
2. Observation
3. Experimentation
4. Simulation.

Personal interviews
Benefits

- ○ Interviewer can select a good quality sample.
- ○ Interviewer can interpret strange answers and ask for clarification.
- ○ The interviewer can classify interviewees to save time.
- ○ Longer questionnaires can be asked with this method.
- ○ Can use visual images.

Problems

- ○ Costly.
- ○ Possible interviewer bias.
- ○ Possibility of fake interviews.

Focus groups
This is one of the most frequently used techniques in marketing research. Successful research requires a skilled moderator (i.e. the person who directs the topics of discussion and creates a balanced environment to encourage the contribution of all members of the group). Members of the focus group should be selected from the target population for the firm's products and services.

Benefits

- ○ A wide range of ideas can be obtained.
- ○ In-depth understanding of consumer attitudes and purchase motivations may be obtained.
- ○ Ideal when managers are looking for ideas or need to clarify some details.
- ○ A certain synergy can be obtained from a group discussion that allows a deeper probing of issues.
- ○ Can use visual images.
- ○ Relatively easy to record (video and audio tape) for future analysis.

Problems

- ○ Costly.
- ○ Success is highly dependent on the skill of the interviewer and on the selection of the sample to attend the focus group.
- ○ Possible problem of domination of the group by a strong and forceful individual, which will result in group conflict or only the views of the forceful individual being obtained.

Focus groups can be used to cover a variety of topics, but they are best used to understand 'why' a particular group feels or acts in a particular way. If an interviewee says something of particular interest during a focus group, the interviewer can probe deeper into the topic, uncovering the information. Topics often covered in focus groups include reactions to product ideas and product prototypes, messaging tests, ad testing and customer-needs identification. The groups are taped (video and audio) for later analysis and can be observed during the focus group – either at a specially designed facility, or via a videoconference or Web-based hook-up when the session proceedings can be viewed remotely. Sometimes hard-to-reach people will not come to a focus group but they may be reached by depth interviews which are one-on-one discussions with a researcher. While qualitative data is very accessible, it can fall short on reliability.

Telephone surveys

Benefits

- Quick and easy to do.
- Reach geographically dispersed sample.
- Ease of sampling, for example random digit dialling.
- Complex routing through questionnaire is automated.
- Low cost.
- Possibility of recording to confirm that interview took place.

Problems

- Method can only handle very short, simple questionnaires.
- Sample obtained can be biased, depending on the type of people who are willing to complete a telephone interview.
- Lack of access to households without telephones.

Insight

Skills survey

It is billed as the largest fact-finding mission of its type, the mother of all surveys – so big that it will take not one but a trio of polling organizations to pull it off. Squads of questioners will be bashing the phones of 70 000 employers of all sizes across England asking whether or not they train their workforces, how and why. No doubt it will yield an unprecedented cornucopia of data. But is it all necessary? There seems to be a rough consensus that, despite all the quizzing of industry and the results this throws up such as the Labour Force surveys produced by the Office of National Statistics, there are things we still need to know; the sorts of data which are reputedly easily available in the Netherlands and Germany. The CBI director applauds the new survey, 'I think it's good that they are drilling down in more depth.' However, there are some sceptics who feel that we need to know the fine detail of the sorts of training that people are getting, how well it fits their needs and how likely it is to raise their skills levels. However, they feel that this is the sort of information that won't be gleaned from a telephone survey. The researchers who conducted a survey of mathematical skills in the workplace said, 'What we found out, we found out by talking to people on the shopfloor. There's absolutely no way we would have got that depth of information from a telephone survey. They concluded that it was vital to ask open-ended questions rather than the typical questionnaire enquiries which ask the respondent to select one of a range of ready-made answers.

Source: Adapted from Questions Remain, Peter Kingston, *Guardian*, 18 March 2003.

(A) Activity 6.5

What do you think of the advantages and disadvantages of using a telephone survey for this kind of work? Do you think the sceptics are being unrealistic in expecting in-depth interviews in the workplace, or do they have a point?

Postal surveys
Benefits

- ○ Low cost.
- ○ Ease of contacting geographically dispersed sample.
- ○ More complex questions can be asked.

Problems

- ○ Usually quite a low response rate.
- ○ The interviewee can misinterpret the questions.
- ○ It can take a long time to get back replies.
- ○ Minimal chance of interpreting the extent to which the respondent is answering truthfully.

Internet surveys
Benefits

- ○ Very fast: instant analysis may be undertaken.
- ○ Very low cost.
- ○ Highly targeted.
- ○ Ease of contacting the sample.

Problems

- ○ Method can only handle very short, simple questionnaires.
- ○ Very limited potential for 'open' questions.
- ○ People with access to the Internet are not representative of the total population for all markets. They tend to be higher income and higher socio-economic groups. This is less of a problem for business–Internet surveys.

Qualitative approaches
- ○ Fewer people.
- ○ Deals with data difficult to quantify – concerned with 'why' rather than 'how many', or 'how often'.
- ○ Concerned with attitudes and motivations.

Some of the more important criteria, when selecting research method, include:

- ○ Cost
- ○ Speed
- ○ Access to target population (including ability to sample the target population)
- ○ Type of questions that can be asked
- ○ Quantity of data
- ○ Response rate.

Qualitative research tends to be exploratory and directional in nature. It is designed to bring out issues associated with the subject matter as well as the best general direction to proceed. Qualitative methods can be useful in all stages of development and are very tangible to marketers and developers.

Observation

This is literally where the individual's behaviour is monitored and recorded. One of the most popular applications of this technique recently is in researching in-store shopping. Consumer movement through the store is observed and recorded. Researchers have been able to classify individuals in supermarkets according to their speed of movement through the store, their willingness to scan the shelves for products and to divert from a pre-planned shopping list, where one exists.

In-depth interviews involve one-to-one contact with respondents and are usually conducted face to face, although telephone interviews are sometimes used. The in-depth interview is different from the tightly structured interview used in quantitative surveys or opinion polls – it is not only longer (45–60 minutes), but also more discursive and open-ended. The interviewer also has a greater level of flexibility since they are not constrained by the order or wording of questions; she or he is able to cover the issues specified in the topic guide in a more context-sensitive way, as they 'naturally' emerge, and to probe responses to gain a full understanding of their meaning and/or implications.

Experimentation

This is where the researcher attempts to establish causality between two factors by varying one factor and holding all other factors constant.

Laboratory experiments

Laboratory experiments take place in an artificial environment created by the researcher, which allows one factor to be varied. For example, an advert can be placed within a magazine that has been created specially for research purposes. Consumers can be given the magazine to look through, and are then asked to comment on the advertising. If unfavourable comments are made, then the advert is changed and consumers are asked to repeat the procedure. In this way, researchers are able to assess changes in advertising on consumer response.

Field experiments

Field experiments take place in a more natural environment. Researchers often change a factor in order to observe the influence on purchase quantity/sales revenue. Examples of experimentation in a retail environment include changing:

- Shelf location
- Price
- Pack design
- Sales promotion activity.

As each of these factors is varied, the researcher observes the effect on sales volume and on revenue.

Simulation

Simulation is where researchers build a model (usually a computer model) of an environment and use this as the basis for experimentation. Simulation is employed when a problem is judged to be too complex for ease of mathematical formulation. In building a simulation, the researcher sets the framework (parameters) of the model and within that framework, the researcher or business manager may experiment.

Insight

The power of images

Pictures selected by tongue-tied shoppers can help companies learn what consumers really want. When words fail, the images consumers choose can serve as a window into their thoughts. These images can be used to tap non-verbal reactions and to probe below the surface for deeper feelings. The insights gleaned can be incorporated into marketing campaigns that resonate with consumers on an emotional level.

Source: *American Demographics*, November 2001, p. 32.

Cross-section versus longitudinal research

Researchers need to be clear about the type of data they require. Cross-sectional data is where a 'snapshot' picture of the current situation is obtained. A survey undertaken this month reports on the situation *as it is* for this month. For various reasons, the results may not be relevant at any other time. Longitudinal data is obtained over a period of time, often over many years.

Tracking studies

A tracking study may involve conducting a survey every month, or even every week, to establish and track consumer reaction. In such studies, advertising managers want to assess the peak level of response, such as awareness, and the rate at which this decays between advertising activity. As longitudinal research is very expensive for individual companies to buy, groups of companies join together to purchase the same data using 'syndicated research'.

Syndicated research

Only companies within the syndicate have access to the data. A relatively low-cost method of collecting 'cross-sectional data usually' is the omnibus survey. A company will run a regular survey (say, every month) with a specified target population. Often a theme is specified, such as financial services or children. Any company is then able to pay to add their own questions.

Stage 4 – Data collection

The most common approach to collecting information is the questionnaire. There are two main types of questions used in questionnaires: open questions and closed questions.

Open questions are used when the researcher wants to explore some ideas. They may be used when trying to design a new product or explore consumer opinion about the company brand, for example what features would you like in a robot vacuum cleaner?

Closed questions are most frequently used to count the number of people who exhibit a particular trait.

Closed question, for example:

Do you buy products made by the firm?

- ○ Never?
- ○ Once per year?
- ○ Once per month?
- ○ More frequently than once per month.

There are many types of closed and open questions. Some closed questions are able to achieve more than simply a count of people or attributes. They may be used to investigate attitudes held by consumers, in particular the intensity of attitude.

Closed questions
Closed questions may include two (dichotomous) or more (multichotomous) options from which the respondent selects an answer.

Semantic differential scale
Semantic differential scale respondents are presented with a set of bipolar adjectives and asked to indicate the point on the scale which best describes the intensity of their feelings.

Open questions
Open questions gather ideas and attitudes but they are time-consuming to analyse and require knowledgeable analysts.

Open questions invite facts and opinions, whereas closed questions seek either the answer 'yes' or 'no'.

The danger of using too many closed questions is that they:

- ○ Prevent people from expressing views
- ○ Restrict the flow of information.

Simple open questions
These leave the respondent free to answer as they wish.

Leading questions
These are phrased in such a way that makes it clear that you only expect one answer: 'I'm sure we all agree that...?' 'Isn't it true that...?' 'Don't you think that...?'. They are to be avoided because they can cause resentment at trying to put words into their mouths or trying to persuade them, against their own judgement, to agree with you. Ultimately, the data gathered is flawed because it may not represent what the respondent really thinks or believes.

Multiple questions
People can only answer one question at a time, so do not fall into the trap of issuing a stream of questions, such as:

'What's the situation with ... and how will we ... and when by?'.

Listening
Questioning skills will not bring results unless equally effective listening skills are being practised. There are three levels of listening:

1. Hearing the words – You must be able to actually hear and understand the words that are being spoken.
2. Understanding the meaning – You must understand the overall meaning.
3. Perceiving the inference – You must be able to perceive the inferences that lie behind the words.

193

Influence of Researcher

When listening, and when you are being listened to, you should be aware of the stream of signals which are given off by somebody who is speaking. These verbal and non-verbal signals can transmit a significantly different message to other members of the meeting than the literal meaning of the spoken words.

Facial expression – If the speaker's expression does not match the words, it is the expression which carries more weight.

Body language – Shrugged shoulders or dismissive hand gestures have the same impact as facial expression.

Tone of voice – Listeners can perceive strong signals through tone of voice and emphasis on certain words. The tone of voice, consciously or subconsciously, can significantly influence the way in which the question is perceived. For example, the question: 'Do you think this is achievable?' is apparently a neutral, closed question which seeks without expectation the answer 'yes' or 'no'. However, in a different tone, it could also imply that there is the slightest chance that the results can be achieved. Conversely, the same question spoken in an enthusiastic voice would convey the impression that you were looking for a 'yes!' If you want the honest opinion of other members, you should take care to keep any expectation – either positive or negative – out of your voice.

Stage 5 – Present the findings

The market research report should present findings that are relevant to the major marketing decisions facing management.

Online research

Online research covers all digital interactive media, including digital TV, WAP and new entertainment technologies. Online research can be appropriate if the target market is visitors to a specific website or Internet-users in general – but it is still not a medium for general public surveys. This may change eventually as penetration grows among women and older groups. Internet research has an advantage for surveys among staff, employees and customers or subscribers to online services in any situation where the universe is known, and the e-mail addresses are available and up to date. Business e-mail addresses tend to be less volatile compared to consumers. The barriers to conducting online research are very low. The most important issue for research is declining respondent co-operation rates. Approaches like showing interactive stimuli material such as clips from ads all work well on the Internet. But while it is feasible to show TV clips, they can slow download times. With interactive digital TV, there is a lot more potential.

Case study

Online research

It is part of our mission at the Future Foundation to continually seek to innovate new research techniques both at the analysis stage and at the point of data collection. Online research can be used very successfully in our opinion if linked directly to specific sites, for example for site U&As, or if respondents are recruited through other means and then directed to a site to answer a questionnaire. Moving onto qualitative research, we have conducted both online groups and moderated e-mail groups for clients for a range of different projects. For example, for BT we invited a group of people who make purchases on the Internet to a group discussion in a moderated chat room. These individuals had been recruited using traditional techniques from sampling points all around the country. They had undergone a two-stage one-to-one interviewing process both face to face and on the telephone. The third stage was conducted online because it represented the most logical way of getting this group together for a discussion. We have utilized the moderated e-mail groups where more detail is required. We ask respondents a question, which we send to them by e-mail. All the replies are summarized and sent back to every member of the group who then responds again the next day. These groups take place over the course of 1 or 2 weeks. This technique does result in less interaction between group members but on the plus side the level of detail supplied by respondents in their answers can be better than any other research technique – both online and offline.

Source: http://www.futurefoundation.net/

Computer-assisted interviewing (CAI)

Computer assisted interviewing involves the use of a computer to collect, store, manipulate and transmit data relating to interviews conducted between the interviewer and the respondent(s).

Computer-assisted personal interviewing (CAPI)

Computer assisted personal interviewing (personal interview by an interviewer using a portable computer at the home or business of the respondent) is one component of CAI. Other components include computer-assisted telephone interviewing (CATI) and Computer-assisted self-interviewing (CASI). The three chief theoretical benefits of CAPI are: better quality, improved timeliness and lower cost after the initial investment. Computer-assisted personal interviewing has the potential to provide improvements in the areas of data quality, survey timeliness and cost effectiveness, but cost savings directly attributable to CAPI are less well documented than the other benefits. On large-scale continuous surveys and on other operations where the hardware can be efficiently utilized and the costs spread over time, net savings might be expected but otherwise the costs might well be greater for CAPI. Computer-assisted personal interviewing also provides the opportunity to apply experimental design principles to survey testing, and the flexibility to enable collection of important policy-related data for difficult topics.

Online focus groups

An online focus group is essentially a formal chat session. A trained moderator leads a group of participants through a predetermined discussion over the Internet. Participants are often recruited through a research firm's own panel and are paid a fee for participating. A focus group could be set up inexpensively by using a chat room and recruiting your own participants. If a panel is used, the following checklist is useful to note.

Case study

Online panel users

A good online panel can offer real advantages over other approaches. But how do you know it's a good panel?

Here's a checklist of questions to ask a panel supplier.

Recruitment sources – How are the panel members found? What biases does this recruitment approach build in?

Screening – Are prospective panel members screened (off-line) to confirm age, residence, and so on? Many panel members belong to several different panels, to the point where some have become almost professional respondents.

Representative membership – How well does the profile of panel members match an independently derived profile of net users as a whole? Is there a bias toward the heavier or more experienced users?

Maintenance of representativeness – What steps has the panel supplier taken to ensure that the membership profile remains up to date? Drop-out and the changing profile of net users can lead to biases in the panel membership, if it is not regularly monitored.

Sampling methods – How are samples drawn from the panel membership? Is it a random sample from the whole database? Are quotas or over-sampling used to allow for differential response rates?

Differential response rates – What monitoring has the agency done on differential response rates? Some people respond every time, some rarely, so that the achieved sample for any survey may be biased, even if the panel as a whole is representative.

Survey frequency – How often are panel members asked to complete surveys? Professional respondents are not representative.

Lifestyle profiling – Are panel members profiled according to lifestyle criteria? If not, the panel could be less cost-effective if you are only interested in, for example people who have booked travel online, or people who regularly work from home. http://www.mori.com/pubinfo/nep-onlineresearch.shtml

Source: http://www.mori.com/pubinfo/nep-onlineresearch.shtml Online Research – ESOMAR Research World Interview.

Feedback forms

A simple way to conduct ongoing qualitative research is through a feedback form. You can gain valuable insight by asking website visitors for suggestions, and/or asking them their opinions. You can do this through a form directly on your site and/or via e-mail to those on your opt-in list.

Primary quantitative market research

Quantitative research is used when you are looking for hard numbers and precision. To produce a top-quality primary quantitative research study, you must generally work through a research agency. For a small-budget business, this type of research is expensive. The Internet has made more inexpensive means of data collection and analysis possible. With the help of software or Web-based tools, you can perform research through customer surveys and collect visitor-use patterns through Web logs.

Customer surveys

The Internet has made conducting surveys quicker and less expensive. Options range from do-it-yourself programmes to research services with screened panels. You can use surveys in a variety of ways – segmenting your customers, improving/developing your product or site and gauging brand awareness, for example.

Use patterns

Another approach to quantitative research on the Web is to look for visitor-use patterns such as routes taken through your site, pages viewed or ordering behaviour. By studying Web logs, you can know which pages are most popular, how visitors navigate through your site, common entry pages and where visitors often leave the site. You can also determine the number of different visitors to your site as well as the percentage of visitors converted to customers. By using a traffic-analysis service or software (often available through your hosting service), you can streamline the process. An alternative to conducting primary research is to find secondary research, or research that originated elsewhere. You can obtain secondary research either by purchasing the information or finding it through free resources.

Quantitative research

Quantitative research produces results that are more statistically accurate than qualitative research results. Often, companies first conduct qualitative research when developing a concept or looking for ideas, and later complete quantitative research to fine-tune and optimize. It is usually conducted via surveys or behavioural tracking. It is based on the principle that the characteristics of a randomly selected group of people will closely reflect the characteristics of the entire group from which the sample was taken. So, when marketers and site developers need to know, with relative certainty, the answers to specific questions, quantitative methods are used.

Insight

Quantitative research focuses on the left brain – objective, comfortable with logic, numbers and detailed, convergent reasoning rather than divergent reasoning. Qualitative research deals with the right brain – the hemisphere accountable for processing data such as words, emotions, feelings, colour and music. Traditional survey questionnaires are weak at eliciting follow-up data from respondents, as they usually require responses pre-categorized by the researcher. Often managers greeted the receipt of such surveys with the response 'So what?'. They answer questions related to such issues as market share, predicted revenue, statistical trends and past behaviour of customers well, but statistics are not good for answering questions about human behaviour, perceptions, future behaviour and involvement with a product. As a result of the need for companies to obtain richer data about their customers, prospective customers and the market as a whole, qualitative research became more in demand. While data collection techniques are now better developed, data analysis methodologies have not kept up. The new 'So what?' reaction from management is in response to the often confused summaries of the pages upon pages of focus group or interview transcripts. Running quantitative research alongside qualitative research offers a synergy whereby objective data can provide a structure to the analysis of subjective qualitative data. Generally, quantitative and qualitative research are presented as two separate entities. Yet, the smart market researcher knows how to combine both kinds of data.

Source: Adapted from: http://www.asiamarketresearch.com/columns/market5.htm.

The market research industry

The market research industry consists of hundreds of firms and consultancies. Each of these will have their own areas of specialization. The leading agencies, and many of the smaller ones, have directors and executives who are members of the Market Research Society. The Society has a Professional Code of Conduct which lays down rules and good practice with respect to their responsibilities to clients (confidentiality), respondents (anonymity), the public as a whole and to each other. The following case study demonstrates how market research is becoming more complex and needs to become more sophisticated to match the complexity of consumers' lives.

A case study in complexity

An overwhelming majority of marketers surveyed – 92 per cent – believe that marketing has become more complicated as a result of the complexity of consumers' lives. Media fragmentation is identified as the root of their frustration, with 67 per cent of marketers citing it as the driving force behind increased complexity. The modern marketer is faced with a dramatically increased number of channels and platforms to deal with. Two-fifths of marketers believe that the increase in the number of media outlets has made consumers' media consumption less predictable and fostered a decline in consumer loyalty. Marketers are increasingly concerned that targeted outlets, which aim to capture specific consumers, have increased confusion rather than offering clarity. Marketers have to balance the need to develop an overall communications strategy with the need to target niche groups. The relationship between market-ers and consumers embodies the complexity problem. The fragmentation of consumers' lives has led marketers to develop more sophisticated methods of marketing to reach them. This in turn has increased choice, making consumers' lives even more complex. Marketers are realizing that standard market research is no longer sufficient for understanding consumer needs. More than two-thirds of those surveyed agreed that there is a need for more innovative research, although only 20 per cent felt that they were already carrying out such research. Respondents to the survey believe that some companies are already getting it right: Tesco received the most praise, followed by Orange, Virgin, First Direct and EasyJet. Another interesting example is Ronseal, which is seen by marketers as a brand that achieves clarity and precision through the simplicity of its marketing.

Source: Adapted from *Marketing Week*, 18 September 2003, Caroline Parry, Emma Doniger and the Future Foundation.

On the theme of increased choice making consumers' lives ever more complex, the book *Sophisticated Consumers, Intricate Lifestyles, Simple Solutions* (Willmott and Nelson, 2003) reports how fourteen types of dental floss were found in one UK pharmacy, a similar range of brandies in a Spanish supermarket and there were eight kinds of orange juice available under the Tropicana brand alone.

Agency selection

It is possible to buy research and a reputable agency should give advice on the most cost-effective way of researching a target audience. It will discuss the advantages and disadvantages of different research options, and help to design and write questions. It will endeavour to achieve a representative sample and report the main findings in whatever form is preferred. The agency should also be willing to discuss the implications of any findings for the business.

Qualitative and quantitative market research: where the twain meet ...

Why can't advertising agencies and market researchers just get on?

Advertising agencies attract creative people, often innovators and independent thinkers who also often lack pragmatic and rational thinking. On the other hand, market research agencies attract a different sort of person – methodical and objective, often more introvert, detail-minded and conservative in outlook. Advertising agencies think they can do the research better than the market research agencies, and market research agencies think they can do the advertising better than the advertising agencies. Research departments within advertising agencies often lack power and crumble under the pressure of their more extrovert advertising colleagues at meetings. The reverse is true with research-based organizations that venture into advertising. It may be difficult for the extrovert, creative people who make up advertising agencies to listen to market researchers whose research suggests that a wonderfully original and unique ad may cause a negative reaction, and similarly it is difficult for researchers to get excited by new and paradigm-challenging ideas.

Source: http://www.asiamarketresearch.com/columns/market1.htm.

Rod Davies, Orient Pacific Century, 12 February 2000.

Rod Davies, Orient Pacific Century, October 2000.

The British Market Research Association (BMRA) website lists its member agencies with their specialisms. Smaller agencies are good for niche areas but larger agencies will tend to have specialists who focus on particular sectors, such as the voluntary sector, financial services, telecommunications, education, and so on.

Assessing the impact of marketing activity

Advertising
Pre-testing
Pre-testing is the showing of unfinished advertisementss to representative groups of the target audience.

Post-testing
Post-testing is concerned with the evaluation of a campaign once it has been released. Examples include the return of coupons, response cards, requests for further literature or actual orders. Recall tests attempt to assess how memorable particular advertisements are whilst recognition tests are based on the ability of respondents to reprocess information about an advertisement.

Evaluation of sales promotions

Evaluation methods include:

- *Consumer audits* – This will indicate if there has been a change in consumer behaviour as a result of the sales promotion campaign.
- *Sales information* – Increase in sales is one performance indicator.
- *Retail audits* – Specialist organizations can track changes in stock levels, distribution, market share immediately after the promotional campaign. This will provide an insight into the basis of an increase or decrease in sales.
- *Sales force feedback* – This is based on sales force feedback about the uptake of sales promotion opportunities in their area.
- *Voucher/coupon redemption* – Usually based on coding to relate response rate to sales promotion activities – this can be used to endorse the right selection of media, the right kind of sales promotion activity and potentially the most frequently used distribution outlet.

Evaluation of public relations

Haywood (1991) suggested that there are seven commonly used measures of results:

1. *Budget* – An assessment of whether the planned PR activity has been achieved within the budget defined and also within the timescales set.
2. *Awareness* – The measure of awareness can be quite complex and is most likely to be established through a range of marketing research activities to establish the level of brand awareness in the marketplace.
3. *Attitude* – Combined with research on brand awareness can be research on brand attitudes, whether they are positive or negative, and whether they have resulted in any change in consumer behaviour.
4. *Media coverage and tone* – First, it will be essential to establish the level of media coverage achieved as a result of planned-PR activities. Typical measures might include the number of different media which covered the case, the number of columns taken, key headings and perceived importance of the PR information. Second, the nature and tone in which the PR activities have been covered.
5. *Positioning* – Measuring the perception of the position of the organization versus that of the competition.
6. *Response generation* – Many of the enquiries or leads generated may be subject to some degree of code referencing, or sources of the enquiry will be recorded.
7. *Share price* – For large public companies, this is an indicator of public confidence in the organization.

Evaluation of direct and interactive marketing communications

Evaluation is related to the pre-determined objectives of a campaign.

Typical measures for successful implementation of the direct marketing campaign will include:

- Response rate
- Conversion rate
- Order value
- Repeat orders.

This information will be gathered through a range of voucher and campaign response codes that will be able to distinguish the source of the direct mail or promotion. This may establish the most popular direct marketing technique.

Technology is developing quickly and click-through rates are a common measure for online activity. However, this evaluates only behaviour not attitudes.

Evaluation of personal sales

Sales performance needs to be measured against objectives on a regular basis. Other factors relating to sales performance that can be measured include:

- Productivity – calls per day, calls per account, total number of orders versus calls.
- Account development – total of new accounts, total of existing accounts, growth of sales from existing accounts.
- Expenses – expenses versus number of calls made, cost per call.

Sales measurement techniques are becoming more sophisticated and more effective and the speed at which information becomes available is of the essence.

When assessing the impact of the marketing activity it is likely that a combination of measures will need to be used to support future expenditure. These could include:

- Sales growth
- Relationship measurement mechanism within centres (e.g. questionnaires)
- Qualitive and quantitive research
- Customer feedback mechanisms
- Footfall conversion measurement
- Indexed trading data (sales trends)
- Service charge savings
- Press cuttings with impact scoring mechanism (e.g. size of article)
- Car counting
- Dwell time measurement
- Frequency of customer visits
- Retailer demand for units
- Community relationships
- Retailer feedback mechanisms including surveys and retailer consultations
- Use of website, where appropriate.

Source: http://www.rics.org.uk/NR/rdonlyres/025B7E06-7F19-46F4-8D27-547F2095078/0/ shopping_goodpractice.pdf.

Summary

There are many different approaches to market research but the most important aspect is to choose an approach that is fit for the purpose and will deliver the kind of data that will be useful. Sophisticated market research is costly so it is important to conduct a cost/benefit analysis of any proposal. No approach is perfect and the main choice is between knowing a lot about a little, or a little about a lot.

Further study

Boddy, D. (2002) *Management: An Introduction*, Chapter 7 'Managing Marketing'.

Hints and tips

You need to be able to show that you know the issue that needs to be decided when designing a research project aimed at providing information as part of a marketing audit or for marketing and business decisions. On a practical level, you will need to be able to analyse and interpret information and present, as a written report or oral presentation, appropriate conclusions or recommendations that inform the marketing and business decisions for which the research was undertaken.

Bibliography

Housden, M. (2003) *Marketing Research and Information*, Oxford: Butterworth-Heinemann.

Public Sector Benchmarking Service (2004) <http://www.benchmarking.gov.uk>

Willmott and Nelson (2003) *Complicated Lives: Sophisticated Consumers, Intricate Lifestyles, Simple Solutions*, Wiley & Sons.

Wilson, D. (2003) *Marketing Research*, Harlow, Essex: FT Prentice Hall.

Sample exam questions and answers for the Marketing Management in Practice module as a whole can be found in Appendix 6 and past examination papers can be found in Appendix 7. Both appendices can be found at the back of the book.

unit 7

developing and implementing marketing plans

Learning objectives

○ Develop an operational marketing plan, selecting an appropriate marketing mix for an organization operating in any context such as FMCG, business-to-business (supply chain), large or capital project-based, services, voluntary and not-for-profit, or sales support (e.g. SMEs) (4.1).

○ Use the main techniques available for planning, scheduling and resourcing activities within the plan (4.2).

○ Identify appropriate measures for evaluating and controlling the marketing plan (4.3).

○ Review and evaluate the effectiveness of planning activities (4.4).

Related Statements of Marketing Practice

Jc2   Manage and report on delivery against plan and objectives.

Kc.1   Define measurements appropriate to the plan or business case and ensure they are undertaken.

Kc.2   Evaluate activities and identify improvements using measurement data.

Introduction

The Marketing Management in Practice module is intended to give participants some practice in developing and implementing marketing plans at an operational level in organizations. A key part of this is working within a team to develop the plan and managing teams implementing the plan by undertaking marketing activities and projects. Its aim is to encourage you to integrate and apply knowledge from all the modules, particularly as part of a team. The focus should be on implementing a marketing plan as a team activity and careful attention needs to be given to the issues surrounding the actual implementation of a plan.

Strategic planning

In his book *The Rise of Fall of Strategic Planning*, Henry Mintzberg describes how strategic planners make the mistake that the future will resemble the past and tend to gather 'hard' data on their industry, markets and competitors, whilst ignoring 'soft' data such as talking with customers, suppliers and employees. Many organizations now make use of the term 'Strategic Intent' defined by Gary Hamel and C.K. Prahalad in their book *Competing for the Future* as 'an ambitious and compelling dream that provides the emotional and intellectual energy for the journey to the future, conveying a sense of direction and destiny'. Strategic intent is more flexible than a strategic plan and recognizes that the best laid plans may need to change in response to market conditions. The pace of change means that it is not always possible to anticipate change and, for example, cataclysmic events such as September 11th and its aftermath which was not and could not have been anticipated, can completely transform the business context. The upshot of this is that planning is important but it needs to incorporate flexibility. The days when vast resources were put into creating gigantic strategic plans that were out of date by the time they had been produced are probably over for the present.

Marketing planning and corporate planning

How corporate planning is organized in different organizations and sectors is influenced by factors such as the size and structure of the organization. In larger organizations, corporate planning is often set up as a separate function reporting directly to top management, with the specific remit of bringing together and synergising all individual departmental plans into the final corporate plan. It is placed directly under top management. In some organizations it is the managing director or chief executive who has responsibility for planning and this helps to position it as an activity that drives the organization.

Corporate planning or strategic company planning comprises the following sequential steps:

- o *Mission statement* – is a statement of the company's overall business philosophy or purpose. It is normally a set of guidelines, rather than something that is stated in hard and fast quantitative terms.
- o *Situational analysis* – means evaluating external and internal factors that will affect the planning process and asks the question 'Where are we now?'.
- o *Organizational objectives* – describes where an organization wants to be and how it wants to fulfil its mission. They are often expressed in achievable quantitative terms.
- o *Strategies to achieve these objectives* – which are the concrete ideas that set about achieving company objectives and they relate to how the mission will be accomplished.

Different parts of the organization, for example, finance, marketing, human resource management and distribution contribute to planning. Corporate planning provides an overview and brings planning functions together from across the organization. A key aspect of corporate planning is to ensure that there is consistency and coherence across the organization and all plans will contribute to achieving overall organizational objectives.

Marketing planning

Strategic marketing planning is the application of a number of logical steps in the planning process. There are different ways in which this can be done. One specific model would not suit every marketing planning situation. The planning process:

Example of a structure for a marketing plan linked to corporate planning

Mission Statement

Macro-Environment Situational Analysis

Political, Economic, Socio-cultural Audits of all major company and Technological (PEST) functions – Marketing, Finance, HRM, Production, Distribution

Strengths, Weaknesses, Opportunities, Threats, Analysis (SWOT)

Marketing Objectives

Forecast Market Potential

Generate Marketing Strategies

Assumptions and Contingency Plans

Prepare Detailed Marketing Mix Programmes

Budget Resources including Staffing

Agree Timescales

Implement the Plan

Measure and Control

Marketing plan components

The following are examples of what can be included in a marketing plan but it does not necessarily follow that every plan will have all of these components. Marketing plans tend to vary by industry, size of company, stage of growth and organizational goals. The process of preparing it is as important as the particular form it takes. The process should make you think about goals and the marketing strategy that will be used to achieve them. A marketing plan may contain all or just some of the following components.

Executive summary

Introduce the organization:

- o Explain the major points of your plan
- o Describe briefly the nature of the business and the products or services offered
- o Include a mission or values statement and objectives
- o List the structure of your organization and the senior management team
- o Summarize the marketing objectives and strategies that are in the plan.

Marketing audit

A good marketing audit is:

- ○ *Systematic* – It follows a logical, predetermined framework – an orderly sequence of diagnostic steps.
- ○ *Comprehensive* – It considers all factors affecting marketing performance, not just obvious trouble spots. Marketers can be fooled into addressing symptoms rather than underlying problems. A comprehensive audit can identify the real problems.
- ○ *Independent* – To ensure objectivity, outside consultants are used sometimes to prepare the marketing audit. Using outsiders may not be necessary, but having an objective auditor is important.
- ○ *Periodic* – Many organizations schedule regular marketing audits because the environment for marketing is dynamic.

A typical marketing audit consists of a number of sections, for example:

Marketing environment audit

This is based on an analysis of the internal and external environment. It should include information about target markets, including information about other individuals or organizations that offer similar products and services. Identify key issues in the competitive environment, for example challenges, such as new legislation or the impact of technological changes.

The marketing audit is important to the planning process because it provides the analysis that supports the corporate and the marketing decision-making process. An audit should provide information on the external (macro) and internal (micro) environment. Understanding trends and trying to anticipate changes that will have an impact on markets, customers, suppliers and competitors are important aspects of strategic development. Decisions about product and service development and investment decisions should be informed by the outcome of the marketing audit. The challenge is to use data intelligently and be prepared to respond to changes that influence consumer preferences and behaviour as well as to be proactive and try to influence that behaviour.

Environmental scanning

This is the systematic collection and evaluation of information from the wider marketing environment that might affect the organization and its strategic marketing activities. It is undertaken by marketing planners.

Key issues are:

- ○ Making sure that data is up to date, particularly for markets that are volatile and where consumer behaviour can change quickly.
- ○ The ability to identify what is significant amongst a myriad of detail. It is important not to drown in a sea of information.
- ○ Collecting data on a regular basis may be too expensive for an organization to undertake itself but the data that is available to purchase from market research analysts may not be specific enough about particular markets and products.
- ○ Marketing managers need to be able to understand the environment in which they are operating.

Marketing analysis tools

Analysis tools commonly used for this purpose are PESTLE, Porter's 5 force analysis, gap analysis, BCG matrix, GE matrix and so on.

A PESTLE (Political/Policy, Economic, Social/Societal, Technological, Legal and Environmental) analysis is a logical framework for identifying and assessing the various influences on the present and future development of the organization. It is usually a precursor to developing a SWOT analysis of the internal strengths and weaknesses of the organization compared with the opportunities and constraints in the external environment.

Political factors – Such as changes in government and the ramifications of their strategies such as tax levels, education and training issues, employment legislation and so on.

Economic factors – Such as the impact of the trade cycle, levels of disposable income and inflation. Typical questions are:

What are the effects of competitors (their products, services, technologies) on your operation?

What major developments in income, prices, savings, taxation and credit will affect the organization?

Social/cultural issues – Such as the ageing consumer, increases in one-parent families, changing values, attitudes and beliefs to smoking.

Typical questions to ask are:

What population trends are expected to affect existing and planned strategy?

- o What social and psychological patterns (attitudes, lifestyle, etc.) are expected to affect buyer behaviour patterns? How are environmental trends monitored?
- o How are present and pending legal developments affecting your operation?

Technological factors – Such as the increased rate of computer capability, production methods and so on.

Legal issues – Such as changes in advertising legislation for tobacco, regulations and codes of practice for promotions, and so on.

Environmental issues – Such as attitudes towards pollution, energy use, fair trade, slave labour, etc.

The following case study is an extract from a PESTLE analysis carried out by a national training organization that was faced with the loss of government grant and the need to become a commercial organization dependent on winning contracts.

The future development of a training organization: PEST analysis

Political issues

Learning and skills are regarded as central to economic growth and prosperity, and underpinned by government resources.

Employers are central to the Government's agenda but UK employer networks and institutions are weak, limiting opportunities for information sharing, best practice and collaboration.

The environment of audit inspection, information and regulation will become more intense and sophisticated. Developing standards, benchmarks and quality assurance procedures will continue to be important.

Economic issues

Globalization

There will be global markets in skilled workers as well as in investment and trade. Taking advantage of globalization will require people who are able to access the resources of other people and organizations around the world.

Flexible labour markets

Non-standard employment, that is part-time work, flexi-hours, self-employment and home working will become more common.

The information economy

The information economy will be a small business, entrepreneurial economy and small firms will become more important. Knowledge is seen as a resource by businesses, governments and individuals.

Social

Skills

UK labour productivity currently lags behind that of other major industrialized countries. The need for 'softer skills' such as communication and team working is likely to increase because of flatter structures, more team-based operations, greater diversification of job roles and other changes to the workplace.

Demography

Young and skilled people are becoming a scarce resource, particularly in countries with tight labour markets. There is an ageing workforce.

Qualifications

A significant number of individuals and employers are not engaging with the qualifications system at all.

Developing the supply side of training

In a demand-led system, private providers, voluntary sector providers and companies' in-house training facilities will be able to compete with public sector providers.

Technological

Technological developments will mean that the provision of education and learning will become more diffuse, informal and user-driven. The Internet's use as a source of information and education will grow significantly.

SWOT analysis

This should be a summary of the marketing audit and indicate the key issues which need then to be considered further.

SWOT stands for Strengths Weaknesses Opportunities Threats.

Strengths

Every organization has some strength. In some cases this is obvious, for example, dominant market shares. In other cases, it is a matter of perspective, for instance, a company is very small and hence has the ability to move fast. It is important to note that companies that are in a bad position also have strengths. Whether these strengths are adequate is an issue for analysis.

Weaknesses

Every organization also has some weakness. In some cases, this is obvious; say for example, a stricter regulatory environment. In other cases, it is a matter of perspective, for example, a company has 99 per cent market share and is open to attack from every new player. It is important to note that companies that are extremely competent in what they do, also have weaknesses. How badly these weaknesses will affect the company is a matter of analysis.

Opportunities

All organizations have some opportunities that they can gain from. These could range from diversification to sale of operations. Identifying hidden opportunities is the mark of an astute analyst.

Threats

No organization is immune to threats. These could be internal, such as falling productivity. Or they could be external, such as lower priced international competition.

A SWOT analysis is undertaken to help plan the marketing mix, which includes:

- Strengths of the product/service/organization
- Weaknesses of the organization
- Opportunities available to the organization (external factors)
- Threats which may come from the competition.

One way to improve upon the basic SWOT is to include more detailed competitor and business environment information in the analysis. SWOT analysis can also be augmented through surveys, for example customer awareness, interest, trial and usage levels.

GAP analysis

A gap analysis is something which needs to be monitored and considered in terms of filling the gap, should one occur. A gap is where corporate sales and financial objectives are greater than the current long-range forecasts in marketing planning. A gap could be filled in various ways, for example by improving productivity, reducing costs, increasing prices, stimulating increased usage, increasing market share, finding new user groups, developing new market segments, product development.

The marketing audit should ensure that the method chosen to fill the gap is consistent with the company's capabilities and builds on its strengths. For example, it would normally prove far less profitable for a dry goods grocery manufacturer to introduce frozen foods than to add another dry foods product. Likewise, if a product could be sold to existing channels using the existing sales force, this is far less risky than introducing a new product that requires new channels and new selling skills.

Marketing objectives

Corporate objectives are derived from the corporate plan, and inform the direction and focus of the marketing plan. Marketing objectives cover issues such as increasing the awareness of your product or service among your target audience in a particular time frame. The marketing objectives are likely to be linked to market share or sales targets. Long-, medium- and short-term objectives should be identified, some of which should be SMART. Examples of objectives are:

1. *Profitability objectives* – To achieve a 25 per cent return on capital employed by August 2007.
2. *Market share objectives* – To gain 30 per cent of the market for umbrellas by September 2006.
3. *Promotional objectives* – To increase awareness of the dangers of hepatitis to travellers from 15 per cent to 30 per cent by April 2005.
4. *Objectives for survival* – To survive the current double-dip recession.
5. *Objectives for growth* – To increase the size of our operation from $200 000 in 2002 to $400 000 in 2003.
6. *Objectives for branding* – To make Y brand of bottled beer the preferred brand of 21–28-year-old females in North America by February 2006.

Goals and aims tend to be more vague and focus on the longer term compared with objectives. They will not be SMART.

Marketing strategy

Segmentation – targeting and positioning – The key area in the strategic section of the marketing plan will consider these issues. The corporate plan may indicate the markets in which the company will operate, but the marketing plan will consider the segmentation strategy, targeting and resulting positioning strategy. This will be linked to the branding decisions.

Marketing mix decisions

The strategy will inform the decisions in relation to pricing, product, place and the extended Ps – people, process and physical evidence. Here, the marketing communications plan will be developed. This enables the organization to meet the needs of its target markets and achieve its marketing objectives. Consideration should be given to each of the areas of the 'four Ps' plus customer considerations in terms of segmentation, targeting and positioning. All parts of the marketing mix should work together to achieve an organization's objectives. This part of the plan is concerned with who will do what and how it will be done. In this way responsibility, accountability and action over a specific time period can be planned, scheduled, implemented and reviewed. Budget decisions will need to be taken throughout the strategic and operational areas of the plan. Marketing mix decisions describe how you intend achieving your marketing objectives. It is, essentially, the heart of your marketing plan and covers the 4 Ps of marketing.

Product – Describe your product or service in detail. Include product features and benefits.

Price – Describe your pricing strategy and payment policies. There are a range of approaches to pricing strategies considering cost, volume and profit.

There are four key factors that affect pricing decisions, also known as the 4 Cs:

1. *Cost* – Related to the actual costs involved
2. *Consumer/customer* – Related to the price the consumer will pay
3. *Competition* – Related to competitors' prices for substitute or complementary products
4. *Company* – Related to the company's financial objectives.

Promotion – Describe the promotional tools or tactics (a promotion plan) you will use to accomplish your marketing objectives (see Unit 8).

Place – Describe how and where you will place your product so that customers have access to it and how you will make the sale – your sales and distribution methods.

Action plan – Describe what will be done, when it will begin or be completed and who will accomplish the tasks.

Budget – List the cost of the marketing activities you are describing in the marketing plan.

Measurements – Describe the specific numerical targets that will be used to measure the results of implementing your plan. Control involves setting standards and comparing progress against them. Corrective action needs to be taken if it looks like the standards would not be met. Include time limits for achieving goals.

Monitoring and control – The plan will need to identify the methods of monitoring and evaluating the plan. Decide which controls are important, how they should be implemented and who should be involved.

Control factors – There are four main areas where control mechanisms should be considered within the marketing plan, that is management control, financial control, efficiency control and strategic control.

- o *Management control* – This includes areas such as performance appraisal for staff and the workforce, benchmarking procedures and so on against other organizations.
- o *Financial control* – This includes financial controls which most companies are adept at calculating. It could include trend analysis, comparison, liquidity ratios, debt ratios, activity ratios and so on.
- o *Efficiency control* – Here, this area considers the optimum value from marketing assets.
- o *Strategic control* – The easiest method of control is to measure marketing activities against market performance or objectives set.

Some organizations group their analysis into the following areas:

Financial analysis

This would include ratio analysis, variance analysis, cash flow monitoring, and capital expenditure monitoring. Financial analysis of competitors is relatively easy to perform because the financial accounts should be readily available. The main problems arise when the competitor is a division of a major corporation, and is not a limited company in its own right, and so is not obliged to publish its accounts, or when the company is present in markets where accurate financial reporting is not in evidence.

Market analysis

This would cover analysis of total market demand and market share. Market share information may not be as easily obtainable, although most organizations have access to some means of measuring this, such as through marketing database companies, market research periodicals, trade associations and journals.

Sales analysis

Analysis of sales targets and selling cost budgets. As with market share, this information may not be easily obtainable. Checking out the effectiveness of a marketing campaign from a product sales standpoint is critical. Begin the review process early, and repeat it often. The plan can be tweaked along the way to eliminate or shift schedules if some element of the mix is not working.

Physical resource analysis

This would involve analysis of plant and equipment utilization together with other measures of productivity and product quality. Operational effectiveness, for example process technology, people, information systems and so on impact on operational efficiency. This affects costs and business performance, including the speed and efficiency of service, customer perception, quality and reliability of product or service and warranty claims.

Systems analysis

The effectiveness of strategic implementation and analysis of marketing resource applications.

Companies may benchmark best practice at different levels of the organization in a variety of ways:

- o In an organization in another industry
- o Internally, for example comparing operations in business units in different locations
- o With competitors, though they may be unwilling to share the secrets of their success.

The way an organization prioritizes these factors has a bearing on its performance.

This leads to the following questions:

- o Which factors are absent from your organization? Do these need further investigation?
- o Which factors do competitors pay more attention to, compared to your organization and why?
- o Which factors are given low priority by your organization? Do these indicate areas for improvement?

Assumptions and contingency plans

Assumptions relate to external factors over which the company has little control and should be as few as possible. For each assumption, a contingency plan should be formulated. They should consist of a sentence or two that give a general indication of what would happen if assumptions prove to be incorrect.

Budget resources and staffing

Budgeting covers general marketing expenditure and salaries and expenses for staffing. If the plan is based on increasing sales and market share this will normally have resource implications for the marketing department, perhaps in terms of more representation or increased advertising costs. Financial considerations might well cause the organization to tone down its original marketing objectives.

Timescales

Most plans are for a period of 1 year but a plan must also contain timescales which detail marketing activities normally on a month by month, or a quarter by quarter, basis. However longer term issues can also addressed in the marketing plan. This will mean different things in different business sectors. In the case of technology long term may not be longer than 3 years, whereas in car production long term may mean 10 years or more. When long-term planning is addressed as part of a marketing plan it is usually a directional marketing plan which does not contain a lot of detail. Some companies have rolling plans that are modified in the light of experience. As one planning period finishes (1 month, 1 quarter, 1 year) the rolling plan will be modified in the light of what has happened and a further planning period will be added on to the end of the plan.

Implement the plan

The plan is now put into action. Those who are involved in implementation need to know what part they must play in its implementation to ensure its success.

Measure and control

The marketing information system provides information from market intelligence, marketing research and the organization's own internal accounting system. It can also be a control mechanism because customer reactions are also fed into this MkIS from market intelligence through the field sales force or from marketing research studies. Information on sales analyses is also fed into the system so assessments can be made as to whether forecasted sales are being achieved or not. The plan should be reviewed on a regular and controlled basis and then updated as circumstances change. Such controls can address the tactics in terms of sales analyses that will commence with a comparison of budgeted sales revenue against actual sales revenue. Variations might be due to volume or price variances.

Tools for monitoring and control

There are many tools to help with control and monitoring:

- Market share analysis
- Sales analysis
- Budgets
- Marketing research
- Marketing information systems (MkIS)
- Feedback from customer satisfaction surveys
- Cash-flow statements
- Customer relationship management (CRM) systems
- Activities of competitors to aspects of your plan
- Distributor support
- Performance of any promotional activities.

Tracking procedures

This section of the plan should include plans and procedures for tracking each type of media you are using and which seems to be the most effective.

Display advertising – With traditional consumer publications, tracking can be done through the use of different phone numbers, special offers (specific to that advertisement or publication), or reference to a specific department to call for information.

Many trade publications also include Reader Service Cards that allow the reader to circle a number that corresponds to your ad on a mail-in postcard in order to get more information about your product or service.

Direct marketing – With postal mailings, tracking is relatively simple. Include on the mailing label a code (called a key code or a source code) that corresponds with the mailing list. For telemarketing campaigns, tracking is also relatively simple since someone is communicating with the customer throughout the entire process in most cases.

Internet marketing – Usually this is easily tracked because it is based on click throughs, or page impressions.

Promotions – Most closed promotions are basically 'self-tracking' because they require the customer to do something such as fill out an entry form (trackable), turn in a coupon, return a rebate slip (trackable), or log on to a website to claim a prize (also trackable).

Supporting documentation

Include any supporting documents referenced in other plan sections here, such as CVs or key management resumés, spreadsheets, market research results and so on.

Activity 7.1

Read and compare the case studies below and critically appraise them as marketing plans. They differ from each other in some respects. Your task is to decide whether these differences are because the organizations are different in size, and so on and serve different markets with different products and services, or is it because of differences in the usefulness and comprehensiveness of the plan?

Would either of the plans benefit from some of the strengths of the other plan, or is the same level of detail not necessary for both plans?

Use the components of a marketing plan from above and decide:

- o Are there components that have not been used in one plan which would improve the other plan if they were included?
- o What gaps are there in the plans?
- o How could either or both plans be improved?

Case study 1 - Diamond badges

Marketing plan

The following marketing plan is written by the solo owner of a small business. Names of some businesses and cities have been fictionalized at the owner's request.

Mission statement

Technically, the mission statement is in the opening of the entire business plan, of which the marketing plan is a part. It is included here for the reader's information.

Diamond intends to supply Oxford with the most visually interesting badges available today. They will delight their users and provide a springboard for creative activity. Diamond believes artistic expression enhances life. It appreciates the skill of human hands and the sensitivity of human hearts. It regards badges as small works of art in which we are able to see ourselves.

Diamond's marketing plan

Diamond is a specialty retail store offering a collection of antique, contemporary and hand-crafted badges from around the world. These badges are distinguished from those available in the market place by the quality of materials, workmanship and design.

Diamond addresses the need to have fun! Badges are wonderfully expressive objects that add unexpected vitality to clothing. Apparel manufacturers are witnessing a competitive advantage to using fun and distinctive badges.

With growth, Diamond will also establish a working studio.

Diamond opened for business on 5 August 1999, with an inventory valued at £2050. In the first 8 months of operation, another £2290 of inventory was added. Sales totalled £2376 for the same period with the average monthly total being £172. Sales have increased steadily over this 8 month period.

Organizations and businesses served include:

Oxford Badgemakers Guild
Badge for Profit of Oxford
Intercom Designers
The Workroom.

215

Funding for the company has come from the personal income of the sole proprietor and from the income generated by sales. Additional funding is sought for the expansion of inventory and for advertising.

Product or service description

Diamond offers hand-crafted and manufactured badges in a range of materials and finishes. A high percentage of these badges are made of natural materials such as horn, bone, wood, glass and clay. These badges are hand-crafted by artisans throughout the world and are of original design. Manufactured metal and synthetic badges are also offered, together with a collection of vintage and antique badges.

Badges are often purchased for their beauty, and collections of antique badges represent a significant investment and historical rise in value.

Location

Diamond is located in Oxford on the second floor of the Tower Building. With growth, it would like to relocate to the building's south end. The benefits of this location are first floor access, room for expansion, higher visibility from large arched windows, more convenient parking, closer proximity to area retailers and reasonable cost.

Market analysis

The industry

According to the British Badgemakers Craft Association, the home badge-making industry contributes £2.5 million in retail sales to the economy. In the 5 years from 1995 to 2002, first-time buyers of badge-making machines increased from 40 per cent to 55 per cent. In the last 5 years (1991–1996), membership in the British Badgemakers Guild has doubled in size with a 55 per cent increase in the number of local chapters. Today's badge-making is technologically advanced and computer memories have also enhanced the creative potential of the badge-making machine.

Badge-making is one of several creative industries served by Diamond. As this country reassesses its priorities, home-oriented leisure activities enjoy increased levels of interest.

The target market

The Badgemaker's profile, as reported by the British Home Badge-making and Craft Association, looks like:

- o 75 per cent female
- o 35–64 years of age
- o household income of £35 000 and more
- o artistic, values originality.

This profile is supported by direct observation of Diamond's customers.

People who pursue the creative industries value objects made by hand, and purchase them for themselves, their friends and their families. They are deeply involved in home-based leisure activities such as reading and gardening. Badges are used increasingly in the home as an element of interest and design.

The competition

Direct competitors exist in three nearby cities. They are the badge factory, a high-end of the market shop located in York and two badge shops in Bath – Antique Badges and Renewal Badges. The strength of these competitors lies in the length of time they have been in business. Awareness of their product is well established.

Badges are displayed prominently at Diamond in a manner consistent with their quality and character. Again, Diamond will compete by focusing on badges. The company will also compete on the basis of location.

Antique Badges and Renewal Badges offer a product impressive in its range of quality, price and character. They are both centrally located and are the model upon which Diamond patterns itself.

Diamond will entice fans away from these shops by diligently procuring badges of high originality. Independent badgesmiths will be showcased whenever possible. Diamond will also maintain a large collection of vintage and antique badges. Indirect competition comes from Northeast Fabrics. Diamond offers badges that cannot be found in these stores and priced generally higher. Diamond will attract customers who may be willing to spend more on badges than on fabric to achieve a higher level of style and expression.

Promotional objectives and strategies

One of the greatest challenges facing Diamond in its first year of operation is lack of awareness. At this time, the customer base is 200 people. The company's goal is to double this number over the months of June through October for an overall goal of 400 customers.

Strategies for achieving this goal include:

- o Establishing an auxiliary sales display at the local farmer's market on Saturdays throughout the summer. This can be done at a cost of £110.
- o Distributing business cards and reprints of an article about Diamond which appeared in *Lifelike Magazine*. Distribution points will be the farmer's market, the Arts Alive Gallery and the Underground Studio.
- o Publishing a quarterly newsletter to existing customers and selected businesses. The newsletter will solicit referrals, advertise additions to inventory and notify readers of current sales promotions.
- o Establishing quarterly sales promotions in May, August, November and February.
- o The April sales promotion will be in honour of Mother's Day. Customers will be treated to an afternoon tea; discounted gift certificates for mothers will be offered.
- o November will focus on year-end festivities.
- o February will highlight Valentine's Day.
- o Advertising in the newsletters of the Woodbrook Weavers, the Oxford Guild. Costs range in the area of £10 per issue.
- o Continuing to advertise in the Yellow Pages at a cost of £15.75 per month.
- o Another goal which Diamond needs to address is that of building inventory. Summer months will allow a greater portion of the company's resources to be directed towards augmenting inventory.
- o Diamond will advertise in the area weeklies, such as *Retreat*, as wanting to buy old badges.
- o Diamond will solicit handmade badges by advertising in the 'Opportunities' section of *The Art Calendar* as a consignor.

Pricing policy

Three categories of badges are purchased by Diamond for resale. They are hand-crafted badges, manufactured badges and antique badges. The standard industry mark-up is 100 per cent.

The average retail price of hand-crafted and antique badges is £4.25. Manufactured badges range in price from £1.45 to £2.00, depending on what material is used. Badges of natural materials are more expensive.

Case study 2 – Stormbreaker

Stormbreaker is a small but profitable company in the extremely competitive sportswear market. In order to grow and become even more profitable, it needs to expand its products to a wider market and consider segmenting specific areas of the market place. In 2000, Stormbreaker introduced a fully waterproof, fully breathable outer clothing system, virtually eliminating the condensation problems normally associated with waterproof clothing.

Turnover in 2000/2001 was £16 million, with a net profit of £182 500. The R&D investment is £250 000 with other costs being covered by co-operation with suppliers and customers.

The market environment

It is clear that many individuals will have specialist sports shoes for specialist sports (tennis, running, cycling, etc.). There are many other companies that are now well established in this market. Some specialize in sportswear alone, unlike Stormbreaker, who have a wide range of sports shoes and sportswear.

Distribution

Stormbreaker has recently been considering some options regarding the way their goods reach the final consumer. Although their goods have an established identity amongst the key consumers, most of the goods are actually sold through specialist retail outlets and catalogues to whom they supply leaflets and posters.

With the advent of e-commerce and the possibility of expanding their network, the company has recently been considering web-based activities much more seriously.

Stormbreaker continues to be highly active in pioneering the use of new materials in their product range. The use of 'smart' materials is particularly interesting them at present. The development of heating and cooling the wearer, utilizing specially bonded fabrics is currently being explored.

SWOT analysis

Strengths
- Good brand
- Good range of outdoor items
- Specialist products
- New waterproof material
- Good TV exposure and PR in general
- Innovative organization.

Weaknesses
- o   Not well known
- o   R&D base small
- o   Marketing and branding budget too small
- o   Manufacturing UK oriented
- o   Limited range.

Opportunities
- o   Expand manufacturing base
- o   Creating strategic alliances with companies that have produced new materials and used chip technology
- o   More expenditure on marketing and PR
- o   Segmentation and targeting.

Threats
- o   New entrants with products based on chip technology
- o   Aggressive branding by more established companies
- o   Me-too products.

PESTLE analysis

Political

There are hardly any political issues impinging on the company. The only thing it needs to consider is the possible ethical impact of manufacturing in the Far East. If they handle this sensitively and well, then they will be able to use this in their marketing strategies.

Economic

The possible plateauing of running shoe sales. Also, any impending recession will mean that consumers will rein back spending on possible luxury items.

Social

Society is ageing … certainly in Europe. In considering marketing strategies, the company will have to take into account grey buying power and its impact on their marketing segmentation policies.

Technological

The technology for sports clothing is continuously developing and improving. In the long run, one can see how 'computerized/smart' materials-based clothing will come into being. Various information links within the case show how this technology is evolving. Technological changes are likely to have a far-reaching impact on the company's sportswear. They need to scan the environment continuously to monitor these changes.

Legal

Not too important, unless they produce sub-standard goods or infringe copyright.

Environmental

This usually relates to the production of the sportswear, whether it is environmentally friendly or not. This does not appear to be an issue for Stormbreaker.

However, their products allow a person to visit previously unexplored places, which affects the environment.

Porter's five forces analysis

Threat of new entrants

This could be a significant issue for Stormbreaker. New entrants could appear:

- o Through the web
- o New brand development by some of the major companies: for example, Boots introduced their Botanics range to compete with Bodyshop products.

Power of suppliers

Supplier power largely depends on their strength in bargaining. It appears that this is not a significant issue for Stormbreaker, as the main items of use are leather and other generic materials.

Many new items such as self-wicking clothing are developed by the company itself, or in co-operation with suppliers.

Power of buyers

This is a significant area for Stormbreaker to consider and also impacts on the generic strategies they adopt (see later questions).

The customers have considerable power – whether they are the end-consumers or the retailers.

Threat of substitutes

The threat of substitutes is forever present. 'Smart' materials and 'computerized' clothing accessories could be the future for outdoor pursuits. The company, however, may not have enough R&D clout to undertake product development in this area.

Rivalry between firms

The market is *very* competitive.

Product	Stage of the product life cycle
'Smart' clothing	Introduction
Clothing and accessories	Growth
Walking and climbing boots	Maturity
Sports shoes and football boots	Decline

To gain a deeper understanding of the issues and factors affecting planning and control issues for Stormbreaker, utilize the following as the basis for your group discussions.

- Product life cycle analysis
- The Ansoff Matrix
- The General Electric Matrix
- Innovation/Value Matrix
- The BCG Matrix
- Core Competencies
- Gap analysis.

The life cycle model helps to show how a product may grow and then eventually decline. The Adopter Categorization of innovators, early and late majority and laggards should also be considered in conjunction with this model. Decline is not inevitable and a number of companies halted their decline in sales in the mid-eighties by repositioning their brand and revitalizing their offer to the consumer. Improved marketing and product development, and more investment can help to halt decline.

		Products	
		Existing	**New**
Markets	*Existing*	Football/Running shoes Climbing/Walking boots Accessories/clothing	New waterproof attire Elasticated clothing 'Smart' clothing
	New	Clothing for cyclists	'Smart' clothing for different markets, including the health market

Figure 7.1 Ansoff Matrix for Stormbreaker

This analysis helps you to ascertain whether the company actually has competences within attractive sectors.

Company Strengths

	Low	Medium	High
Low			
Medium	○ Football and running shoes		Walking and climbing boots ○
High		○ Clothing and accessories	

Industry Attractiveness

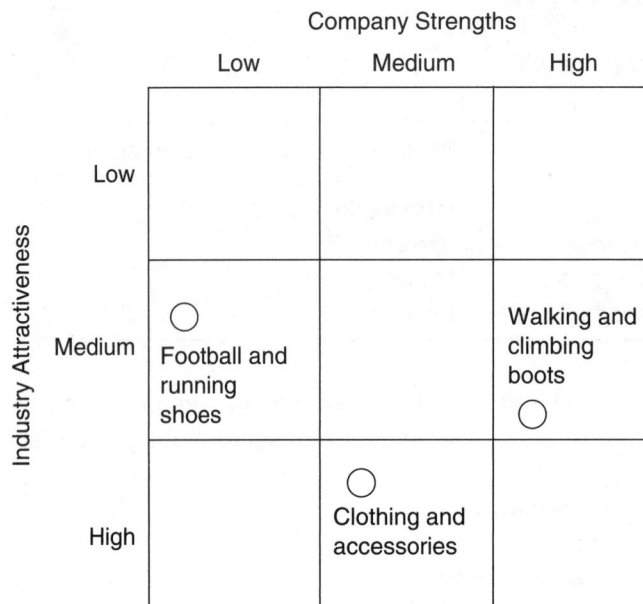

Figure 7.2 Industry/Product Matrix for Stormbreaker (General Electric Matrix)

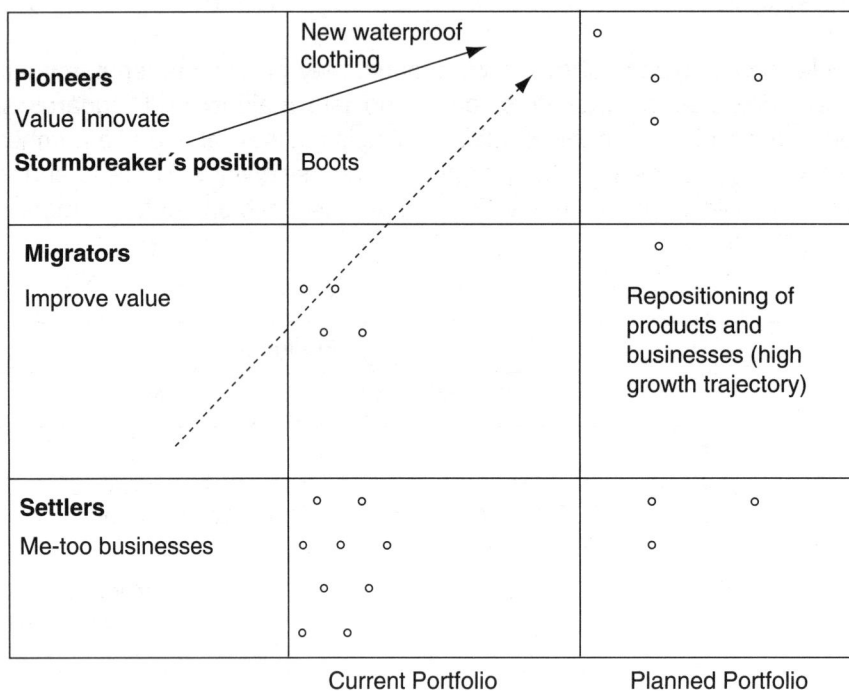

	Current Portfolio	Planned Portfolio
Pioneers Value Innovate **Stormbreaker's position**	New waterproof clothing → Boots	○ ○ ○ ○
Migrators Improve value	○ ○ ○ ○	○ Repositioning of products and businesses (high growth trajectory)
Settlers Me-too businesses	○ ○ ○ ○ ○ ○ ○ ○ ○	○ ○ ○

Figure 7.3 The Innovation/Value Matrix

Stormbreaker needs to consider the Innovation/Value Matrix in terms of the possible threats from the me-too and migrator competitors. If it is to keep its lead then it must innovate. Its large R&D budget is indicative of this. The dotted arrow shows the threat from me-too companies. It is important for Stormbreaker to protect its innovations with a patent.

BCG Matrix

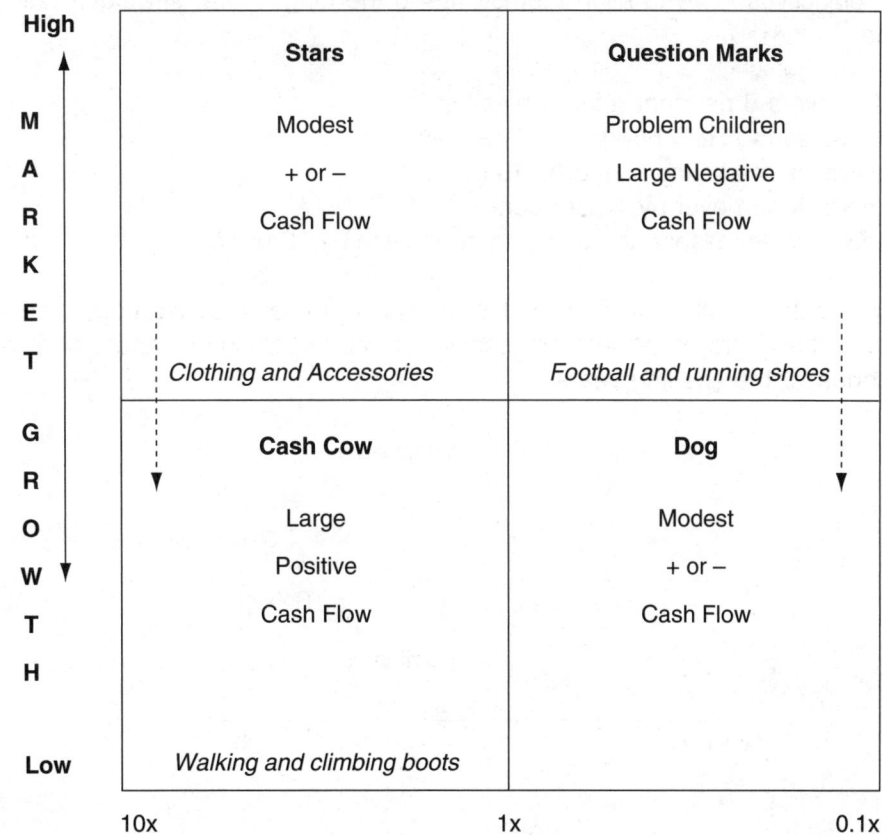

Figure 7.4 Boston Matrix

A possible BCG analysis is presented for Stormbreaker, taking into account industry growth and potential growth for Stormbreaker products. In undertaking this analysis, it would be hopeless to consider the whole market. We have to make the assumption that Stormbreaker is competing within a small sector of the specialist market and therefore the idea of a market share actually makes some sense! The potential trajectories for the products are shown in the matrix.

Market share

In addition to this, it is useful to gauge what products/markets meet the above criteria. Whatever strategy Stormbreaker undertakes, these criteria should be met to ensure continued success in the market place. The above analyses show the positioning of the company *vis-à-vis* its product portfolio and market attractiveness. You could continue analysing a company's situation *ad nauseum*, ending up with paralysis through analysis. You should consider issues such as available time and the most relevant models. From these analyses, Stormbreaker has several potential routes that it could follow. The route chosen will depend on the strategies that it is likely to follow.

(a) Possible mission statement

Stormbreaker's mission is to be the leading niche player in the outdoor footwear, clothing and accessories market, providing high-quality differentiated products that delight the customer.

(b) SMART objectives

SMART objectives have to align themselves to the longer term strategy. Examples of these would be:

o   Achieve a 5 per cent return on sales
o   Increase the R&D budget by 5 per cent
o   Increase marketing spend by 10 per cent
o   Increase turnover by 10 per cent
o   Increase accessory and climbing boot sales by 20 per cent.

All these should be achievable within 1 year. Market forces may lead the company to change direction in the future. It is therefore sensible to have tight boundaries for 1 year and more flexible ones for the ensuing years.

Figure 7.5

(c) Possible option for Stormbreaker to follow

o   Drop the football and running shoe market
o   Expand research into 'smart' clothing technology (computerized clothing)
o   Consider a strategic alliance
o   Concentrate on pushing forward the focused strategy (Porter)
o   Improve return on sales by concentrating on the most profitable items
o   Develop a communications plan that fits with the strategies adopted.

The company could decide to follow all these options or some of them, depending on its resource base. A differentiated strategy, with more manufacturing taking place in the Far East, would certainly help to increase its market share, but would it then have a negative impact on its specialist market? Once an option has been decided and the strategy set actions need to be considered. For instance:

o   Dropping the football and running shoe market will mean considerable loss in revenue.
o   No one can predict the potential market for 'smart' clothing. A basic calculator now has more computing power than the Apollo spacecraft which landed on the moon in 1969.

Mobile phones, smart cards, digital cameras and many more everyday items are the results of continuing developments in, and combinations of, technology.

○ Alliances are usually within distribution networks for the sports and clothing industry. Whilst Stormbreaker collaborates with suppliers in the development of materials, it does not have a sufficient volume of output to have exclusive use of such materials. Stormbreaker gains a reputation for innovation from these relationships.

○ Concentrating on the more profitable items can improve return on sales, but not always. Porsche improved their position by cutting back on diversity in the mid-1990s and improved their position considerably. Triumph motorcycles withdrew from the smaller bike market in the 1970s. The consequent loss of 'novice' customers led to a decline in sales of larger bikes.

Stormbreaker should not only set targets and measure performance against them, but should also benchmark these against the industry, specific competitors and best practice. Any aspect of the business can be benchmarked, providing opportunities for measurement and improvement at the tactical and local level. From this comparison, the essential attributes for delivering value to customers can be derived.

(A) Activity 7.2

Implementation

It is important to schedule the events in your plan and assign responsibilities for implementation. Using some of the components of a marketing plan above and previous chapters in the book, draw up a simple action plan for implementing the Stormbreaker marketing plan. Try using a Gantt chart to schedule the activities.

Pay particular attention to who should be involved in the implementation. Identify the positions of people involved, for example finance manager, marketing manager and so on.

The plan should include information about:

○ What needs to be done (tasks and activities)
○ Who needs to do it (assembling the team)
○ When does it need to be done (scheduling).

Summary

This unit has provided examples of marketing plans and demonstrated that there is no uniform pattern. However, there are key issues that a marketing plan needs to address even if the formats are sometimes different.

Sample exam questions and answers for the Marketing Management in Practice module as a whole can be found in Appendix 6 and past examination papers can be found in Appendix 7. Both appendices can be found at the back of the book.

unit 8 marketing communications and customer service

Learning objectives

- Plan the design, development, execution and evaluation of communications campaigns by a team of marketers, including external agencies and suppliers (5.1).

- Use appropriate marketing communications to develop relationships or to communicate with a range of stakeholders (5.2).

- Manage and monitor the provision of effective customer service (5.3).

- Use marketing communications to provide support for members of a marketing channel (5.4).

- Use marketing communications techniques for an internal marketing plan to support management of change within an organization (5.5).

- Review and evaluate the effectiveness of communications activities and the role of the individual and the team in this process (5.6).

Introduction

Marketing communications strategy is concerned with how an organization can successfully communicate and deliver its marketing strategy. The Marketing Communications units of the CIM syllabus are intended to provide the skills and knowledge that enable marketers to manage marketing communications and brand support activities within organizations. The Marketing Management in Practice Module builds on the underpinning knowledge developed in the CIM Marketing Communications module. Three in four British companies confess they are not easy to do business with – and the majority look destined to remain that way.

Formats for a Marketing Communications Plan

There are a range of formats that can be used for developing a marketing communications plan. The following is an example from a university:

Deciding where, when and how to get the right message to the right audience at the right time is the essence of a marketing communications plan. The plan is a tool to promote an event, unit or activity and is based on the following fundamentals:

- Targeted audience
- Perceived university image
- Overall marketing strategy
- Results/expected outcome
- Resources available and capabilities
- Timing of these activities
- Measuring results.

Checklist to complete a Marketing Communications Plan

Do your homework – Before you contact your account executive to begin planning, assemble the relevant background information for review. Think through your key messages and audiences, timeline, budget, challenges, resources, measurable goals, sources to contact and what you want accomplished.

Plan – Meet with your account executive and other appropriate personnel to think through communication strategies linked to the university's marketing goals, past efforts and external factors.

Assign responsibilities – Determine who will communicate all vital information, facilitate meetings among key staff, faculty and students and ensure timely approvals and reviews through plan completion.

Write – Determine who will gather information, read reports, interview key sources, review what has been done and how project relates to the university marketing goals.

Approve plan – Identify who will edit, update and approve the plan at various administrative levels.

Assign responsibilities – Determine who will carry out the plan's tactics on time, on budget and within university identity and style compliance and ensure payment of services.

Distribute – Send plan to all appropriate personnel.

Evaluate – Track, monitor and evaluate plan's effectiveness and distribute evaluation. Ensure goals are successfully met.

Source: http://www.map.wayne.edu/checklists/marketing.pdf.

Designing a communications campaign

A communications campaign is the dissemination of messages using appropriate channels, to a well-defined audience in order to educate and create an informed public. Designing and implementing a communications campaign could be carried out entirely in-house, or it could be devolved to an agency, or the campaign could involve a combination of internal and external input. Obviously the size of the campaign and that of the budget, as well as its aims and objectives, will be important factors in determining which approach to use. The key barrier to integrating the communications mix is people, and the way they work. The best way to overcome this barrier is to motivate the key players to work as a team. An effective team is one that includes client and agency, across the entire communications mix.

Full-service agency

When using an external agency the most straightforward approach is to use the services of a full-service agency that is able to assemble a team including representatives from all the agency services that the client needs. Full-service agencies can provide a comprehensive range of services such as creative, strategic planning, production, media planning and buying and market research. The advantage of using a full-service agency is the range of skills that can be drawn upon when needed, and the fact that all the elements of the promotional mix and marketing communications operation can be brought together making the whole process easier to manage and control. However, this strength is also a potential weakness because if the relationship breaks down, it will be difficult to find another agency to take on the work at short notice and still keep to the envisaged timescale.

Limited service agency

An alternative to the full-service agency is a limited service agency that specializes in particular elements of the marketing communications process. For example, an advertising agency may specialize in the design of advertisements. The advantage in using a limited service agency is that a client can use different agencies for the different skills that best suit his needs. This gives choice and flexibility but it can take a lot of time to manage the different relationships involved. Selecting an agency should be based on explicit criteria based on the aims and objectives of the communications. Key issues are whether the agency fully understands the requirements of a brief, and whether it will be able to work with the client as a team. In some cases, companies are establishing online communication services which may make it more difficult to tell whether or not the chemistry is right between the client and the agency.

Developing an Agency brief

Elements that could be contained in an agency brief are:

Current situation – The history of the brand, previous campaign successes (or failures) and the reasons for mounting the new campaign.

Promotional objectives – Having set marketing objectives, the promotional objectives need to be identified. These will vary but could include, for example, encouraging product trial or direct sales or increasing distribution outlets.

Target markets – This should include socioeconomic details (e.g. age, class, sex) and also psychographic information on users. This will have a bearing on the focus and content of the promotional activity.

Product/service – In providing the agency with a detailed brief, this section should include any available research that has been used to establish the perceived benefits so that these can be promoted strongly.

Budget – The budget should include funds for the cost of the media and the production of promotional material.

Competitors – Find out about these and include the results of your findings in the brief.

Timescales – Media scheduling will play an important role at this stage.

The creative team will be responsible for the direction of the artwork, ensuring that visualization and copywriting match the needs of the organization, and they will be directed by the accounts manager within the agency who will also brief the media and planning functions.

When agencies are used, the process of briefing will be followed by the 'agency pitch'. An agency will carry out research into the marketing and communications situation, and then present creative and media plans to the client.

What type of campaign is it?

There are different types of marketing communications campaign. An educational campaign targets a specific audience with information that benefits the consumer, for example health-related matters, or how to obtain benefits. A marketing campaign promotes, for example, a new service or product, or repositions an old service or product, and focuses on price, promotion and product. A public relations campaign would focus on image and name recognition. The following is an example of an integrated campaign that was the result of extensive research carried out over a year involving marketers and professionals working in the anti-drug field.

National youth anti-drug media campaign

The campaign's 5-year initiative to reduce and deglamorize youth drug use targets middle-school-age adolescents (approximately 11–13 years old), parents and other influential adults. The integrated communications campaign delivers anti-drug messages to kids and parents where they live, work and play through advertising, the Internet, movies, music and television, public education efforts and community partnerships. The campaign will spend about $180 million per year in advertising – and receive a pro bono match of equal value from the entertainment industry, media, corporations and other advertisers – to expose young people to innovative anti-drug messages that reinforce the ads. For more than a year, TV ads have run nationwide during prime time. Nearly a year of research went into designing the campaign. Hundreds of specialists were consulted, including experts in behaviour change, drug prevention, teen marketing and advertising communications, as well as representatives from professional, civic and community organizations. The campaign will be constantly monitored, evaluated and updated to ensure that it effectively reaches teens and their parents.

Who is the target audience?

Communication should be tailored to meet the needs and interests of a given audience. Is the audience potential buyers, current users, deciders or influencers, individuals groups, or the general public? Are the members of the target audience consumers, businesses, non-profit organizations or government agencies? The target audience is a critical influence on decisions about what to say to whom, when and how.

What are the aims and objectives of the campaign?

Try to devise both quantitative (measurable) and qualitative objectives. A quantitative objective would be, for example, to increase the number of users by 20 per cent per year. A qualitative objective would be to improve public understanding of the benefits of recycling by the autumn, measured by pre- and post-survey responses. The campaign may be trying to elicit a cognitive (attention), affective (feeling) or behavioural (doing) response.

Designing the message

This is concerned with what to say, how to say it and who should say it. The aim is to find a theme, idea, appeal or unique selling proposition. The message can try to appeal on moral, rational or emotional grounds. Rational grounds emphasize the benefits of a product or service such as quality, value or performance. Emotional appeals try to stir up negative or positive emotions to motivate purchase. Moral appeals to the audience's sense of propriety and the right way to behave. The structure of a message is important, that is, whether it is a one-sided or two-sided presentation mentioning benefits and shortcomings, and the order in which arguments are presented. The credibility of the message source depends on expertise, trustworthiness and likeability.

Select the channels

This involves choosing between a range of personal communication channels, for example face to face or through telephone or e-mail, and non-personal communication channels which include the media.

Activity 8.1

Think of a marketing campaign that you have been involved in or which is memorable to you.

What type of campaign was it?
Who do you perceive was the target audience?
What was the key message?
What channels were used?
What made it stand out for you?

Internet Marketing

Companies that have achieved the greatest success with Internet marketing have leveraged the strength of multiple marketing and sales channels. This includes the use of more traditional marketing and sales channels: brand advertising in broadcast media, demand generation and promotional communications in print media, direct mail and e-mail channels, and sales and service support from field sales, telesales and business partners.

What is the single biggest pre-requisite for successful Internet marketing? – Customer-centric thinking and delivery. Marketers still talk about 'campaigns' whereas customers want to take control of the relationship. And the second biggest lesson for successful online marketing? It's a multi-channel process, not just a collection of separate web pages. Customers experience you as a journey that is a sequence of interactions across any number of channels towards their end goal.

The really successful marketers really understand that journey and how the channels, including the Internet, best work together. The real challenge here is getting your organization galvanized and incentivised to work together, as opposed to by channel or departmental silo, to help the customer towards his or her end destination, wherever that may be within your company.

Companies that have achieved the greatest successes also have defined and deployed Internet marketing strategies from a cross-functional perspective and leveraged the strength of multiple marketing and sales channels. In these companies customer-facing marketing, sales and service activities have not simply been automated or moved to the Internet. Instead, they first have been freshly re-designed to provide greater value, reliability, responsiveness and service quality to customers – and secondly to provide improved transaction economics to the company. Such a re-design, of course, suggests that the company has already gained a thorough understanding of customers' buying behaviours and their channel preferences.

The Internet has been an integrated element of the marketing mix, not an isolated or stand-alone marketing activity. Years of management research and practical experience have demonstrated that changing customers' buying behaviours and motivating them to accept and adopt innovations, like Internet marketing, can be difficult and costly. The most successful 'Internet marketing' companies have recognised that integrating new e-channel capabilities with traditional marketing and sales channels can accelerate the innovation process for customers and themselves.

Source: http://www.insightexec.com/cgi-bin/item.cgi?id=130982&u=pnd&m=phn. http://www.insightexec.com/cgi-bin/item.cgi?id=130983&u=pnd&m=phnd.

Media planning

Media planning needs to be co-ordinated with marketing strategy and with other aspects of an advertising strategy. The strategic aspects of media planning involve four steps:

1. Selecting the target audience towards which all subsequent efforts will be directed.
2. Specifying media objectives, for example, in terms of reach (What proportion of the target audience must see, read, or hear our advertising message during a specified period?), frequency (How often should the target audience be exposed to the advertisement during this period?), gross rating points or GRPs or effective rating points or ERPs (How much total advertising is necessary during a particular period to accomplish the reach and frequency objectives?).
3. Selecting general media categories and specific vehicles within each medium.
4. Buying media.

The concept of media neutral planning has been developed to counteract the perceived power of creative teams that may be regarded as considering only itself and its peers when developing new ideas. This has led to media choice, being biased towards those options deemed to show off creative talent to best effect, rather than necessarily being the best at meeting the needs of the consumer.

Media Neutral Planning Just Today's Buzz Word or a Genuine New World Order?

Looking back for a moment we can see that each decade through the second half of the twentieth century brought our predecessors face to face with their own key issues. Starting in the 50's with the development of the creative team as we now know it, which then contributed in the 60's to the move away from linear models of communication to a more humanistic approach, through the advent of account planning in the 70's, to the break up of the full-service agency in the 80's which, in turn, led directly to the issue of integration in the 90's. So here we are in a new century facing our own particular issue – media neutral planning. But what is it? What, if anything does it owe to these preceding trends? And is it just a passing fad or is it here to stay? To set my stall out from the beginning ~I should say that, in my view, media neutral planning is probably the biggest issue of all, being a culmination of all those issues that came before. To put it in its own context, I believe that media neutral planning is far greater than merely a creative or 'advertising' issue. It is fundamental to the way in which a brand does and should touch consumers' lives. It is the planning of those brand touchpoints without bias toward or against any particular mediums or channels, from conventional above the line media, through traditional below the line options to new media, ambient media, pr, sponsorship, events, design, point of sale, collateral material, etc. Currently, planning tends to be heavily media centric dependent on where the planner sits, who pays his/her wages and what his/her particular prejudices are. Media neutral planning, on the other hand, seeks to put the consumer firmly at the centre of the planning process, viewing media from his/her perspective as defined by the particular brand relationship in question.

Source: Tina Kaye, http://www.marketing-society.org.uk/downloads/MEDIA-NEUTRAL-PLANNING.pdf.

Determining the marketing communications budget

A key task within the framework of marketing communications is the appropriate determination of the levels of expenditure required to fulfil the task established. The amount of money spent on marketing communications differs widely among companies, even within the same industry. There are various methods to choose from, each with a slightly different focus, and different advantages and disadvantages.

Percentage of sales – A widely used method of budget determination is based on the calculation of a ratio between past expenditure and sales. The model creates a situation in which the budget only increases against an expectation of higher sales and fails to acknowledge that marketing can create sales for a brand.

Percentage of product gross margin – A percentage of either the past or expected gross margin – net sales less the cost of goods – is used.

Percentage of anticipated turnover – This approach is based on the allocation of a fixed percentage of future turnover to the marketing communications budget.

Unit or case/sales ratio method – This method is based on estimating sales volumes, and a fixed sum per unit is allocated towards marketing communications expenditure. Multiplying the expected sales volume by the fixed allocation gives producers the size of the budget. The expenditure patterns reflect past achievement and tends to benefit growth brands and disadvantage those that are declining.

Competitive expenditure – Another frequently used approach is to base a brand's expenditure levels on an assessment of competitors' expenditures. However, the difficulty is how to make an accurate assessment of the level of competitors' spend. While it is possible to obtain a reasonable fix on advertising spend from published information, the same is not true of sales promotional spend and other categories of marketing communications.

Share of voice – This approach is based on the relationship between the volume share of the product category and the expenditure within the category as a whole. It is primarily related to advertising expenditure.

Media inflation – This makes the assumption that the previous year's budget should be increased in line with the growth in media costs.

Objective and task method – This method is based on the specific objectives that the marketing plan needs to achieve. The objective and task method requires that specific objectives for the campaign are defined; for example, increasing brand awareness, encouraging sampling and trial, promoting repeat purchase and so on. A numerical target is given and the costs of achieving this target are calculated. The budget is based on present goals rather than past or future results.

What can be afforded – This is based on a management assessment of, for example, the return on investment, and the marketing communications budget is the amount that remains after calculating that level and other claims on the budget.

When engaging in media planning

There are multiple issues to consider. Some of the most important ones are:

The nature of advertising is changing: customers want to be more informed about the choices they are making, especially when the product of their interest is a costly one.

Doing some additional research on the Internet before making the final decision on a purchase is therefore more rule than exception these days. That's why a web presence with a reliable appearance and solid information about your product is a must these days.

Ratings from various sources always harbor a certain amount of error. For starters, the ratings are based on a sample of the population, which always entails the possibility of deviations from real outcomes. Besides, up till now, the strategies that were used to establish the ratings could be questioned for all media.

And on top of that, ratings are always a retrospective picture in a world where everything changes at the speed of the wind. One of the most risky acts in the media decision-making process is therefore: linear planning.

The act of planning which media to use for an advertising campaign should therefore be done with consideration of the numbers available, but also with a certain amount of vision and intuition.

Comparing the performance of the designated brand with that of its competitors is a good way to go, but should not be the ultimate determining factor in developing your media strategy. After all, your competitors may have a different marketing strategy – and perhaps also an entirely different budget – lying at the foundation of their campaign than you have for yours.

Length of impact of the particular media-vehicles should also be looked at. Will your product still be around or in season by the time a particular media vehicle of your choice reaches its last important group of viewers? Keep the average duration of the media vehicles you want to select in mind when planning, and compare them with the availability and seasonableness of your product.

Keep multiple factors in mind when comparing and contrasting index numbers: even if your brand seems to do greatly in a certain market, you cannot solely rely on the indices: market size and purchasing power of the group under consideration should also play an important role in determining your final choice.

Considering the markets where you want your campaign to be executed is also a multi-faceted issue: what are your competitors doing, and why? If your brand is not doing well in a market but your competitors' are, you may want to find out what the reasons are before increasing your advertising budget in that market. And if neither your brand nor your competitors' are doing well in a market, you may think even harder before initiating a campaign there.

When you compare data from various sources, make sure you also consider the geographic divisions these sources handle: there are many divisions in use by various data sources. You don't want to compare apples and oranges.

Make sure you remain on top of the developments: digital is the key word of the near future. You want to be on that train. And not just with regards to new media, but also when it comes to old media going digital, such as online newspapers.

Keep all factors in mind when making final decisions. Everything is important and intertwined these days: the right time, the right audience, the duration of the impact, the availability of the product, your intuition, and the way your audience makes its decisions. Just be where they go.

Source: *Marketing* Monthly, November 2004, http://www.onevision.co.uk/xq/ASP/id.1078/qx/default.htm?CT=LeftNav.

Evaluating channel effectiveness

It is essential that having selected an appropriate distribution channel and intermediaries, their efficiency, effectiveness and performance are continually managed.

Key performance and evaluation measures include:

- Regular reviews
- A forum for problem review and solution
- Monthly, quarterly and yearly sales data analysis
- Average stock levels
- Lead and delivery times
- Zero defects
- Customer service complaints
- Marketing support – achieving marketing objectives, level of marketing activity, sales promotions, distributor incentives
- Spot-check of distributions further down the supply chain
- Annual performance audit.

From an Internet perspective, typical evaluation methods of marketing effectiveness might include:

- o Number of leads
- o Increased sales
- o Customer retention
- o Increased market share
- o Brand enhancement and loyalty
- o Customer service.

A marketing communications manager could expect to be involved in all these stages. The following case study shows the wide range of responsibilities of a marketing communications manager.

Senior marketing communications manager

Responsibilities

Actively help to develop and implement a marketing communications plan that effectively reaches target users, and facilitates the job of product marketing and business development teams by generating quality customer and partner leads.

Design, co-ordinate production and implement ongoing advertising, direct mail and other promotional programmes.

Maintain overall responsibility for management of and changes to company website.

Actively contribute to the development of and regular updates to corporate and product messaging, as well as to public relations materials.

Track newsworthy events and co-ordinate with public relations agency to publicize.

Gather information for press releases and co-ordinate approval and distribution processes.

Help co-ordinate the creative process, development and production of the company's collateral materials.

Help manage development, writing and production of company newsletter.

Co-ordinate with sales teams to collect leads, integrate with salesforce and manage the appropriate follow-up.

Manage development of the process to measure marketing communications results, including quality of leads generated and so on.

Hold primary responsibility for managing the company's various advertising, design and public relations agency relationships, including negotiating contracts, managing administrative and billing issues and so on.

Marketing communications are important for all types of organization and a wide range of contexts.

Planning a social marketing campaign

When planning programmes or awareness campaigns, it is important to target programmes and messages to reach and meet the needs of the intended audience. In health communications, these concepts take on the following meanings:

Product – is the knowledge, attitudes or behaviour you want the audience to adopt.

Price – can be interpreted as what the target audience must give up in order to receive the programme's benefits.

Promotion – is the means for persuading the target audience that the product is worth the price.

Place – refers to how the message is disseminated, such as through electronic or print media, or community programmes.

Stage 1 – Planning and selecting the strategy

This stage provides the foundation for the entire social marketing process. An assessment of the problem, the target audience and the available resources is conducted before moving ahead. During this planning process, the target audience should become increasingly segmented. This segmentation will aid in the development of appropriate messages. Goals and objectives for the programme will be developed at this time.

Stage 2 – Selecting channels and materials

Channels are how the message will be delivered, whether it is face to face, group, mass media, or a combination of channels. The more the channels selected, the more the target audience will be exposed to the message. Determining the channel prior to producing materials is important because different materials work better in different channels.

Material selection involves using what you have learned about your target audience to your advantage. Time and money can be saved by selecting materials that are specific to the audience you are trying to reach.

Stage 3 – Developing the materials and pre-testing

Draft the materials, pre-test them with the target audience and, if necessary, revise them. Determine if materials get the intended results, or revise them accordingly. Pre-testing adds time to the project but it can help to avoid producing materials that the target audience do not read.

Stage 4 – Implementing the programme

A method for tracking and evaluating the programme should be in place before it starts. The tracking method should help to identify those areas where changes may be needed.

Stage 5 – Assessing effectiveness

The type of evaluation conducted at this stage will depend upon several factors, including money, time, policies regarding the ability to gather information, the level of support for evaluation and the overall design of the programme.

Types of evaluation

- *Formative evaluation* – includes pre-testing of materials, and is designed to test the strengths and weaknesses of a programme before it is ready for implementation.
- *Process evaluation* – reviews the tasks of implementing the programme.

     ◦ *Outcome evaluation* – is used to gather descriptive information. It gathers information about knowledge and attitude changes, expressed intentions of the target audience and the initiation of policy changes.

     ◦ *Impact evaluation* – is the most comprehensive of the four types of evaluation. It focuses on the long-term outcomes of the programme and long-term behaviour change.

Stage 6 – Refining through feedback

If the programme is to be continued, revisions of the programme should be undertaken. If this is the end of the programme, documentation of what was learned should be made so as to assist others who may undertake a similar project in the future. An evaluation report should be prepared that could be used to secure funding to continue the programme and assist others conducting similar activities.

Integrated marketing communications

Creating an integrated marketing communications (IMC) plan is important for achieving maximum effectiveness.

Using the elements of the communications mix in a co-ordinated way so as to achieve the objectives of a promotion. Usually, a combination of marketing communications tools are used to meet specific campaign objectives. For example, advertising campaigns are often supported with sales promotions activities, or public relations or both. The role of marketing communications is to:

     ◦ Differentiate a product/brand (to make it different to a competitor's brand or seem different through effective positioning)

     ◦ Remind and reassure a target audience with regard to benefits (to encourage (re)purchase)

     ◦ Inform a target audience by providing new information (e.g. of a new brand or flavour)

     ◦ Persuade an audience to take a particular set of actions (e.g. visit a theatre, stop smoking).

The following two examples show how companies see the advantages of an integrated approach.

Why create an Integrated Marketing communications (IMC) plan? The answer should be 'to be able to get the best co-ordinated message to your potential customers and stakeholders at the right place and at the best time'. You may have the world's best product but if potential customers never learn about it, you cannot move them to 'purchase' stage, let alone think of 're-buy'. Ever been to a concert and the orchestra when it is warming up? Spurts of music are heard left and right, bits and bars of the soon-to-be performed symphony are played pell-mell, trumpets tap their part out and the second violins test their pizzicato. Traditional marketing methods used to date are much like this. An IMC plan is your orchestra and can help make lovely philharmonic music out of your marketing communications effort. After researching your market's needs, a good starting point is to ensure there is a set of marketing and corporate messages so you can carry out a co-ordinated dialogue with your stakeholders. Yes, the 'integrated' in marketing communications works. A well-structured IMC plan ensures a common thread throughout everything you do. For example, if the plan calls for direct marketing, that theme should be cascaded onto your website and potentially into other vehicles. IMC takes a broad perspective. Look at your communications on a macro level – similar to the artist's palette – rather than at the individual components. Typically this is a suite of the following parts: advertising; direct marketing; interactive/Internet marketing; sales promotion; publicity and PR; and attractive communication – also called 'personal selling'. Work on this by setting clear top level goals and a plan for considerable co-ordination between the different channels and activities. One pitfall to avoid is becoming too top down and, in the case of larger companies, 'killing local creativity'. You can mitigate this with a master IMC calendar to make sure everyone knows what is going avoiding 'off-track' or parallel activities. Track success – a company-wide measuring system is a tool that can be used to gather information on a respective campaign (a benefit for local users) while aggregating this data into a central database (a boon for central marketing co-ordination). A good marketing communications plan can take your Company's marketing efforts to the next level. Test what works and feed the information back into the plan.

Source: Orchestrating Integrated Marketing Communications, Robert-Charles Kahn.

Marni Media – integrated marketing communications

Marni Media is an online information and creative marketing service. The firm's services integrate marketing strategy and creativity into written copy, sales presentations, website design and media management projects. Marni Media's objective is to provide professional marketing and creative media expertise to a client's communication team. Effective marketing communications depends upon team work between marketers, designers and programmers. Marni Media provides marketing and creative services to small and medium size businesses, advertising agencies, corporate marketing departments, web design teams and web content producers. Our services integrate marketing strategy with written and visual content. We create and produce effective front-end website design and content based upon search engine marketing strategies. Marni Media's objective is to deliver the right message to the right audience for business clients. Our approach to marketing communications is based upon experience in creating and producing messages to customers in web-based, e-mail, print, trade show, radio and television formats. We start by clearly defining marketing objectives and target audiences before the creative process begins, and we follow up with research and analysis to improve the efficiency of the media project. We believe that business should make it easy for customers to buy products and services.

Types of marketing communications

There are many different terms used to describe the various methods used by organizations to communicate with customers and other stakeholder groups. They include personal selling and non-personal selling (advertising, sales promotion, public relations and direct marketing). Advertising is any paid form of non-personal presentation by an identified sponsor. Sales promotion is a short-term incentive to encourage the purchase or sale of a product. Public relations aims to build and sustain good relations with the organization's stakeholders and publics through favourable publicity, building up a good 'corporate image', and handling or heading off unfavourable rumours, stories and events. Direct marketing is direct communications with carefully targeted individual consumers to obtain an immediate response through the use of non-personal tools (mail, telephone, fax and e-mail).

With *push strategies*, marketers use personal selling to promote their product to retailers and wholesalers, not the end-user. They include special incentives such as discounts, promotional materials and cooperative advertising. Advertising and sales promotions are part of pull strategies, which build consumer awareness so that the consumer will ask retailers to carry the product. The strategies are not exclusive and, in fact, most companies use both to increase their promotional effectiveness. By selecting a combination of promotional mix elements, marketers attempt to achieve the organization's promotional objectives: to provide information, differentiate a product, increase demand and add to a product's value.

Personal selling

Personal selling is often the most expensive element of the marketing communications mix because it is resource-intensive, and involves high contact and customer maintenance costs. In some instances, personal sales have been replaced by direct mail, telemarketing and e-mail. Personal selling includes activities such as:

Prospecting – Gathering information in order to gain sales leads and prospective clients.

Communicating – Being the provider of information about the organization, its products, services and after-sales care.

Selling – Persuading a potential customer to adopt the product.

Market research/information gathering – Environmental scanning, competitor intelligence, customer intelligence.

Servicing of accounts – Maintaining and providing ongoing customer service, including technical support, financial contractual arrangements and logistical arrangements.

Allocating – Ensuring that the allocation of products to customers is undertaken at all times, in particular in times of production shortages.

Customer relationship building – Building and sustaining long-term customer relationships.

Evaluation of personal sales

Evaluating and measuring sales performance is based upon the sales objectives set for the organization. But the objectives set will be SMART, and therefore clearly defined and clearly linked with marketing objectives and overall corporate performance goals.

It is likely that sales performance will be measured against objectives on a regular basis, anything from weekly to quarterly. However, in most organizations sales performance against actual planned achievement is measured on a monthly basis.

It is also likely that other factors relating to sales performance will be measured, such as:

- o *Productivity* – calls per day, calls per account, total number of orders versus calls.
- o *Account development* – total of new accounts, total of existing accounts, growth of sales from existing accounts.
- o *Expenses* – expenses versus number of calls made, cost per call.

With the evolution of IT, sales measurement techniques are becoming more sophisticated and more effective, and the speed at which information becomes available is of the essence. A drastic reduction in sales performance can mean that other elements of the promotional mix might be subject to increased activity to compensate for the drop in sales. However, the drop in income often inhibits too much marketing expenditure of a contingency nature to be undertaken.

Advertising

Advertising is one of the most influential forms of communication within the promotional mix and is particularly effective at reaching large audiences with specific messages. Depending on the media used, costs of reaching individuals can be lowered compared to other forms of communications. It can be used at different stages of purchasing, or for awareness creation at the early stages of a new product launch. Its main purpose is to inform, persuade and remind customers to purchase products and services. Advertising objectives are expressed in terms of promoting products, organizations and services, or stimulating demand, increasing sales, brand and product awareness, and reminding and reinforcing perceptions of a product or service.

Measuring advertising effectiveness is important for understanding how well ads are performing and what changes need to be made to improve performance. Promotion research consists of media and message research. Media research measures audience composition and size for media vehicles as a basis for determining ratings. Audience measurement services include magazine, local radio, national radio and television. Multiple measurement methods are usually preferable to single techniques to assess advertising effectiveness. There has been a trend towards greater use of sales promotion in comparison with advertising. This shift is part of the movement from pull- to push-oriented marketing, particularly in the case of consumer packaged goods. The factors that underpin this shift include increased brand parity, growing price sensitivity, reduced brand loyalty, the fragmentation of the mass market, reduced media effectiveness, growing short-term orientation, and favourable consumer responsiveness to sales promotions.

Sales promotions

Sales promotions often complement advertising, and may be planned and executed in parallel with associated advertising and possible public relations campaigns. They are used to encourage customers to trial products and services, and then to purchase them. The main aims and associated objectives of sales promotions are, for example, to increase brand and product awareness, attract new customers, increase trial and adoption of new and existing products, increase brand usage and to encourage trading up to the next size or the next range. Sales promotions can be a highly targeted and flexible form of communications and evaluation of their effectiveness is usually an integral part of the communication through, for instance, coupon redemption, money-off vouchers/coupons, buy one get one free, discounts, trial-sized products and so on.

Public relations

Some commonly used measures of results are:

Budget – Has the planned activity been achieved within budget and timescale?

Awareness – Established through using market research activities.

Attitude – Positivity or negativity and whether there is any change in consumer behaviour.

Media coverage and tone – Coverage in a range of media – number of column inches, key headings and the tone.

Positioning – Comparative information about the relative position of the organization and the competition.

Response generation – Enquiries or leads linked to reference codes or enquiry sources, for example a particular newspaper.

Share price – Recent highly publicized scandals such as Enron and WorldCom show that share prices can be manipulated, especially when exceeding a particular level is a management target, the achievement of which means that large bonuses can be earned. During the so-called 'dotcom boom', some worthless stock was also heavily promoted by brokers. A share price can also be affected by a myriad of external factors outside a company's control so, all in all, a healthy degree of scepticism is needed before relying on share price as a guide to anything.

Sales – When an organization suffers from negative perception, sales tend to drop. The challenge is to rehabilitate the image in order to increase sales.

Direct marketing activities

Direct marketing may take the form of direct mail, telemarketing, electronic marketing and online marketing. It is immediate, customizable to individual consumers or groups of consumers, and interactive. Direct e-mail marketing includes unsolicited bulk e-mail and opt-in direct email. Generally, direct marketing allows for easy measurement of effectiveness. Data mining (the extraction of hidden predictive information from large databases) is used to 'drill down' into the data to any level of detail needed to identify common characteristics of high-volume users. Clusters of consumers who share specific characteristics, such as income, education and brand loyalty, can be identified as targets for marketing efforts. Direct mail is the most commonly used direct-marketing advertising medium and marketers are able to target messages to specific market segments and quickly evaluate the success of a mailshot. It also enables greater personalization compared to mass media advertising.

Evaluation of direct marketing activities is based upon the predetermined objectives of the campaign. Typical measures for successful implementation of the direct marketing campaign will include:

- o Response rate
- o Conversion rate
- o Order value
- o Repeat orders.

Often, this information will be gathered through a range of voucher and campaign response codes that will be able to distinguish the source of the direct mail or promotion. However, the cost per enquiry and per order needs to be identified. Click-through rates are a common online measurement.

Trade promotions

Good trade promotions, that is a good 'push strategy', highly incentivized, backed up by appropriate merchandising and appropriate advertising, may be advantageous. Specific methods might include, for example, allowances and discounts, free merchandise, selling and marketing assistance, co-operative advertising, merchandising allowances, market information and product training. The following case study from Nortel demonstrates a range of incentives available if the value of sales is forecasted to be more than $1 million.

Case study

Nortel Networks

The Nortel Networks Partner Support Plan is designed to simplify your relationship with the company and make it easier for both parties to work together. The end result is that meshing your business goals with Nortel Networks is easier, more cost-effective and more advantageous than ever before. The Nortel Networks Premium Partners is associated with specific plan criteria that establish the basic guidelines for the relationship. Participants with annual forecasted purchases of Nortel Networks products greater than $1 million are eligible to register as a Premium Partner – the highest level within the plan. Premium Partners have access to the broadest spectrum of products, services and support programmes including:

- Eligibility for the Volume Discount Plan
- Assigned resources for sales and marketing support
- Access to new or restricted products if authorization requirements are met
- Marketing support funds
- Participation in all channel partner events.

The Nortel Networks Enterprise Solutions Co-op Fund is available to reimburse Premium Partners for pre-approved marketing activities. The funds can be used to create market and product awareness, increase sales and support your marketing efforts through a wide variety of marketing communications including advertising, direct mail, trade shows, promotional items and other marketing communications. Having access to new products can enable you to be first to market.

You will have access to:

Volume discounts, Promotional funds, Direct purchase, Indirect purchase, Assigned resources, Access to restricted products, Marketing programmes access, Pre-sales support, Post-sales support and Partner event access.

Retailer to consumer sales promotions

The key aims and objectives of this process will be to increase sales through a range of promotional techniques such as increasing in-store trade and customer traffic through, for example, the use of coupons and money-off vouchers, discounted promotions for next purchase, the use of storecards and rewards systems.

Manufacturer to consumer sales promotions

Typical sales promotion activities might include encouraging trials through the use of samples and gifts, disseminating information packs door-to-door and encouraging customers to trade up from their existing models.

Marketing channels

Increasingly, organizations are examining the whole demand chain that links raw material, components and manufactured goods, and how they are moved to their customers. The starting point should be the customer needs for which the organization needs to mobilize its resources. However, the term 'supply chain' is challenged because it suggests too linear a view of purchase, production and consumption. A more contemporary term is 'value network'. Philip Kotler in his book *Marketing Management* (Kotler, 2003) expresses the wish that marketers will look more widely than the customer side of the value network and participate in upstream activities. This would mean that they became network managers, not only customer and product managers.

Marketing channels are an integral part of the marketing mix, and they provide the means by which products and services are made available to end-user customers. They link manufacturers with their target markets, and are the means by which customers can access the products and services that they want. They consist of a number of different organizations each of which fulfils a particular role. Typically, a conventional channel will consist of a producer, wholesaler, retailer and end-user customer who need to collaborate and co-operate with each other. Intermediaries assume particular roles in relation to the other members of the marketing channel according to their position.

Hybrid channels

There are also 'hybrid' channels with different strategies used to reach different types of customers. For example, IBM uses its salesforce for its largest accounts, telemarketing for medium-sized accounts, direct mail for small accounts, retailers to sell to even smaller accounts and the Internet for speciality items. The Internet has had a major impact on established marketing channel structures because it allows direct contact between, for example, a service provider and the customer. Low-cost airlines is an example of this. Overall, the effect of more direct selling has been to reduce the number of intermediaries.

Distribution channels

A distribution channel consists of individuals and organizations who ensure that a product or service is available to the customer at the right place and time. A channel comprises marketing intermediaries, for example transportation companies, merchants, agents, wholesalers, warehouses and retail outlets. The successful management of the supply chain depends on motivating and controlling distributors and distribution outlets. Investing in intermediaries and their activities motivates them to undertake marketing within their network, thus adding value to the customer–supplier relationship. Traditionally, manufacturers operated within the area of production and marketing of brands, and retailers focused on selling activities. Interaction between the two was often based on manufacturers acting as 'order takers' and retailers as 'sales outlets'.

The challenge of making products and services available to customers around the world when, where and how they want them is complex. Technology transfer has made product advantages difficult to maintain but distribution is seen as having the potential for achieving a competitive advantage if marketing channels can be designed to provide excellent customer service. This means that members of the channel need to work together to create added value. A competitive advantage gained through better distribution is not so easily copied and may offer more of a sustainable competitive advantage. The main objective of physical distribution is to decrease costs while increasing service to the customer. The manager will need to consider the order processing, materials handling, warehousing, inventory management and transportation issues. Managers strive for a good balance of service, costs and resources. Therefore, effective planning is paramount to ensure that this happens by determining what level of customer service is acceptable, yet realistic in terms of costs. As physical distribution affects every element of the marketing mix, it is important that the customers needs are at the top of the list. An effective physical distribution programme should have a positive impact on customer satisfaction; for example, some companies offer guaranteed 'next day' delivery.

The following case study shows how 'category management' in the small convenience store sector is based on a collaborative approach between manufacturer and retailer.

Category management

Category management is based on a more collaborative approach and means that manufacturer and retailer interact actively together. Together they evaluate sales data to determine who buys what in a particular category, how often and how much they spend. Based on this shared data, they are able to develop customized strategies for individual categories in specific stores so that shelf-space, pricing, promotions and so on, maximize sales and profits. This means that manufacturer and retailer share, and are committed to, common goals.

Retailers should consider several criteria when evaluating the impact that categories have on their businesses, including: category sales, category gross profits, the category's ability to draw store traffic, and the impact on store image. Selecting the right supplier partner is critical. An ideal supplier partner should possess the following qualifications:

- *Track record* – The supplier partner should have a history of successfully driving the retailer's business.
- *Data management* – The supplier partner should have the skills and resources to deliver state-of-the-art, business-building information, insights and ideas.
- Does the candidate have access to data for use in better understanding category dynamics and benchmarking performance?
- Can the candidate interpret data and develop business-building recommendations?
- *Personnel* – Does the proposed team have high-quality members? Do you get along with the candidate's team members?

Wholesaler

Wholesalers buy products from the manufacturer, store them within their warehouses and sell the products on to the trade. Producers try to increase demand, and support marketing activity through various push and pull strategies. Both wholesalers and retailers want their respective customers to perceive a high level of service and value in the goods and services they purchase.

Retailer

Nowadays, retailers often have a presence on the high street and the Internet. They provide the link between the customer and the producer, and may require a lot of technical support, customer services backup, stock ordering facilities, systems underpinning the sales process, information and merchandise. Retailers provide wholesalers with sales contacts and outlets and help them by purchasing small quantities of stock on a regular basis. Retailers focus on end-user consumers and consider their buying motivations.

Distributors and dealers

Distributors and dealers stock products for manufacturers and sell them on, including after-sales service, warranties and credit facilities. Dealers often specialize in a particular brand and sell them to the end-user, making the channel shorter.

Agents, brokers and facilitators

Agents and brokers act on behalf of the manufacturer and bring buyers and sellers together.

Franchisee

A franchisee holds a contract to market and supplies a product or service that has been very strictly designed and developed by the franchiser. There are often restrictions on store design and layout, and what is sold within the retail outlet.

Merchandiser
Merchandisers are responsible for promotional displays in stores relating to different products.

Value-added activities
Examples of the kinds of value-added activities that intermediaries can undertake are: analysing information such as sales data, evaluating channel activities, co-ordinating advertising, personal selling, promotions and so on, facilitating communication, maintaining relationships between manufacturer and retail outlets, and providing advice, technical support, after-sales service and warranties.

Channels perform most effectively when they co-operate, co-ordinate and integrate their activities. Vertical channel management is where two or more channel members are connected by ownership or legal obligation. Marketing mix activities are more integrated, and often more effective because of this. Horizontal channel integration is the merging of organizations at the same level of channel operation under one management, for example, through mergers and takeovers.

Channel management

Power is not distributed evenly in most distribution channels and conflict can occur which is either horizontal, involving disagreements between channel members at the same level in the distribution chain, or vertical, occurring between channel members at different levels. Conflict in marketing channels can occur for a variety of reasons over issues such as stock levels, pricing and sales order processing. Sometimes it is because channel members have different priorities, and are focused on different business elements. A manufacturer might be focused more on products and processes, and a retailer may be focused more on customers and the processes necessary to meet their needs. Poor communication between channel members can be a cause of conflict but communication is an important co-ordinating mechanism for all members of a marketing channel. The willingness of members to share information and associated resources is an important factor because it enables an openness between parties, through which full information can be exchanged. This means that the producer must be willing to share sensitive information, and the distributor must be willing to share information about themselves, their customers and markets.

Horizontal conflict occurs among companies at the same level of the channel. For example, dealers in an area can complain about other dealers who are too aggressive in their pricing and advertising or by selling outside their assigned territories. Vertical conflict occurs between different levels of the same channels.

To overcome this, sometimes companies implement a vertical marketing system (VMS), a planned network of distribution channels designed to reduce conflict among channel members and resolve other distribution problems. This is where producers, wholesalers and retailers act as a unified system. One channel member owns the others, has contacts with them, or has so much power that they all co-operate.

The promotional mix in the marketing channel
A marketing channel is an organized network of agencies and institutions which in combination perform all the functions required to link producers with end-customers to accomplish the marketing task. It enables goods and services to be moved from producers and providers to consumers. Within a channel, upstream trading partners for a retailer are, for example, wholesalers, manufacturers and producers. Downstream activity takes place along the distribution chain, for example, from manufacturer to retailer to customer.

Channel communications help to hold together a channel of distribution and they are important in the development of channel relationships. However, the nature of marketing communications in a marketing channel is different from communications aimed at consumers because different audiences have different information needs. For example, in comparison with consumers, distributors tend to make a smaller number of high value orders less frequently. The promotional mix in a marketing channel is aimed mainly at conveying information relating to product features and benefits. For this purpose, advertising is expensive and relatively inefficient whereas personal selling, combined with activities such as direct marketing, the Internet, exhibitions and sales literature, could provide an effective promotional mix.

Difference between consumer and business-to-business marketing communications

	Consumer-orientated markets	Business-to-business markets
Message reception	Informal	Formal
Number of decision-makers	Single or few	Many
Balance of the promotional mix	Advertising and sales promotions dominate	Personal selling dominates
Specificity and integration	Broad use of promotional mix with a move towards co-ordinated mixes	Specific use of below-the-tools but with a high level of co-ordination and integration
Message content	Greater use of emotions and imagery	Greater use of rational, logic and information-based messages although there is evidence of a move towards the use of imagery
Length of decision time	Normally short	Longer and more involved
Negative communications	Limited to people close to the purchaser/user	Potentially an array of people in the organization and beyond
Target marketing and research	Great use of sophisticated targeting and communication approaches	Limited but increasing use to targeting and segmentation approaches
Budget allocation	Majority of budget allocated to brand management	Majority of budget allocated to sales management
Evaluation and measurement	Great variety of techniques and approaches used	Limited number of techniques and approaches

Source: Fill (2002) cited in Beamish, K. (2003) CIM Advanced Certificate Coursebook, Butterworth-Heinemann, *Marketing Communications*. Used with kind permission

Marketing communications in the b2b sector have been transformed by technological advances (Beamish, 2003). In the b2b sector, marketing communications can fulfil a variety of specific objectives which will vary according to the circumstances:

1. To create and maintain awareness
2. To generate sales leads
3. To pre-sell sales calls
4. To contact minor members of the decision-making unit
5. To build corporate and product images
6. To communicate technical information
7. To support the promotional effort.

The CIM Advanced Certificate 2003–2004 coursebook on Marketing Planning (Beamish, 2003) uses the DRIP acronym to describe the use of marketing communications in a marketing channel.

Focus of the message	Potential needs
Differentiation	Downstream so that channel members understand how a particular manufacturer (or particular products) adds value and is different from its competitors and other products that they carry
	Upstream to flag attention and to secure stock, support and resources
Reinforcing	Reminding downstream members of any superior product features and support facilities that are available
	Reassuring them of the benefits of continuity and reliability
	Reminding upstream members of their needs, problems and the support that is available
	Reassuring them that the business is working hard on their behalf, that they have their interests in mind
Informing	Providing downstream members with suitable levels of customer support and upstream members with market and performance information
Persuading	Encouraging downstream members to carry extra stock, provide facilities and meet service levels
	Stimulating upstream members to allocate stock, promotional support and favourable financial arrangements

Personal selling is a major communications tool in the marketing channel because face-to-face meetings between buying and selling organizations helps to develop and maintain inter-organizational relationships. The willingness of organizations to share information is important to the development of sustainable relationships.

Intranet

An intranet uses a company's internal network to publish, distribute and display information for anyone directly connected to the network. Intranets allow authorized staff to access the information they need and it can encourage the sharing of knowledge from the different parts of an organization. Different types of information, prepared by different people in different parts of the business can be integrated into a single document. Staff can have easy access to information at their computer, even photographic images and technical drawings. Information can be shared rapidly when transmitted through e-mail, either within a company or outside via the Internet.

Extranets

Extranets can be used to engage distributors and producers, and allows for fast, accurate, low cost exchange of information. It involves building bridges between the public Internet and private corporate intranets, and can be seen as part of a company's intranet that is made accessible to other companies, to the public, or comprises components that enable the collaboration with other companies. Maximizing accessibility will mean that many partners can be involved and the more the participants, the greater the rates of return from the system. Extranets can also help companies to finally realize the benefits of Just-In-Time (JIT) inventory systems.

Other uses of extranets include:

o Private newsgroups that co-operating companies use to share valuable experiences and ideas.
o Groupware collaboration in the development of new products or services.
o Training programmes that companies develop and share.
o Shared product catalogues accessible only to wholesalers or those in the trade.
o Project management and control as part of a common work project.

247

The following case study shows examples of the use of an extranet.

Automotive Network eXchange (ANX)

Chrysler, General Motors and Ford Motor Co. have a collaborative extranet called the Automotive Network eXchange (ANX) which links them to their suppliers. Communications between suppliers and manufacturers are quicker, and the system is used for product shipment schedules, order information, files for product designs and purchase orders.

Federal Express' Tracking System (www.fedex.com).

On FedEx's public site, a tracking number can be entered and any package still in their system can be located. In one session, all the information needed to prepare a shipper form, obtain a tracking number, print the form and schedule a pick up can be entered. The processes on their site have been copied by many other companies.

The following case study shows a typical working day for a marketing channel executive in a mobile phone manufacturing company.

Channel Marketing Executive: a day in the life

Toria works for a mobile phone company as a Channel Marketing Executive. She provides channel marketing/retail support to dealers and channel members (managing and planning merchandiser programme, dealers' roadshow and events, POS fulfilment, etc.). She manages product launches and marketing collaterals' fulfilment to channel members.

9:00 a.m. – My morning begins with replying to dealers' fax and e-mail requests of the company's channel marketing/retail support. The most exciting part of my day is when we have an active discussion with channel members on how to implement activities and formulate strategies.

10:00 a.m. – Meeting with channel members to discuss new promotional activities or events. Today, we discussed the upcoming dealer roadshow.

11:00 a.m. – I am contacting dealers about any updates pertaining to the company or their shops. I work with the rest of my colleagues as a team to implement dealer events and sales training. My time is mostly spent meeting with channel members to work out dealer events. I also visit them at retail shops to ensure that there is retail support and wide exposure of the company's brand presence.

3:00 p.m. – Meeting with a dealer to discuss his roadshow.

7:00 p.m. – Time to go home. This is the usual time I leave from the office. However, when I am on site at a roadshow, I leave around 9 p.m. so that I can ensure logistic arrangements are met before the event starts.

Consumer and business-to-business marketing communications

The importance of b2b communications is underpinned by buoyant Internet-based marketing communications compared with relatively slow growth in the b2c market.

The most important difference, however, is that organizational buying decisions are taken by *groups* of people rather than individuals. A key issue is to identify the individuals who comprise the decision-making unit.

Communications in marketing channel networks

A planned, channel-orientated communications strategy should contribute to and reinforce the partnerships in the network. There are many factors that can influence channel communication strategy, for example:

- o *Power* – Are some organizations more important than others?
- o *Direction* – Are communications one-way or two-way?
- o *Frequency* – How often should messages be sent?
- o *Timing* – Should messages be sent to all members simultaneously or serially?
- o *Style and content* – Should messages be formal/informal? What must be included?
- o *Distortion* – Will messages be received, stored and acted upon as the originator intends?

Review and evaluate the effectiveness of communications activities

The apocryphal quote about half of all advertising being a waste of money but it is not clear which half serves as a reminder that measuring the success of communications activities can be difficult. However, there are techniques that can be used for different purposes.

Many organizations measure the effectiveness of their marketing communications, and there are a range of techniques and procedures available. Increasingly, it is the synergy that derives from effective co-ordination of all activities that determines overall success. Single elements of the communications mix are not used in isolation. Different parts of a campaign can be assessed and the evaluation process can be carried out at different stages of a marketing campaign, that is, before, during and after a campaign has been launched. However, the overall impact of a co-ordinated marketing communications campaign and the degree to which the promotional objectives have been achieved are key measures that interest stakeholders.

Whilst the primary focus is upon ascertaining whether objectives have been met and the strategy has been effective – efficiency is also of interest. There should be a strong emphasis on 'efficiency', 'effectiveness' and 'value for money', which means making the best use of the available resources to achieve the best possible outcomes. However, some aspects of marketing are notoriously difficult to evaluate; for example, advertising. Whilst communications is one element of the marketing mix, the other elements should be evaluated as well.

Pre-testing is about showing unfinished advertisements, often to focus groups to gather their reactions and to understand their reasoning. Post-testing is concerned with the evaluation of a campaign once it has been released. A typical measurement is the number of enquiries or direct responses elicited by a single advertisement or campaign. Recall and recognition tests are common post-testing procedures for advertisements.

Tracking studies involve collecting data from buyers on a regular basis in order to assess their perceptions of ads. Sales promotion evaluation includes methods such as *consumer audits* and general s*ales information, retail audits* including, for example, changes in stock levels, distribution, market share and so on immediately after a promotional campaign. *Salesforce feedback* is also a common measure.

Voucher/coupon redemption – Usually coded so that the different response rates in different media can be tracked.

Calculating ROI

Obviously, the power of metrics diminishes if the information is merely distributed, and not intelligently assessed and acted upon by management. Return on Investment is the most critical measure of marketing programmes for making decisions that will help maximize company profits. Return on Investment in its simplest form is: {Net Profit (pre-marketing investment) – Net Profit (post-marketing investment)} – Investment = Return. Return/Net Profit (pre-marketing investment) = ROI.

Victorian government communication evaluation guidelines key principles
- Evaluation involves assessment of the degree to which an activity's objectives have been met as a result of the activity.
- Evaluation is an internal part of all communications projects, not an optional extra.
- Evaluation should be planned at the outset of a communications project.
- Evaluation must be properly budgeted for. As a rule of thumb, 10 per cent of a project's budget should be allocated to evaluation.
- A good test of the usefulness of an evaluation is to ask the following questions:

  - Does it effectively identify the *success/failure* of the project?
  - Does it effectively identify *the reasons for success/failure* of the project?
  - Does it effectively identify the *cost-effectiveness* of the project?

Broadly speaking, evaluation can address:

- *Activity* – what was done (for example, wrote, designed and produced brochures).
- *Output* – what communication took place (for example, distributed each brochure to 1000 people).
- *Outcome* – what was achieved in terms of knowledge, attitudes and behaviour. Outcome evaluation is far more important, useful and relevant than activity or output evaluation. All significant projects should be evaluated on their outcomes.

Evaluation tools
Methods commonly used to measure project outcomes and outputs include:

- Surveys
- Focus groups
- Web statistics
- User feedback.

The choice of method in any case depends principally on the objectives being measured against and the budget available.

1. *Accountability* – The evaluation should identify an individual, responsible, office holder who is accountable for the overall programme/activity.
2. *Situation analysis* – A situation analysis should provide sufficient rationale for the program purpose and objectives. It should include background to the activity, including the source of the original reason for the project.
3. *Rationale for approach* – Research/evidence should be cited in support of the approach taken, its form and extent.
4. *Aims and objectives* – The over-arching *aim* from the original project plan should be provided.
5. *Target audience/s* – Target audience should be identified, and a rationale provided for them.
6. *Communications activities* – All project communications activities should be listed and a rationale provided for the choice.
7. *Selected media* – Media used should be listed and a rationale provided for the selection.
8. *Key messages/creative* – Key messages/creative should be cited/described, and a rationale/ evidence provided for their selection.
9. *Output/outcome measurement tools* – Measurement tools used as part of the evaluation should be specified and a rationale provided, if necessary.
10. *Evaluation findings* – Findings should be clearly stated, and address the objectives.
11. *Key Success Factors* – Factors critical for the success (or failure) of the activity to achieve its objectives should be identified.
12. *Recommendations* – The evaluation should make recommendations for the future, reflecting learnings gleaned from the evaluation.
13. *Budget* – Budget and expenditure figures should be provided, and a statement should be made in respect of the cost-effectiveness of the activity.

Customer service

Customer service can be interpreted as any contact, whether active or passive, between a customer and a company that influences customer perceptions. Customer's make positive or negative judgements according to whether companies meet or exceed their expectations and meet their wants and needs. This involves more than the face-to-face contact or direct service that a customer receives. It includes all the elements that are part of the production and distribution of products and services. Mark McCormack in his book on selling describes customer service:

> *You can be doing the best job in the world for your client but if there's something missing, if the client is unhappy, then all your opinions about your performance are worthless. Great service is a matter of perception. Great service is what the client thinks it is.*

Trends in customer service

In November 2003, The Customer Care Alliance conducted an online survey to investigate current trends and performance levels in delivering customer care in Great Britain. Following an e-mail invitation, 10 957 British consumers took part in the study that examined the problems they experienced with products and services they used, what they did to address such problems and, if they contacted the organization responsible, the effectiveness of the response they received.

- o Eighty-one per cent of consumers experienced at least one problem in the past year with the products and services they consumed.
- o The top ten industry sectors responsible for problem experience were banking, eating and drinking out, holidays, car purchase and servicing, cable and satellite TV, air travel, rail/bus/coach travel, large electrical goods and home.

251

o Improvements and maintenance.
o The five most frequent problem issues were product or service did not meet expectations (41 per cent), poor product or service quality (34 per cent), unsatisfactory service – unrelated to repair (29 per cent), misleading information/advertising.
o Delivery delay (19 per cent)/non-delivery (17 per cent).
o Eighty-five per cent complained to the organization responsible, 54 per cent shared their experience with friends/colleagues and 34 per cent decided never to do business with the organization again.
o Of those who did not complain, 31 per cent felt that nothing would be done and 17 per cent felt that nothing could be done to resolve their problem.
o Of those who complained, 70 per cent contacted by telephone, 37 per cent by letter, 35 per cent face-to-face to frontline staff, 17 per cent by e-mail, 16 per cent face-to-face to management, 9 per cent by complaint form or comment card, 4 per cent by the Internet and 3 per cent by fax.
o It took an average of 3.8 contacts to resolve a problem.
o Satisfaction dropped from 31 per cent for one contact to 5 per cent if three or more were required.
o Only 11 per cent of problems were resolved within one day – 20 per cent took more than 30 days and 38 per cent of respondents felt that their problem had still not been resolved.

Conclusions
o Consumers are very likely to complain when they experience bad products or service but are unlikely to receive an effective and acceptable response from the organization responsible.
o Many only want non-monetary remedies that cost little to provide but do not get them.
o Delay, in terms of time and multiple contacts, undermines customer satisfaction but also increases organizational costs.
o Many organizations may be more interested in short-term cost reductions and productivity improvements than in providing effective customer care.
o Whilst standards appear low throughout Great Britain, there is a major opportunity for those that take customer satisfaction and retention seriously to gain a significant competitive edge.

The following case study highlights the results of a 2004 survey of senior managers with customer service responsibility. Three in four British companies say that they are not easy to do business with.

Customer dis-service built into British Business

77 per cent of businesses admit they are not easy to deal with.

71 per cent fail to gather data on their customers' total experience.

56 per cent of companies fail to incentivise managers to improve the customer experience.

When asked why they fail to understand the causes of bad customer experiences, the top two reasons given are lack of internal resource and poor cross-departmental collaboration. This is the conclusion of the 'Fast + Simple' research report from Budd, the customer service consultancy. The report paints a picture of British business systematically failing its customers, by failing to close the loop from customers' reported frustrations to actual improvements they can feel. Companies need to jettison 'silo' thinking and collaborate across business units and departmental boundaries to act quickly and systematically to interpret customer feedback. Says Peter Massey, CEO of Budd. Just 3 in 10 businesses have regular cross-department reviews and just 1 in 20 of organizations implement formal programmes to exchange learning.

The report highlights seven principles which underpin any approach to systematic excellence. By effectively linking hard and soft processes companies can close the loop between the customer and operations.

To be successful and prevent customer frustration businesses need to:

o Actively listen to the customer – rather than just hearing them
o Make the right people accountable for improvement
o Fix the things that make a difference to customers – addressing root causes not symptoms
o Measure projects and operations with the same success-indicators – so it is clear what makes a difference to customers
o Collaborate end-to-end across the business, to ensure the frontline can deliver what the customer wants
o Track what happens and make sure the customer can see the difference
o Put in a consistent process, not a one-off.

Source: http://www.insightexec.com/cgi-bin/item.cgi?id=131008.

There is a growing recognition of the strategic importance of customer service to business success. As industries mature and companies can no longer easily differentiate themselves by attributes such as products or pricing and technological innovations are widely available, customer service becomes a critical competitive advantage. Service and support interactions are often the only direct contact the company has with the customer and the quality of those interactions has a significant impact on long-term success. Organizations are facing increased pressures to do more with less. Many are being asked to provide service to more customers and/or support a wider range of products and services as budgets are reduced or remain flat.

There is a growing emphasis on the common management of diverse customer service communications channels, which include the phone, e-mail and web. Managing the channels as separate 'silos' makes it difficult to integrate information and gain a holistic view of a customer's preferences and purchasing profile. Organizations are looking for ways to treat all incoming service requests as a single, manageable queue so they can optimize efficiency.

An integrated customer service process can reduce cost, save time and improve profitability. Linking customer service information with sales data improves business scheduling and helps target potential customers. It helps to avoid duplication of effort and presents a unified, informed image.

The benefits of good customer service

The whole of an organization is implicated in customer service although some companies have dedicated customer service departments. Customer service is a link in a chain between buyer and seller and one of a series of links between stages in a marketing channel.

Increased customer retention rates

It has been repeatedly shown that good service leads directly to increased customer retention rates but the service has to be of a high standard to genuinely keep customers.

Reduced costs of running the business

Increased customer retention rates means the resources associated with setting up the customer's details are reduced to only one over a long time period, compared to a constant stream of new customers coming in as others leave. Regular customers can be serviced more efficiently. Good service means lower complaint rates, and therefore less time and cost involved in dealing with such complaints.

Reduced marketing costs

Many studies have shown that it costs around three to five times as much to attract a new customer compared to making the same sale to an existing customer. Customers can take on part of the marketing function by making recommendations and referrals. Personal referrals are one of the strongest influences on service adoption, and hence the strongest form of marketing.

Stronger position in the competitive marketplace

Companies identified as being good service providers tend to have higher revenue growth compared with poor service competitors. Customers that stay with a company for a long time are more profitable. They are more likely to make repeat purchases of the same goods and services, more likely to purchase other products or services, and often maintain higher balances/accounts.

Improved internal communication, staff relations and morale

Employees who receive positive feedback from their interactions with customers and a reduction in the number of complaints are bound to feel more satisfied with their work than working in a hostile climate. In turn this contributes to better customer service, and a virtuous circle is set in train. Being part of a service that is recognized as poor is damaging to morale.

Customer care

The culture of the organization is the basis of good customer service because it embodies the values of the organization, including how customers and employees should be treated. Motivated and valued staff is the basis of good customer care. Customers may interact with a number of different people during any transaction. The pre-transaction, transaction and post-transaction activities are the customer's chain of experience. An organization committed to customer service should try to understand and gain feedback about the customer's chain of experience.

Developing customer service

Sometimes, customer-care training focuses on superficial issues such as 'have a nice day' and doesn't look at the underlying causes of poor service; for example, management style, lack of empowerment of customer facing staff and lack of continuous training. If you are truly a customer-centric organization, you will literally live and breathe your customers' needs. Every activity should be tuned into making profit for all stakeholders, particularly customers, by maximizing the benefits available to them throughout the delivery and post-delivery processes. That means you have to work towards improving the 'life' of the individual or organization, and this also requires a system of needs and business improvement prioritisation across the supply and value chain. So, Hood explains, you first of all must undertake a needs definition analysis of both your organisation and customers. The next step is to ascertain which activities are going to have a greater impact on ROI for all of your stakeholders, which activities are necessary and in what order they must be achieved according to their potential impact and benefits. So measure not just inside your company, measure the customer too. Customer-centricity has to enhance the value of the relationship to create a win-win situation otherwise it isn't customer-centricity. The question is: how are you going to become customer-centric? To be customer-centric, you need to manage your total marketing – taking a broader, holistic approach to profit and strategy-making.

Source: By Graham Jarvis, Editor, CIMTech International, editor@cimtech.org http://www.insightexec.com/cgi-bin/item.cgi?id=131131.

Essentials of customer care

Customer audit

Who are your current customers?
What proportion of the business does each represent?
Who is the 'buyer'?
Are their needs satisfied?
How can the service offered to them be improved?

If employees are expected to deliver high-quality customer care, their views should be canvassed for ideas about how customer service could be improved. They also need access to good quality training in areas such as dealing with telephone calls and managing customer complaints efficiently and effectively. A website can be used to give customers the services and information they want. A good database can also help with the organization and planning of customer contacts.

Moments of Truth by Jan Carlzon (Carlzon, 1987) is an account of how the Scandinavian airline SAS was saved by promoting excellence in customer service. He put forward the view that any time a customer comes into contact with any aspect of a business, it provides an opportunity to form a good or a bad impression. Carlzon identified a series of critical transactions, for example initial contact, first use, ongoing support and further purchases, that he called 'Moments of Truth' because they had the potential to affect customer satisfaction and value. He sent SAS managers on training courses so that they would be able to better manage these moments of truth and this had a positive effect on the company.

Monitoring and evaluating customer service

A number of issues that impact upon quality measurement are:

o The difference in perception between employees and customers
o The inseparability of production and consumption
o The individuality of employees' performance and customers' perceptions.

There is a proposed formula for measuring these components:

o *Customer expectations* – service organizations' perceptions of customer expectations
o *Customer experience* – service organizations' perceptions of customer experience.

255

The following are examples of processes that can contribute to the monitoring and evaluation of the service that customers receive:

- o *Marketing research* – gather information about services, and delivery of them
- o *Observing customer* – staff interactions as the latter receive a service
- o Interviews to understand their perceptions and expectations versus their experience
- o *Customer satisfaction surveys* – questionnaires to monitor customer satisfaction
- o *Mystery consumer experience* – include a mystery person in the delivery of the service
- o *Evaluating dissatisfaction* – examine the main causes of customer dissatisfaction
- o *Monitoring image* – how is the image of the service perceived
- o *Performance appraisals* – of staff involved in the delivery of a service
- o *Employee group discussions* – internal marketing practice.

SERVQUAL

Measuring customer satisfaction is important for many organizations. The SERVQUAL Methodology was developed originally by customer satisfaction researchers Valarie Zeithaml, A. Parasuraman and Leonard Berry (*Delivering Quality Service*, Free Press: 1990). The Methodology helps organizations to better understand what customers value and how well their current organizations are meeting their needs and expectations. SERVQUAL provides a benchmark based on customer opinions of an excellent company, on your company, on the importance ranking of key attributes, and on a comparison to what your employees believe customers feel. It provides a detailed information about: customer perceptions of service (a benchmark established by your own customers); performance levels as perceived by customers; customer comments and suggestions and impressions from employees with respect to customers' expectations and satisfaction.

ServQual Model

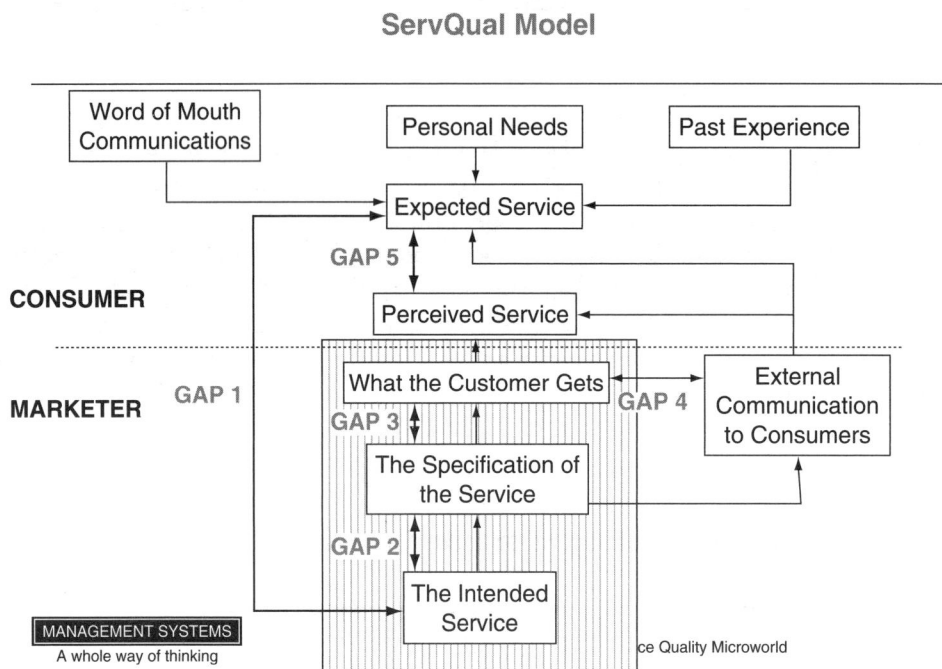

GAP 1 What managers and customers see as important; GAP 2 What managers see as important and the specifications; GAP 3 The specification and the delivery; GAP 4 The delivery and the claim/promise; GAP 5 Expectations and perceptions

Examples of the kinds of questions that can be asked are:

Desired level – The excellence level of service desired. Please consider the level of service you would desire for each of the statements below. If you think a feature requires a very high level of service quality, choose number nine in the second column. If you think a feature requires a very low level of service quality, choose number one in the second column. If your requirements are less extreme, choose an appropriate number in between.

Perceived level – Your perception of the service quality that is provided (see third column). Please use the same nine-point scale to evaluate the level of service you perceive.

With regard to	My DESIRED service level is: LOW 1 2 3 4 5 6 7 8 9 HIGH	My PERCEPTION of service level is: LOW 1 2 3 4 5 6 7 8 9 10 HIGH
1. Providing services as promised		
2. Dependability in handling client's problems		
3. Performing services right at the first time		
4. Providing the service at the promised time		
5. Keeping clients informed of when something will be done		
6. Prompt service to clients		
7. Willingness to help clients		
8. Readiness to respond to clients' requests		
9. Personnel who instill confidence in their clients		
10. Making clients feel assured		
11. Personnel who are always courteous and considerate		
12. Personnel who have the expertise to look after clients' needs		
13. The individual attention that clients get		
14. Personnel who deal with clients in a caring fashion		
15. Personnel who have the clients' best interest at heart		
16. Personnel who understand the needs of their clients		
17. The modern equipment and apparatus available		
18. The visually appealing facilities		
19. Convenient office hours		
20. How would you rate the *overall quality of service* provided?		

Case study

Monsoon is a design-led retailer operating two chains – Monsoon and Accessorise. Monsoon aims to provide its customers with an experience that is distinctively different, in terms of product offering and levels of customer service. The company recognizes that its people, and in particular its continuing ability to inspire, motivate and reward them, are critical to the achievement of this aim.

Monsoon has ten service standards to ensure that a consistently high level of service is provided in all their branches. They are:

1. Every customer should be acknowledged within two minutes of entering the branch.
2. Every branch will have a 3-hour window (customer service time).
3. If a customer is holding an item of stock, a member of staff must always approach and offer assistance.
4. When a customer is trying on an item of stock, a member of staff must always be actively working with them.
5. Every customer that an assistant is working with must be offered a secondary product.
6. The telephone should not be answered when serving a customer, except if no one else is free and staff excuse yourself first.
7. If an item is out of stock an alternative item should be found or a solution offered, for example phone another branch or mail order.
8. Every purchasing customer must have the account card mentioned to them at the till point.
9. A positive comment must be made to all customers at the till point; where possible this should be a feature or benefit.
10. Customers should always be thanked and given a smile on the completion of the sale.

Monsoon has a customer service award scheme for its staff, including an employee of the month award. Pay rises and performance related pay are also connected with superior levels of customer service.

Source: http://www2.monsoon.co.uk/.

Because Monsoon's service standards are clearly set out they can be evaluated comparatively easily through direct observation. Obviously, the methods of monitoring and evaluating customer service that are used depend on the type of business and the organizational context. Large companies are more able to introduce sophisticated monitoring systems compared to smaller organizations. Business sectors such as finance, insurance, call centres often record customer telephone calls for training purposes.

Ways to improve customer service

Personalize communications – For example, greeting a customer by name, personalize the e-mail addresses of customer-facing employees.

Create opportunities for feedback

Find out from new customers why they chose the company over the competition. Ask existing customers what could be better. Enable online feedback by putting an e-mail response form or newsgroup on the website. Encourage complaints, as only one in ten dissatisfied customers bothers to complain, usually dissatisfied customers just take their custom elsewhere. Carry out occasional customer satisfaction surveys. Contact any customer who has stopped buying and keep a record of customer feedback to help identify problem areas.

Establish a customer hotline, and make sure the number is on every piece of paper sent out.

- ○ Monitor and analyse the contact you have with customers.
- ○ Use software to discover which webpages are most popular.

Differentiate between different customer segments

When marketing, if appropriate, differentiate between different market segments.

- ○ Potential customers who have not yet purchased anything. For example, someone who has made an enquiry as a result of an advertisement where the aim is to build interest in what you have to offer.
- ○ Another segment is customers who have already made a purchase, where your aim is to increase the frequency of their buying and to sell them other products and services.
- ○ Premium customers who already make regular purchases. Sometimes, a few large customers generate a high proportion of profits and it is important to make sure that their needs are being met. Invite key customers to special events. Try to reinforce the idea that they are valued customers but without being unduly obtrusive or obsequious. Above all, don't be like Uriah Heep who was ever so 'umble'.

Added-value schemes

A successful loyalty scheme pays for itself by encouraging more frequent purchases. The most common loyalty schemes are based on offering rewards to loyal customers. Several businesses can collaborate to support the same loyalty scheme. An accounting system may need to track the purchasing activity of each customer and recognize when discounts have been earned. The following case study is an example of service standards and also shows how customers with special needs are catered for.

Inland revenue customer service standards

We aim to provide a prompt, efficient and courteous service to our customers.

Our aims and what they mean – We aim to provide you with the best possible customer service and we set targets to measure our success in providing that service.

Answering the telephone – We aim to answer 90 per cent of all calls to local offices within 20 seconds.

Answering post – We aim to respond fully to 80 per cent of post within 15 working days. Where we cannot do this, we will let you know the reason for the delay, and when you can expect a full reply.

Attending to callers at our Enquiry Centres – We aim to see 95 per cent of our callers without an appointment within 15 minutes.

Attending to repayment claims – When tax has been correctly taken at source from investment income but the recipient is not liable to tax, we aim to repay that tax within 20 working days of receiving a claim.

If you have a complaint, you should write to the area director of the office you are dealing with; most problems can be settled at this level. You can get his or her name from the people who have been dealing with your complaint, or at any Inland Revenue office.

Customers with special needs.

We will do everything reasonably possible to help you. The full range of services include:

- ○ The use of Textphones, their locations and telephone numbers.
- ○ Handling Typetalk and Minicom calls from deaf customers through a telephone operator.
- ○ Providing an induction loop for people with hearing aids and lighted magnifier for the partially sighted in all of our Enquiry Centres.
- ○ Our website at www.inlanderevenue.gov.uk is compatible with speech output software used by people with impaired vision.
- ○ Specialist help, such as sign language interpreters and other language interpreters.
- ○ Publishing leaflets in other languages.
- ○ Providing some forms and leaflets in braille, large print, on audio tape and disk.
- ○ Home visits to customers who are unable to call at our offices and cannot be helped over the phone or by correspondence.

Plan for introducing better customer service

1. Review other organizations with good reputations for good customer service. Look at how this compares with practices in the target organization.
2. Agree what customer service means and how it will be interpreted in the target organization.
3. Agree customer service standards and procedures.
4. All staff should participate in the process of change. Establish a working group or project team that has representation from all the parts of the organization that have an influence on customer service.
5. Review strengths and weaknesses.
6. Agree and communicate customer satisfaction performance targets.
7. Develop plans to implement changes, including an internal marketing plan.
8. A training programme aimed at everyone who has an influence on customer service should be devised or outsourced and implemented.

The following case study highlights the need to target and retain their most attractive customers and expanding their base of profitable customers. This is necessary because the cost of acquiring new customers greatly exceeds the cost of retaining existing customers.

Case study: Cisco Systems

Customer care refers to the processes, software, hardware and Internet capabilities used to gather and manage information about customers and potential customers. While companies can differentiate themselves from their competition with the scope and quality of their products and services and with their physical or virtual surroundings, the best way to generate customer loyalty is to ensure that customers have a positive, satisfying experience every time they interact with your company.

To meet this challenge, today's progressive companies are adopting a new business model – one that emphasizes a customer's lifetime value. They are executing this model by integrating new Internet initiatives and Web-based application. Specifically, companies can:

Integrate customer interactions across marketing, sales, e-commerce, fulfillment, billing and provisioning, service, learning, and online communities.

Create a flexible, effective channel for communicating with existing customers and reaching out to new customers.

React quickly to customers' changing needs and increase brand awareness.

Enable customers to do business at their convenience – let them order online, find technical information, check order status, or configure products online at any hour of the day.

Create online tools for the sales force that allow them to access product information, communicate with other groups, create proposals, and check availability.

Allow the sales organization to focus on the customer, provide more value-added services, and pursue additional sales opportunities.

Maintain order processing and customer support at a steady headcount despite an increasing customer base.

Reduce the time for handling orders, resolving customer issues, and transferring knowledge to and from a customer or to partners across the supply chain. Move transactions away from agents to automated fulfillment.

Eliminate redundant infrastructure.

Source: http://www.cisco.com/global/UK/solutions/ent/bus_solutions/cc_home.shtml.

Customer retention management

There are a number of techniques for measuring customer satisfaction linked to profitability. Established customers tend to be more profitable because:

- ○ They place frequent, consistent orders, and cost less to serve
- ○ They tend to buy more
- ○ Satisfied customers may sometimes pay a premium price
- ○ Retaining customers makes it difficult for competitors to enter a market or increase their share
- ○ Satisfied customers often refer new customers to the supplier at no extra cost
- ○ A higher retention rate implies fewer new customers need to be acquired.

Customer retention in business-to-consumer (b2c) markets

In consumer markets, customer retention schemes are focused around loyalty cards. Loyalty schemes are based on accessing information from customer databases, and making use of direct response media such as direct mail and telemarketing. Product-based sales promotion advertising is more widely used by retailers who do not use loyalty schemes.

Retaining customers in business-to-business (b2b) markets

The basic principles that a b2b market should consider in relationship development:

Technical support – providing added value to clients in industrial markets.

Technical expertise – providing expertise can be a good selling point for the organization.

Resource support – making available a range of cost-effective resources to support the relationship.

Service levels – these appear to be of growing importance and will relate in particular to time, delivery and product quality.

Reduction of risk – using exhibitions, trial use and product delivery guarantees.

Relationship marketing

Key dimensions that provide a basis for a relationship:

Reliability – ability to perform the promised service dependably and accurately.

Responsiveness – willingness to help customers and provide prompt service.

Assurance – knowledge and courtesy of employees, and their ability to inspire trust and confidence.

Empathy – caring, individualism, attention the firm provides its customers.

Tangibles – physical facilities, equipment and appearance of personnel.

Relationship marketing and mass customization

Mass customization enables companies to focus on what customers want, rather than what the company can produce. It also allows companies to produce individually tailored products. There is a longer history of using this approach with services such as banking stockbroking rather than products. Mass customization is also more common in b2b markets and the simplest approach is to design a product that buyers can customize themselves. Dell Computers allows the buyer to design an individual computer and then track it through to delivery. Much of Dell's production, up to the point of final assembly, is outsourced which means that suppliers at every link in the chain need good timely information about what customers want, and when. Speed and good communications are essential if mass customization is to work.

The Age of E-tail (Birch, Gerbert and Schneider, 2000) conveys the message that the future of shopping is online and the result of this will be the need for companies to offer almost everything in ways that are specifically tailored to the customer. Personalized products, such as cars and PCs, are made to individual specifications and soon all successful e-tailors will offer almost everything tailored individually to the customer. E-tailors need repeat business to achieve profitability but e-customers are fickle.

Internal marketing

This topic is covered in more detail in Unit 4 Managing Change. You should be able to demonstrate that you are able to use marketing communications techniques for an internal marketing plan to support the management of change within an organization. The basis of internal marketing is focusing on the relationship that exists between the organization and its employees. One of the success factors for the implementation of the marketing plan is to treat internal staff as if they are customers who all need the same consideration and attention as external customers. The aim of internal marketing is to develop a unified sense of purpose among employees. It plays an important role in ensuring that the organization is marketing- and customer-focused. Internal marketing is based on a communications programme, and there are a number of steps that an organization can take in order to achieve internal synergy and employee co-operation:

- Creating an internal awareness of the corporate aims, objectives and overall mission
- Determining the expectations of the internal customer
- Communication to internal customers
- Changes in tasks and activities
- Internal monitoring and control.

It is as important to segment the market internally, as it is segmented externally. A key aim of the marketing plan should be the successful motivation and retention of the internal customer so that the organization can meet the needs of the external market.

Internal marketing aids communication and can help to overcome resistance to change. It can be used to help inform and involve staff in new initiatives and strategies.

The Internet can help to foster the sharing of information but an extranet, that is a computer network that provides communication across selected organizations, enables sharing in a more controlled and secure manner. Often, companies use extranets as part of a search for better ways to communicate with their channel members and reduce costs. Because the extranet is interactive and easily accessible it has the potential to transform the way channel members communicate with each other. For example, it can make information sharing and communication frequency more timely than the same information obtained from more traditional methods of communication.

Internal relationship marketing techniques

Internal marketing projects can be considered in four phases:

Understanding the nature of the internal market
An assessment phase that aims to find out the attitudes and beliefs of employees and managers towards each other, the company, customers and marketing mix components.

Communicating with staff
A review of communications activities and their effectiveness, including a 'mapping' of communications channels.

Developing the plan
Devising strategies for meeting the objectives of the internal marketing campaign.

Evaluation

Evaluating the success of the plan according to the set objectives.

Internal marketing can contribute to helping organizations achieve good relationships with their external customers. The key success factors of internal marketing success are:

- o Create an internal awareness of the corporate aims, objectives and overall mission.
- o Determine the expectations of the internal customer.
- o Communicate to internal customers.
- o Provide appropriate human and financial resources to underpin the implementation of the marketing strategy.
- o Provide training in order that employees have the appropriate skills and competences to undertake the task at hand.
- o Implement a change in tasks and activities appropriate to the objectives of the organization.
- o Provide a structure whereby cross-functional integrated teams across business units can work together, in order to aid communication of business activity relating to the achievement of corporate goals.
- o Provide the systems and processes that enable successful delivery of services and products, enabling employees to successfully implement them and achieve organizational success.
- o Maximize the opportunity for customer interaction through effective management of service levels, for example response times, reply processes.
- o Internal monitoring and control.

For internal marketing to be successfully implemented, a planned approach is essential to allow evaluation and measurement of the successful execution of a plan. The plan could be designed with the following headings:

- o Internal vision
- o Aims and objectives
- o Internal marketing strategy
- o Segmentation, targeting and positioning
- o Marketing programme (to include all elements of the marketing mix)
- o Implementation.

Planning for a change programme

Ensure that there is a receptive climate towards the proposed change.

Identify a champion or a team of champions that will help to promote change and oversee its implementation.

Audit team capabilities and competences and identify any gaps that may need to be filled through training and development.

Market the change to the target audience.

Develop the plan, including a budget.

Try to anticipate arguments against change, and identify positive responses to them.

Before we can effectively market our libraries to our customers, we have to market within to library staff. Each member of staff markets the library with every single interaction they have with customers. Friendly staff can often make up for short-comings elsewhere in the service. Staff are also the most potentially damaging part of the marketing equation. Customers do not always notice good service, but they invariably notice and remember poor service, which is often a consequence of limited interpersonal skills. If employees do not care about their company, they will in the end contribute to its demise. Even if you don't have the time, staff, or budget for a formal, full-blown marketing plan, you can make progress on internal marketing.

Step 1: Staff buy-in

Get staff involved, energized, and feeling ownership for your library. Your staff members have a personal stake in your library, and therefore in this process. Every customer interaction is a marketing moment.

Step 2: Mission statement

Do you have a mission statement? Does it explicitly support the mission of your organization? The needs of your customers? Link the work of individual staff members to your mission. Post your mission statement prominently in your library; use it on documents such as fax cover sheets, e-mail, business cards, etc.

Step 3: Image/Brand

A brand is the emotional connection you have with your customers.

Your library's image is created by the collective actions of the library staff.

What expectations do you want to create for your customers?

How will you deliver on those expectations?

Step 4: Identity

Create an identity for your library – Place your identity stamp on intranet banner ads, library brochures and publications, presentations, e-mail signatures, and partner intranet sites.

Step 5: Key customer messages

Identify the key messages you want to communicate to your customers, for example I know the library has an intranet site; I can easily navigate the library's site; I know the library staff can provide consulting and analysis for my projects.

Step 6: Vision

Do you have a vision of where your library is going? What it will look like in 2 years? In the real world, you need to have a clear picture of your vision – and then communicate that vision to your staff.

What will success look like? – library staff will understand that they are selling or hurting your library during every interaction with customers? – feel increased personal ownership for your library? – know how your mission supports your organization's goals?

In conclusion, every customer interaction is a marketing moment. All staff must know, support, and be able to articulate your library's mission, vision, and key customer messages.

Source: Adapted from: Internal Marketing: Inside Job. Laura Zick, Library and Information Services, Lilly University, Eli Lilly and Company. http://www.sla.org/division/dpht/Spring2003/presentations2003/Laura_Zick.ppt.

Summary

There are a variety of approaches to planning the design, implementation and evaluation of communications campaigns. Marketing communications are used to develop relationships or communicate with a range of stakeholders including the provision of support for members of a marketing channel. There are also a variety of ways to review and evaluate the effectiveness of communications activities.

Bibliography

Beamish, K. (2003) 'Communication strategies and planning', *Marketing Communications*, Harlow: Butterworth-Heinemann.

Birch, A., Gerbert, P. and Schneider, D. (2000) *The Age of E-tail*, 4th European edition, Milford, CT: Capstone.

Carlzon, J. (1987) *Moments of Truth*, Harper.

Kotler, P. (2003) *Marketing Management*, 11th edition, New York: Prentice Hall.

Sample exam questions and answers for the Marketing Management in Practice module as a whole can be found in Appendix 6 and past examination papers can be found in Appendix 7. Both appendices can be found at the back of the book.

appendix 1
guidance on examination preparation

Preparing for your examination

You are now nearing the final phase of your studies and it is time to start the hard work of exam preparation.

During your period of study you will have become used to absorbing large amounts of information. You will have tried to understand and apply aspects of knowledge that may have been very new to you, while some of the information provided may have been more familiar. You may even have undertaken many of the activities that are positioned frequently throughout your Coursebook, which will have enabled you to apply your learning in practical situations. But whatever the state of your knowledge and understanding, do not allow yourself to fall into the trap of thinking that you know enough, that you understand enough, or even worse, that you can just take it as it comes on the day.

Never underestimate the pressure of the CIM examination.

The whole point of preparing this textbook for you is to ensure that you never take the examination for granted, and that you do not go to the exam unprepared for what might come your way for 3 hours at a time.

One thing is for sure: there is no quick fix, no easy route, no waving a magic wand and finding you know it all.

Whether you have studied alone, in a CIM study centre, or through distance learning, you now need to ensure that this final phase of your learning process is tightly managed, highly structured and objective.

As a candidate in the examination, your role will be to convince the Senior Examiner that you have credibility for this subject. You need to demonstrate to the examiner that you can be trusted to undertake a range of challenges in the context of marketing and that you are able to capitalize on opportunities and manage your way through threats.

You should prove to the Senior Examiner that you are able to apply knowledge, make decisions, respond to situations and solve problems.

Very shortly we are going to look at a range of revision and exam preparation techniques, and at time-management issues, and encourage you towards developing and implementing your own revision plan, but before that, let's look at the role of the Senior Examiner.

A bit about the Senior Examiners!

You might be quite shocked to read this, but while it might appear that the examiners are 'relentless question masters' they actually want you to be able to answer the questions and pass the exams! In fact, they would derive no satisfaction or benefits from failing candidates; quite the contrary, they develop the syllabus and exam papers in order that you can learn and then apply that learning effectively so as to pass your examinations. Many of the examiners have said in the past that it is indeed psychologically more difficult to fail students than pass them.

Many of the hints and tips you find within this Appendix have been suggested by the Senior Examiners and authors of the Coursebook series. Therefore, you should consider them carefully and resolve to undertake as many of the elements suggested as possible.

The Chartered Institute of Marketing has a range of processes and systems in place within the Examinations Division to ensure that fairness and consistency prevail across the team of examiners, and that the academic and vocational standards that are set and defined are indeed maintained. In doing this, CIM ensures that those who gain the CIM Professional Certificate Professional Diploma in Marketing and Professional Postgraduate Diploma in Marketing, are worthy of the qualification and perceived as such in the view of employers, actual and potential.

Part of what you will need to do within the examination is be 'examiner friendly' – that means you have to make sure they get what they ask for. This will make life easier for you and for them.

Hints and tips for 'examiner friendly' actions are as follows:

o Show them that you understand the basis of the question, by answering *precisely* the question asked, and not including just about everything you can remember about the subject area.
o Read their needs – how many points is the question asking you to address?
o Respond to the question appropriately. Is the question asking you to take on a role? If so, take on the role and answer the question in respect of the role. For example, you could be positioned as follows:

'You are working as a Marketing Assistant at Nike UK' or 'You are a Marketing Manager for an Engineering Company' or 'As Marketing Manager write a report to the Managing Partner.'

These examples of role-playing requirements are taken from questions in past papers.

o Deliver the answer in the format requested. If the examiner asks for a memo, then provide a memo; likewise, if the examiner asks for a report, then write a report. If you do not do this, in some instances, you will fail to gain the necessary marks required to pass.
o Take a business-like approach to your answers. This enhances your credibility. Badly ordered work, untidy work, lack of structure, headings and subheadings can be off-putting. This would be unacceptable in the work situation, likewise it will be unacceptable in the eyes of the Senior Examiners and their marking teams.
o Ensure the examiner has something to mark: give them substance, relevance, definitions, illustrations and demonstration of your knowledge and understanding of the subject area.
o See the examiner as your potential employer or ultimate consumer/customer. The whole purpose and culture of marketing is about meeting customers' needs. Try this approach – it works wonders.

    o Provide a strong sense of enthusiasm and professionalism in your answers; support it with relevant up-to-date examples and apply them where appropriate.

    o Try to do something that will make your exam paper a little bit different – make it stand out in the crowd.

All of these points might seem quite logical to you, but often in the panic of the examination they 'go out of the window'. Therefore it is beneficial to remind ourselves of the importance of the examiner. He/she is the 'ultimate customer' – and we all know customers hate to be disappointed.

As we move on, some of these points will be revisited and developed further.

About the examination

In all examinations, with the exception of Marketing Management in Practice at Professional Diploma level, the paper is divided into two parts.

    o Part A – Mini-case study = 50 marks
    o Part B – Option choice questions (choice of two questions from four) = 50 per cent of the marks (each question attracting 25 per cent).

For the Marketing Management in Practice paper, the same approach is taken. However, all of the questions are directly related to the case study and in this instance the case material is more extensive.

Let's look at the basis of each element.

Part A: The mini-case study

This is based on a mini-case or scenario with one question, possibly subdivided into between two and four points, but totalling 50 per cent of overall marks.

In essence, you, the candidate, are placed in a problem-solving role through the medium of a short scenario. On occasions, the scenario may consist of an article from a journal in relation to a well-known organization.

Alternatively, it will be based upon a fictional company, and the examiner will have prepared it in order that the right balance of knowledge, understanding, application and skills is used.

Approaches to the mini-case study

When undertaking the mini-case study there are a number of key areas you should consider.

Structure/content
The mini-case that you will be presented with will vary slightly from paper to paper and, of course, from one examination to the other. Normally, the scenario presented will be 250–500 words long and will centre on a particular organization and its problems or may even relate to a specific industry. However, please note, for Marketing Management in Practice, the case study is more significant as all the questions are based upon the case materials.

The length of the mini-case study means that usually only a brief outline is provided of the situation, the organization and its marketing problems, and you must therefore learn to cope with analysing information and preparing your answer on the basis of a very limited amount of detail.

Time management

There are many differing views on time management and the approaches you can take to manage your time within the examination. You must find an approach to suit your way of working, but always remember, whatever you do, you must ensure that you allow enough time to complete the examination. Unfinished exams mean lost marks. A typical example of managing time is as follows:

Your paper is designed to assess you over a three hour period. With 50 per cent of the marks being allocated to the mini-case, it means that you should dedicate somewhere around 100 minutes of your time to both read and write up the answer on this mini-case, leaving a further 80 minutes for the remaining questions. Some students, however, will prefer to allocate nearly half of their time (90 minutes) on the mini-case, so that they can read and fully absorb the case, and answer the questions in the context of it. This is also acceptable as long as you ensure that you work extremely 'SMART' for the remaining time in order to finish the examination.

Do not forget that while there is only one question within the mini-case, it can have a number of components. You must answer all the components in that question, which is where the balance of time comes into play.

Knowledge/skills tested

Throughout all the CIM papers, your knowledge, skills and ability to apply those skills will be tested. However, the mini-cases are used particularly to test application, that is your ability to take your knowledge and apply it in a structured way to a given scenario. The examiners will be looking at your decision-making ability, your analytical and communication skills and, depending on the level, your ability as a manager to solve particular marketing problems.

When the examiner is marking your paper, he or she will be looking to see how you differentiate yourself, looking at your own individual 'unique selling points'. The examiner will also want to see if you can personally apply the knowledge or whether you are only able to repeat the textbook materials.

Format of answers

On many occasions, and within all examinations, you will most likely be given a particular communication method to use. If this is the case, you must ensure that you adhere to the requirements of the examiner. This is all part of meeting customer needs.

The likely communication tools you will be expected to use are as follows:

- ○ Memorandum
- ○ Memorandum/report
- ○ Report
- ○ Briefing notes
- ○ Presentation
- ○ Press release
- ○ Advertisement
- ○ Plan.

Make sure that you familiarize yourself with these particular communication tools and practise using them to ensure that, on the day, you will be able to respond confidently to the communication requests of the examiner. Look back at the Customer Communications text at Certificate level to familiarize yourself with the potential requirements of these methods.

By the same token, while communication methods are important, so is meeting the specific requirements of the question. This means you must understand what is meant by the precise instruction given. *Note the following terms carefully*:

○ *Identify* – Select key issues, point out key learning points, establish clearly what the examiner expects you to identify.

○ *Illustrate* – The examiner expects you to provide examples, scenarios and key concepts that illustrate your learning.

○ *Compare and contrast* – Look at the range of similarities between the two situations, contexts or even organizations. Then compare them, that is ascertain and list how activities, features and so on agree or disagree. Contrasting means highlighting the differences between the two.

○ *Discuss* – Questions that have 'discuss' in them offer a tremendous opportunity for you to debate, argue, justify your approach or understanding of the subject area – *caution* it is not an opportunity to waffle.

○ *Briefly explain* – This means being succinct, structured and concise in your explanation, within the answer. Make your points clear, transparent and relevant.

○ *State* – Present in a clear, brief format.

○ *Interpret* – Expound the meaning of, make clear and explicit what it is you see and understand within the data provided.

○ *Outline* – Provide the examiner with the main concepts and features being asked for and avoid minor technical details. Structure will be critical here, or else you could find it difficult to contain your answer.

○ *Relate* – Show how different aspects of the syllabus connect together.

○ *Evaluate* – Review and reflect upon an area of the syllabus, a particular practice, an article and so on, and consider its overall worth in respect of its use as a tool or a model and its overall effectiveness in the role it plays.

Source: Worsam, Mike, *How to Pass Marketing*, Croner, 1989.

Your approach to mini-cases

There is no one right way to approach and tackle a mini-case study, indeed it will be down to each individual to use their own creativity in tackling the tasks presented. You will have to use your initiative and discretion about how best to approach the mini-case. Having said this, however, there are some basic steps you can take.

○ Ensure that you read through the case study at least twice before making any judgements, starting to analyse the information provided, or indeed writing the answers.

○ On the third occasion read through the mini-case and, using a highlighter, start marking the essential and relevant information critical to the content and context. Then turn your attention to the question again, this time reading slowly and carefully to assess what it is you are expected to do. Note any instructions that the examiner gives you, and then start to plan how you might answer the question. Whatever the question, ensure the answer has a structure: a beginning, a structured central part and, finally, always a conclusion.

○ Keep the context of the question continually in mind: that is, the specifics of the case and the role which you might be performing.

○ Because there is limited material available, you will sometimes need to make assumptions. Don't be afraid to do this, it will show initiative on your part. Assumptions are an important part of dealing with case studies and can help you to be quite creative with your answer. However, do explain the basis of your assumptions within your answer so that the examiner understands the nature of them, and why you have arrived at your particular outcome. *Always ensure that your assumptions are realistic.*

o Only now are you approaching the stage where it is time to start writing your answer to the question, tackling the problems, making decisions and recommendations on the case scenario set before you. As mentioned previously, your points will often be best set out in a report or memo type format, particularly if the examiner does not specify a communication method.

o Ensure that your writing is succinct, avoids waffle and responds directly to the questions asked.

Part B: Option choice questions

Part B is comprised of four traditional questions, each worth 25 per cent. You will be expected to choose two of those questions, to make up the remaining 50 per cent of available marks. (Again please note that the structure is the same for Marketing Management in Practice, but that all questions are applied to the case study.)

Realistically, the same principles apply for these questions as in the case study. Communication formats, reading through the questions, structure, role-play, context and so on – everything is the same.

Part B will cover a number of broader issues from within the syllabus and will be taken from any element of it. The examiner makes the choice, and no prior direction is given to students or tutors on what that might be.

As regards time management in this area, if you used about 100 minutes for the mini-case you should have around 80 minutes left. This provides you with around 40 minutes to plan and write a question, to write, review and revise your answers. Keep practising – use a cooker timer, alarm clock or mobile phone alarm as your timer and work hard at answering questions within the time frame given.

Specimen examination papers and answers

To help you prepare and understand the nature of the paper, go to www.cim.co.uk/learningzone or to access Specimen Answers and Senior Examiner's advice for these exam questions. During your study, the author of your Coursebook may have, on occasions, asked you to refer to these papers and answer the questions. You should undertake these exercises and utilize every opportunity to practise meeting examination requirements.

Each of the Professional Diploma coursebooks has, at the end of it, some examination questions and guidance provided by the authors and Senior Examiners, where appropriate, to provide you with some insight into the types of questions asked.

The specimen answers are vital learning tools. They are not always perfect, as they are answers written by students and annotated by the Senior Examiners, but they will give you a good indication of the approaches you could take, and the examiners' annotations suggest how these answers might be improved. Please use them.

Other sources of information to support your learning through the learning zone are 'Hot Topics'. These give you scope to undertake a range of associated activities related to the syllabus and study areas, and will also be very useful to you when you are revising.

Key elements of preparation

One Senior Examiner suggests the three elements involved in preparing for your examination can be summarized thus:

1. Learning
2. Memory
3. Revision.

Let's look at each point in turn.

Learning

Quite often students find it difficult to learn properly. You can passively read books, look at some of the materials, perhaps revise a little, and regurgitate it all in the examination. In the main, however, this is rather an unsatisfactory method of learning. It is meaningless, shallow and ultimately of little use in practice.

For learning to be truly effective it must be active and applied. You must involve yourself in the learning process by thinking about what you have read, testing it against your experience by reflecting on how you use particular aspects of marketing, and how you could perhaps improve your own performance by implementing particular aspects of your learning into your everyday life. You should adopt the old adage of 'learning by doing'. If you do, you will find that passive learning has no place in your study life.

Below are some suggestions that have been prepared to assist you with the learning pathway throughout your revision.

- ○ Always make your own notes, in words you understand, and ensure that you combine all the sources of information and activities within them.
- ○ Always try to relate your learning back to your own organization.
- ○ Make sure you define key terms concisely, wherever possible.
- ○ Do not try to memorize your ideas, but work on the basis of understanding and, most important, applying them.
- ○ Think about the relevant and topical questions that might be set – use the questions and answers in your Coursebooks to identify typical questions that might be asked in the future.
- ○ Attempt all of the questions within each of your Coursebooks since these are vital tests of your active learning and understanding.

Memory

If you are prepared to undertake an active learning programme then your knowledge will be considerably enhanced, as understanding and application of knowledge does tend to stay in your 'long-term' memory. It is likely that passive learning will only stay in your 'short-term' memory.

Do not try to memorize in parrot fashion; it is not helpful and, even more important, examiners are experienced in identifying various memorizing techniques and therefore will spot them as such.

Having said this, it is quite useful to memorize various acronyms such as SWOT, PEST, PESTLE, STEEPLE, or indeed various models such as Ansoff, GE Matrix, Shell Directional

Policy Matrix and so on, as in some of the questions you may be required to use illustrations of these to assist your answer.

Revision

The third and final stage to consider is 'revision', which is what we will concentrate on in detail below. Here just a few key tips are offered.

Revision should be an ongoing process rather than a panic measure that you decide to undertake just before the examination. You should be preparing notes *throughout* your course, with the view to using them as part of your revision process. Therefore, ensure that your notes are sufficiently comprehensive that you can reuse them successfully.

For each concept you learn about, you should identify, through your reading and your own personal experience, at least two or three examples that you could use; this then gives you some scope to broaden your perspective during the examination. It will, of course, help you gain some points for initiative with the examiners.

Knowledge is not something you will gain overnight – as we saw earlier, it is not a quick fix; it involves a process of learning that enables you to lay solid foundations upon which to build your long-term understanding and application. This will benefit you significantly in the future, not just in the examination.

In essence, you should ensure that you do the following in the period before the real intensive revision process begins.

- o Keep your study file well organized, updated and full of newspaper and journal cuttings that may help you formulate examples in your mind for use during the examination.
- o Practise defining key terms and acronyms from memory.
- o Prepare topic outlines and essay answer plans.
- o When you start your intensive revision, ensure it is planned and structured in the way described below. And then finally, read your concentrated notes the night before the examination.

Revision planning

You are now on a critical path – although hopefully not too critical at this time – with somewhere in the region of between 4 and 6 weeks to go to the examination. The following hints and tips will help you plan out your revision study.

- o You will, as already explained, need to be very organized. Therefore, before doing anything else, put your files, examples, reading material and so on, in good order, so that you are able to work with them in the future and, of course, make sense of them.
- o Ensure that you have a quiet area within which to work. It is very easy to get distracted when preparing for an examination.
- o Take out your file along with your syllabus, and make a list of key topic areas that you have studied and which you now need to revise. You could use the basis of this book to do that, by taking each unit a step at a time.
- o Plan the use of your time carefully. Ideally, you should start your revision at least 6 weeks prior to the exam, so therefore work out how many spare hours you could give to the revision process and then start to allocate time in your diary, and do not double-book with anything else.

o   Give up your social life for a short period of time. As the saying goes 'no pain – no gain'.
o   Looking at each of the subject areas in turn, identify which are your strengths and which are your weaknesses. Which areas have you grasped and understood, and which are the areas that you have really struggled with? Split your page into two and make a list on each side. For example:

Planning and control	
Strengths	**Weaknesses**
Audit – PEST, SWOT, Models	Ratio analysis
Portfolio analysis	Market sensing
	Productivity analysis
	Trend extrapolation
	Forecasting

o   Break down your list again and divide the points of weakness giving priority in the first instance to your weakest areas and even prioritizing them by giving each of them a number. This will enable you to master the more difficult areas. Up to 60 per cent of your remaining revision time should be given over to that, as you may find you have to undertake a range of additional reading and also perhaps seeking tutor support, if you are studying at a CIM Accredited Study Centre.
o   The rest of the time should be spent reinforcing your knowledge and understanding of the stronger areas, spending time testing yourself on how much you really know.
o   Should you be taking two examinations or more at any one time, then the breakdown and managing of your time will be critical.
o   Taking a subject at a time, work through your notes and start breaking them down into subsections of learning, and ultimately into key learning points, items that you can refer to time and time again, that are meaningful and that your mind will absorb. You yourself will know how best you remember the key points. Some people try to develop acronyms, flowcharts or matrices, mind maps, fishbone diagrams and so on, or various connection diagrams that help them recall certain aspects of models. You could also develop processes that enable you to remember approaches to various options. (But do remember what we said earlier about regurgitating stuff, parrot fashion.)

Figure A1.1 is just a brief example of how you could use a 'bomb-burst' diagram (which, in this case, highlights the uses of advertising) as a very helpful approach to memorizing key elements of learning.

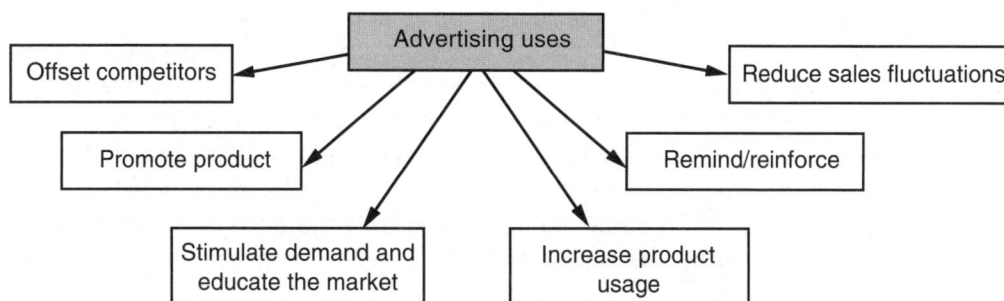

Figure A1.1 Use of a diagram to summarize key components of a concept
Source: Adapted from Dibb, Simkin, Pride and Ferrell, *Marketing Concepts and Strategies*, 4th edition, Houghton Mifflin, 2001

o Eventually you should reduce your key learning to bullet points. For example: imagine you were looking at the concept of Time Management – you could eventually reduce your key learning to a bullet list containing the following points in relation to 'Effective Prioritization'.

- Organize
- Take time
- Delegate
- Review.

o Each of these headings would then remind you of the elements you need to discuss associated with the subject area.
o Avoid getting involved in reading too many textbooks at this stage, as you may start to find that you are getting confused overall.
o Look at examination questions in previous papers, and start to observe closely the various roles and tasks they expect you to undertake, and importantly, the context in which they are set.
o *Use the specimen exam papers and specimen answers* to support your learning and see how you could actually improve upon them.
o Without exception, find an associated examination question for the areas that you have studied and revised, and undertake it (more than once, if necessary).
o Without referring to notes or books, try to draft an answer plan with the key concepts, knowledge, models and information that are needed to successfully complete the answer. Then refer to the specimen answer to see how close you are to the actual outline presented. Planning your answer, and ensuring that key components are included and that the question has a meaningful structure, is one of the most beneficial activities that you can undertake.
o Now write the answer out in full, time constrained and written by hand, not with the use of IT. (At this stage, you are still expected to be the scribe for the examination and present handwritten work. Many of us find this increasingly difficult as we spend more and more time using our computers to present information. Do your best to be neat. Difficult handwriting is often off-putting to the examiner.)
o When writing answers as part of your revision process, be sure to practise the following essential examination techniques:

- *Identify and use the communication method* – Requested by the examiner.
- *Always have three key parts to the answer* – An introduction, a middle section that develops your answer in full, and a conclusion. Where appropriate, ensure that you have an introduction, main section, summary/conclusion and, if requested or help-ful, recommendations.
- *Always answer the question in the context or role set.*
- *Always comply with the nature and terms of the question.*
- *Leave white space* – Do not overcrowd your page; leave space between para-graphs, and make sure your sentences do not merge into one blur. (Don't worry – there is always plenty of paper available to use in the examination.)
- *Count* – How many actions the question asks you to undertake and double-check at the end that you have met the full range of demands of the question.
- *Use examples* – To demonstrate your knowledge and understanding of the parti-cular syllabus area. These can be from journals, the Internet, the press, or your own experience.
- *Display your vigour and enthusiasm for marketing* – Remember to think of the Senior Examiner as your Customer, or future employer, and do your best to deliver what is wanted to satisfy their needs. Impress them and show them how you are a 'cut above the rest'.
- Review all your practice answers critically with the above points in mind.

Practical actions

The critical path is becoming even more critical now as the examination looms. The following are vital points:

- Have you registered with CIM?
- Do you know where you are taking your examination? CIM should let you know approximately 1 month in advance.
- Do you know where your examination centre is? If not, find out, take a drive, time it – whatever you do don't be late!
- Make sure you have all the tools of the examination ready. A dictionary, calculator, pens, pencils, ruler and so on. Try not to use multiple shades of pens, but at the same time make your work look professional. *Avoid using red and green as these are the colours that will be used for marking.*

Summary

Above all, you must remember that you personally have invested a tremendous amount of time, effort and money in studying for this programme and it is therefore imperative that you consider the suggestions given here as they will help to maximize your return on your investment.

Many of the hints and tips offered here are generic and will work across most of the CIM courses. We have tried to select those that will help you most in taking a sensible, planned approach to your study and revision.

The key to your success is being prepared to put in the time and effort required, planning your revision, and equally important is planning and answering your questions in a way that will ensure that you pass your examination on the day.

The advice offered here aims to guide you from a practical perspective. Guidance on syllabus content and developments associated with your learning will become clear to you as you work through this Coursebook. The authors of each Coursebook have given subject-specific guidance on the approach to the examination and on how to ensure that you meet the content requirements of the kind of question you will face. These considerations are in addition to the structuring issues we have been discussing throughout this Appendix.

Each of the authors and Senior Examiners will guide you on their preferred approach to questions and answers as they go. Therefore, where you are presented with an opportunity to be involved in some activity or undertake an examination question either during or at the end of your study units, do take it. It not only prepares you for the examination, but also helps you learn in the applied way we discussed above.

Here, then, is a last reminder:

- Ensure you make the most of your learning process throughout.
- Keep structured and orderly notes from which to revise.
- Plan your revision – don't let it just happen.
- Provide examples to enhance your answers.
- Practise your writing skills in order that you present your work well and your writing is readable.
- Take as many opportunities as possible to test your knowledge and measure your progress.

- Plan and structure your answers.
- Always do as the question asks you, especially with regard to context and communication method.
- Do not leave it until the last minute!

The writers would like to take this opportunity to wish you every success in your endeavours to study, to revise and to pass your examinations.

Karen Beamish
Academic Development Advisor

appendix 2
assignment-based assessment

Introduction – the basis to the assignments and the integrative project

Within the CIM qualifications at both Professional Certificate and Professional Diploma there are several assessment options available. These are detailed in the outline of modules below. The purpose of an assignment is to provide another format to complete each module for students who want to apply the syllabus concepts from a module to their own or a selected organization. For either qualification there are three modules providing assessment via an assignment and one module assessed via an integrative work-based project. The module assessed via the integrative project is the summative module for each qualification.

	Entry modules	Research & analysis	Planning	Implementation	Management of Marketing
Professional Post Graduate Diploma	Entry module – Professional Post Graduate Diploma	Analysis & Evaluation	Strategic Marketing Decisions	Managing Marketing Performance	Strategic Marketing in Practice
Professional Diploma	Entry module – Professional Diploma	Marketing Research & Information	Marketing Planning	Marketing Communications	Marketing Management in Practice
Professional Certificate		Marketing Environment	Marketing Fundamentals	Customer Communications	Marketing in Practice
Introductory Certificate		Supporting marketing processes (research & analysis, planning and implementation)			

Outline of CIM 'standard' syllabus (© The Chartered Institute of Marketing, September 2003)

The use of assignments does not mean that this route is easier than an examination. Both formats are carefully evaluated to ensure that a grade B in the assessment/integrative project route is the same as a grade B in the examination. However, the use of assignments does allow a student to complete the assessment for a module over a longer period of time than a three-hour examination. This will inevitably mean work being undertaken over the time span of a module. For those used to cramming for exams, writing an assignment over several weeks which comprises a total of four separate questions will be a very different approach.

Each module within the qualification contains a different assignment written specifically for the module. These are designed to test understanding and provide the opportunity for you to demonstrate your abilities through the application of theory to practice. The format and structure of each module's assignment is identical, although the questions asked will differ and the exact type of assignment varies. The questions within an assignment will relate directly to the syllabus for that particular module, thereby giving the opportunity to demonstrate understanding and application.

The assignment structure

The assignment for each module is broken down into a range of questions. These consist of a core question and a selection of optional questions. The core question will always relate to the main aspects of each module's syllabus. Coupled with this are a range of four optional questions which will each draw from a different part of the syllabus. Students are requested to select two optional questions from the four available. When put together these form the assessment for the entire module. The overall pass mark for the module is the same as through an examination route, which is set at 50 per cent. In addition, the grade band structure is also identical to that of an examination.

Core question

This is the longest and therefore the most important section of your assignment. Covering the major components of the syllabus, the core question is designed to provide a challenging assignment which both tests the theoretical element and also permits application to a selected organization or situation. The word limit for this task will be indicated to you by the CIM and will be included in the rubric on the front of the assignment. It also outlines the regulations for including additional materials in the form of appendices. However, the appendices should be kept to a minimum. Advice here is that there should be no longer than five pages of additional pertinent information.

Optional questions

There are a total of four questions provided for Professional Certificate and Professional Diploma of the syllabus from which a student is asked to select two. Each answer is expected to provide a challenge although the actual task required varies. Again the word count for these tasks will be in the rubric on the front of the assignment.

These are designed to test areas of the syllabus not covered by the core question. As such it is possible to base all of your questions on the same organization although there is significant benefit in using more than one organization as a basis for your assignment. Some of the questions specifically require a different organization to be selected from the one used for the core question. This only occurs where the questions are requiring similar areas to be investigated and will be specified clearly on the question itself.

Within the assignment there are several types of questions that may be asked, including:

- o *A report* – The question requires a formal report to be completed, detailing an answer to the specific question set. This will often be reporting on a specific issue to an individual.
- o *A briefing paper or notes* – Preparing a briefing paper or a series of notes which may be used for a presentation.

o *A presentation* – You may be required either to prepare the presentation only or to deliver the presentation in addition to its preparation. The audience for the presentation should be considered carefully and ICT used where possible.

o *A discussion paper* – The question requires an academic discussion paper to be prepared. You should show a range of sources and concepts within the paper. You may also be required to present the discussion paper as part of a question.

o *A project plan or action plan* – Some questions ask for planning techniques to be demonstrated. As such, the plan must be for the timescale given and costs shown where applicable. The use of ICT is recommended here in order to create the plan diagrammatically.

o *Planning a research project* – Whilst market research may be required, questions have often asked for simply a research plan in a given situation. This would normally include timescales, the type(s) of research to be gathered, sampling, planned data collection and analysis.

o *Conducting research* – Following on from a research plan, a question can require the student(s) to undertake a research gathering exercise. A research question can be either an individual or a group activity depending upon the question. This will usually result in a report of the findings of the exercise plus any recommendations arising from your findings.

o *Gathering of information and reporting* – Within many questions information will need gathering. The request for information can form part or all of a question. This may be a background to the organization, the activities contained in the question or external market and environmental information. It is advisable to detail the types of information utilized, their sources and report on any findings. Such a question will often ask for recommendations for the organization – these should be drawn from the data and not simply personal opinion.

o *An advisory document* – A question here will require students to evaluate a situation and present advice and recommendations drawn from findings and theory. Again, any advice should be backed up with evidence and not a personal perspective only.

o *An exercise, either planning and/or delivering the exercise* – At both Stage One and Stage Two, exercises are offered as optional questions. These provide students with the opportunity to devise an exercise and may also require the delivery of this exercise. Such an activity should be evidenced where possible.

o *A role-play with associated documentation* – Several questions have asked students to undertake role-plays in exercises such as team-building. These are usually videoed and documentation demonstrating the objectives of the exercise provided.

Each of these questions relate directly towards specific issues to be investigated, evaluated and answered. In addition, some of the questions asked present situations to be considered. These provide opportunities for specific answers relating directly to the question asked.

In order to aid students completing the assignment, each question is provided with an outline of marking guidance. This relates to the different categories by which each question is marked. The marker of your assignment will be provided with a detailed marking scheme constructed around the same marking guidance provided to students.

For both the core and optional questions, it is important to use referencing where sources have been utilized. This has been a weakness in the past and continues to be an issue. There have been cases of plagiarism identified during marking and moderation, together with a distinct lack of references and bibliography. This becomes more important at Stage Two where the nature of the syllabus lends itself to a more academic approach. It is highly recommended that a bibliography be included with each question and sources are cited within the text itself. The type of referencing method used is not important, only that sources are referred to.

Integrative project structure

The integrative project is designed to provide an in-company approach to assessment rather than having specified assignments. Utilized within the summative module element of each level's syllabus, this offers a student the chance to produce a piece of work which tackles a specific issue. The integrative project can only be completed after undertaking other modules as it will rely on information in each of these as guidance.

Professional Diploma Assignments – Marketing Management in Practice

Marketing planning assignments CIM briefs and student work

This section commences with the instructions for the Marketing Planning assignments, which are issued by CIM, to a CIM centre and then despatched to the candidates wishing to undertake the assessment via coursework. After each question, there is a critique of what is required and at the end there is a discussion of strengths and weaknesses found in the work from the candidates who undertook these assignments.

Marketing Management in Practice: Integrative Project

There are *Two* separate elements to the complete assignment, as detailed below:

- o The *Core Section* is compulsory and worth 50 per cent of your total mark. It should be approximately 3000 words.
- o The *Elective Section* has four options from which you must complete *Two*. Each of these options is worth 25 per cent of your total mark and should be approximately 1500 words.

Please note: As these assignments have been designed to test the application of knowledge, it will be insufficient to rely on theory alone for your answers. All work should be professionally produced, with arguments presented that are compelling and well reasoned. Your assignment must be an individual piece of work with any sources of information, definitions, methodologies and applications clearly referenced.

It is suggested that the answers for all the sections should be based on an organization of your choice, preferably your own, and that you should use the same organization throughout. This will present a more holistic account and involve you in less research.

If you are not in a position to use your own organization, you may use an alternative organization with which you are familiar, but your choice should be made following discussion with your tutor, to ensure the best use of your study time.

You should submit your assignment by securing pages in the top left hand corner with a treasury tag – do not use staples as these can come apart. No folders or wallets will be accepted.

The above word counts are guides only and you will not be penalized if you do exceed this recommendation. However, the professionalism of the presentation or your assignment, which includes producing concise and appropriate work, will be taken into consideration.

CORE SECTION – The role of marketing in the organization – 50 per cent weighting

QUESTION NO. 1

Your report should be based on your own organization or an organization of your own selection with tutor advice. This integrative project is not marked at the centre by your tutor but anonymously marked at the CIM. You should provide a brief (around one page) overview of the nature of the selected organization and its marketing environment to provide the marker with the context to understand your development of issues in your report.

In formulating a marketing plan using relationship-marketing concepts, stakeholders need to be identified and their attitudes to the organizations reviewed. If their attitudes are positive, it is necessary to maintain and develop these. If the attitudes are not positive, marketers may need to build actions into the marketing plan to develop more favourable attitudes.

You are required to prepare a report to address the following:

1. Evaluate the stakeholders' possible concerns and attitudes to the organization.
2. What objectives does the organization need to achieve in its relationship with the stakeholder groups identified?
3. What initiatives can be incorporated into the organizations' marketing plan to develop the relationships favourably? You may evaluate current activities and/or propose new ones.
4. An often-neglected critical element of a marketing plan is the incorporation of appropriate feedback and control systems. For the stakeholders identified, what methods would you use to monitor the quality of the relationship and the key stakeholder group? Again you may evaluate current methods and/or propose new ones.

In a large organization it may be necessary to be selective and use examples to illustrate general points. If in doubt, discuss this with your tutor.

Note: This is an individual assignment, as such the report must be completed individually and not as part of a group. Recommended word count 3000 words, excluding relevant appendices.

Syllabus references
1.2, 2.1, 2.2, 3.1, 3.4, 4.1, 4.3, 4.4, 5.2, 5.5, 5.6

Assessment criteria

	Marks available
o Identification and selection of appropriate *key* stakeholders	4
o Identification and analysis of stakeholder issues	13
o Evaluation of stakeholder relationship initiatives	18
o Control and feedback evaluation	12
o Presentation, format and tone of plan and report	3
Total marks	50

Question 1

Candidates were required to write a formal report for this and other questions. Some guidance notes on structuring reports are given below. Three marks are allocated for the presentation and tone of the report.

1. Submission Cover Sheet: Ensure that all the relevant sections of the CIM cover sheets have been completed with any necessary declarations.

2. Title page, including title of project and candidate number. It is suggested that you do not engage in lavish colour graphics. Colour can be expensive and time taken over graphics here is no substitute for content in the body of the report where grades are won.

3. Contents: Good housekeeping – makes it easy for readers to find their way round a report. For a project report this may be in sections such as Contents, Figures, Illustrations, Tables, Appendices. All reports should be page numbered.

4. Brief illustration outlining the nature of the selected organization for the first question.

5. Body of report in report format with headings and subheadings. Literature sources should be referenced. The literature used should be appropriate and may include textbooks, academic papers, trade press, other press sources and web-based research. Clear referencing is important, the Harvard system is recommended. For websites it is suggested that you give the web (URL) reference and the date of access. A broad range of relevant references should be given as appropriate. Note that a bibliography of relevant literature is different to references. More recent references are appreciated, as it is an indication of current reading around the subject. Arguments should be based on evidence and be logically developed. The use of and reference to relevant course materials and tools of analysis is important to gain as many marks as possible.

6. Only relevant material should be included in the appendices. Adding lengthy bundles of company literature or printouts of the results of web-based research is not appropriate and does not gain additional credit.

7. Diagrams, models flow, charts, tables, graphs, etc. as appropriate are encouraged. Clearly housekeeping is important so use the grammar and spell check.

8. A focused treatment is appropriate and 'scatter gun' approaches of writing everything that I can think of is not appropriate and does not gain good grades. The X factor for maximum marks is a convincing report with professional polish (note this does not necessarily mean extravagant and expensive coloured graphics).

This core question integrates a number of aspects of the syllabus. The information and data gathered to support the report should be in-depth, rather than a superficial reproduction of tutor-based notes. The report should be based on evidence not just opinions. Primary research may not be necessary if full and appropriate secondary sources exist. However, it is expected that in the majority of cases some primary research would be needed. Sources of information should be evidenced with appropriate referencing.

Candidates were expected to identify the range of stakeholders relevant to their specific selected organization. To manage stakeholder expectations, it is necessary to evaluate the relevant stakeholder issues from the stakeholders' point of view (e.g. in a commercial company it may be necessary to move a group perception of the organization from unfavourable to favourable). This follows the typical marketing approach of firstly defining the objectives and then formulating strategies to achieve these objectives.

The next section of the report should identify the strategies undertaken by the selected organization with a critical analysis. At this level candidates are expected to be able to apply the theory and bring professional judgement to situations and to formulate mature, balanced and professional views based on the relevant theory and the evidence collected.

ELECTIVE SECTION – 25 per cent weighting for each of TWO options

You are required to complete TWO of the four options within this section. As previously stated, it will be most beneficial in terms of research, etc., if the organization chosen for the Core Section is also used in this section where appropriate.

OPTION – The Management of a marketing project – 25 per cent weighting

QUESTION NO. 2

To be successful, a project manager has to use hard skills (e.g. Critical Path Analysis) and soft skills (e.g. team building):

- o Review the applicability of selected project management theory in the context of your selected organization or organization of your choice, giving relevant examples to illustrate your answer.
- o Discuss what you consider to be the successful skills and attributes of a good project manager in the context of your selected organization?

Note: This is an individual assignment, as such the report must be completed individually and not as part of a group. Recommended word count 1500 words, excluding relevant appendices.

Syllabus references

1.2, 1.3, 1.4, 1.5, 1.6, 1.8, 2.1, 2.2, 2.3, 2.4, 2.6

Assessment criteria

	Marks available
o Selection and use of suitable examples	3
o Depth of consideration of human aspects of project management	7
o Depth of consideration of 'hard' aspects of project management	7
o Consideration of attributes of successful project managers	6
o Presentation, format and tone of report	2
Total marks	25

Question 2

Too often, project management is seen as an exercise in the use of computer-based project management tools. Clearly these tools have their place but are only effective if implemented with 'soft' interpersonal skills. This elective project element requires candidates to consider both aspects of project management in the context of their selected organization.

The final aspect of the task is intended to provide the candidate with an opportunity to critically consider the attributes of successful project managers and from this process to better understand the role. The hope is that this depth of understanding will not only gain the candidate good grades in the assessment but also improve their performance in the work place.

ELECTIVE SECTION: OPTION – Marketing research and information needs – 25 per cent weighting

QUESTION NO. 3

Organizations need to respond to the activities of other organizations in the environment (e.g. competitors).

Write a report (using relevant examples from your own organization or one of your choice to illustrate your points) that identifies the information needing to be obtained, how it may be obtained and what use can be made of it.

Note: This is an individual assignment, as such the report must be completed individually and not as part of a group. Recommended word count 1500 words, excluding relevant appendices.

Syllabus references

3.1, 3.2, 3.4, 3.5, 3.6, 4.3

Assessment criteria

	Marks available
o Selection of appropriate examples	3
o Identification of information needs for the issue	7
o Critical evaluation of the collection methods	7
o Critical evaluation of management use of the information	6
o Presentation, format and tone of report	2
Total marks	25

Question 3

Competitive intelligence is vital to organizations; even charities have competitive pressures (given the wide range of potential organizations candidates may select, some flexibility was allowed in the selection of organizations).

The organizations selected should be of key significance to the selected organization and provide an appropriate platform to evaluate the data and information issues, with the use of appropriate theory. In most cases it is expected that the competition would be appropriate. However, for some organizations, e.g. not-for-profit, some other group might be more relevant.

One of the major problems in research is to ask the right questions. The first section of the project assignment was intended to develop the candidate's skill in evaluating what information is needed.

Given that the actual collection of data and information is a marketing role, the second section should have been straightforward with relevant comments on the organization's data collection methods and data analysis. Marketing reports should not be for the shelf and so the final section was an opportunity for candidates to critically consider the management use of the information. The overall purpose of the task was to give candidates an opportunity to reflect on the intelligence process and deepen their perspective and skills.

ELECTIVE SECTION: OPTION – Delivering a communications programme – 25 per cent weighting

QUESTION NO. 4

The element of the marketing mix 'promotion' is about communications and developing relationships. The failure of many of the 'dotcom' operations has demonstrated that often a balanced mix of traditional and new technology (e.g. websites) communications initiatives is needed. Using relevant examples illustrates how an integrated communications mix can be successfully developed.

Write a report that covers:

o Relevant traditional mix elements.
o Relevant 'new technology' mix elements.
o Issues in achieving integration.

Note: This is an individual assignment, as such the report must be completed individually and not as part of a group. Recommended word count 1500 words, excluding relevant appendices.

Syllabus references
5.1, 5.2, 5.3, 5.4, 5.6

Assessment criteria

	Marks available
o Selection of appropriate examples	3
o Appraisal of traditional mix elements	7
o Appraisal of 'new technology' mix elements	7
o Appropriate consideration of integration issues	6
o Presentation, format and tone of plan and report	2
Total marks	25

Question 4

Most marketers will be involved in communications initiatives. There are a number of dangers in implementing communications plans including:

o Selection of a number of discrete initiatives without considering the integration issues.
o Use of traditional methods such as posters without considering the possibilities of 'new technology' elements.
o The reverse of this within 'technical myopia' where the new media and methods are considered to have completely replaced traditional mix elements.

Candidates were expected to select an appropriate range of examples. Then critically appraise the traditional mix elements and the use of 'new technology' methods. The seamless integration of new and old elements is important and the issues in achieving this formed the final element for candidates to review in their report.

ELECTIVE SECTION: OPTION – Customer service – 25 per cent weighting

QUESTION NO. 5

Often there is a mismatch between perception of the management of an organization regarding its customers' quality needs and wants, and what the customers actually do demand.

Using relevant examples from your own organization or an organization of your choice to illustrate your points, write a report on what the management's view of quality issues is, how they form this view and what actions need to be taken to discover the real needs and wants of the customers.

Note: This is an individual assignment, as such the report must be completed individually and not as part of a group. Recommended word count 1500 words, excluding relevant appendices.

Syllabus references

1.1, 1.8, 3.2, 3.4, 4.3, 4.4, 5.3, 5.6

Assessment criteria

	Marks available
o Selection of appropriate examples	3
o Identification and appraisal of management quality/service objectives	7
o Evaluation of customers' quality needs and wants	6
o Critical review of process for evaluation of customer satisfaction	7
o Presentation, format and tone of report	2
Total marks	25

Question 5

A critical issue in successful marketing is the management of quality expectations. In the context of service marketing approaches such as the SERVQUAL model have been developed. Given the wide diversity of candidate's experience, some candidates selected 'internal' customers. Many candidates focused on 'service' aspects but a focus on products where appropriate was equally acceptable.

This elective question requires the candidate to explore what management set as their quality objectives in their selected organization. The second aspect demands consideration of the customers' quality needs and wants. In the final section candidates are then required to appraise how well the organization understands the effectiveness of its processes in accessing actual customer satisfaction. Marketers have a role in appraising the experience from the customer viewpoint as part of the process in gaining a marketing orientation in the whole organization.

Overall strengths of candidates' work

The characteristics of good candidates' work in this integrative project were:

- o Selection of good relevant examples to illustrate points.
- o Selection of relevant aspects of theory.
- o Demonstration of more than knowledge of theory but also understanding.
- o Understanding of the practical aspects of implementation of theory including overcoming problems.

- ○ Good, well-structured reports within 20 per cent of indicative word count.
- ○ Small but relevant appendices, but only where necessary.
- ○ Understanding of the textbook theory and evidence of reading around the subject to find latest developments.
- ○ Appropriate referencing for sources.
- ○ Use of an appropriate range of sources including original research articles, current textbooks, marketing and general press and appropriate use of Internet sources.
- ○ Focus on the specific aspects demanded by the integrative project tasks.

Overall weaknesses of candidates' work

The characteristics of less good submissions for this integrative project were:

- ○ Poor selection of examples and a failure to use them in the illustration of points.
- ○ Theory 'dump' of all the notes that the candidate had acquired in and around the topic area with little understanding of what was relevant demonstrated.
- ○ Listing of theory rather than a demonstration of depth of understanding.
- ○ Little understanding of problem-solving issues and the creative use and interpretation of theory.
- ○ Long rambling reports much in excess of 20 per cent of indicative word count with little structure and focus on the key aspects.
- ○ Long and often numerous appendices, including printouts of websites and material such as complete brochures and annual reports. Only strictly relevant material should be appended. The inclusion of appendices without relevance just wastes candidate's time without gaining additional credit.
- ○ Lack of understanding of the textbook theory and little evidence of reading around the subject.
- ○ Referencing that is inadequate or missing. It should be noted that inclusion of material without appropriate referencing might be interpreted as plagiarism, which is an academic offence. To avoid this risk, all sources should be acknowledged. What is required is a focused expression of the candidate's critical insight. A mosaic formed by 'cutting and pasting' a selection of web research material without attribution will result in failure.
- ○ Restricted range of sources sometimes apparently limited to lecture notes.
- ○ A lack of specific focus on aspects demanded by the integrative project tasks; more of a dump of everything in the candidate's notes, apparently in their hope that enough will be relevant to gain a pass grade.

Conclusion

These integrative project assignments are created so that candidates can use their own organization or an organization of special interest. The purpose is that this should maximize the value of the learning experience in exploring aspects of the academic material that will be of direct relevance to the development of candidates' work performance as well as gaining the CIM qualification.

Take care with your selection of examples and when appropriate, seek your tutor's advice. Do not just rely on just your lecture notes or books. Do read a round the subject. Do discuss your work with colleagues and fellow students (keeping due regard to any confidentiality issues). It is this additional depth of insight developed by this that yields high grades.

These assignments are marked at the CIM centre and all work is regarded as confidential. Given that the person marking these integrative assignments has not been associated with the tutorial support, it is important to provide a brief (around one page) overview of the nature of the selected organization and its marketing environment. This provides the marker with the context to understand your development of issues in your report.

It is intended that this should be one of your most interesting and valuable learning experiences. Good luck and enjoy researching and writing your project. It should help you to improve career prospects as well as gaining your CIM qualifications.

Assignment regulations

There have been a number of changes to the assignment structure compared with previous years, timed with the introduction of the new syllabi. These have been designed to provide consistency in approach for a student whether they are completing the assessment for a module by examination, assignment or integrative project. The more significant changes include:

- For the current academic year tutors at CIM centres will mark assignments. These are then moderated by CIM assessors. An integrative project is marked by CIM assessors only.
- No resubmission of assignments, as per an examination. In previous years a range of assignments were being submitted. Where a student does not achieve the 50 per cent pass mark, they were requested to re-take the assessment for the module through examination or an assignment/integrative project.
- Whichever assessment route is selected is fixed rather than having the option to change at the last minute. Past history has shown that students sometimes begin on an assignment route, change to an examination at the last minute due to not meeting the deadline and then score badly in the examination. The paths to an assignment or examination are different and therefore it is unadvisable to switch, which is the reason for the change of rule.
- In the 2002–2003 academic year word limits for questions and assignments were introduced. This was introduced due to assignments being submitted which were of a wide variety of lengths. These ranged from under 2000 words to over 25 000 words. Where a student is completing four modules by assignment this would equal over 100 000 words – the equivalent of a medium-sized textbook or novel. As such, it became impossible for two assignments to be considered together. Therefore the word limit guidance was introduced in order to provide equality for all students undertaking the assessment by assignment.
- Two sets of assignments per year as with the examination route. With this change, students are required to complete the assignment aimed at the nearest examination session. Previously students had between 3 and 9 months to complete an assignment depending upon whether it was given out in September for a June deadline or in March for the June deadline. Therefore a decision was made to follow the examination route with the intention of giving all students equal time to complete an assignment.

These summarize the key changes which have occurred due to the introduction of new syllabi with the assignment/integrative project route in order that there is parity of assessment at all levels and using all formats. Some of these changes have been significant, others minor. However, all the changes have been considered thoughtfully and with the best intentions for the students in mind.

Use of case studies

For anyone who is not working or has difficulty in accessing information on their or another organization, there are a number of case studies available which allow the completion of a module using a case-based approach rather than basing it upon an organization identified by the student. These case studies are provided on a request-only basis through your accredited CIM centre and should only be used as a last resort. Using a case study as the basis for your assignment will not mean an easier approach to the assignment. However, they do provide an opportunity to undertake assignments when no other alternative exists. Each case study comes with a certain amount of information that can be used specifically for the completion of a question. Additional information may need to be assumed or researched in order to create a comprehensive assignment.

Submission of assignments/integrative project

The following information will aid not only yourself and your tutor who marks your work but also the CIM assessor who will be moderating your work and moderating the integrative project. In addition, the flow diagram represents the process of an assignment/integrative project from start to final mark.

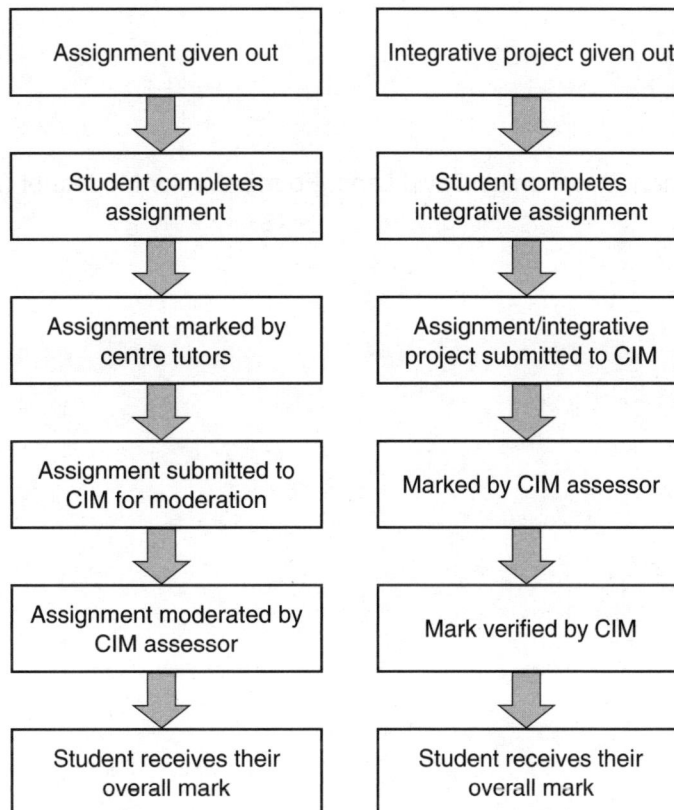

Assignment given out	Integrative project given out
Student completes assignment	Student completes integrative assignment
Assignment marked by centre tutors	Assignment/integrative project submitted to CIM
Assignment submitted to CIM for moderation	Marked by CIM assessor
Assignment moderated by CIM assessor	Mark verified by CIM
Student receives their overall mark	Student receives their overall mark

When completing and submitting assignments or the integrative project, refer to the following for guidance:

- Read through each question before starting out. Particularly with the core question there will be a considerable amount of work to undertake. Choose your optional questions wisely.
- Answer the question set and use the mark guidance given regarding the marking scheme.
- Reference each question within the assignment and use a bibliography.
- Complete all documentation thoroughly. This is designed to aid both the CIM and yourself.
- Ensure that the assignment is bound as per instructions given. Currently, assignments are requested not to be submitted in plastic wallets or folders as work can become

291

detached or lost. Following the submission instructions provided aids both the CIM administrators and the CIM assessor who will be marking (integrative project) or moderating (assignments) your work.

o Complete the candidate declaration sheet showing that you have undertaken this work yourself. *Please note that if you wish the information contained in your assignment to remain confidential you must state this on the front of the assignment.* Whilst CIM assessors will not use any information pertaining to your or another organization, CIM may wish to use the answer to a question as an example.

An assignment will be marked by a tutor at your CIM centre followed by moderation by a CIM assessor. The integrative project will be marked by a CIM assessor as per an examination with moderation by the CIM. To ensure objectivity by CIM assessors there exists a mark-in meeting prior to any marking in order that standardization can occur. The senior assessor for each subject also undertakes further verification of both examinations and assessments to ensure parity between each type of assessment.

Tony Curtis
Senior Examiner
February 2004

Based on the appendix written by David Lane, Former Senior Moderator (Advanced Certificate), February 2003.

appendix 3
how to pass the case study exam

Figure A3.1 shows the case study exam process.

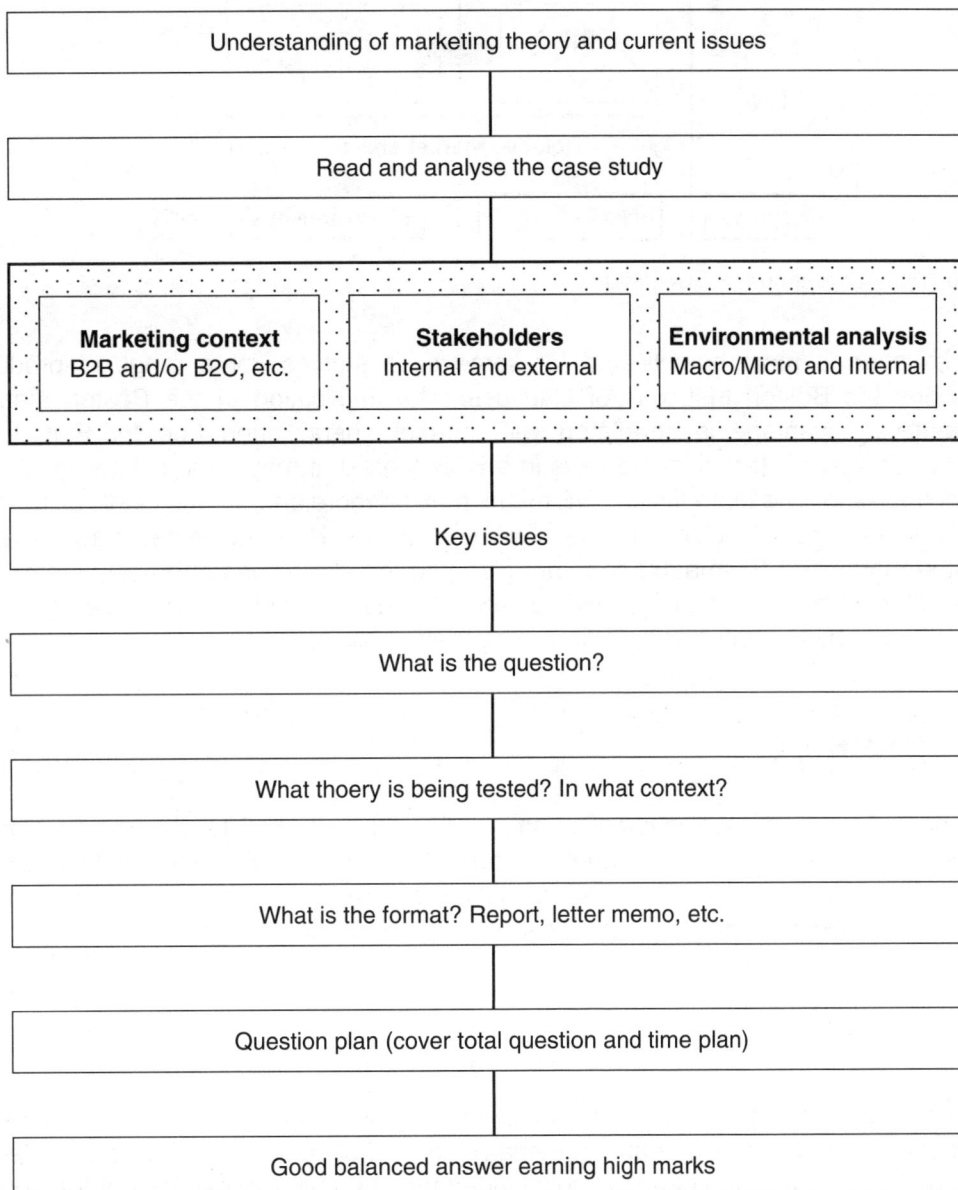

Understanding of marketing theory and current issues

Read and analyse the case study

Marketing context B2B and/or B2C, etc.	**Stakeholders** Internal and external	**Environmental analysis** Macro/Micro and Internal

Key issues

What is the question?

What thoery is being tested? In what context?

What is the format? Report, letter memo, etc.

Question plan (cover total question and time plan)

Good balanced answer earning high marks

Figure A3.1 An approach to a case study exam

Understanding marketing theory

Take great care that you understand how to use the models and marketing theories. Figure A3.2 shows a generalized version of the Boston matrix. In the box marked 'Dog', it is noted that often a product is in the decline phase; that is to say the market growth is negative, find a textbook that indicates this possibility. Relative market share to who? What 'market' are we talking about? Aston Martin does not compete with the Ford Ka. The implication of this is that we know and understand the segmentation structure for the market situation.

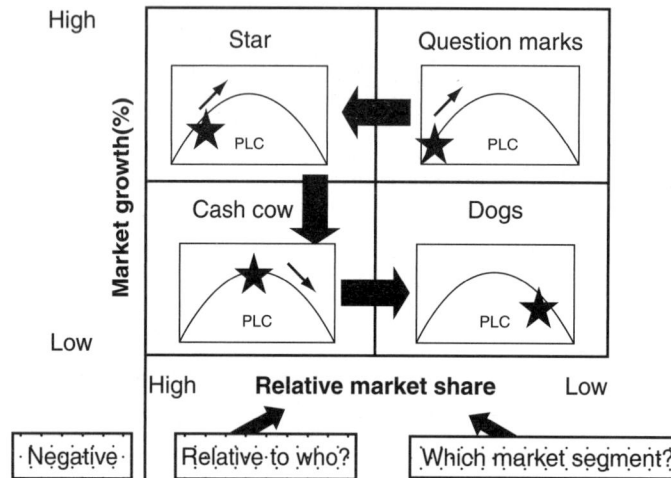

Figure A3.2 Adapted Boston (BCG) Matrix

The situation is more complicated for some case studies, for a range of product/market situations the Boston matrix is of little use. The implication of the Boston matrix is that competitive advantage is correlated with market share, often true for FMCG products. However, for highly technical products in a B2B context, it may be a technological advantage that is the issue. The more flexible GE matrix may be more appropriate in this case. Know your tools (theory). Know which one to use, in what situations. Knowing how to draw the two models (Boston matrix and GE matrix) does not give you the skill to use and apply them. A sculptor does not learn how to create by reading a book alone. You only gain proficiency in the use of tools (theory) by reading and then practising their application.

Current issues

The marketing environment is turbulent. In the UK, at the start of 2005, the numbers of digital TV viewers were overtaking the traditional, analogue viewers. The value of £1 could be $2 at the end of 2005. In these professional exams, candidates are expected to have a general understanding of the international business climate. This comes from reading magazines and papers.

What is a case study?

A case study is a brief overview of a business situation. The purpose of the case study is to allow you to demonstrate your ability to analyse a marketing situation. To do this effectively, for this integrative paper, you need to know, understand and have experience of the application of the relevant theory. This is an active process not a memory exercise. So, practice on a range of case studies is essential, two are given in this coursebook. The specimen answers are available on the CIM website. However do not be tempted to look at these too early. They are the 'winning post'. If you do not learn how to 'run the race' (analyse the case study, etc.) when you get into the exam you will not know how to win through. Simply memorizing past case studies is not a strategy to pass this exam. You need to learn analysis and problem-solving skills. This needs active practice, not just passive reading revision. On analyzing the case study you may need to make realistic assumptions (in a 3-hour exam the case study has to be simplified to keep to a readable length). A wide knowledge of current marketing and business climate developments, demonstrated in the exam, will gain you marks. In any case, theory, if you have no understanding of the continuously evolving international business climate, will not gain you career success.

After the general analysis there can be a diagnosis of the situation. What are the key issues? Read the questions carefully to see just what is required. What theory is being tested? What is the context? In what format is the answer required? Plan your answer before you start writing. The whole process, shown in Figure A3.3, will allow you to develop a balanced, insightful, approach.

Read and analyse the case study

With a highlighter pen read the study. Highlight key words and make brief notes as to what are the key issues. What is the marketing context? Note this is not an issue of 'or'. A case study is not one dimensional. A case study can be international and service, and B2B and B2C (e.g. a bank). Below is an outline of areas and factors that may apply:

- o B2C and/or
- o B2B and/or
- o Product and/or
- o Services and/or
- o International and/or
- o Not-for-profit/social and/or
- o Relationship marketing and/or
- o Consumer issues and/or
- o Green issues and/or
- o Limited budget and/or
- o ?

Stakeholders

Who are the key stakeholders? What are the issues relevant to them and the case study organization? Note just as with customers stakeholders can segment. Some typical examples of potential stakeholders are given below:

- o Customers (B2B: segmented and/or B2C: segmented). Possibly customers' customers (e.g. P&G marketing to TESCO, then to ultimate customers – Push and Pull strategy)
- o Suppliers
- o Distributors and agents
- o Internal (segmented, e.g. management, technical, full time, part time, shift worker, etc.)
- o Owners (note different types of ownership are possible, e.g. individual, co-operative, trustee, shareholder, etc.)
- o Industry (competitors, trade associations, etc.)

  o Media (may segment, e.g. TV, radio, press. International, national, regional, local)
  o Political (may segment, e.g. international (e.g. EU), national, local)
  o Regulatory
  o Pressure groups
  o General public.

In particular, it is necessary to identify, from the stakeholders analysis, who the communication targets might be. This is required for tasks such as 'Write a marketing plan' or 'Write a communications plan'.

Environmental analysis

Focused use of STEEPLE (or one of its variants), Porter competition and segmentation issues should be considered for the external environment. The value chain can be used if the internal issues are an important aspect of the case study scenario. As noted, with the portfolio models it is not the ability to remember STEEPLE that is required, you need to develop practice in its application.

Key issues

A SWOT analysis helps focus the range of issues uncovered in the above analysis. This will then indicate the key imperatives that face the organization (e.g. gain new customers, introduce new products, move into international markets, etc.).

What is the question?

Specimen answers to past questions are not for 'learning' in parrot fashion. They are for you to be able to compare your solution to a situation. They are an aid to practice, not another textbook. This issue is important as candidates must answer the question asked in the exam, not the specimen answer from last time. Take care to answer the question fully. In an outline context of a marketing plan, for example, is the 'product' simply 'a product', or are there elements of service? If service is an element, the service-extended marketing mix should be used.

What theory is being tested? In what context?

Question 2 of the 'Picasso Perfumes' case study (June 2004) was:

 (a) Picasso Perfumes operates in a b2b context. Its target customers are manufacturers of fragranced products such as cosmetics, detergents etc. (see Appendix 1 in the case study). What information does Picasso Perfumes need to obtain to identify likely profitable customers? How would you collect this information?
 (b) Having identified a potential client, what additional information would the sales team require about the target client's business and key staff?

Part 'a' is about information and market research (what information? how to collect it?). The question reminds you that the context is B2B and the target customers are in the business of manufacturing FMCG products for the consumer market (there is an ultimate B2C element at the end of the chain). Part 'b' is about gaining more insight into potential customers business (e.g. buying processes). The 'key staff' indicated in the question suggests that some research into the targets' DMU's make-up would be appropriate.

What is the format?

The two most common formats for this exam are 'report' (default format for all CIM questions unless otherwise indicated) and 'plan' (e.g. Marketing or communications). Plans should be written in report format. Outline heading structures are given below for marketing and communications plans. These basic outlines may need adaptation. Some exam issues are added as comments.

Outline structure for a marketing plan

Report heading [*very short, marks not gained here.*]

Mission aims and objectives [*very brief note of overall business mission and objectives.*]

Environmental analysis

> **STEEPLE** [*or variant*]

> **Competition** [*porter five forces recommended*]

> **Segmentation/stakeholders** [*May not be a separate heading but some explicit understanding of these issues should be demonstrated in the case study context.*]

SWOT [*Short and focused. A key factor in marginal fail papers is to spend far too much time on the above headings. Balance your plan and allow time to develop your strategy, mix and control sections.*]

Objectives [*Context specific, for example do not write 'implement SMART' objectives. Give some context specific SMART objectives.*]

Strategy [*Needs relevant, context-specific use of strategy theory. Selective use of models such as Ansoff, Porter generic strategies, Boston matrix, GE matrix. You must be selective. Marks are not gained for remembering how to draw all the models. You must make the model used relevant and context specific. To be able to do this quickly takes skill. Practice on past case studies.*]

Marketing mix

> **Product** [*Relevant context specific points – not 'superior quality product', this may be true but could apply to any situation. It has not demonstrated any context-specific application of marketing theory.*]

> **Price** [*Relevant context-specific points – not 'superior value', this may be true but could apply to any situation: it has not demonstrated any context-specific application of marketing theory.*]

> **Place** [*Relevant context-specific points – not 'saturation distribution', this may be true but could apply to any situation. It has not demonstrated any context-specific application of marketing theory.*]

Promotion [*Relevant context-specific points – not 'Mass TV advertising' in every case. A major mistake is to suggest 'mass TV advertising', when the organization is small. There is not enough money in the budget for it. Another error is to suggest TV advertising for a focused B2B context. Communications must be relevant to the context and the stakeholders. Know the difference between a communications plan and a marketing plan. You must demonstrate your application of relevant marketing theory to the given case study context with relevant insightful proposals.*]

People [*Is the context 'service' or containing elements of service? If so develop the service extension in a relevant context-specific way. If not just write a line, 'Product context so service extension (People, Physical evidence and Process) is not relevant'. This demonstrates to the examiner that you know the full mix and have made a positive decision to exclude its development, a correct decision in a product-only situation. However, by noting the service extension you are indicating that this was a positive decision and not that you do not know about the service extension to the marketing mix.*]

Physical evidence [*Relevant context-specific points.*]

Process [*Relevant context-specific points.*]

Budget and schedule [*Make context specific.*]

Control and feedback [*Balance scorecard type approach is fine. Do not make too long but try to make some context-specific points, look back at your objectives.*]

Outline structure for a communications plan

The broadest structure is much the same as for a marketing plan but the business objectives are replaced with the marketing objectives. We are operating at the next level of detail. In real life there would be parallel detailed plans for product, price, place and service extension. However, much work in other marketing mix areas may be done by other parts of the organization, for example R&D (product development), finance (pricing and credit systems) and production/logistics (manufacture and physical distribution). The communications plan is very much the 'baby' of marketing and rightly gets more focus in marketing books. Not all of the elements given below may be needed. In some circumstances (e.g. an 'e' based strategy), sections may need expansion. This is a rough outline that needs to be adapted to suit the given case study circumstance.

Report heading [*very short, marks not gained here.*]

Mission aims and objectives [*Very brief, note of overall marketing mission and objectives.*]

Environmental analysis

STEEPLE [*or variant. Focused on the communications issues, so builds on from that for the overall marketing plan. We are into the next level of detail.*]

Competition [*A note on what the competition are doing and how this affects communications planning for the organization.*]

Segmentation/stakeholders/target publics/audiences [*It is not possible to write a communications plan without considering with whom you are communicating.*]

SWOT [*Possibly a very brief SWOT focused on communications issues.*]

Objectives [*Context specific, do not write 'implement SMART' objectives. Give some context-specific SMART objectives. Objectives should be linked to the key stakeholder/target publics. It is not possible to frame communications objective without some consideration of the communications target(s).*]

Strategy [*Needs relevant, context-specific use of strategy and theory. Selective use of concepts and models such as branding, 'Push–Pull' and AIDA, etc.*]

Communications mix [*Note this may need to be adapted for different segments and 'push and pull' elements of the communications strategy.*]

Advertising [*Relevant context-specific point. Note the comments about TV advertising in the section on marketing plans. Develop detail as appropriate. Potential headings are given below.*]

TV

Radio

Print

Newspapers [*Develop detail, such as daily/weekly, as necessary.*]

Magazines [*Develop detail as necessary.*]

Directories [*Develop detail as necessary.*]

Outdoor

Cinema

Other

PR [*Relevant context-specific points.*]

Publicity [*Relevant context-specific points. Publicity is not free. The media may be. It does have costs, PR to generate it.*]

Personal selling [*Relevant context-specific points.*]

Point of sale [*Relevant context-specific points.*]

Sales promotion [*Relevant context-specific points.*]

Direct marketing [*Relevant context-specific points.*]

E-communications (websites etc.) [*Relevant context-specific points.*]

Sponsorship [*Relevant context-specific points.*]

Exhibitions [*Relevant context-specific points.*]

Other [*Relevant context-specific points.*]

Integration [*How do the communications activities integrate with the other six elements of the service extended marketing mix? All elements of the mix can participate in communication. What contributions are being made to your plan by the other six elements, e.g. packaging.*]

Media schedule [*Make context specific.*]

Budget [*Make context specific.*]

Control and feedback [*Do not write 'primary and secondary research' and leave it as such. Do not make it too long but try to make some context-specific points, look back at your communications objectives.*]

Other formats

Other formats used in CIM exams include memos, letters, budgets, schedules and briefing notes.

Question plan

In the analysis of marginal fail papers against good pass papers, it was noted that marginal fail candidates tend not to question plan. Students in the upper quartile of performance tend to question plan. A UK training manual for meetings had a cartoon where the caption was: 'Before opening your mouth, put the brain in gear': before your write an answer, think and plan. This is important as in the time stress of the exam, it is easy to cover 5Ps, not 7Ps, as an example. If you have question planned, mark the Ps off as you cover them, so you shouldn't forget one.

Time

A common reaction, when looking through the above process, is that there is not enough time. There is enough time but only if you practice case studies and exam technique. Better to practice now than fail an exam and then have all the time, expense and trouble of a re-sit.

The successful exam process

Figure A3.3 gives the outline of the successful exam process.

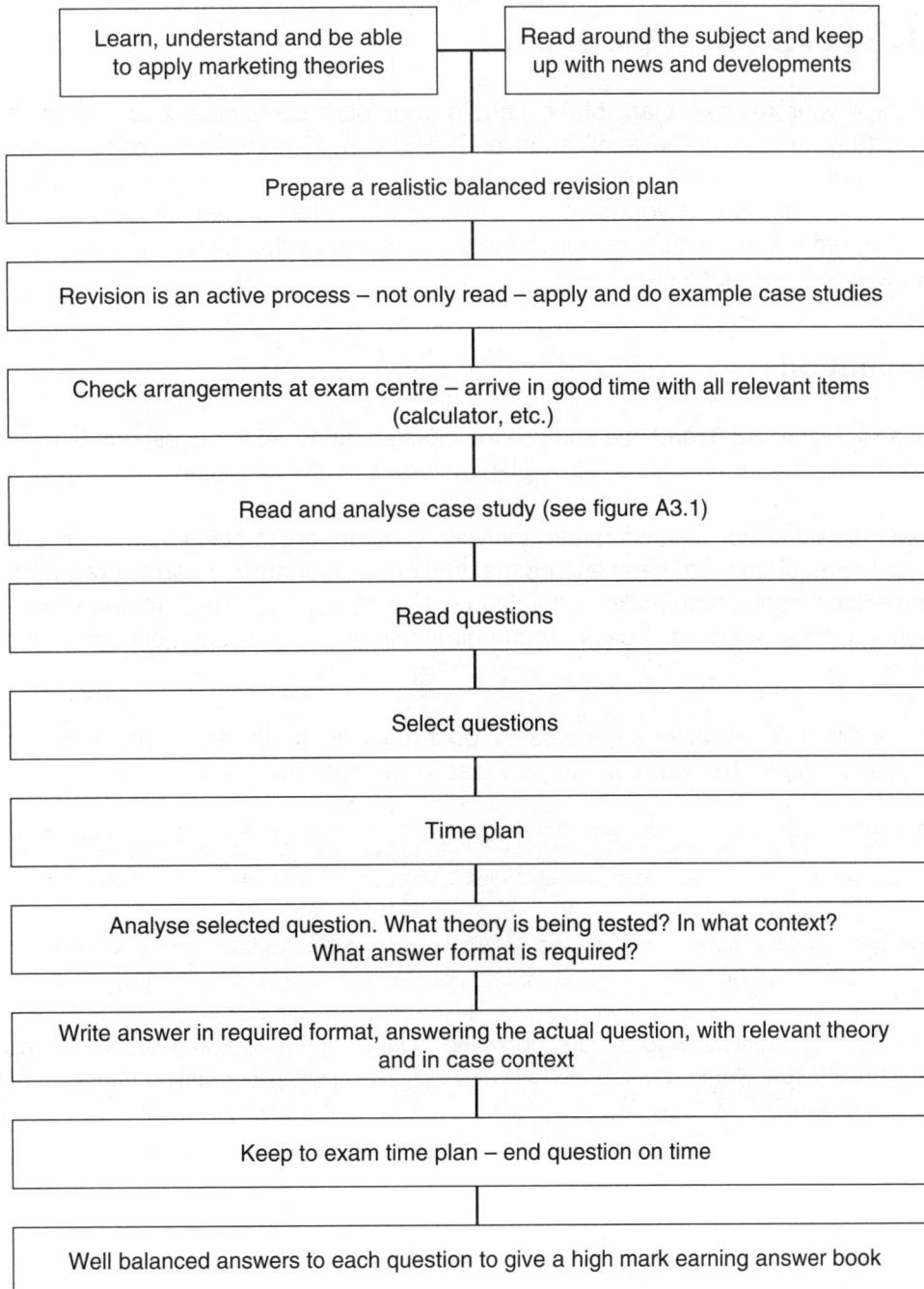

```
┌──────────────────────────┐    ┌──────────────────────────┐
│ Learn, understand and be │    │ Read around the subject  │
│ able to apply marketing  │────│ and keep up with news    │
│ theories                 │    │ and developments         │
└──────────────────────────┘    └──────────────────────────┘

┌────────────────────────────────────────────────────────────┐
│          Prepare a realistic balanced revision plan         │
└────────────────────────────────────────────────────────────┘

┌────────────────────────────────────────────────────────────┐
│ Revision is an active process – not only read – apply and   │
│ do example case studies                                      │
└────────────────────────────────────────────────────────────┘

┌────────────────────────────────────────────────────────────┐
│ Check arrangements at exam centre – arrive in good time     │
│ with all relevant items (calculator, etc.)                  │
└────────────────────────────────────────────────────────────┘

┌────────────────────────────────────────────────────────────┐
│        Read and analyse case study (see figure A3.1)        │
└────────────────────────────────────────────────────────────┘

┌────────────────────────────────────────────────────────────┐
│                       Read questions                        │
└────────────────────────────────────────────────────────────┘

┌────────────────────────────────────────────────────────────┐
│                      Select questions                       │
└────────────────────────────────────────────────────────────┘

┌────────────────────────────────────────────────────────────┐
│                        Time plan                            │
└────────────────────────────────────────────────────────────┘

┌────────────────────────────────────────────────────────────┐
│ Analyse selected question. What theory is being tested?     │
│ In what context? What answer format is required?            │
└────────────────────────────────────────────────────────────┘

┌────────────────────────────────────────────────────────────┐
│ Write answer in required format, answering the actual       │
│ question, with relevant theory and in case context         │
└────────────────────────────────────────────────────────────┘

┌────────────────────────────────────────────────────────────┐
│      Keep to exam time plan – end question on time          │
└────────────────────────────────────────────────────────────┘

┌────────────────────────────────────────────────────────────┐
│ Well balanced answers to each question to give a high mark  │
│ earning answer book                                          │
└────────────────────────────────────────────────────────────┘
```

Figure A3.3 The successful examination process

Before revision

Learn and understand the theory and content of the programme as you progress. An attempt to cram in knowledge in the last few weeks will not work. This exam requires understanding and application as well. This must be developed throughout the programme with the skills of case study analysis and answer writing. You need to set this all in the current business context so keep reading marketing magazines and business pages of newspapers during your programme, do not leave this to the revision time; this is too late. Before you start your revision, time plan to ensure you cover all the topics and practice all the skills that will be tested in the exam. Ensure that you keep a time/work/personal-life balance.

Revision and before the exam

Implement your revision plan. Make certain your plan contains active learning as well as reading (e.g. practising the application of STEEPLE). Continue with case study and exam question practice. If you have the opportunity (if offered by your tuition centre) do a mock examination. Ensure that you have your examination pack sorted (spare pens, highlighters, calculator, etc.). Know where and when the exam is to be held. Allow for problems (e.g. difficult traffic) and arrive in good time.

Examination

As given in Figure A3.3 read and analyse the case study. Read the questions, analysing what is required. Select your questions. Time plan and keep to the time plan.

For each selected question complete analysis. What theory is being tested? In what context? Keep to the required format and ensure that you make your answer context relevant (e.g. if you use an Ansoff matrix, then make certain you put some key case study material into it). End the question on time. A common cause of marginal failure is not to leave enough time for the last question.

After the exam do not have a depressing 'post-mortem'. If you have another exam, focus on what you can do in the future. If it is your last exam, you have earned some R&R!

Summary

Examination success does not depend on two weeks cramming before the exam and memorizing past case study answers. What is required is the development of knowledge, understanding and application of marketing theory into the given case study context. This requires the development of skills in analysis and problem solving to recommend appropriate marketing actions. In this section a structured approach is outlined which will allow you to develop this skill and achieve success, not only in the exam but also in your marketing career.

Further study

In this workbook there are a selection of recent exam case studies. Further case studies are available on the CIM website. The more case studies you work through the more you will develop your skills.

Hints and tips

Do not 'zap through' to look at the specimen answers when working through past case studies. Work through the case study and develop your own answers. Only then compare these with the specimen answers provided and the senior examiner's comments. Discuss your approach with your tutor and other students. Only by this process you will fully develop your skills.

Bibliography

Cameron, S. (2005) *The Business Students Handbook: Learning Skills for Study and Employment*, 3rd edition, FT Prentice Hall.

how to pass the integrative assignment

The process to compete a successful assignment is given in Figure A4.1.

Understanding of marketing theory and current issues

General research into your selected organization

Marketing context B2B and/or B2C, etc.	**Stakeholders** Internal and external	**Environmental analysis** Macro/Micro and Internal

Key issues

What is the task?

What theory is being tested? In what context?

Further primary and/or secondary research in the context of the task

Plan the report (cover total task and use word count wisely, remember to reference sources)

Good balanced answer earning high marks

Figure A4.1 An approach to an integrated assignment

Understanding of marketing theory and current issues

This is covered in p. 294 and is not repeated here.

General research into your selected organization

An important first task before you start to complete any of the detailed assignments is to prepare the ground and do some general research. However, it has its parallel in a challenge facing an engineer to build a bridge (Figure A4.2a,b). Faced with this situation the engineer does not say 'no problem just send me down 20 000 tonnes of steel and 100 000 tonnes of concrete and I will have it sorted! There are reasons why the Sydney Harbour Bridge is different to the San Francisco Golden Gate Bridge in construction. Some research and planning is needed. So, it is with an integrative project.

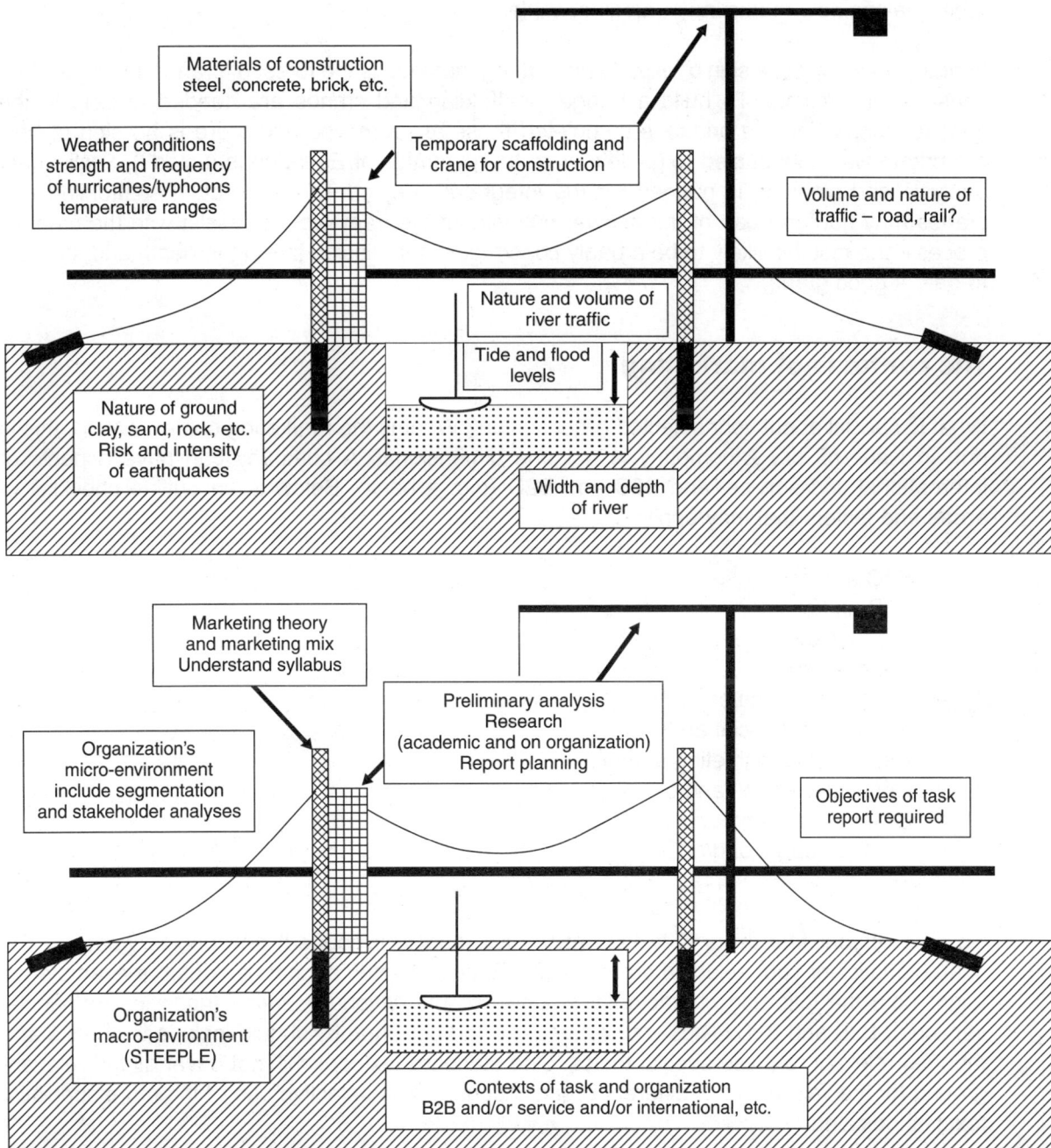

Materials of construction steel, concrete, brick, etc.

Weather conditions strength and frequency of hurricanes/typhoons temperature ranges

Temporary scaffolding and crane for construction

Volume and nature of traffic – road, rail?

Nature and volume of river traffic

Tide and flood levels

Nature of ground clay, sand, rock, etc. Risk and intensity of earthquakes

Width and depth of river

Marketing theory and marketing mix Understand syllabus

Preliminary analysis Research (academic and on organization) Report planning

Organization's micro-environment include segmentation and stakeholder analyses

Objectives of task report required

Organization's macro-environment (STEEPLE)

Contexts of task and organization B2B and/or service and/or international, etc.

Figure A4.2 (a) Engineering issues in the construction of a bridge; (b) Integrated assignment task viewed in the context of the bridge building model

305

One preliminary question is: What are the characteristics of the river to be bridged? (width, depth, rate of flow, tidal and flood levels, nature and volume of river traffic, etc.). In a marketing context, what are the characteristics of the marketing problem? (Does it have elements of B2B and/or services and/or international and/or···?).

The nature of the bridge will be affected by the ground conditions (clay, sand, rock, frequency and intensity of earthquakes, etc.) and the weather conditions (frequency of hurricanes, typhoons and temperature extremes to be expected, etc.). In the marketing task, the shape and content of the output will be affected by the macro- and micro-environment.

The way in which the bridge is built will depend on the development of building theory and materials of construction (e.g. the replacement of steel reinforced concrete with carbon-fibre composites reducing weight and reducing maintenance). This can be viewed as a parallel to the arrival of the Internet for marketers. One is making new forms of construction possible, the other making new marketing strategies viable.

In many major cities, a sign of expansion and regeneration is the forest of cranes involved in the construction projects. To build a bridge, scaffolding and cranes are needed to help in the construction. When the bridge is completed these are removed and there is no sign of how the bridge was constructed (e.g. How were the pyramids of Egypt constructed?). Preliminary analysis and planning is needed for the integrated project. The intellectual scaffolding and cranes may not form part of the answer but without the framework to assist with the creative process, the result is likely to be a badly constructed submission lacking in depth and strength to gain a good grade.

The contexts of marketing

What is special about your selected organization? What is the marketing context? Note, this is not an issue of 'or'. A company is not one dimensional. A company can have aspects of international and service, and B2B and B2C (e.g. a bank). Below is an outline checklist of areas and factors that may apply:

- o B2C and/or
- o B2B and/or
- o Product and/or
- o Services and/or
- o International and/or
- o Not-for-profit/social and/or
- o Relationship marketing and/or
- o Consumer issues and/or
- o Green issues and/or
- o Limited budget and/or
- o ?

So, one of your first tasks is to look at the list (add to if needed) and decide what are the characteristics of your selected organization. Taking an international bank as our example we might note the following characteristics/contexts: international, service (specifically financial services), B2B and B2C. Thus your references and bibliography should include textbooks and theories relevant to these special topics. One standard textbook will not cover all the relevant ground for the vast range of different organizations. Some selective use of the more specialist texts is indicated.

Stakeholder analysis

As part of your general research you should draw up a stakeholder analysis table. A suggested format with some indicative stakeholder types is given in Table A4.1. Stakeholder segment: it is a good exercise to analyse the internal structure of stakeholders. Some illustrative examples are given below:

- ○ *Customers* – B2B: segmented and/or B2C: segmented. Possibly customers' customers (e.g. P&G marketing to TESCO, then to ultimate customers – Push & Pull strategy).
- ○ *Internal* – Management, technical. Full time, part time, shift worker, etc.
- ○ *Media* – TV, radio, press. International, national, regional, local, etc.
- ○ *Political* – International (e.g. EU), national, local, etc.

Table A4.1 Outline stakeholders for a typical organization

Stakeholder	Stakeholder agenda	Organization's objectives	Comments
Customers	Good marketing mix offering	Promotion of mix, building relationship (RM)	Full analysis need this for each key customer segment
Consumers	Good marketing mix offering	Promotion of mix, building relationship (RM)	The buyer need not be the consumer, for example gifts
Owners	Development of stakeholder value	Reassurance on how value is being built	Note not always shareholders. Private companies and charities with trustees, etc. as well. Note not-for-profit 'value' as well
Employees	Stakeholder value (pay, prospects, pension, etc.)	Development of commitment, attraction and retention of key staff	Note segmentation issues (e.g. management, front line, etc.). May be taken to include potential employees
Suppliers	Stakeholder value (continued profitable business)	Relationship marketing: building and maintaining supply chain partnerships	Not only raw materials but all goods and services. May segment, for example small and international
Political	Balancing competing pressures (e.g. job and green issues)	Understanding pressures and providing reassurance about corporate objectives	May segment, for example for a supermarket National: about consumer credit Local: problems with car parking at new supermarket centre
Pressure groups	Often focused agenda (e.g. green issues) with not-for-profit elements	Understanding agenda and providing reassurance and conflict resolution where possible	Need proactive rather than reactive management. Note, may also segment, for example national over packaging, local back to that car park and location of bottle bank

Table A4.1 (continued)

Stakeholder	Stakeholder agenda	Organization's objectives	Comments
Media	Want a story to build circulation. Some publications' significant not-for-profit issues	Develop long-term positive relationship to give out good news and manage bad news	Segments (e.g. TV, radio, press; international, national and regional, etc.)
Partners	Stakeholder value (continued profitable partnership)	Often full mix delivery requires partners (e.g. hotel and an airline collaborating on packages)	Often occurs in B2B, e.g. several companies may work collaboratively with a computer company developing an integrated range of hardware/software components

Environmental analysis

Complete a focuses STEEPLE (or one of its variants) analysis. Do not leave as 'Exchange rate: £ moving up, the £1 = $2 is a possibility'. Go on: *Exchange rate: £ moving up the £1 = $2 is a possibility, Implication is trading will be – better (UK company selling USA holidays) – worse (UK manufacturer exporting to the USA).* A Porter competition analysis should be completed. The segmentation issues should be evaluated. A value chain analysis can be useful.

Key issues

A SWOT analysis helps focus the range of issues uncovered in the above analysis. This will then indicate the key imperative that face the organization (e.g. gain new customers, introduce new products, move into international markets, etc.).

What is the task? What theory? What context?

Figure A4.3 outlines the integration of the various threads to produce a coherent submission. The organizational audit will give you the context for your organization. This will direct you into the right selection of theory (e.g. for a charity organization, specialist texts on not-for-profit marketing). The review of the organization's marketing mix again provides a foundation for the specific assignments. Over your studies, on this and the other CIM modules, you will have developed your marketing skills and kept up with the current trends in the industry by reading the marketing and business press.

```
                        ┌─────────────────────────┐
                        │      CIM success        │
                        │  Integrative assignment │
                        └─────────────────────────┘
                                   ▲
                                   █
┌───────────────────────┐   ┌─────────────────────┐   ┌──────────────────────────┐
│  Organizational audit │   │                     │   │  Evaluation of Integrated│
│                       │   │                     │   │     Mix for organization │
│   Macro-environment   │   │ Integrated          │   │         Product          │
│   Micro-environment   │ ► │ assignment task     │ ◄ │         Price            │
│  (STEEPLE and Porter) │   │                     │   │         Place            │
│  Internal environment │   │ Aims and objectives │   │         Promotion        │
│  Segmentation, etc.   │   │                     │   │         People           │
└───────────────────────┘   │ Format              │   │     Physical evidence    │
                            │ (often report for   │   │         Process          │
                            │  MMIP)              │   └──────────────────────────┘
┌───────────────────────┐   │                     │   ┌──────────────────────────┐
│   Marketing context   │   │ Integration         │   │                          │
│    for organization   │   │                     │   │                          │
│   Consumer Services   │ ► │ Referencing         │ ◄ │    Marketing skills      │
│    B2B marketing      │   │                     │   │    Clear language        │
│     Not-for-profit    │   │ Proofing            │   │    Grasp theory          │
│   International, etc.  │   │                     │   │   (relevant to syllabus) │
└───────────────────────┘   └─────────────────────┘   └──────────────────────────┘
```

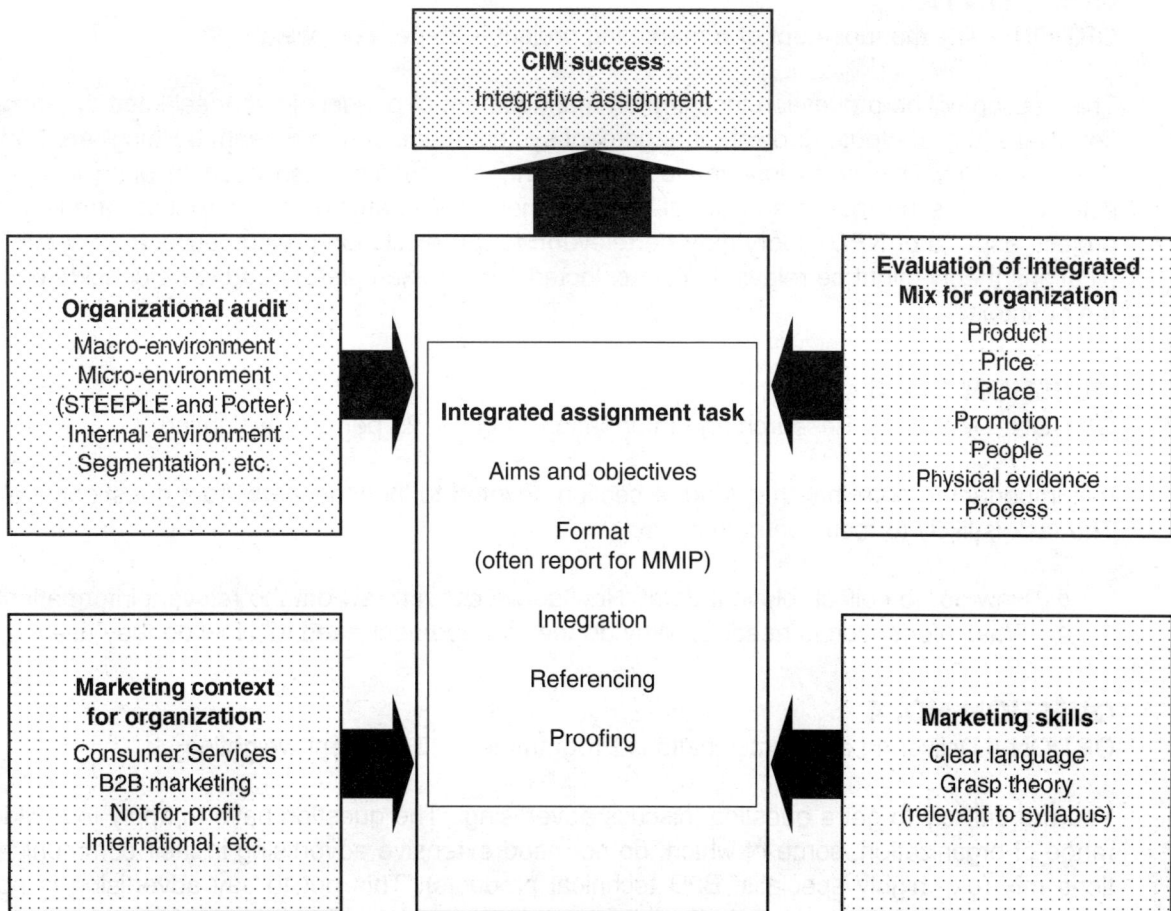

Figure A4.3 Elements of integration for a MMIP assignment

The first part of the assessment is the core section, 'the role of marketing in the organization' and covers a wide spectrum of the syllabus content.

CORE SECTION – The role of marketing in the organization – 50 per cent weighting

QUESTION NO. 1

In this you will be required to demonstrate the application of a relevant body of theory to your selected organization. This does not imply a 'sandwich cake' structure, a descriptive layer of theory, followed by a description of the company. What is required is an integrated application of the theory. Something like Smith's theory (reference) is helpful in considering this xxxxxx aspect of xxxxx. The implications are xxxxxx.

ELECTIVE SECTION – 25 per cent weighting for each of TWO options

You are required to complete TWO of the four options within this section. It is most beneficial in terms of research, etc. if the organization chosen for the core section is also used in the elective section. These optional questions are more focused on specific areas of marketing management than the core question. This allows you to work in an area that interests you and will allow you to improve those skills that are relevant to developing your career.

309

QUESTION NO. 2
OPTION – The management of a marketing project – 25 per cent weighting

This section will be a question focusing on management of projects in your selected organization. Hard (e.g. computer project management systems) and soft (e.g. team building) are likely to be relevant. This is an integrative assignment, so you may also need to bring in other selected marketing theory as part of the treatment, for example for a product introduction project, aspects of NPD theory may be relevant; for an exhibition project, aspects of communications theory might be relevant. Your selected project example(s) need to be considered in their context.

QUESTION NO. 3
OPTION – Marketing Research and Information Needs – 25 per cent weighting

It is important to note that this is not a section devoted to 'how do we write a questionnaire?' The task is likely to focus on both aspects.

- o How do we collect relevant data? How do we convert raw data to relevant information?
- o What information is needed? Why do the management need it? How do they use it?

QUESTION NO. 4
OPTION – Delivering a Communications Programme – 25 per cent weighting

You are unlikely to get a question 'discuss advertising'. The question have to apply to a wide range of organization, some of which, do not need extensive advertising in their communications mix (e.g. highly specialist B2B technical products). This not to say advertising is not important, in the right context. A candidate setting their submission in the context of a major FMCG brand might well focus on advertising. Given the integrative nature of this module and the perceived importance of relationship marketing (RM), some explicit cover of all relevant stakeholders is likely to be appropriate. Customer communications are important but communication to other key stakeholders may also be important (e.g. internal and channel).

QUESTION NO.5
OPTION – Customer Service – 25 per cent weighting

A broader rather than a narrower view of 'customer' is taken in this integrative module. A focus on internal customers, in certain circumstances and task settings, might well be appropriate. Relevant marketing theory, such as SERVQUAL, should be integrated into your treatment. The old definition of marketing: 'Selling products that do not come back to customer who do come back' has a lot of truth. However some more development is required. What contributes to customer satisfaction? In RM terms, what makes a profitable relationship?

The most frequently required submission format is a 'report'. The issues for this are covered in the next section. As noted in Figure A4.3 more primary or secondary research and additional reading may be needed, once you have defined your approach. For a financial services context, some reference to specialist writing and theories, in that area, would be appropriate. Discussions with senior management may be appropriate, to understand how the processes are intended to work, in your selected organization. It is not possible to be prescriptive given the wide range of organizations and contexts that might be selected. In most cases, some additional research work will be required, once the approach and shape of the submission has become clear from your preliminary analysis.

Academic reports

The single most important format for a CIM candidate is report format. Unless otherwise stated all assignment projects should be submitted in report format. Different contexts demand different approaches styles and the general framework (Figure A4.4) given below should be adapted as required. Comments are also made about general academic reports, for the interest of candidates who might wish to proceed to a university higher degree qualification later.

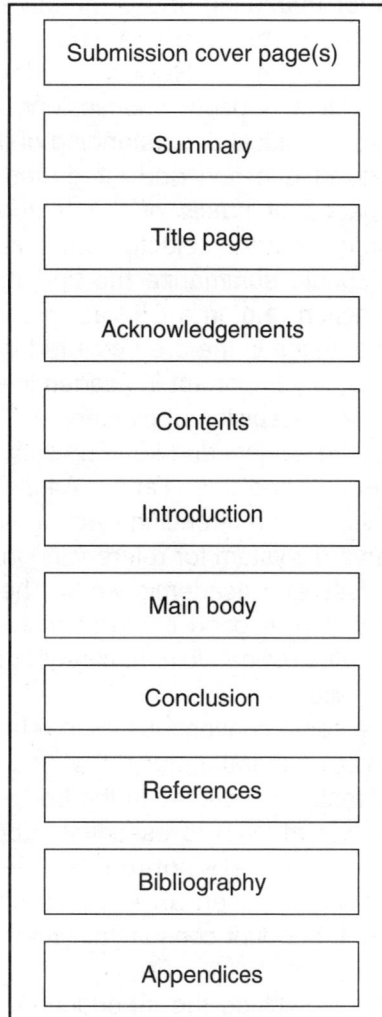

Submission cover page(s)

Summary

Title page

Acknowledgements

Contents

Introduction

Main body

Conclusion

References

Bibliography

Appendices

Figure A4.4 General outline of a report for an academic project

1. Submission cover sheet(s) contains all the necessary information for submission of the assignment. As cover documentation, it is not part of the formal report. Full instructions are given on the CIM website. In any doubt consult your tutor.
2. Title page including title of project and date. For CIM integrative assignments the question number should be included. Lavish colour graphics are not required; presentation is no substitute for content. A good clear professional presentation is required.
3. Summary, focused and brief (150–300) words, should include key words for computer indexing of the project for more formal academic reports.
4. For acknowledgements assistance may have been given with resources (e.g. assistance with running focus groups) or other support. It is good manners to acknowledge support.

5. Contents helps people find their way around a longer project. Longer academic projects might include page numbers of main topic headings, appendices and lists of diagrams, figures, tables and illustrations. Reports should be page numbered.

6. Brief introduction gives a clear definition of the hypothesis, issue(s) or problems covered in the report. For CIM company-based assignments, a brief overview of the company context is helpful. Lengthy descriptive sections do not earn high grades and eat into the word count.

7. Body of the report with full use of headings and subheadings. In academic reports, the more formal style should be used (e.g. 'the view is advanced' rather than 'I suggest'). Typical frameworks for marketing and communications plans are given in the CIM specimen answers to case studies. For a typical academic project, the major section headings might be 'Literature Review', 'Primary Research', 'Conclusions & Recommendations'. Cut and paste submissions are in danger of a marginal fail. What is required is some critical understanding of the relevant theory with application in the light of the given question and integrated into the context of the selected organization. Two pages of précis of the textbook theory, with a few pages of unrelated description of what the selected organization does, are not sufficient.

8. Conclusion section should summarize the findings and if appropriate give recommended courses of action (e.g. in a CIM assignment how the selected organization might improve its operations in the area covered in the report).

9. References are particularly important in academic work. Failure to properly reference work quoted can leave a suspicion of plagiarism. The CIM framework excepts candidates to read around the subject and keep up with development. References provide evidence that you have done this. Tables A4.2 (books), A4.3 (journals) and A4.4 (websites) give the accepted referencing system used professionally and in academic institutions. The 'Harvard' system for referencing in the body of the report is the most widely used in business and academic work. There are many good websites from various universities that give good comprehensive guidance on referencing; http://library.open.ac.uk/help/helpsheets/cite.html#eg1) is the address for The Open University's guidance site.

10. Bibliography uses the same conventions as in referencing, the sources are the same type but this is the more general material that you consulted in your overall research but have not used directly and quoted in the body of your report.

11. Appendices should be restricted to essential support material. Complete copies of annual reports, etc. are generally not required. If some primary research was conducted with a questionnaire, then an example copy of a completed questionnaire might be appropriate. If in doubt consult your tutor.

Usually a word count is taken to include the introduction, body and conclusion of a report. Greatly exceeding the word count can result in failure in academic work. You are strongly advised to consult the precise regulations covering your submission. Length is not the test of quality (one kilogramme of cold, soggy chips is not a good eating experience; quality and quantity are different issues). What is required is a focused delivery of knowledge, understanding and application of relevant theory in the light of the given question/task and in the context of the selected organization.

Table A4.2 Outline of how to reference a book (*Source*: Elsevier author guideliness with adaptation) Kopperl, D. (1965), *Manual of Document Microphotography*, Boston, Focal Press.

Field	Example
Author(s) or editor's surname followed by initials	Kopperl, D.
Year of publication in brackets	(1965)
Book title in italics	*Manual of Document Microphotography*
City where published	Boston
Publisher name	Focal Press

Table A4.3 Outline of how to reference a journal (*Source*: Elsevier author guidelines with adaptation) Kopperl, D. (1965), 'Techniques of Photography', *J. Appl. Photogr. Engng*, 2, 2, 1 pp. 117–120.

Field	Example
Author(s) surname and initials	Kopperl, D.
Year of publication of journal in brackets	(1965)
Paper title in inverted commas	'Techniques of Photography'
Journal title in italics (abbreviations or acronyms are acceptable here)	*J. Appl. Photogr. Engng*
Voulme	2
Issue number	2
Part/section (if applicable)	1
Page numbers plus date article written if available	117–120

Table A4.4 Outline of how to reference an Internet source (*Source*: Elsevier author guidelines with adaptation) Kopperl, D. (1965), *Techniques of photography [online]*, The Online Journal of Applied Photographic Engineering www.JAPE.co.uk/Kopp/TechPhot.html (03/07/04).

Field	Example
Author(s) surname and initial	Kopperl, D.
Year the website was constructed in brackets	(1965)
Title of the document (in italics) followed by [online]	Techniques of photography [online]
Website title plus complete URL	www.marketingonline.co.uk
Date you accessed the site in round brackets	03/07/04

Further study

Most colleges keep a bank of past projects. Look at past projects to get ideas to develop your own approach. These are not only useful for style and structure. Be selective and look at projects in your selected area. These may give you useful key references. Past projects in a library are just like journals and may be used as such. Remember it is essential to reference any material you directly use.

Hints and tips

Do not rush to start to write your report. Complete the analysis of your selected organization's marketing environment and read around the relevant theory. Remember to read articles or textbooks in your selected area (e.g. if your selected organization is a bank, look at some textbooks on financial services). Draw up a project time plan to allow you to do this preliminary groundwork.

Bibliography

Anderson, J. and Poole, M. (2001) *Assignment and Thesis Writing*, 4th edition, Wiley.

appendix 5
answers and debriefings

Unit 1

Debriefing Activity 1.1

Managers are likely to differ in how they perceive demands, choices and constraints, and they may have more choices than they perceive. Different perceptions arise out of a combination of personal factors such as personality and previous experience, cultural factors such as views about how managers and other staff should interact and who has the authority to make decisions, and job factors relating to the work context and the people with whom the manager interacts. In some contexts, such as retailing, it can be very important for front-line staff to have the discretion to respond to customers and clients rather than to apply a rigid set of rules. 'More than my job is worth' is the embodiment of a lack of both choice and responsiveness to customers. However, in some other areas of work, the rigid application of a set of rules is necessary to ensure that people are treated fairly or that health and safety procedures are followed. Therefore, whether or not different perceptions about demands, choices and constraints is a problem or not depends on the context.

Debriefing Activity 1.2

Most managers have strengths and weaknesses, and few managers are strong in all respects and an awareness of personal strengths and weaknesses is an important aspect of management. Different management styles can be effective and efficient, and views about what makes an 'effective' manager might vary depending on your role or where you 'sit' in the organization. Being popular and being effective are not the same. The television series 'The Office' provides a humorous example of the embarrassing consequences of a manager who feels that being 'a chilled out entertainer' is what people are looking for in a 'boss'.

Debriefing Activity 1.3

In looking at the time you spent on interpersonal roles, decisional roles, informational roles – does this match the priorities of your job? After completing your chart, are there any less developed management roles you need to improve? If you were promoted tomorrow what roles are you likely to have to perform in addition to those you have already?

Debriefing Activity 1.4

The Spiderman website is more geared up for advertising the merchandise that is available. The Lord of the Rings site seems to focus more on providing in-depth information about the characters and the films. However, whilst the Spiderman website looks to be more sophisticated technologically, is it as quick to navigate this site compared with the Lord of the Rings site? – What is your view? Which site is the most effective from a marketing perspective is a matter of opinion but criteria to look at are, for example, ease and speed of navigation, how well different parts of the site are signposted and how straightforward it is to find what the site is marketing. You might think of other criteria that could be used to compare marketing effectiveness.

Debriefing Activity 1.5

Likely problems:

For managers – supervision and control, communications, understanding employees' needs/concerns, and so on, building and maintaining relationships, motivation, evaluating performance, and so on.

For employees – isolation, lack of interaction, home distractions and protecting work space (both physical and mental), personal development, lack of sense of belonging, and so on.

Implications for the business – insurance, health and safety, also redesigning/reducing office space, providing space for team events/meetings, ensuring steelworkers have the necessary equipment and maintaining this equipment, use of technology, for example videoconferencing, intranet, fostering the work ethic and protecting reputation and brand.

Debriefing Activity 1.6

In many organizations, functions such as sales and marketing are combined in one role but in some organizations, sales and marketing departments can work against each other, with each group planning their strategy, training their team and implementing their plan without considering each other's plans, gathering their input, providing feedback or gaining support from each other. If co-ordination is a problem in your organization, what are the causes of the problem and how could they be improved?

Debriefing Activity 1.7

One of the benefits of the site is the Special Reports on CRM but there are other benefits as well. However, you may find that the site is too specific to the USA and the ideas that are discussed may need to be adapted to your own context.

Debriefing Activity 1.8

The USA site has information about campaigns such as child labour in the chocolate industry but the UK site does not seem to contain similar information. Maybe this is based on a view of what is important in the USA compared to the UK, or maybe it says something about the use of social causes in marketing. You decide.

Debriefing Activity 1.9

It should be clear that in many organizations, the effective performance of marketing roles requires good working relationships with a wide range of people inside and often outside the organization. This means that there is also a need to develop a range of other social skills as well as marketing expertise. Marketing managers need skills in the following areas:

- Communication
- Project development
- Team leadership
- Delegation
- Time management
- Working across organizational boundaries
- Negotiation and conflict resolution
- Project planning
- Managing people
- Performance management
- Coaching.

Debriefing Activity 1.10

1. Definition

Your answer should begin with a definition of service marketing, for example Kotler, 'Any activity of benefit that one party offers to another, which is essentially intangible and does not result in the ownership of anything.'

2. Characteristics of services marketing

Heterogeneity – Service provision varies.

Intangibility – A need for tangible proxy evidence such as environmental quality, friendliness of staff, and so on.

Perishability – A service cannot be stored like a product can be kept.

Inseparability – Service and consumption cannot be separated.

3. Explain the 7 Ps

1. Product
2. Place
3. Promotion
4. Price
5. People
6. Process
7. Physical evidence.

Mention the need for good training and development to help make the service have some standardized components but also leave room for staff to add their individual flourish to the service.

Point out the need for physical evidence – stationery, uniforms, the general environment and ambience.

Focus on areas that will help the customer remember the service and help to differentiate it from competitors' services.

Process is important because needs have to be anticipated and met.

Promotion helps to reduce, for example, under-occupancy, wasted food, and so on.

4. Service quality

Set SMART objectives and try to close the gap between what the service offers and what customers need. Use, for example, Parasuraman's service quality model.

Identify the factors that can lead to a breakdown in service quality, for example expectations, perceptions, actual service delivered, the service brief and the way that changes are communicated to the customer.

5. Benchmarking

Explain the concept of Christopher, Payne and Ballantyne to recruits.

6. Service criteria

Discuss generic service criteria:

Responsiveness – Can cleaning take place at short notice?

Reliability – Does someone turn-up at the agreed time?

Empathy – Is awareness shown of busy office practice?

Assurance – Are there SMART objectives?

Tangibles – Are we professional?

7. Conclusion

Conclude by asking recruits to use Parasuraman's model to establish a service performance matrix for the company. Conclude with an opportunity for discussion and questions.

Senior Examiner's comments:

Answers showed a clear understanding of the five characteristics of services and the extended marketing mix. Better students discussed the GAP model.

They applied the characteristics of the business-to-business cleaning context using a presentation format and a tone that would be suitable for new recruits. Those who failed did not provide enough detail or forgot that the cleaning company existed, preferring to give no examples at all or standard hotel and airline responses.

Unit 2

Debriefing Activity 2.1

Were you able to answer this question easily, or did it take a long time to think about the whole range of stakeholders involved with your organization? Your list should have included internal and external people. In some organizations, the expectations of different parts of the organization will be explicit but, in others it may only be implicit. Sometimes there is a disdainful view of other parts of the organization that contribute to the overheads but whose contribution to frontline activities is not so visible – for example, what is your view of personnel/HRM? finance? – Were you able to identify your key stakeholders' expectations of your team? Who did you identify as your customers? – Do you see people internal to the organization as your customers?

Debriefing Activity 2.2

In what areas does your team work well and in what areas does it need to improve? If you identified any barriers to effectiveness, how much of this is within the power of the team to overcome? – Usually, teams can improve if one of their goals is to improve how they work together. However, this may not be spoken about even though there may be a recognition that the team does not work well.

Debriefing Activity 2.3

There are many aspects of culture to pay attention to, particularly in marketing activities. The use of language can be a barrier even when the same language is spoken. Unit 1 provided some examples of this but business cultures can vary a lot. Every organization manifests patterns of member behaviours and values which together may be said to form a 'culture'. Organizational effectiveness and decision-making processes are influenced by cultural expression e.g. attitudes and responses of employees, styles of management, etc. Interpreting and understanding organizational culture is an important activity for managers because it affects strategic development, productivity and learning at all levels. Cultural assumptions can both enable and constrain what organizations are able to do. A key role for culture is to differentiate the organization from others and provide sense of identity for its members. A strong culture is one that is internally consistent, is widely shared, and makes it clear what it expects and how it wishes people to behave. Sometimes different disciplines or departments within organizations develop their own sub-culture which can make it difficult when there is a need for people to work together to achieve the goals of the organization. Understanding what cultural differences exist within organizations is important for achieving a common approach and managing change.

Debriefing Activity 2.4

Employee specification

Factor	Essential	Desirable
Attainments	Degree preferably in a media or marketing discipline	CAM qualifications to Diploma level
Specific professional skills	Written composition and presentation skills. Media and communications strategies	–
Experience	5 years or more in a media/PR role	Preferably in a non-profit organization or consultancy
Reasoning abilities	Capacity for strategic media analysis and event management	–
Personality	Calm, proactive, assertive, confident, representative personality. Empathy with NHS values	–
Aptitudes	Networker, promoter, persuader, win rapport with clients. Create and develop promotional material	–
Physical make-up	Professional, well-groomed image. Stamina and good health	–
Circumstances	Weekend and evening work	–

Essential – Attributes essential for adequate job performance. Job cannot be performed unless these factors are present.

Desirable – Attributes that are not essential but if present will enhance effective work performance.

Source: Adapted from http://sol.brunel.ac.uk/~jarvis/bola/jobs/mediajob/perspec.html.

Debriefing Activity 2.5

1. The correct answer: Cannot tell
   You have no idea how many animals were used in any year apart from the previous one.
2. The correct answer: True
   It says that some products can only be tested on live systems.
3. The correct answer: Cannot tell
   There is no information on whether testing makes people angry.
4. The correct answer: False
   It says that Vistek simulates the reaction of the eye.
5. The correct answer: False
   It says that 10 000 ingredients can be used without the need for animal testing.
6. The correct answer: True
   It says that kidney transplants would not exist if it were not for animal testing.

Unit 3

Debriefing Activity 3.2

Were you able to identify your needs and people in the organization that could help? Will you need any assistance to be able to access this help? Is your line manager likely to be supportive or will he or she see this as a threat because they may feel it makes them look like a poor manager – or is your line manager more secure about themselves and likely to be more supportive?

Unit 4

Debriefing Activity 4.1

What kind of issues did you identify? We all need to learn from our experience of being involved in change so that the same mistakes aren't repeated. Gathering feedback after a change has been implemented could be tried providing that the raw feelings associated with change have died down. Otherwise, there is a risk of stirring things up again.

Unit 5

Debriefing Activity 5.1

How easy was it to devise a GANTT chart? – Did you find it useful? – Can you think of examples of how you could use it at work?

Debriefing Activity 5.2

There should be a lot of examples where a project management approach may be useful in a marketing context, such as developing a communications campaign or working with external agencies, for example in market research projects.

Debriefing Activity 5.3

Examples of the key areas could be as follows:

The project timetable, with particular reference to critical event times and potential bottlenecks. There should be feedback on activity times achieved and their effect on the whole project. If network analysis is used, then it is vital that the network is reworked and updated to take into account the actual performance achieved.

The project budget; budgetary control procedures can be used as in respect of any other form of budget.

Quality and performance standards; these need to be monitored against the original project specification subject to changes agreed with stakeholders in the course of project development.

Unit 6

Debriefing Activity 6.1

These are examples of the kinds of questions that can be asked. Developing and maintaining an MkIS system can be expensive so it is important that it is fit for purpose and meets the identified needs. An MkIS system should serve the whole company not a single department and integrate data from across business functions and from many sources. Data often exists already in an organization but not in a form that is useful to marketing.

Debriefing Activity 6.2

How easy did you find it to use the model? Do you see any advantages in distinguishing between what is written about approaches on paper and collecting information about what is actually being implemented? Do you have any examples of where there is a gap between theory and practice in your own organization? Would a model like EFQM be appropriate in your situation – or, if you already use such a model, how successful is it at promoting improvements?

Debriefing Activity 6.3

It is a self-selecting audience and there must be doubts about how representative it is of a wider population. However, there is no reason to think what interests these women would not interest other women as well, bearing in mind that nothing will please everyone, all of the time. On a limited scale, it is market research and the personal endorsement of some viewers that will encourage other viewers to buy the product.

Debriefing Activity 6.4

Were there any gaps, that is information you would like that is not available? How could this information be obtained from other secondary sources?

Debriefing Activity 6.5

A balance needs to be struck between breadth and depth. Usually, it is possible to find out a lot about an issue from a small sample, but not as much from a larger sample. Sometimes different approaches can be combined so that, for example, a focus group can precede or follow a larger survey to probe certain issues in more detail. However, with a large survey, it is important that there is a consistency of approach, and at least some comparative data can be gained. This means that the questioners need to ask the same questions of employers, something that wouldn't happen if in-depth interviews were being held on the shopfloor, not to mention the added expense. A survey of 70 000 employers is a large survey and should enable some useful conclusions to be drawn. The use of the telephone will provide data in greater depth than could be achieved by a questionnaire.

Unit 7

Debriefing Activity 7.1

Case study 1 has rather less detail than the second, and is not organized as systematically. However, the size of the organization is a lot smaller in Case study 1 and it could be argued that the type of case study is 'fit for purpose'. Case study 2 is an example of a comprehensive approach and shows how some well-known marketing models can be applied. Gathering the information to do this would have incurred an expense that the company in Case study 1 may have found difficult to emulate.

Debriefing Activity 7.2

Did you manage to construct a Gantt chart to schedule the activities? The Gantt chart should show how complex the scheduling can be and how there are bottlenecks and troughs in activity, that is sometimes everything needs doing at the same time and sometimes there is a lull in activity. The aim is to try and smooth this out as far as possible whilst still keeping to deadlines. What range of people were there in your team? – Did you include finance and human resources – or are these line management responsibilities in your organization?

Unit 8

Debriefing Activity 8.1

Are there any conclusions or criteria that you would draw from the campaign that you identified that could be used in other campaigns? What kind of appeal was being made through the campaign? – Was it appealing to 'the rational' or 'the emotional' you? Were you able to associate the product or service with the campaign? Often, we seem to be able to remember advertisements but cannot remember the brand that is being sold.

appendix 6
sample exam questions and answers

The exam

The exam is based on a mini case study. The section A questions are compulsory and account for 50 per cent of the marks for the paper. Two questions must be selected from the four section B questions (25 marks each). The mini case study gives you a role and a context within which you can demonstrate your knowledge of the relevant theory and the skills in applying the techniques to a specific area.

Study Guide

The successful application of marketing theory is like driving a car. You can read many books on the subject but this is no substitute for getting behind the wheel and practising under guidance. Marketing demands the application of theory. The way to develop this skill is to work with your tutors' guidance through relevant case studies. Practice at specimen questions and comparison with outline answers will develop your skills to pass the exam.

Before the exam

Knowledge of the theory is vital, so go over the various models well before the exam date to ensure that you fully understand them and you have practised their application. The Chartered Institute of Marketing is a professional exam, and on qualification, employers will expect you not only to know the relevant theories but also to apply them creatively to real situations. To gain this level of skill it is not sufficient to sit in class or passively read textbooks. Work on case studies and study of real marketing situations are vital. Marketing is a fast-developing area so there is a need to read the current press. Exams require specific skills so do not make your first practice the actual exam. Work through specimen case studies and questions under simulated exam conditions, and discuss your answers and approaches with your tutor. In a busy life there may be a temptation to question spot and 'cherry pick' in the hope that your favourite questions will turn up. Questions will be set across the entire range of the syllabus and in a variety of contexts such as service, not-for-profit and b2b marketing.

In the exam

Do not repeat the question or complete long environmental and SWOT analyses. These waste valuable time without gaining much marks. What is required in the exam is a structured answer demonstrating the knowledge and application of theory to the specific context of the mini case study. Brainstormed ideas without structure and application of theory are likely to yield a marginal fail mark. Theory without context-specific application will also be likely to not gain a pass mark. Report format (unless otherwise indicated in the exam paper) is required in your answers.

Take care to answer the entire question and spend appropriate time on all aspects, e.g. on a question including some cover of the marketing mix, consider all aspects of the service-extended marketing mix with case study relevant points. Standard template answers with little or no context are not acceptable. It is vital to plan your answer so take a few minutes considering your answer structure. Take care to leave enough time for the last question.

Marketing Management in Practice

Time

Date

3 Hours Duration

This examination is in two sections.

PART A – Is compulsory and worth 50 per cent of total marks.

PART B – Has **FOUR** questions; select **TWO**. Each answer will be worth 25 per cent of the total marks.

DO NOT repeat the question in your answer, but show clearly the number of the question attempted on the appropriate pages of the answer book.

Rough workings should be included in the answer book and ruled through after use.

Marketing Management in Practice

The Eden Project – The eighth wonder of the world

In the 90s there was a vision to turn a disused industrial site in Cornwall into a world centre of plants with the largest conservatory in the world – 200-m long and 100-m wide. Even before completion, the project captured the world's imagination and the Eden Project has become one of Europe's most visited attractions and has placed Cornwall well and truly on the map. In 2000, 200 000 visitors were anticipated, but more than double the number came. At present visitors average 1.8 million a year.

The project is owned by The Eden Charitable Trust, a registered charity. It is not a green theme park. Some pre-eminent academic staff have joined the project to develop the academic excellence on site and achieve the educational objectives of the trust.

The world media have acclaimed the project, and in its short life the Eden Project has become in its sector a global brand. Not content with this success, the trust has imaginative ideas for future developments for 2004 and beyond.

325

Disclaimer – The factual information contained in this case study has been taken from the Eden Project's published sources. The management issues below have been written for the needs of the Chartered Institute Qualifications and are not intended to reflect the detailed management plans of the Trust. *Candidates are specifically requested not to contact the Eden Project's management.*

March 2003

Your Role

You are James Smith, a marketing consultant. The CIM scenario is that given the ambitious expansion plans, the Eden Project is considering retaining you as a marketing consultant.

Appendix One

James Smith's fact file

The Eden Project is located in Cornwall in the West Country of the UK, 270 miles west from London. It is located close to major roads but the outstanding success has caused some congestion at peak visiting times. Buses link the project to nearby towns and the main rail station. The 'green' platform consideration has been given to provide good access by coach and bicycle (the Eden Project is on the UK National Cycle Network).

The existing attraction consists of the Humid Tropics Biome, the Warm Temperate Biome and the outdoor landscape. Towering rainforest trees are included in 100 000 plants representing some 5000 species, a truly world class attraction.

There is, at present, no hotel as part of the complex. Plans are being developed to build a conference-based hotel to host major international conferences.

The Project has a good shop and it is possible to buy Eden Project merchandise. Appropriate facilities are provided for refreshments with two restaurants.

The Eden Project has had a major impact on the local environment. The Eden Trust is concerned to take full account of the legitimate concerns of local stakeholder groups.

Education is a major aim of the Eden Trust providing a resource for learning, a living curriculum for schools and colleges.

As a not-for-profit organization, maximizing profits is not the key objective. However, to finance the scientific and education activities, the Eden Project must generate significant earnings. The original project cost £86 million. Although a charity, an effective and efficient commercial operation is needed to generate the cash flow to fund the not-for-profit activities.

The Eden Project has been successively used to host major events such as concerts.

The Eden Project can be used as the ultimate in corporate entertainment and has been hailed as the eighth wonder of the world. It provides clients with an unforgettable experience.

Appendix Two

Future plans

Additional space has recently been purchased to provide room for extra facilities such as the Education Resource Centre.

Designs for a third 'semi-arid' biome have been developed.

Plans are under consideration for a 'Meeting House' for conferences and seminars.

A hotel is also included in the potential new developments.

Appendix Three

Private functions

The Biome Link is situated between the giant conservatories. There is an impressive open area with a first floor viewing gallery. This has been successively used for a variety of events such as banquets and award ceremonies.

Visitor centre gallery

This spectacular location overlooking the Project is available for evening use for receptions and meetings.

Eden as a leading live music and theatre location

The summer 2002 season established the Eden Project as spectacular setting for special performances.

PART A
Question 1
a.   Corporate events and concerts can generate vital revenue to fund the plans. If the Eden Project was to consider appointing a Marketing Manager with specific responsibility for marketing the project for corporate events and concerts, what advice would you give on the recruitment, selection and induction of this person?

(25 Marks)

b.   Outline a marketing plan to develop profitable corporate business for the project. Lengthy environmental analysis and SWOT analysis are NOT required.

(25 Marks)

PART B – Answer TWO questions only
Question 2

What Marketing Information System would you implement to monitor and develop visitor satisfaction of the Eden Project experience? What information would you collect, and how would you obtain it?

(25 Marks)

Question 3

The Eden Project is concerned to be sensitive to the needs and wants of the local stakeholder groups. Outline the marketing communications activities you would undertake for the Eden Project locally.

(25 Marks)

Question 4

Clearly with almost two million visitors a year, the Eden Project has got off to a spectacular start. However, maintaining interest and visitor numbers will be key to the future. Using Relationship Marketing and other relevant marketing techniques, what initiatives would you consider appropriate to maintain and grow visitor numbers?

(25 Marks)

Question 5

You have decided that you wish to produce a new brochure for the corporate hospitality business, and complete a direct mail shot in the UK to expand this business. Using appropriate project management concepts, outline an action plan for the production of this brochure.

(25 Marks)

The outline answers provided are not intended to be the only appropriate treatment, and do not cover all possible points and approaches. Research on past high-mark earning answers written under exam conditions indicates that some 600–900 words provide scope for an appropriate treatment in the time available. These answers have been kept to this length to indicate approaches that are practical under actual exam conditions.

Answers

Question 1

a. Corporate events and concerts can generate vital revenue to fund plans. If the Eden Project were to consider appointing a Marketing Manager with specific responsibility for marketing the project for corporate events and concerts, what advice would you give on the recruitment, selection and induction of this person?

(25 Marks)

To   Marketing Manager – Eden Project

From   James Smith

Date   March 2003

Appointment of Marketing Manager for Corporate Marketing and Concerts

Introduction

This will be an important revenue-earning activity, working with high-profile clients and delivering exciting events. This is a critical appointment demanding an able operational manager who will be able to creatively exploit the potential but with ability to manage the details as well. The issues will be considered under the headings below:

- o   Drawing up the specification
- o   Finding the right candidates
- o   Short-listing
- o   Selection process/event
- o   Induction.

Drawing up the specification

The secret for successful management action as always is pre-planning. Actions that need to be resolved before the candidate search gets underway include:

- o   Senior management agreeing how the new manager will fit into the organizational structure, reporting relationships and responsibilities.
- o   Agreement at senior management regarding level of pay and overall benefits package to be offered.
- o   Working with the Personnel Manager, a job description needs to be drafted.
- o   Again personal specifications need to be drafted including 'must-haves' (e.g. relevant experience) and desirables (e.g. attainment of Chartered Institute of Marketing qualifications).
- o   Agreement of the selection process.
- o   Agreement reached as to who should be involved in the selection process.
- o   A plan agreed to attract suitable candidates (see below). As this is a relatively senior position, a national search may be appropriate. In which case any re-location package to be offered should be agreed.
- o   The candidate package should be agreed with the wording of any intended advertisements.

Note: There are many legal implications in this process. Use of personnel experts is essential. It is assumed that standard rules exist for the payment of candidates' expenses.

Finding the right candidates

The problem with finding the right candidates for more responsible positions which demand experience is that many attractive candidates are not actively searching for work and thus not scanning the recruitment pages.

- o   Given the costs of advertising in the national press, and the likely situation that many strong candidates are not in active job search (i.e. not looking through the jobs pages), this option should be rejected.

329

    ○ A marketing recruitment specialist should be appointed. This is not a low-cost option but may be a more certain way of getting a range of suitable candidates for interview.

    ○ The job should be posted on the website.

    ○ The job should be advertised internally (there may be suitable candidates and an open process is needed to maintain a good working atmosphere).

Short-listing

    ○ The use of a standard application form is recommended. This makes the checking for 'must-haves' easier. Candidates that fail to satisfy these criteria can be eliminated.

    ○ The 'desirable' characteristics can be used to rank the remaining candidates to draw up a long/short-list.

    ○ The candidate information for the long/short-list can be circulated to the selection panel and the final short-list agreed.

    ○ The candidates can then be contacted regarding the arrangements for the selection event. It is advisable to also note a couple of 'reserves' in case at this stage a candidate should decide to withdraw.

Note: All candidate information should be treated in the strictest confidence.

Selection process/event

    ○ Candidates should be given an appropriate briefing and a tour of the facilities.

    ○ In consultation with the Personnel Manager, appropriate aptitude tests can be used to contribute information for the panel.

    ○ It is suggested that candidates should be asked to make a presentation on an appropriate marketing topic (in the corporate selling situation this will be a key skill). In consultation with the personnel function, other activities that might provide useful information are a group activity and an in-tray exercise involving writing some marketing copy.

    ○ The formal interviews should be conducted in a friendly and supportive atmosphere.

    ○ Candidates should be informed of the outcome as quickly as reasonably possible.

Induction

This can be considered under three headings:

Formal induction process
There are legal requirements such as the Health & Safety Act, and full use should be made of the Personnel Management to ensure that all the legal issues are properly covered.

Induction to the job role
Cover of the full range of roles and responsibilities, and relevant organizational procedures, etc.

Informal induction
Introductions to others in the management team and people working in support roles.

Conclusion

Of necessity the above is an outline only. Good preparation and clear objectives and processes should ensure that the position is filled by a good marketing person, who can rapidly make a full contribution to the organization.

Guidance notes The above is a structured review of the issues and processes. Candidates are not expected to be full experts in Employment Law (this is for the Human Resource specialists and lawyers) but are expected to have a general awareness of the issues, in particular, when there are specific legal issues that need specialist involvement (e.g. contracts of employment). The rejection of press advertising may be seen as controversial by some people. It was introduced here to make the point that sometimes it is appropriate for a candidate to propose a negative action. A good answer could use press advertising as an alternative approach. These outline answers are intended to be indicative not prescriptive. Other issues could be considered such as a probationary period. Clearly, in the exam timescale, candidates cannot be expected to cover every possible issue. What is required is a demonstration of a balanced professional level of understanding of the issues.

b.   Outline a marketing plan to develop profitable corporate business for the project. Lengthy environmental analysis and SWOT analyses are NOT required.

(25 Marks)

To   Marketing Manager – Eden Project

From   James Smith

Date   March 2003

Outline Marketing Plan for Corporate Business

Brief situation analysis

There is great scope to generate revenue to support our educational and other charitable activities by the sympathetic use of the facilities for corporate use. A lengthy environmental analysis is not given here but in brief we need to note the following focused SWOT issues.

Strengths

- o One of the most exciting locations in Europe
- o Perceived as new and where it is happening.

Weaknesses

- o Somewhat outposted from London
- o Full facilities required for corporate users – still not fully in place, e.g. hotel yet to be built.

Opportunities

Chance to exploit the unique platform and brand, not just another Disney theme park or another 5 star 'bed factory' hotel chain.

Threats

- o Economic downturn reducing corporate hospitality spend
- o Crowded market with many other offerings.

331

Mission

To bring the Eden experience and values to the corporate sector.

Aims

To develop a profitable corporate activity for national and international clients.

Objectives

At this early stage, detailed objective is yet to be formulated but the working objective is to achieve one profitable corporate event a week after 1 year.

Segmentation

In the detailed future development of this outline plan, the following segmentation variables need to be considered:

○ Size and location of company (e.g. small and national – large and international)
○ Nature of the event such as: product launch, corporate hospitality, management conference, training events, etc.

Positioning

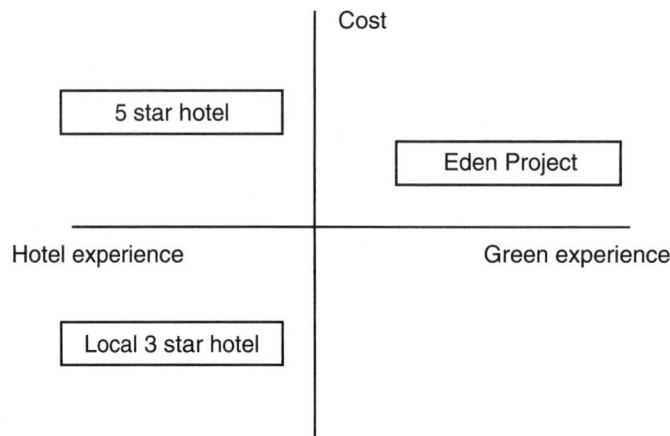

In a crowded market place, it is suggested that we maximize the unique attributes and position of the Eden Project. We will of course accept 'normal' activities but will actively promote green theme corporate events as our competitive advantage. This is also in keeping with the not-for-profit part of our agenda.

Research

○ *Secondary research* – To identify event organizers from trade directories, etc.
○ *Primary research* – Interviews with potential clients to see needs and validate projected mix offering. Research of the mix including price of other event locations.

Provisional service extended marketing mix

Product
All the normal conference facilities (we will need to check out when a client requires special facilities such as three-phase electricity supply).

Given that we do not have our own hotel accommodation at present, we will have to form strategic alliances with local hotels for this part of the offering.

If required, we can offer expert speakers on 'green' issues to clients.

Price
We need the revenue to support our other activities so a market-based price based on the 'going rate' for good national locations as indicated on the positioning map.

Place
Access by car is satisfactory.

For delegates arriving by rail etc. we need a contract with a local taxi company for personal pick-up.

Promotion
In this b2b context, the identification of the key decision-makers in the clients' DMU will be key. To conclude the sale, skilled personal selling will be essential.

Target stakeholder publics will include:

- DMU in potential client organizations
- Media publics (vital for our publicity-driven strategy)
- Local publics (e.g. local partner hotels)
- Internal publics (we must keep all the employees informed as they are a critical part of the service offering).

Advertising
Limited to key trade magazines and trade directories.

Publicity
Work with early clients to gain publicity as 'the' place to hold your company event.

PR
Press releases to get the above publicity.

Internet
Need to maintain a lively section on our website for this aspect of our activities.

Personal selling
This will be key to close the sale. We should seek to recruit a person who has past experience in selling to the corporate event sector.

Direct mail
Rejected as probably expensive and lots of other 'junk mail' are cluttering up the desks of key decision-makers in the major companies. We will rely on a pull strategy with clients attracted by good publicity and then gaining further information from our website.

Physical evidence

The buildings speak for themselves.

We should have a good event organizers' pack to convey our professionalism in this type of activity.

Process

Personal service. Single person to call on to organize things and resolve problems.

People

Briefing session with all front-line staff in the special needs of these clients to develop empathetic client care.

Availability of top 'Green' experts to speak at events to add status.

Other clients: post list of top companies who have used the facilities on the website, 'If it is good enough for BT, it is good enough for us to use.'

Outline action plan

- o Research
- o Recruit manager and develop mix elements
- o Have promotional literature printed and website updated
- o Place advertisements
- o Launch
- o Ongoing marketing support.

Budget

Too early to draw up a formal budget. To do this, we will need estimates for the printing and other media costs. We will need to recruit a person for this role and this must also be in the budget. Revenue can be estimated after the primary research.

Feedback and control

Normal plan against budget.

Key in relationship marketing terms will be a good debriefing process with event organizers to build on success and eliminate bugs.

Guidance notes Writing an outline marketing or communication plan is a frequent task within the CIM exams. The above is suggested as one suitable framework for this. This answer takes a specific view to focus on the green platform. Taking this specific stance is not intended to indicate that this is the single 'right' answer. What is needed for a good pass mark is a practical self-consistent plan that could be developed into a full operation plan. In a mini case study context, it is not possible to give all the figures to draw up a detailed budget. Some indication of the information is needed to start to construct a budget of appropriate size.

Question 2

What Marketing Information System would you implement to monitor and develop visitor satisfaction of the Eden Project experience? What information would you collect and how would you obtain it?

(25 Marks)

To   Marketing Manager – Eden Project

From   James Smith

Date   March 2003

Report for Marketing Information System for Visitor Satisfaction

Introduction

Kotler (2003) defines a Marketing Information System to consist of the people, equipment and procedures to gather, sort, analyse, evaluate and distribute needed, timely and accurate information to marketing decision makers. Components identified by Kotler are:

- o Marketing research system
- o Internal records system
- o Market intelligence system
- o Marketing decision support system.

This report outlines some approaches for such a system to monitor visitor satisfaction and identify directions to improve the Eden Project visitors' experience.

The aim will be to identify what features contribute to a positive experience, and what aspects cause dissatisfaction. In addition, also to provide some pointers to developments and management policies that would enhance a visit.

Research

Secondary research is used to establish general factors in the marketing environment that affect visitors and primary research to gain specific information of the quality of the visit.

Secondary research

General information on the PEST environment such as:

- o *Political/legal* – Issues such as disabled access, what is the law so we can work within both the letter and the spirit?
- o *Economic* – Spending on leisure activities and prices expected for comparable leisure activities
- o *Social* – Demographic information about regional tourism. Who comes to the region? Where do they come from? How do they travel to the region?
- o *Technical* – Developments in Internet, how is penetration progressing, what use are people making of the new technology for planning and booking trips?

Information will be available from government sources and regional tourist organizations.

335

Primary research

Ongoing quantitative research to track satisfaction and qualitative research to probe issues further.

Quantitative research

A questionnaire to a sample of visitors, on an ongoing basis, to track visitor satisfaction with the attractions and other relevant information such as:

- o Visitor demographic information such as age, etc.
- o Travel and access to the project (e.g. by coach. Also 'satisfaction'; e.g., 'Is access satisfactory for groups with small children?')
- o Queuing time/issues
- o Length of stay
- o Satisfaction with facilities such as restaurants and the shop
- o Overall satisfaction
- o Would they visit again?
- o Value for money.

Qualitative research

Focus groups from target groups to probe 'deeper' issues such as attitudes to green issues.

Observation research to see how people move round the site, and time spent in specific attractions.

Internal information

Tracking all the normal sources of information from the commercial systems such as:

- o Ticket purchase (how many, where purchased, advance purchase, collaborative travel and entry packages, e.g. group purchase). Numbers and trends
- o Spend levels and patterns in restaurants and shops.

Other sources of information:

- o Front-line staff on questions (an indication where there may be issues such as poor direction signs)
- o Tracking formal and informal complaints (tracking formal letters of complaint is vital but getting front-line staff to report informal expressions of dissatisfaction will be useful to identify irritating aspects not sufficient to cause a formal complaint).

Market intelligence

Tracking press cover as this affects people's attitudes prior to their visit.

Satisfaction is a comparative issue. What are other attractions such as zoos and theme parks doing to provide a good day out?

- o Visits to other centres
- o Web-based research

- ○ Review of press cover of competition
- ○ Analysis of advertising platform of competition.

Marketing decision support system

Detailed analysis of the data from all the sources is necessary to convert data to useful marketing management information such as:

- ○ Statistical analysis of data, for example, to appraise if certain user groups are more or less satisfied (e.g. families as against adult only groups).
- ○ Analysis to evaluate if time (e.g. day of week or time of day) or weather conditions have an effect on enjoyment.
- ○ Tracking of trends, both internal and external, against other parameters such as general level of holiday activity (e.g. visitor numbers to other attractions).
- ○ If queuing is identified as an issue, modelling of queue lengths under different conditions and marketing strategies (e.g. modelling the effect of a promotional offer for pre-purchase of tickets to avoid on-site queuing for entry).

Conclusion

The above system will identify negative issues to be resolved (e.g. if facilities do not provide a good day out in wet weather) and provide pointers to new developments that will enhance the visit and encourage repeat attendance.

Guidance notes The answer illustrates an appropriate structured approach. Various writers indicate slightly different structures and classifications. The key issue in a good answer is to propose an appropriate range of data with an indication as to how it could be collected and then used.

Question 3

The Eden Project is concerned to be sensitive to the needs and wants of the local stakeholder groups. Outline the marketing communications activities you would undertake for the Eden Project locally.

(25 Marks)

To   Marketing Manager – Eden Project

From   James Smith

Date   March 2003

Proposed Local Marketing Communications Activities

Introduction

The Eden Project has a significant impact on the local environment. There is an overall benefit to the local economy boosting the local tourist industry. This is not all good news as this has caused problems with local road congestion on busy days.

The local stakeholders that are relevant to the Eden Project include:

o *Media* – local radio, TV and papers
o *Political publics* – local elected representatives
o *Local services* – e.g. police
o *Supplier publics* – local suppliers of products such as catering products to the restaurants
o General public
o Friends and relations of people working at the Eden Project
o People seeking employment
o Given the educational aims – local schools and colleges
o Given this is a charity with not-for-profit aims, potential donors and volunteers (existing volunteers covered in our internal marketing plan)
o Visitors to the Eden Project who live locally.

Note: Internal stakeholders are excluded as they are covered by our internal marketing activities.

Key issues are considered first and then some specific activities are suggested for each of the above stakeholders.

Media: local radio, TV and papers

Their need is for news and to service the needs of their readers. A positive attitude from this group is vital, especially in the event of a PR disaster such as an accident to one of the visitors. Key to build relationships with local journalists:

o Special briefings to provide background information
o CD fact file including images to provide resource material
o Press releases and invitations to special events
o Make certain that the local press publics are not ignored when national press events are taking place
o Have a contingency crisis management PR plan.

Political publics

This group shape and respond to local opinion. The legitimate concern is that the international stature should not be built at the expense of the local community. A key influencer group for the local general public. Key to build relationships before there are problems.

o Meetings to brief them with the senior management to solve problems before they become major issues.

Local services

Large events need security. This group will have a legitimate concern that large numbers of visitors do not cause public order problems (e.g. as has happened in the past at rock festivals).

o Relationship-building to ensure effective communications when there is an issue (e.g. larger than normal visitor numbers for an event)
o E-mails to provide up-to-date information about plans that might affect their activities.

Supplier publics

Modern supply chain management invites the organization to make suppliers part of the extended structure. As a major local buyer, we must be sensitive not to be seen to be exploiting this Porter-type power (e.g. recent controversies with supermarkets and small food producers).

- o Build relationships in a Relationship Marketing context, e.g. catering manager to visit food suppliers to build relationships.
- o Local newsletter sent to suppliers to make them feel involved and part of the extended team.
- o An invitation to the 'local friends' evening' (special open evening for key local publics to be invited to).

General public

Local pride in the new attraction is balanced with concerns about traffic congestion. Key that we appear sensitive and responsive, and do not become a local 'Big Brother'.

Local general public will, of course, use the website, so make certain it has any special information that might be relevant.

- o Key activity will be communication through publicity generated press releases. As a charity, we have a limited budget.
- o A responsive attitude to local people when they complain; communication is also about listening.

Friends and relations

Simply an extension of the internal publics. We wish to gain and retain the reputation as a local 'family-friendly' employer.

- o Invitation to the 'local friends' evening' outlined above
- o A friends' newsletter.

People seeking employment

The unemployed are vulnerable, and we must be seen as fair and caring in our treatment. Poor procedures here could damage positive attitudes built up by other activities.

- o Job section on the website
- o Relationship marketing view of the recruitment process. Even if we do not employ, we wish applicants to still view us as fair and a good local corporate citizen.

Given the educational aims – local schools and colleges

Education is a key objective of the Trust; an ideal opportunity to build deep and positive links with the local community. Good attitudes from students are likely to be shared by their friends and families.

- o Special educational visits to the site
- o Local education resource pack to complement the general education resource pack
- o Education visits by research staff to schools.

Potential donors and volunteers

Many charities use voluntary assistance to reduce costs and widen local participation in the broader objectives.

- ○ Information pack for prospective volunteers
- ○ Special web pages for prospective volunteers.

Visitors to the Eden Project who live locally

Key to a service is gaining use at off-peak times.

- ○ Loyalty passport for entry all the year for local people
- ○ Concessionary rates for out-of-holiday season visits.

Conclusion

We should monitor local attitudes by periodic surveys. We should subscribe to a 'clippings service' so that we are fully aware of media cover.

With the above actions, we should build and maintain good relationships with our local stakeholders.

Guidance notes The above structure considers the publics, some issues and then some action points. Clearly, this is not the only possible structure. These outline answers are not intended to be prescriptive. An alternative approach would be to consider communications actions and then consider their impact on various stakeholders.

Question 4

Clearly with almost 2 million visitors a year, the Eden Project has got off to a spectacular start. However, maintaining interest and visitor numbers will be key to the future. Using Relationship Marketing and other relevant marketing techniques, what initiatives would you consider appropriate to maintain and increase visitor numbers?

(25 Marks)

To   Marketing Manager – Eden Project

From   James Smith

Date   March 2003

Relationship Marketing Approaches to Building and Maintaining Visitor Numbers

Introduction

Gummesson defines relationship marketing as 'marketing seen as relationships, networks and interaction'. The traditional marketing focus tended to:

- Focus on short time-scales
- Be product-driven
- Have sales as the objective
- Have discontinuous customer contact.

The relationship marketing focus tends to move marketers:

- To longer time-scales and lifetime value of the relationship
- To focus on customer benefits and value more than just product
- To see sales as part of the broader issue of customer orientation and relationship building
- To pursue more frequent customer contacts not restricted to just sales interactions.

This can be expressed in Payne's relationship ladder. Traditional marketing takes people from step one (a prospect) onto step two (a customer), the so-called 'customer catching'. The relationship ladder seeks to move people through the full five steps:

1. Prospect
2. Customer
3. Client
4. Supporter
5. Advocate.

The marketing activity changes from simply selling to developing and enhancing relationships, and customer retention.

In the context of the Eden Project, we need to move people from a single visit to repeated visits by suitable promotional activities (e.g. discount price for a second visit). Ultimately, we wish to move people to advocates not only of the Eden Project but also in the context of the overall green movement. Marketing activities could include a 'Friends of the Project' scheme with a newsletter and a special section of the website to maintain and develop relationships. Thus, drawing people into the deeper not-for-profit objectives of the Eden Project.

Morgan and Hunt propose that it is not only the buyer partnerships that are important but also:

- Supplier partnerships
- Internal partnerships
- Lateral partnerships.

In this discussion, I will focus on the lateral partnerships.

Competitors

One can regard competitors as strategic partners. We could consider a packaged ticket, which provides entry to a number of attractions and engage in collaborative marketing communications.

Non-profit organizations

Other not-for-profit organizations are not so much competitors but partners. We should ensure good web links from such organizations and again consider collaborative marketing communications such as a 'save the rainforest week'.

Government

Given the expansion plans, a favourable view is needed by national and regional government for support such as local infrastructure development, e.g. improvement of the access roads. Good strategic PR to lobby key political decision makers will be important.

A visit to the Eden Project is a leisure activity in a service marketing context. Services have four main characteristics:

1. Intangibility
2. Inseparability
3. Perishability
4. Heterogeneity.

These characteristics are addressed by marketers by the use of the service-extended marketing mix. However, the quality of 'people–people' interactions, etc. are much more difficult to measure than the weight of a bag of sugar. The SERVQUAL model seeks to address these issues. Gap analysis can help the Eden Project consistently achieve a quality experience for visitors.

Gap 1: Consumer expectations – managers' perceptions of consumer expectations. Need to research that we are creating the right service experience for our visitors.

Gap 2: Managers' perceptions of consumer expectations – service quality specifications actually set. Again research that service level specifications such as target queuing times are appropriate.

Gap 3: Service quality specifications – actual service delivery. We must ensure that internal records systems monitor levels of performance and flag up when these fall below specification.

Gap 4: Actual service delivery – external communications about the service. We must conduct research to check we are not creating expectations – visitor expectations, which we later fail to deliver.

Gap 5: We must check from our internal systems, where resources have to be adjusted such as additional attendants at peak periods.

Conclusion

By integrating a range of these actions, we should ensure that we build up long-term relationships with our key stakeholders; ultimately, converting a casual visitor to a supporter of the Eden Project and an advocate of the green movement.

Guidance notes   The above provides a structured outline using some appropriate approaches with selective use of the theory. Candidates in the exam setting are not expected to cover all the theory and use all the elements of all the possible tools. Good answers will indicate selective use of the theory to address the practical issues in the case study situation.

Question 5

You have decided that you wish to produce a new brochure for the corporate hospitality business and complete a direct mail shot in the UK to expand this business. Using appropriate project management concepts, outline an action plan for the production of this brochure.

(25 Marks)

To   Marketing Manager – Eden Project

From   James Smith

Date   March 2003

Project Management for New Brochure Production

Introduction

There are many methods of project management such as critical path analysis (e.g. activity-on-arrow or activity-on-node) and Gantt charts. Such approaches are vital to Marketing Managers as many plans have time-critical events. A new summer brochure published in the autumn will not achieve much. Even a modest marketing initiative involves a group of people and a failure of one of the supporting staff can have a knock-on effect. This can provide a fatal delay in project completion much later. Explicit methods of project management allow the identification of 'pressure points' and prompt the project manager to provide appropriate communications. This will co-ordinate the activities of the extended project team and bring in the project on time.

For a relatively simple project such as the production of a brochure, the activity plot against time format (Gantt chart) may be all that is required. For increased complexity, a network-type approach such as activity-on-arrow with critical path analysis will provide an analysis of the logic sequence and identify the critical path. Therefore, focus management time and energy on critical activities, where modest delays could affect the completion of the whole project.

For convenience in this report, the brochure production will be considered under the following headings:

- o   Pre-planning
- o   Collection of material
- o   Integration of material
- o   Production of brochure (it will be assumed an external printer will be contracted for this)
- o   Distribution and post-production.

Pre-planning

It is vital to start the process early, and to establish key parameters and responsibilities. Issues that need to be considered include:

- o   Setting of publication deadline
- o   Setting budget and identifying budget responsibilities
- o   Establishing house style (possibly with design consultant)

- o Guidance on must-haves (e.g. good images) and must-not-haves (e.g. things outside the house style)
- o Appointing project leader
- o Establishing communications objectives
- o Defining the theme for authors to work to
- o Establishing outline structure (e.g. number of pages and images, size of sections)
- o Budgetary estimates should be obtained from printers, etc.
- o The nature and costs of any copyright should be established
- o Legal experts should be consulted about any contracts that are to be used like contract for photographers (e.g. who will own the copyright of the images).

Collection of material

This can be an 'explosive' phase of the project with many different people involved. Firm briefing and good project management skills are required, as there is no such thing as 90 per cent ready material. Either you have it or you do not. Actions that need to be managed include:

- o Firm briefing instructions to authors and photographers
- o Checking that where contracts are needed for providers, they have been agreed and signed
- o Milestone checking with the contributors that work is progressing satisfactorily
- o Checking that where library resources are to be used (e.g. an image bank library), the material is of adequate quality, if an appropriate format and establishing if copyright clearance may be used
- o Once a firm definition of what is required is established, firm tenders can be sought for printing and the contract placed.

Integration of material

Here the diversity of material has to be checked and assembled. It is assumed that the final process of producing the files will be completed by a printer. Issues to be considered and actions to be completed include:

- o Checks that images are acceptable and are in the required format for the printers
- o Check that texts to be integrated are correct for factual content, typographical errors and house style issues
- o Integration of texts into appropriate file format for the printer
- o Where work is completed ensure fees are paid.

Production of brochure

The physical production will be the responsibility of the printer but the project manager still has work to do including:

- o Checking that the printer has received all the materials and files in good order
- o Distribution of the proofs to the various authors for final proofing
- o Checking that all proofs have been 'signed off' by the appropriate responsible people (note the need of cover for sickness or holidays)
- o Authorizing the print run.

Distribution and post production

The project is not over until the brochures are in the hands of the intended recipients. Actions in the final lap include:

- Checking that all stock points have received the number of brochures required
- Ensuring that all remaining bills have been paid
- Ensuring that authors and other relevant people have their courtesy copies
- Most importantly, a review of the process to see what areas caused problems (was a particular contractor poor on quality or consistently missing deadlines, etc.).

Conclusion

Project management of even a modest project is a demanding challenge needing the ability to see both the big picture (the completed product) and meticulous attention to detail where one small error (e.g. failure to gain copyright clearance) can cause a disaster. Modern software for project management helps the busy operational marketing manager in this process.

Guidance notes   It is impossible in the exam setting to cover every detailed point and it is suggested that in the time allowed detailed construction of networks or charts is too time-consuming. What a good answer needs to demonstrate is an appreciation of project management tools and a practical understanding of actions and their control in a typical project situation that an operational level marketing manager may be faced with in their day-to-day job.

appendix 7

past examination paper and examiners' report

The Chartered
Institute of Marketing

Professional Diploma in Marketing

Marketing Management in Practice

44:     Marketing Management in Practice

Time: 09.30-12.30

Date: 11th June, 2004

3 Hours Duration

This is a generic paper to cover the following qualifications: -

• **Diploma in E-Commerce and Marketing**

• **Diploma in Tourism**

This examination is in two sections.

PART A – Is compulsory and worth 50% of total marks.

PART B – Has **FOUR** questions; select **TWO**. Each answer will be worth 25% of the total marks.

DO NOT repeat the question in your answer, but show clearly the number of the question attempted on the appropriate pages of the answer book.

Rough workings should be included in the answer book and ruled through after use.

© The Chartered Institute of Marketing

Professional Diploma in Marketing

44:   Marketing Management in Practice

PART A

Picasso Perfumes

Picasso Perfumes is a North American-based company with US revenues in fragrance compounds of $100,000,000 in the last financial year. Picasso Perfumes Perfumery Raw Materials was sold two years ago, generating free capital for expansion. Picasso Perfumes wants to join the top international billion dollars a year club. Construction is almost complete for their first green field international expansion. The South Island site is located close to road, rail and air transport terminals. It has state-of-the-art automated production facilities and has laboratory and office facilities to match.

Note: in the above context the South Island site can be considered to be located in any non-North American country of your selection.

Your Role

You are Pat Jones and have just been appointed Marketing Manager for Picasso Perfumes at the South Island site. You have been appointed for your local market knowledge. You have no previous experience of working for a creative perfumery house.

Appendix One gives an overview of the Perfume Industry.

347

Appendix One

The Creative Perfumery Industry

The creative perfumery houses are a hidden industry, creating fragrances for famous brands and also 'own label' products made under contract for the major supermarkets. The vertical industry value chain is given below.

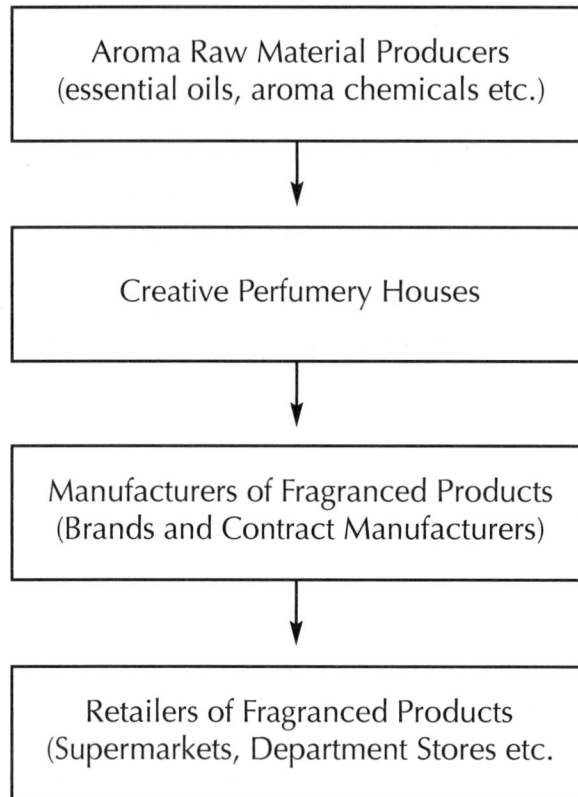

```
┌─────────────────────────────────────┐
│      Aroma Raw Material Producers    │
│   (essential oils, aroma chemicals   │
│                etc.)                 │
└─────────────────────────────────────┘
                   │
                   ▼
┌─────────────────────────────────────┐
│       Creative Perfumery Houses      │
└─────────────────────────────────────┘
                   │
                   ▼
┌─────────────────────────────────────┐
│   Manufacturers of Fragranced        │
│   Products                           │
│   (Brands and Contract Manufacturers)│
└─────────────────────────────────────┘
                   │
                   ▼
┌─────────────────────────────────────┐
│   Retailers of Fragranced Products   │
│   (Supermarkets, Department Stores   │
│                etc.                  │
└─────────────────────────────────────┘
```

The range of products containing fragrances is vast and includes premium fashion fragrances, mass fragrances, cosmetics, personal care products (shampoos, hair conditioners etc.), laundry products (detergents, fabric conditioners), air fresheners and household products (cleaners, disinfectants etc.).

The Role of Fragrances in Functional Products such as Hair Conditioners

With perfumes the perfume (with the package) is the product. However in functional products the fragrance acts as a 'signal' attribute. The consumer knows that the product is working and that their hair is clean, as it smells clean. The fragrance acts as a marketing communication to impart brand values and provide a lifestyle association. As such, fragrances are very culture sensitive. A fragrance that succeeds in the USA may not be successful in Japan. Local marketing knowledge is critical. Thus major perfumery companies maintain a network of creative centres to provide the needed regional focus and support.

The Creative Perfumery House and Staff Roles

The structure and activities of a creative perfumery house are not unlike that of an advertising agency, except that the mechanism of communication to the ultimate consumer is based on smell rather than visual/audio.

Creative Perfumers (the 'noses'): create the perfumes.

Marketing/Evaluators: they act as the link between the marketplace and the perfumers; translating clients' marketing needs into directions for the perfumer to create the required perfume. The Marketing/Evaluator will conduct panel tests etc. to select the best fragrance. Research will be conducted to provide a platform for the fragrance to demonstrate to the client how the fragrance will fit into the integrated communications mix for the final product. So although the context of the marketing activity is business-to-business, a key selling point is an intimate understanding of the consumer market for fragranced products (a classic FMCG context).

Account Managers: these people stay in contact with the clients to gain new briefs and maintain relationships with the client decision-making unit, so vital in this business-to-business context.

Other functions such as production and quality assurance will ensure that the fragrance, once selected by the client, is made to specification and delivered to fit the client's production schedule.

Product Life Cycles and Winning Fragrance

Typical products such as fabric conditioners have relatively short life cycles; there will be just a few years before technical and/or competitive pressures require a re-launch with a new perfume, to fit new fashion styles. Thus the perfumery house has to provide product (the perfume) and marketing service to assist the client in positioning the product. The marketing research and support for the fragrance can be the vital factor to induce the client to select one company's perfume rather than another's.

The industry in the international context has become polarised consisting of a small group of major international companies with sales revenues of around $100,000,000 a year.

Appendix Two

Excerpt of Job Description for Marketing Manager Picasso Perfumes – South Island

Reports to General Manager Picasso Perfumes – South Island.

Role

- To be responsible for implementing Picasso Perfumes' marketing plans for the region operating from South Island.

- To prepare local marketing initiatives in support of the global expansion plans.

- To research the local consumer markets for product developments including all aspects of the marketing mix.

- To research the local market for the development of the b2b marketing activities.

- To co-ordinate the marketing activities with other functions both locally and internationally.

- To be responsible for the local marketing communications of Picasso Perfumes.

- To prepare client presentations and where appropriate give presentation to clients.

- To be responsible for the management and development of two Marketing Assistants.

Appendix Three

Notes Made by Pat Jones in the First Week Working at Picasso Perfumes

One marketing assistant is to be locally recruited.

The other marketing assistant will be appointed from the USA as part of the programme to give staff international experience. This person has three years experience of working for Picasso Perfumes but this will be the first time they have worked outside the USA.

Production is just starting to serve a customer previously supplied by importing.

The recruitment programme for staff in the laboratories and office will be largely complete by the end of August.

The President of Picasso Perfumes will be visiting the site in the second week of September. It is the Marketing Manager's responsibility to arrange a series of events to mark the formal opening of the South Island facility.

Note: The above data is based on a fictitious company for assessment purposes.

PART A

Question 1.

a.   Outline a marketing communications plan to cover the opening of the new South Island site and the six months after the launch.

(25 marks)

b.   As this is a new market for Picasso Perfumes, there is a need to evaluate the local macro-environment. Outline the information you would need to obtain and the procedure you would follow in order to collect it.

(10 marks)

c.   How would you select and then train your new Marketing Assistant?

(15 marks)
(50 marks in total)

PART A

PART B – Answer TWO Questions Only

Question 2.

a.   Picasso Perfumes operates in a business-to-business context. Its target customers are manufacturers of fragranced products such as cosmetics, detergents etc. (see Appendix One). What information does Picasso Perfumes need to obtain to identify likely profitable customers? How would you collect this information?

(15 marks)

b.   Having identified a potential client, what additional information would the sales team require about the target client's business and key staff?

(10 marks)
(25 marks in total)

Question 3.

a.   You have been given the responsibility for planning the opening event. Who are the key publics (stakeholders) for this event? What would be your objectives for the day? What schedule would you plan?

(10 marks)

b.   Viewing this opening event in project terms and using project management tools, how would you plan for and run the event successfully?

(15 marks)
(25 marks in total)

Question 4.

A key activity for companies in this business is to track developments in the market such as new product launches and new advertising campaigns. Outline a suitable MkIS framework to achieve this for Picasso Perfumes.

(25 marks)

Question 5.

You have been asked by the Human Resources Manager to devise a one-day 'Customer Care' workshop to involve all staff who will be in front-line contact with customers. Outline your objectives and programme for the event and justify these.

(25 marks)

The Chartered
Institute of Marketing

Professional Diploma in Marketing

Marketing Management in Practice

44:       **Marketing Management in Practice**

SENIOR EXAMINER'S REPORT FOR JUNE 2004 EXAMINATION PAPER

SENIOR EXAMINER'S REPORT FOR
JUNE 2004 EXAMINATION PAPER

MODULE NAME: MARKETING MANAGEMENT IN PRACTICE

AWARD NAME: ADVANCED CERTIFICATE LEVEL 2

DATE: JUNE 2004 EXAMINATION

1. **General Strengths and Weaknesses of Candidates**

Some improvement in the pass rate in the June 2004 examinations was noted over December 2003.

Common causes of poor exam performance include:
- Generic answers with little application of the selected theory to the specific context of the case study and question. Good answers require a selection of the relevant theory. Template answers (e.g. a marketing communications plan with generic points failing to take account of the BtoB context with recommendations for heavy national TV and radio advertising) are likely to result in a marginal fail grade.
- Unstructured lists of action points without any underpinning of relevant theory. Good comprehensive solutions need the theory to ensure the complete cover of the issues. Lack of knowledge and understanding of the relevant theory results in superficial answers that will not achieve a pass grade at this level.
- Reproduction of answers from previous case study work. Each case study has distinctive aspects requiring a judged and tailored approach. A memorised answer from a previously viewed case study will not be appropriate. The purpose of providing specimen answers to case studies is not to provide 'template' answers but to provide a benchmarking framework to which students can compare their solutions. They are intended to provide guidance and assistance in the development of skills, not to provide proforma answers.
- Failure to answer the question as presented. Each question has specific context.
- Time management. Time should be allocated according to the marks for a given question or sub question. Failure to leave enough time for the last question will cause problems.
- Failure to note the developments of the syllabus and marketing theory in general. Specific areas of concern were: Confusion of the structure and focus of a communications plan. Lack of appreciation of the difference in communications in a BtoB context (as compared to a FMCG context), lack of application of communication theory alongside lack of customer care / quality theory and lack of awareness and application of RM theory.
- Failure to develop answers.
- Failure to structure answers (report format is required for all answers unless indicated otherwise) and/or leaving gaps in the treatment of the issues. It is

vital to plan answers. Just a few minutes to quickly rough out a question plan provides a vital perspective to ensure focus on the specifics of the question, developing planned cover of all the relevant issues. The danger of rushing into the answer without planning is that the development can drift away from the specific focus required. Also the key issues can be overlooked. Thus important gaps are left in the answer.

- Unless otherwise stated all answers are required in report format style. However, lengthy introductions, title pages and contents listings for every question and sub question are not required. They can waste valuable time.

In the next section the strengths and weakness of answers are reviewed. In some cases the same point appears in both sections. Good answers consisted of good application of the theory. Weaker submissions missed or omitted to cover some of the issues, e.g. in the present case study good answers had appropriate focus on the BtoB context. Poor answers were more general and failed to move away from a FMCG type emphasis.

2.   Strengths and Weaknesses by Question

Question 1a

Task: To outline a 'marketing communications plan' covering the opening of the South Island site and the 6 months after the launch.

Strengths
- Appreciation of the BtoB context with application of RM concepts.
- Development of a BtoB communications mix with emphasis on elements other than advertising e.g. personal selling.
- Where advertising was considered, concentration on BtoB media such as trade journals rather than national TV campaigns.

Weaknesses
- In some cases production of a marketing plan rather than a communication plan. This resulted in a lack of depth of cover in the development of the communication mix detail.
- Failure to demonstrate the integration of the various elements of the communication mix.
- Inappropriate mix development such as national TV advertising or 'buy one get one free' promotions for a BtoB context.
- Essay review of the issues – a structured plan was required (including control aspects).
- Surprisingly little mention was made of 'e' - based communications by most candidates.

Overall
Candidates who clearly appreciated the BtoB context produced good well-considered plans. Candidates who reproduced a standard generic FMCG communication plan did not achieve a pass grade.

Question 1b

Task: To review the information needed on the local macro environment and indicate how this information could be collected.

Strengths
- Most candidates used one of the standard models (e.g. PEST) to structure their answer and this was welcomed.
- Good answers indicated sound secondary sources that might be used.

Weaknesses
- Often the information overview was rather general and lacked context specific depth.
- Some candidates did not question plan and forgot the end part of the question 'and the procedure you would follow in order to collect it' thus failing to gain valuable marks.

Overall
Most candidates produced a fair overview of the issues and appropriate procedures for data collection. Better answers were more context specific (e.g. Social: cultural trends in perfume preferences).

Question 1c

Task: To select and train a new member of staff.

Strengths
- Good general awareness of the recruitment process.
- Fair understanding of the training issues.

Weaknesses
- Lack of context depth. Some of the poorer answers might state 'Advertise the vacancy'. The better answers were more context developed and more context specific 'Given the specialist nature of the position advertising in the specialist perfumery press'.
- Candidates with poor time management and/or lack of question planning tended to provide inadequate cover of the training aspects.

Overall

In general, answers to the question were satisfactory, apart from the context issues discussed above. High mark-earning answers applied appropriate theory to the situation.

Question 2a

Task: To collect information needed to identify profitable customers.

Strengths
- An appreciation of the factors that would make a customer attractive (e.g. annual use of perfume in the manufacture of their consumer products).
- Appreciation of appropriate data sources such as company annual reports, import statistics etc.

Weaknesses
- Lack of appreciation of the BtoB context.
- Poor knowledge of secondary sources in a BtoB context.
- Suggestions for primary research more appropriate for a FMCG context.

Overall

Good answers focused on sound points to build a profile of the potential profitability of the account, if Picasso Perfumes were successful.

Question 2b

Task: Having identified a potential profitable target, to profile the company for successful sales development.

Strengths
- Sound appreciation of the need to profile the target companies perfume needs (e.g. range of products made). Best answers used examples such as P&G and Unilever to illustrate their points.
- Good knowledge of the DMU concepts and sound application to the context.

Weaknesses
- The key weakness of poorer answers was the absence of knowledge of DMU concepts and thus these submissions lacked depth and development.

Overall

Performance in this aspect of the question was mixed. Less able candidates did not appear to have knowledge of DMU concepts.

Question 3a

Task: Planning a communications event is a frequent task for the marketing professional. The first aspect here focused on the basics: identification of the publics (stakeholders), objectives and a schedule for the opening event.

Strengths
• Good answers identified each stakeholder group, explained its importance to Picasso Perfumes and listed appropriate objectives for the specific stakeholder group. Where such answers are required a table format may be the best way to outline the core of the answer with a suitable opening paragraph and final schedule of events (in this specific case).

Weaknesses
• Poor identification of stakeholders. A surprising minority of candidates forgot to include future customers in their analysis.
• Lack of focus with a rather general list of objectives (better answers linked objectives more tightly to specific stakeholder groups).

Overall
Key to good answers here was a good foundation of stakeholder analysis.

Question 3b

Task: Even a simple marketing event has hidden complexity and without good project management can go badly wrong. A practical review of how to plan the event with application of theory was required.

Strengths
• Good use of project management theory and illustration with good examples (e.g. specific project management software).

Weaknesses
• General list of points without the use of theory to structure the answer.

Overall
Most submissions made reference to project management theory. Better answers were developed with more context specific points.

Question 4

Task: To outline a framework for the tracking of developments in the market place for Picasso Perfumes.

Strengths
• Most candidates attempting this question had a fair understanding of the nature and role of MkIS.

- The above 'good answers' used relevant examples to illustrate the information to be collected and how the framework would achieve this.
- Good answers realised that the 'market' for Picasso Perfumes included both the retail activities (the ultimate consumer choice drives the industry value chain) alongside the BtoB context in which Picasso Perfumes operates.

Weaknesses
- A minority of submissions were not well structured and did not demonstrate knowledge of MkIS concepts.
- Many submissions failed to note that a company such as Picasso perfumes has to appreciate changes at all the levels of the industry value chain, For example, in Europe consumer pressure groups demanded 'cruelty free' (e.g. not animal tested) cosmetic products. This issue was adopted by retailers such as The Body Shop, who demanded that products were made without animal testing. It was also important that the ingredients and components that were supplied conformed to the same conditions, therefore affecting the fragrances that Picasso Perfumes would have to supply. Clearly candidates cannot be expected to understand all the detail in a given industry under exam conditions. However, often the business activity in the BtoB sector is driven by ultimate needs and wants of the consumer market. For example, the demand for (amounts and types) of microchips is driven by the demand for consumer products e.g. mobile telephones, alongside the functionality consumers demand in these products. Candidates are expected to appreciate the need for many BtoB organisations to understand their customers' customers' requirements if they are to succeed.

Overall
Sound understanding of MkIS but some lack of depth in the application of the theory to the given context.

Question 5

Task: To develop with justification the objectives and programme for a customer care workshop.

Strengths
- Knowledge and application of customer care theory.
- Objectives with justification (linked to the application of the above theory)
- An appreciation that in this BtoB context, the 'product' = product + service.
- A sound programme for the event.

Weaknesses
- Lack of customer care/quality theory (customer care is more than 'always be polite to the customer').
- In some answers there was a drift of focus from 'customer care' to exclusive concentration on 'team building'. Clearly 'team building' is a relevant aspect but again customer satisfaction needs more than just a 'happy team'.

Overall

Candidates who applied customer care/quality theory to the situation achieved good grades. This required more depth of insight than just a 'team building away day'.

3. **Future Themes**

Future case studies will continue to focus on real-life situations and require candidates to apply their knowledge to provide context specific solutions. The application of knowledge requires more than textbook reading. Frantic cramming for the month before the exam is not only stressful but is not a guarantee of a good grade. Application of knowledge requires practice, so tutors and candidates are strongly advised to practice and develop their skills on past case studies. The specimen answers are intended to be a guide to aid in the process. It is not intended that specimen answers are 'textbook' answers to be learned and reproduced in the next exam. Each exam case study has a different context and will need context specific application of marketing theory. The need is to develop skills in this process.

Of increasing importance to all aspects of marketing is the impact of e-commerce. Surprisingly few answers made any specific reference to e-commerce and related issues in their answers (e.g. the provision of marketing intelligence to people in the Picasso Perfumes by an internal Intranet rather than by hard copy reports). Future case studies will require candidates to demonstrate knowledge of e-commerce and related issues.

Marketing is conducted in a range of contexts including FMCG, BtoB, Not for Profit and services. Future case studies will range across this spectrum. This case study focused on a large global organisation but future case studies will also include focus on small organisations.

appendix 8
curriculum information and reading list

Aim

The Marketing Management in Practice unit practises students in developing and implementing marketing plans at an operational level in organizations. A key part of this unit is working within a team to develop the plan and managing teams implementing the plan by undertaking marketing activities and projects. Its aim is to assist students in integrating and applying knowledge from all the units at Professional Diploma, particularly as part of a team. This unit also forms the summative assessment for the Professional Diploma.

Related statements of practice

Jc.1   Plan marketing projects and prepare budgets.
Jc.2   Manage and report on delivery against plan and objectives.
Kc.1   Define measurements appropriate to the plan or business case and ensure they are undertaken.
Kc.2   Evaluate activities and identify improvements using measurement data.
Lc.1   Manage a marketing team.
Lc.2   Maintain relationships with other functions and disciplines within the organization.
Lc.3   Encourage and help others to develop their competencies relevant to a marketing role.
Lc.4   Embrace change and modify behaviours and attitudes.

Learning outcomes

Students will be able to:

- Explain the roles and structure of the marketing function and the nature of relationships with other functions within various types of organization.
- Plan and undertake or commission marketing research for an operational marketing plan or business decision.
- Interpret qualitative and quantitative data and present appropriate and coherent recommendations that lead to effective marketing and business decisions.

- o Develop marketing objectives and plans at an operational level appropriate to the organization's internal and external environments.
- o Develop an effective plan for a campaign and supporting customers and members of a marketing channel.
- o Use appropriate management techniques to plan and control marketing activities and projects.
- o Use appropriate techniques to develop, manage and motivate a team so that it performs effectively and delivers required results.
- o Define measures for, and evaluate the performance of, marketing plans, activities and projects and make recommendations for improvements.

Knowledge and skills requirements

Element 1: Managing people and teams (30 per cent)

1.1 Describe the functions, roles of marketing managers and typical marketing jobs and the nature of relationships with other functions in organizations operating in a range of different industries and contexts.

1.2 Develop and maintain effective relationships with people in other functions and disciplines within the organization.

1.3 Identify and explain the key challenges of managing marketing teams in a multi-national or multi-cultural context.

1.4 Explain how you would use the techniques available for selecting, building, developing and motivating marketing teams to improve performance.

1.5 Allocate and lead the work of marketing teams, agreeing objectives and work plans with teams and individuals.

1.6 Respond to poor performance within a marketing team by minimizing conflict, supporting team members, overcoming problems and maintaining discipline.

1.7 Explain the sources and nature of change affecting organizations and the techniques available for managing change.

1.8 Evaluate individual and team performance against objectives or targets and provide constructive feedback on their performance.

Element 2: Managing marketing projects (10 per cent)

2.1 Describe the main stages of a project and the roles of people involved at each stage.

2.2 Describe the main characteristics of successful and less successful projects and identify the main reasons for success or failure.

2.3 Explain the importance of, and techniques for, establishing the project's scope, definition and goals.

2.4 Use the main techniques available for planning, scheduling, resourcing and controlling activities on a project.

2.5 Explain the importance of preparing budgets and techniques for controlling progress throughout a project to ensure it is completed on time and within budget.

2.6 Explain the main techniques for evaluating the effectiveness of a project on its completion.

Element 3: Managing knowledge and delivering marketing research projects (20 per cent)

3.1 Explain the concept, and give examples, of the application of information and knowledge management, highlighting the role of marketing and employees within the organization.

3.2 Design a research project aimed at providing information as part of a marketing audit or for marketing and business decisions.

3.3 Manage a marketing research project by gathering relevant information on time and within the agreed budget.

3.4 Make arrangements to record, store and, if appropriate, update information in the MkIS, a database created for the purpose or another system.

3.5 Analyse and interpret information and present, as a written report or oral presentation, appropriate conclusions or recommendations that inform the marketing and business decisions for which the research was undertaken.

3.6 Review and evaluate the effectiveness of the activities and the role of the individual and team in this process.

Element 4: Developing and implementing marketing plans (20 per cent)

4.1 Develop an operational marketing plan, selecting an appropriate marketing mix for an organization operating in any context such as FMCG, business-to-business (supply chain), large or capital project-based, services, voluntary and not-for-profit, or sales support (e.g. SMEs).

4.2 Use the main techniques available for planning, scheduling and resourcing activities within the plan.

4.3 Identify appropriate measures for evaluating and controlling the marketing plan.

4.4 Review and evaluate the effectiveness of planning activities and the role of the individual and team in this process.

Element 5: Delivering communications and customer service programmes (20 per cent)

5.1 Plan the design, development, execution and evaluation of communications campaigns by a team of marketers, including external agencies and suppliers.

5.2 Use appropriate marketing communications to develop relationships or communicate with a range of stakeholders.

5.3 Manage and monitor the provision of effective customer service.

5.4 Use marketing communications to provide support for members of a marketing channel.

5.5 Use marketing communications techniques for an internal marketing plan to support management of change within an organization.

5.6 Review and evaluate the effectiveness of communications activities and the role of the individual and team in this process.

Related key skills

Key skill	Relevance to unit knowledge and skills
Communication	Develop a research brief
	Develop a research proposal or plan
	Present research results to decision-makers
	Present and justify a marketing or communications plan
	Produce effective marketing communications
	Assess the impact of a campaign
Application of number	Determine information requirements for a business or marketing decision
	Plan a research project
	Use quantitative research methods, analysis and calculations
	Conduct a marketing audit
	Use forecasting techniques
	Set objectives
	Set and justify a budget
	Forecast likely response rates
	Measure marketing performance and communications effectiveness
Information technology	Use IT tools for research planning
	Use IT tools to acquire, store, retrieve and communicate research data
	Use IT tools for forecasting, modelling options, budgeting and measuring performance for a marketing plan or a communications campaign
Working with others	Work as part of a team in planning, undertaking, and measuring and evaluating results for a research, planning or a communications project
Improving own learning and performance	Review current capabilities
	Identify opportunities and set realistic targets for development and learning
	Plan how these targets will be met (methods, timescales, resources)
	Use a variety of methods for learning
	Seek feedback, monitor performance and modify approach
	Assess effectiveness of learning and development approach
Problem solving	Use research to establish the critical features of a business or marketing problem
	Formulate a marketing solution within defined constraints
	Select a marketing mix appropriate to a specific context
	Recommend changes to marketing processes
	Formulate a communication solution within defined constraints

Assessment

As the summative assessment at this level, the assessment will require students to demonstrate knowledge and skills in all areas covered by the four units of Professional Diploma. CIM will normally offer two forms of assessment for this unit from which study centres may choose: written examination (a 'midi' case study) and an integrative assignment. Specimen papers and guidance on the structure, format and approach of these assessments will be published separately.

CIM may also recognize, or make joint awards for, units at an equivalent level undertaken with other professional marketing bodies and educational institutions.

Recommended support materials

In addition to the texts from the other units at Professional Diploma, the following texts and resources are available to support this unit.

Core texts

Boddy, D. (2002) *Management: An Introduction*, 2nd revised edition, London: FT Prentice Hall.

Martin, P. (2002) *Getting Started in Project Management*, Chichester: John Wiley.

Workbooks

BPP (2003) *Marketing Management in Practice,* London: BPP Publishing.

CIM revision cards (2004/2005) *Marketing Management in Practice*, Oxford: Butterworth-Heinemann.

Williams, J. and Curtis, T. (2004) *Marketing Management in Practice*, Oxford: Butterworth-Heinemann.

Supplementary readings

Adair, J. (2002) *Inspiring Leadership*, London: Thorogood.

Belbin, R.M. (1996) *Management Teams: Why they Succeed or Fail*, Oxford: Butterworth-Heinemann.

Brown, A. (1998) O*rganizational Culture*, 2nd edition, London: FT Prentice Hall.

Handy, C. (1993) *Understanding Organizations.* London: Penguin.

Hilton, S. and Gibbons, G. (2002) *Good Business: Your World Needs You*, London: Texere.

Trompenaars, F. and Hampden-Turner, C. (1997) *Riding the Waves of Culture*, 2nd revised edition, London: Nicholas Brealey.

Woodcock, M. (1989) *Team Development Manual*, 2nd revised edition, Aldershot: Gower.

Marketing and management journals

Students can keep abreast of developments in the academic field of marketing by reference to the main marketing journals, a selection of which are listed in the Appendix to this document.

Press

Students will be expected to have access to current examples of marketing campaigns and so should be sure to keep up to date with the appropriate marketing and quality daily press. A selection of marketing press titles is given in the Appendix to this document.

Websites

A list of websites that tutors and students may find useful is shown in the Appendix at the end of this document.

Additional resources

There are many useful diagnostic tools for those interested in learning more about themselves and the workings of teams, a few of which are mentioned here. Permission should be obtained from the appropriate sources for use of these tools.

- o Learning styles questionnaire, Honey and Mumford
- o Team roles questionnaire, Belbin
- o Leadership style questionnaire, Hersey, Blanchard, Reddin, Blake, Mouton
- o Work Motivation Inventory, Chartwell Bratt
- o Strengths Deployment Inventory, E. Porter, S. Maloney.

Overview and rationale

The Marketing Management in Practice syllabus requires a broad and practical demonstration of marketing at an operational level and an awareness of the strategic context. It provides an opportunity for students to develop and implement an operational marketing plan, so applying, as part of a team, the theory of research, planning and marketing communications provided in the previous three units. This unit also provides the final assessment of students' ability to create an operational marketing plan. As such, it forms an important measure of the students' ability to meet organizations' requirements of an operational marketer.

From an educational standpoint, this unit seeks to integrate learning from the full Professional Diploma syllabus. As such, it is best suited to delivery after the other units of the Professional Diploma. It should be lively and fun for all involved. It rounds off the Professional Diploma and so provides a springboard for Professional PG Diploma at the next level, which goes on to develop students for a role in strategic marketing.

Approach

Marketing Management in Practice is about developing and managing teams to add value to the organization's activities and deliver effective results. Like members of other functions and disciplines within organizations, marketers work towards departmental and broader organizational objectives. They work in teams, both within the marketing function and, importantly, with people in other functions.

It is important to recognize that the context within which marketers are operating is continually changing as a result of both external and internal influences. No organization is detached from international influences, even if the organization does not have to deal with international customers. Organizations source materials from around the globe, access international markets from a desk, compete with other organizations from around the world, and imitate global behaviour. It is therefore appropriate in this unit to cover international issues as part of everyday marketing life in organizations.

Marketers and marketing managers must be able to work effectively themselves, for example managing time and problem solving. They must also be able to manage and motivate people and teams to produce results. Using Adair's model of leadership, effective team performance is contingent on a balance between:

- The needs of the task.
- The needs of the individuals within the team.
- The maintenance needs of the team as a whole.

Syllabus content

The syllabus for this unit uses Adair's concept. It provides underpinning theory on managing teams to help with managing individual needs and team needs to get the most from the team. It also provides basic project management techniques to help with managing the task. These two elements provide the final skills and knowledge for marketers to develop and implement marketing plans at an operational level. The remainder of the syllabus for this unit is about the development and implementation of an operational marketing plan, including the management of information, communications and human resources. In other words, students should apply within a marketing team the theory of marketing research and information, planning and communications covered in the earlier units. This should be achieved through a project.

A syllabus can contain only so much and this syllabus assumes that, on entry to the unit, students have the skills to manage themselves (defined in the key skill 'Improving own learning and performance') and the principles of motivation, leadership, power and influence relevant to the team context. If students do not have these skills, then study centres may wish to impose additional required learning or provide additional sessions and materials.

Element 1: Managing people and teams

This element provides the underpinning knowledge required for the selection, development and maintenance of effective marketing teams. It is particularly important to stress the organizational and global context within which marketing teams are operating and how different organizations adopt different approaches to marketing depending on their context and culture. In cases where this subject is taught by a HR tutor, it is important that it is set within a marketing context. This subject is developed further in the Professional PG Diploma. It is also important to use this element to build on the Key Skills 'Working with others' and 'Improving own knowledge and performance'.

Element 2: Techniques for managing marketing projects and activities

Managing the planning and performance of a marketing task by a team requires skills in planning, scheduling, directing, motivating and monitoring. The techniques of project management equip marketing managers to manage marketing activities and projects effectively. This element provides the underpinning knowledge of the techniques, which are then applied in the marketing activities that make up the rest of the syllabus for this unit.

Element 3: Managing knowledge and delivering market research projects

Knowledge management is about people. We need to motivate and enthuse the people we manage with a willingness and desire to share and exchange knowledge. We cannot do this by simply presenting them with a piece of IT equipment. It requires a cultural norm of open communication and informing and sharing knowledge and motivating and rewarding knowledge sharing that benefits the business.

This element builds on the underpinning knowledge developed in the Marketing Research and Information unit by providing students with the opportunity to plan and undertake or commission a research project as a team activity as part of a marketing audit feeding into a marketing plan or business decision.

Element 4: Developing and implementing marketing plans

This element requires effective teamwork and a good understanding of the marketing planning process and techniques to produce successful outcomes. This element builds on the underpinning knowledge developed in the Marketing Planning unit by providing students with the opportunity to develop and implement a marketing plan as a team activity. It is important that the implementation issues are explored in some depth. Apart from providing students with valuable learning, this will test the realism of the plans they have developed.

Element 5: Delivering communications and customer service programmes

This element builds on the underpinning knowledge developed in the Marketing Communications unit by providing students with the opportunity to manage campaigns or communication programmes as a team activity using appropriate techniques to develop or maintain stakeholder relationships, manage the provision of customer service, provide support for a marketing channel or deliver an internal marketing plan.

Delivery approach

This syllabus covers approximately 45 hours of tutor-directed learning, usually fifteen 3-hour sessions if delivered face-to-face. As a guide, study centres should allocate up to one third of these sessions to cover the underpinning theory on and techniques for managing teams and managing projects and any coaching required on the assessment. These can, and indeed should, be active sessions with students using these techniques rather than just lectures.

Two thirds of the sessions should be allocated to a significant practical project involving the formulation and implementation of an operational marketing plan. This should cover the management of information, communications and human resources. It is important that these sessions are of a practical nature. All the necessary theory should have been covered in the previous three units, so the emphasis in this unit should be the application of this theory within a marketing team. The nature of the project undertaken may depend on which form of assessment the students will use. A typical project will consist of:

o   Planning the project to be undertaken to meet the brief given.
o   Undertaking the task. This will involve collecting and analysing information and developing a marketing plan.
o   Planning, scheduling and resourcing marketing activities within the plan, identifying and overcoming problems during implementation.
o   Measuring and evaluating the outcomes.
o   Reflecting on the performance of the team and the individuals in it.

Additional resources (Syllabus – Professional Diploma In Marketing)

Introduction

Texts to support the individual units are listed in the syllabus for each unit. This Appendix shows a list of marketing journals, press and websites that tutors and students may find useful in supporting their studies at Professional Diploma.

Marketing journals

Students can keep abreast of developments in the academic field of marketing by reference to the main marketing journals.

- *Corporate Reputation Review* – Henry Stewart
- *European Journal of Marketing* – Emerald
- *Harvard Business Review* – Harvard
- *International Journal of Advertising* – WARC
- *International Journal of Corporate Communications* – Emerald
- *International Journal of Market Research* – WARC
- *Journal of Consumer Behaviour An International Review* – Henry Stewart
- *Journal of the Academy of Marketing Science* – Sage Publications
- *Journal of Marketing* – American Marketing Assoc. Pubs Group
- *Journal of Marketing Communications* – Routledge
- *Journal of Marketing Management* – Westburn Pubs Ltd
- *International Journal of Market Research* – NTC Pubs
- *Journal of Product and Brand Management* – Emerald
- *Journal of Services Marketing* – Emerald
- *Marketing Review* – Westburn Pubs Ltd

Press

Students will be expected to have access to current examples of marketing campaigns and so should be sure to keep up to date with the appropriate marketing and quality daily press, including:

- *Campaign* – Haymarket
- *Internet Business* – Haymarket
- *Marketing* – Haymarket
- *Marketing Business* – Chartered Institute of Marketing
- *Marketing Week* – Centaur
- *Revolution* – Haymarket

Websites

The Chartered Institute of Marketing

www.cim.co.uk	The CIM site with information and access to learning support for students
www.cim.co.uk/learningzone	Full details of all that's new in CIM's educational offer including specimen answers and Hot Topics

Publications on-line

www.revolution.haynet.com	Revolution magazine
www.marketing.haynet.com	Marketing magazine
www.FT.com	A wealth of information for cases (now charging)
www.IPA.co.uk	Need to register – communication resources
www.booksites.net	Financial Times/Prentice Hall Text websites

Sources of useful information

www.acnielsen.co.uk	AC Nielsen – excellent for research
http://advertising.utexas.edu/world/	Resources for advertising & marketing professionals, students, and tutors
www.bized.com	Case studies
www.corporateinformation.com	Worldwide sources listed by country
www.esomar.nl	European Body representing Research organizations – useful for guidelines on research ethics and approaches
www.dma.org.uk	The Direct Marketing Association
www.eiu.com	The Economist Intelligence Unit
www.euromonitor.com	Euromonitor consumer markets
www.europa.eu.int	The European Commission's extensive range of statistics and reports relating to EU and member countries
www.managementhelp.org/research/research.htm	Part of the 'Free Management Library' – explaining research methods
www.marketresearch.org.uk	The MRS site with information and access to learning support for students – useful links on ethics and code of conduct
www.mmc.gov.uk	Summaries of Competition Commission reports
www.oecd.org	OECD statistics and other information relating to member nations including main economic indicators
www.quirks.com	An American source of information on marketing research issues and projects
www.statistics.gov.uk	UK Government statistics
www.un.org	United Nations publish statistics on member nations
www.worldbank.org	World bank economic, social and natural resource indicators for over 200 countries. Includes over 600 indicators covering GNP per capita, growth, economic statistics, etc

Case sites

www.bluelagoon.co.uk	Case – SME website address
www.ebay.com	On-line auction – buyer behaviour
www.glenfiddich.com	Interesting site for case & branding
www.interflora.co.uk	e-commerce direct ordering
www.moorcroft.co.uk	Good for relationship marketing
www.ribena.co.uk	Excellent targeting & history of comms

© CIM 2005

Index